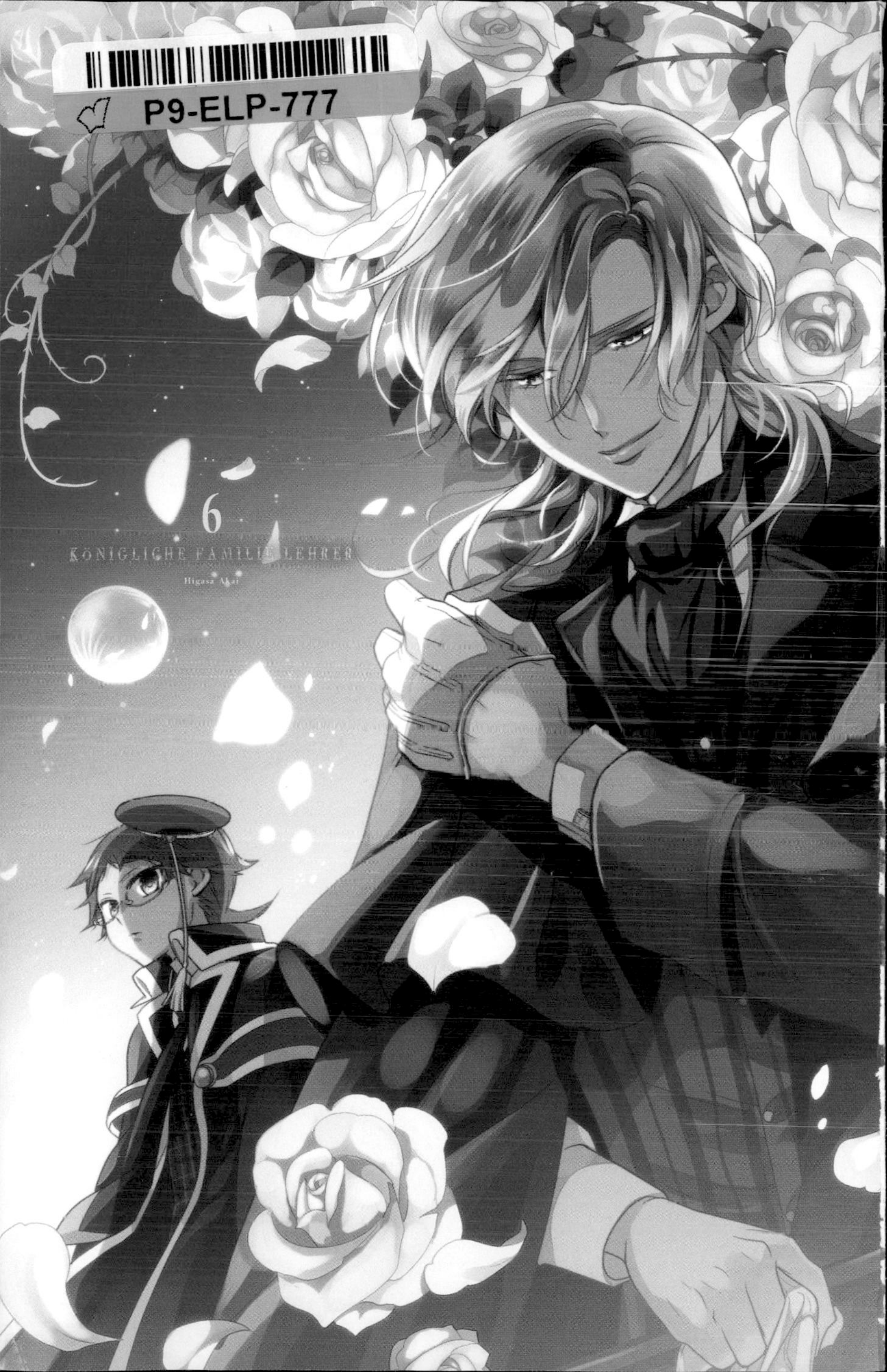
6
KÖNIGLICHE FAMILIE LEHRER
Higasa Akai

CONTENTS

KÖNIGLICHE LEHRMÄHREN

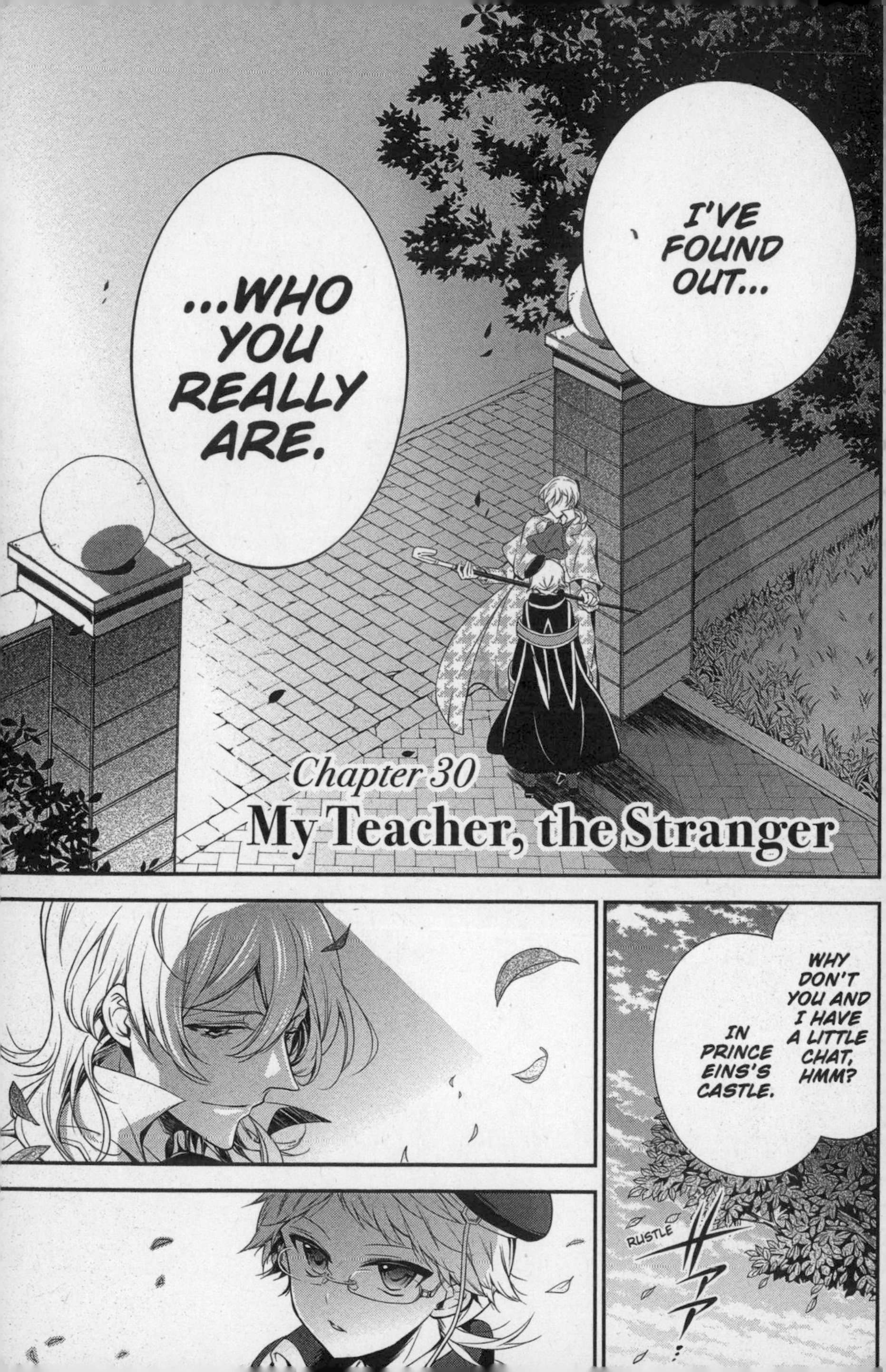
I'VE FOUND OUT...
...WHO YOU REALLY ARE.
Chapter 30
My Teacher, the Stranger
WHY DON'T YOU AND I HAVE A LITTLE CHAT, HMM?
IN PRINCE EINS'S CASTLE.
RUSTLE

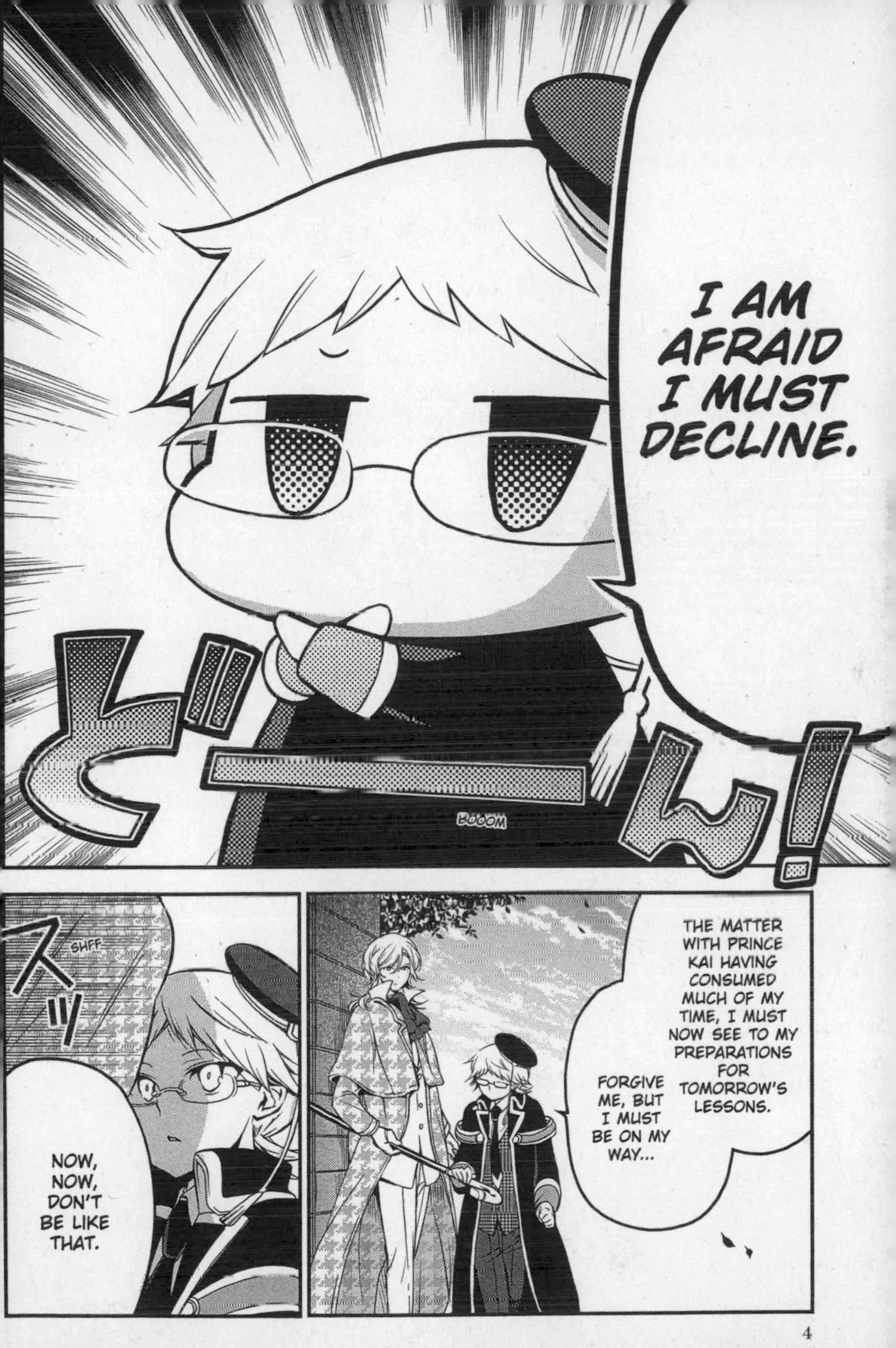
I AM AFRAID I MUST DECLINE.
どーーん!
BOOOM
THE MATTER WITH PRINCE KAI HAVING CONSUMED MUCH OF MY TIME, I MUST NOW SEE TO MY PREPARATIONS FOR TOMORROW'S LESSONS.
FORGIVE ME, BUT I MUST BE ON MY WAY...
スッ
SHFF
NOW, NOW, DON'T BE LIKE THAT.

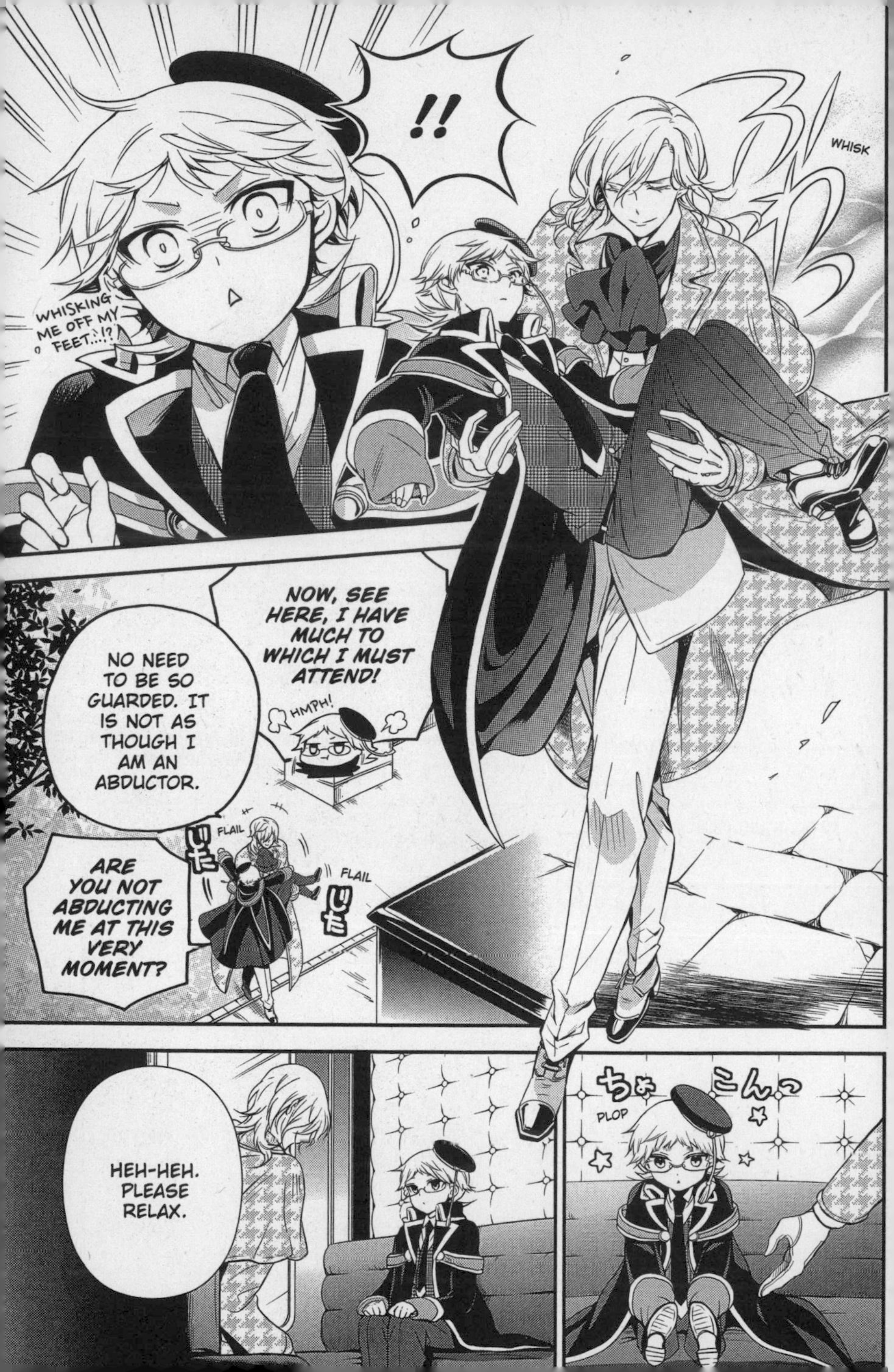
WHISK
!!
WHISKING ME OFF MY FEET...!?
NOW, SEE HERE, I HAVE MUCH TO WHICH I MUST ATTEND!
HMPH!
NO NEED TO BE SO GUARDED. IT IS NOT AS THOUGH I AM AN ABDUCTOR.
じた
FLAIL
じた
FLAIL
ARE YOU NOT ABDUCTING ME AT THIS VERY MOMENT?
ちょこんっ
PLOP
HEH-HEH. PLEASE RELAX.

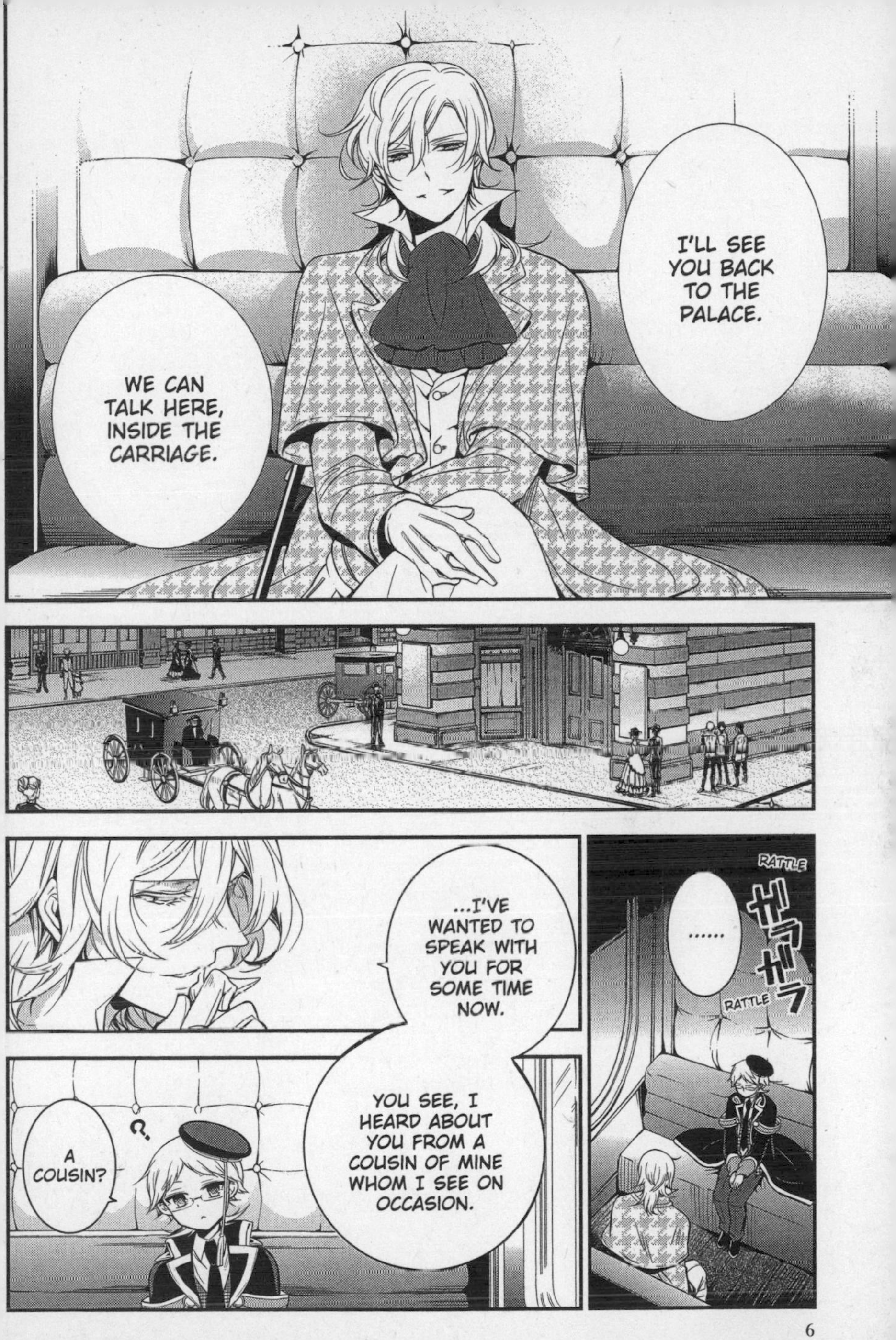
I'LL SEE YOU BACK TO THE PALACE.
WE CAN TALK HERE, INSIDE THE CARRIAGE.
RATTLE
ガラガラ
RATTLE
......
...I'VE WANTED TO SPEAK WITH YOU FOR SOME TIME NOW.
YOU SEE, I HEARD ABOUT YOU FROM A COUSIN OF MINE WHOM I SEE ON OCCASION.
?
A COUSIN?

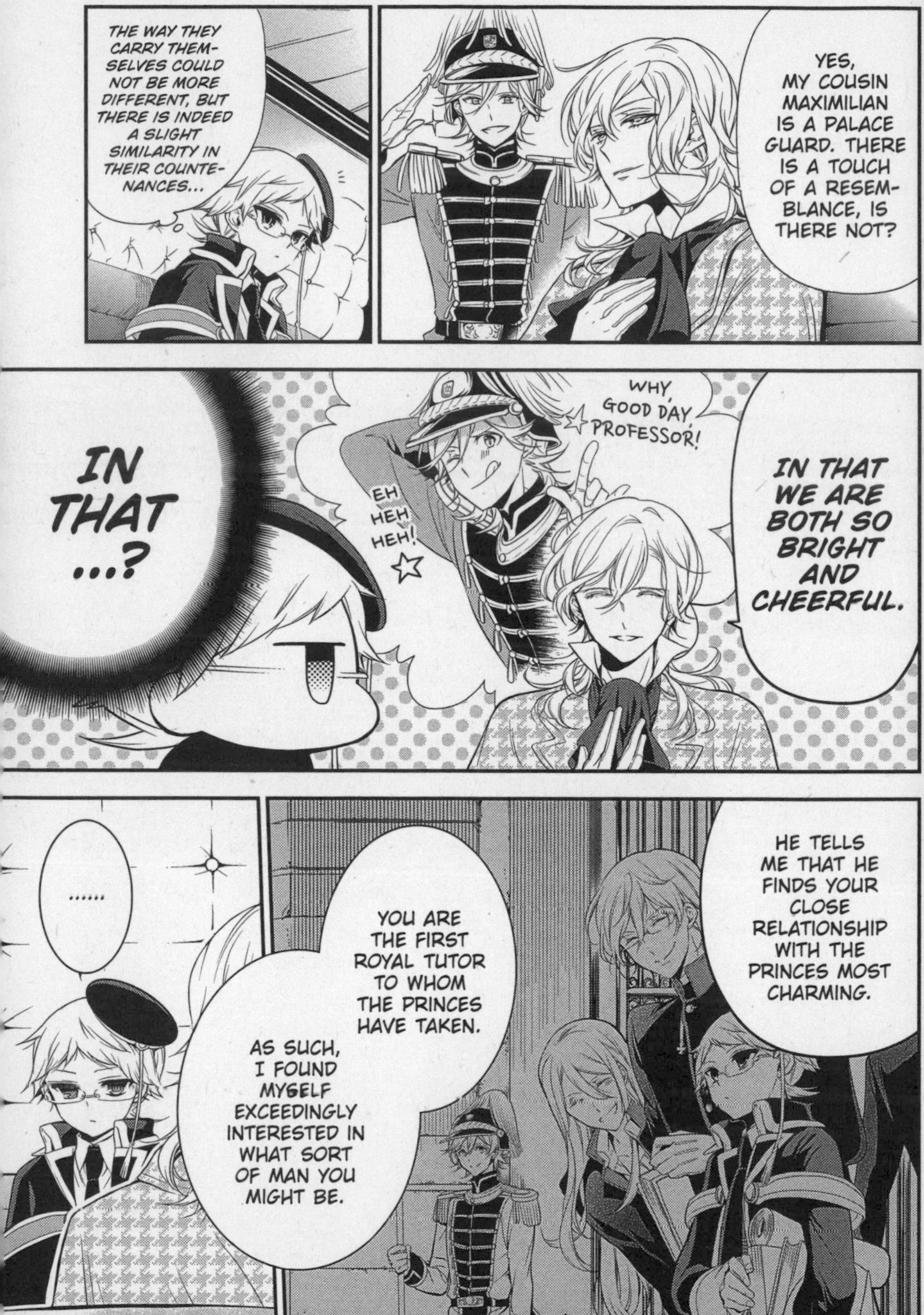
YES, MY COUSIN MAXIMILIAN IS A PALACE GUARD. THERE IS A TOUCH OF A RESEMBLANCE, IS THERE NOT?
THE WAY THEY CARRY THEMSELVES COULD NOT BE MORE DIFFERENT, BUT THERE IS INDEED A SLIGHT SIMILARITY IN THEIR COUNTENANCES...
IN THAT WE ARE BOTH SO BRIGHT AND CHEERFUL.
WHY, GOOD DAY, PROFESSOR!
EH HEH HEH!
IN THAT...?
HE TELLS ME THAT HE FINDS YOUR CLOSE RELATIONSHIP WITH THE PRINCES MOST CHARMING.
YOU ARE THE FIRST ROYAL TUTOR TO WHOM THE PRINCES HAVE TAKEN.
AS SUCH, I FOUND MYSELF EXCEEDINGLY INTERESTED IN WHAT SORT OF MAN YOU MIGHT BE.
......

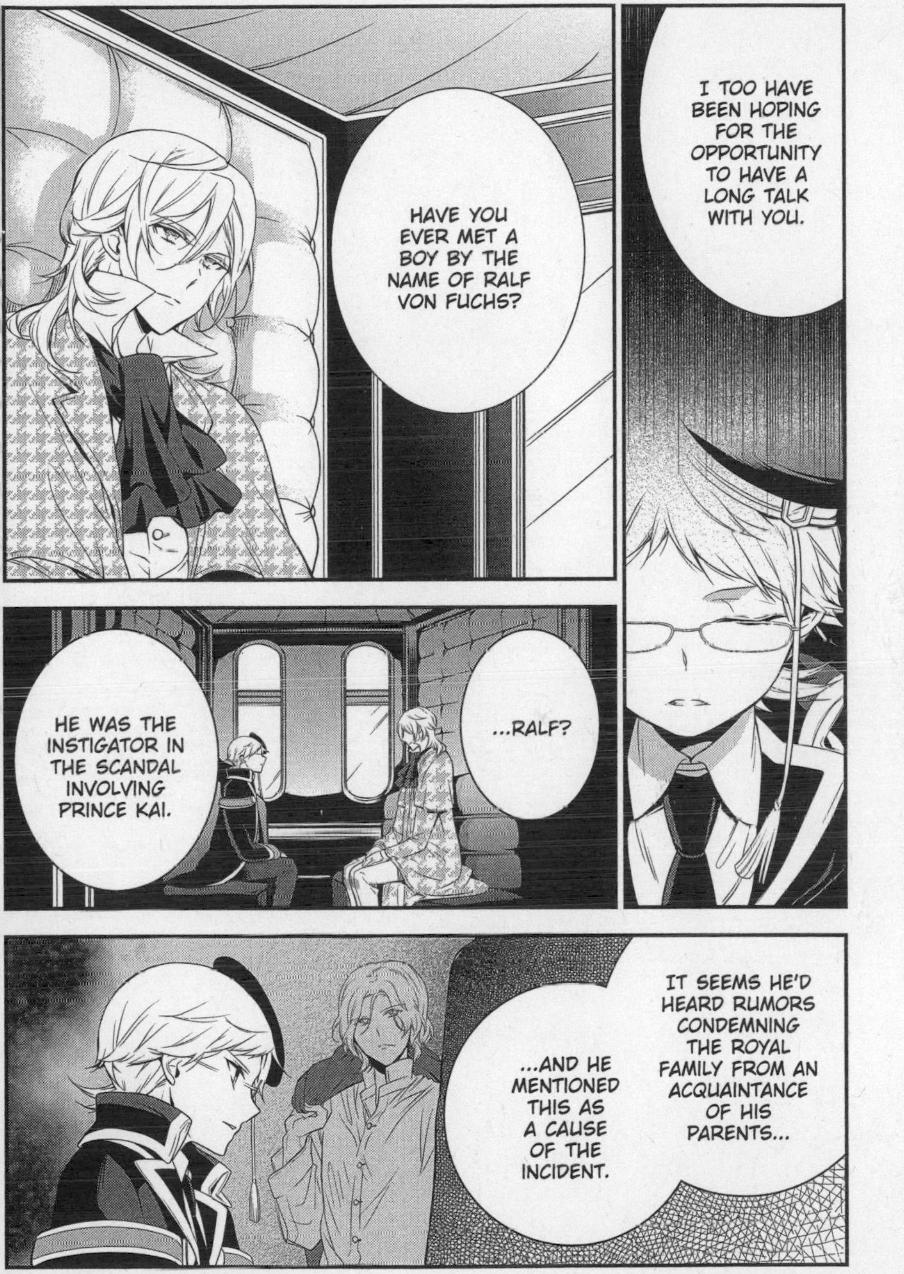
I TOO HAVE BEEN HOPING FOR THE OPPORTUNITY TO HAVE A LONG TALK WITH YOU.
HAVE YOU EVER MET A BOY BY THE NAME OF RALF VON FUCHS?
...RALF?
HE WAS THE INSTIGATOR IN THE SCANDAL INVOLVING PRINCE KAI.
IT SEEMS HE'D HEARD RUMORS CONDEMNING THE ROYAL FAMILY FROM AN ACQUAINTANCE OF HIS PARENTS...
...AND HE MENTIONED THIS AS A CAUSE OF THE INCIDENT.

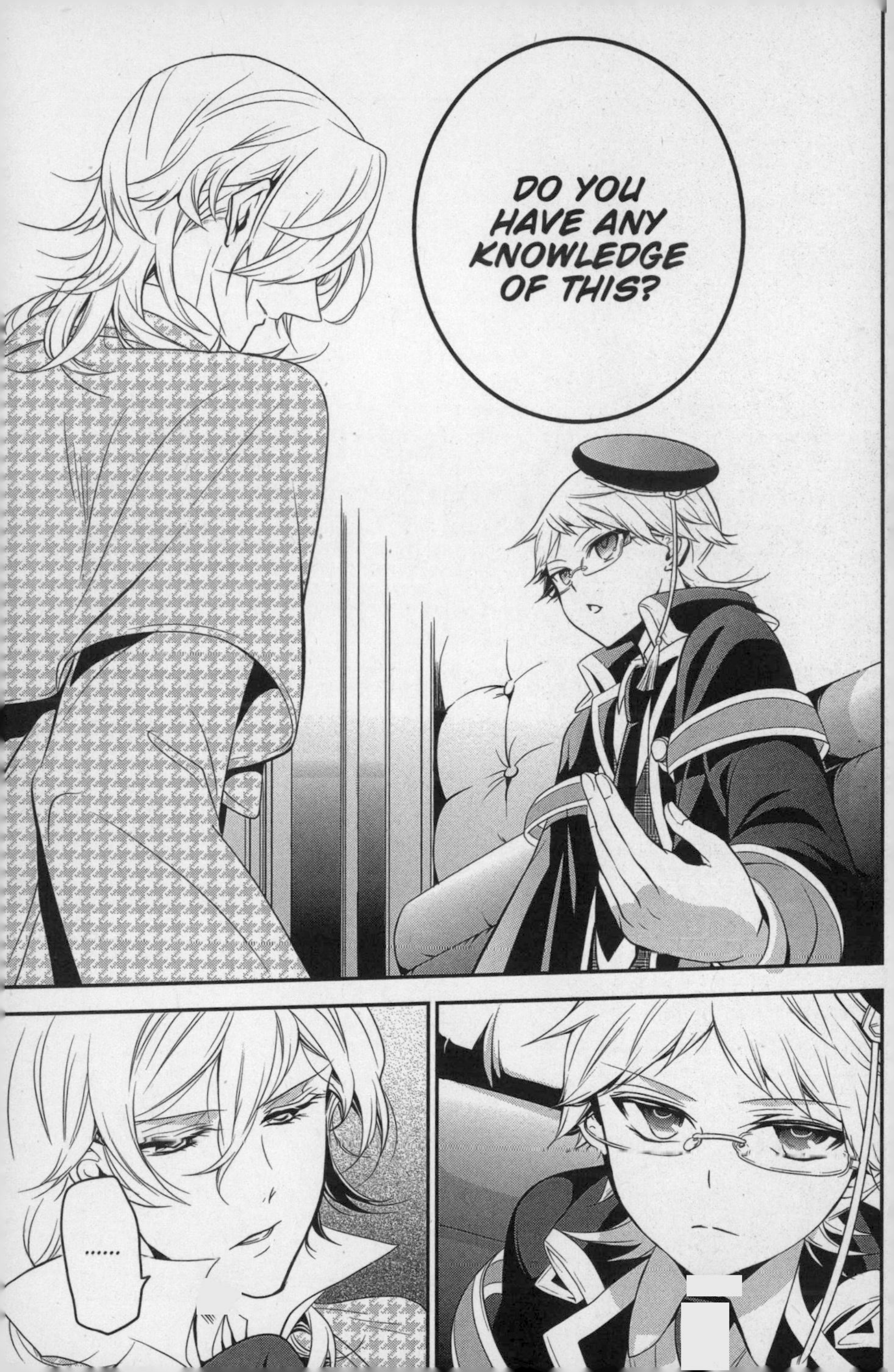
DO YOU HAVE ANY KNOWLEDGE OF THIS?
......

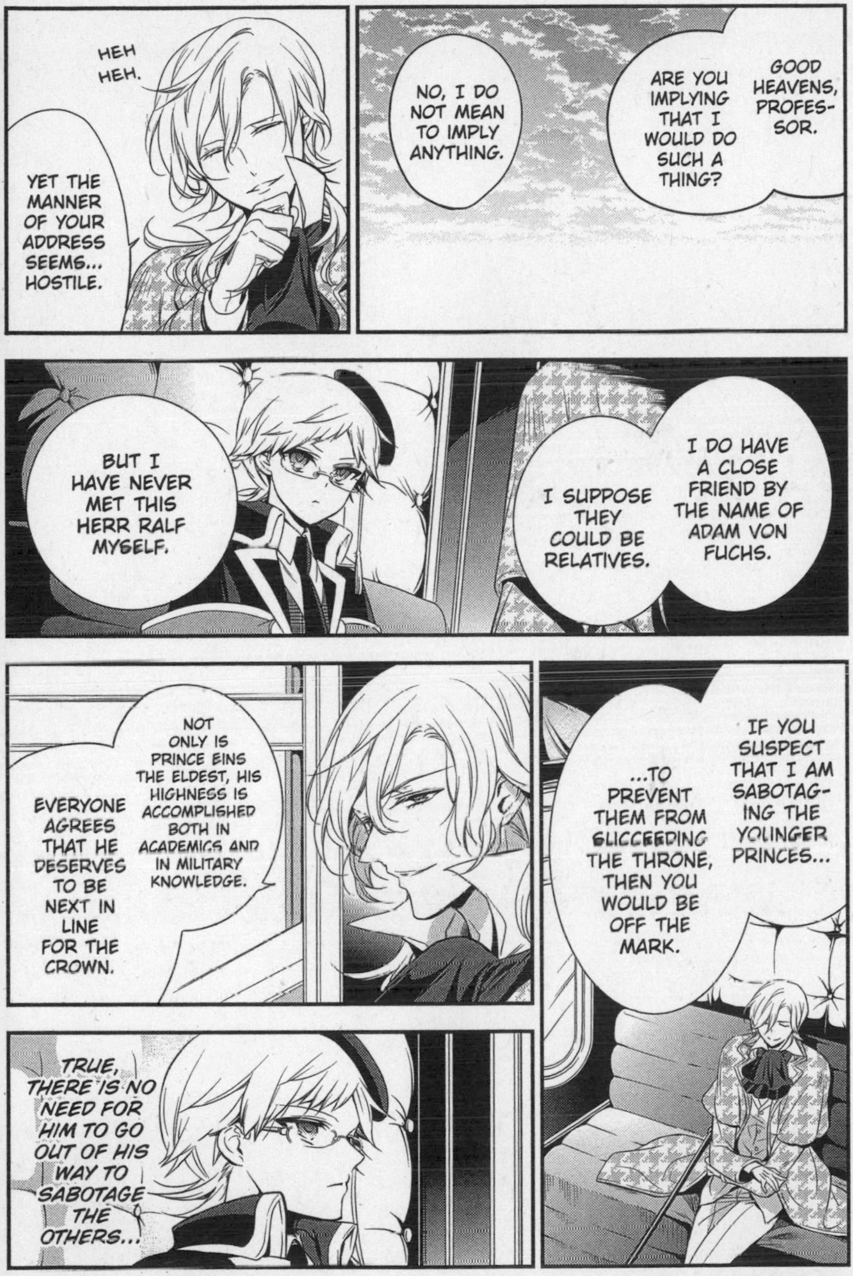
GOOD HEAVENS, PROFES-SOR.
ARE YOU IMPLYING THAT I WOULD DO SUCH A THING?
NO, I DO NOT MEAN TO IMPLY ANYTHING.
HEH HEH.
YET THE MANNER OF YOUR ADDRESS SEEMS... HOSTILE.
I DO HAVE A CLOSE FRIEND BY THE NAME OF ADAM VON FUCHS.
I SUPPOSE THEY COULD BE RELATIVES.
BUT I HAVE NEVER MET THIS HERR RALF MYSELF.
IF YOU SUSPECT THAT I AM SABOTAG-ING THE YOUNGER PRINCES...
...TO PREVENT THEM FROM SUCCEEDING THE THRONE, THEN YOU WOULD BE OFF THE MARK.
NOT ONLY IS PRINCE EINS THE ELDEST, HIS HIGHNESS IS ACCOMPLISHED BOTH IN ACADEMICS AND IN MILITARY KNOWLEDGE.
EVERYONE AGREES THAT HE DESERVES TO BE NEXT IN LINE FOR THE CROWN.
TRUE, THERE IS NO NEED FOR HIM TO GO OUT OF HIS WAY TO SABOTAGE THE OTHERS...

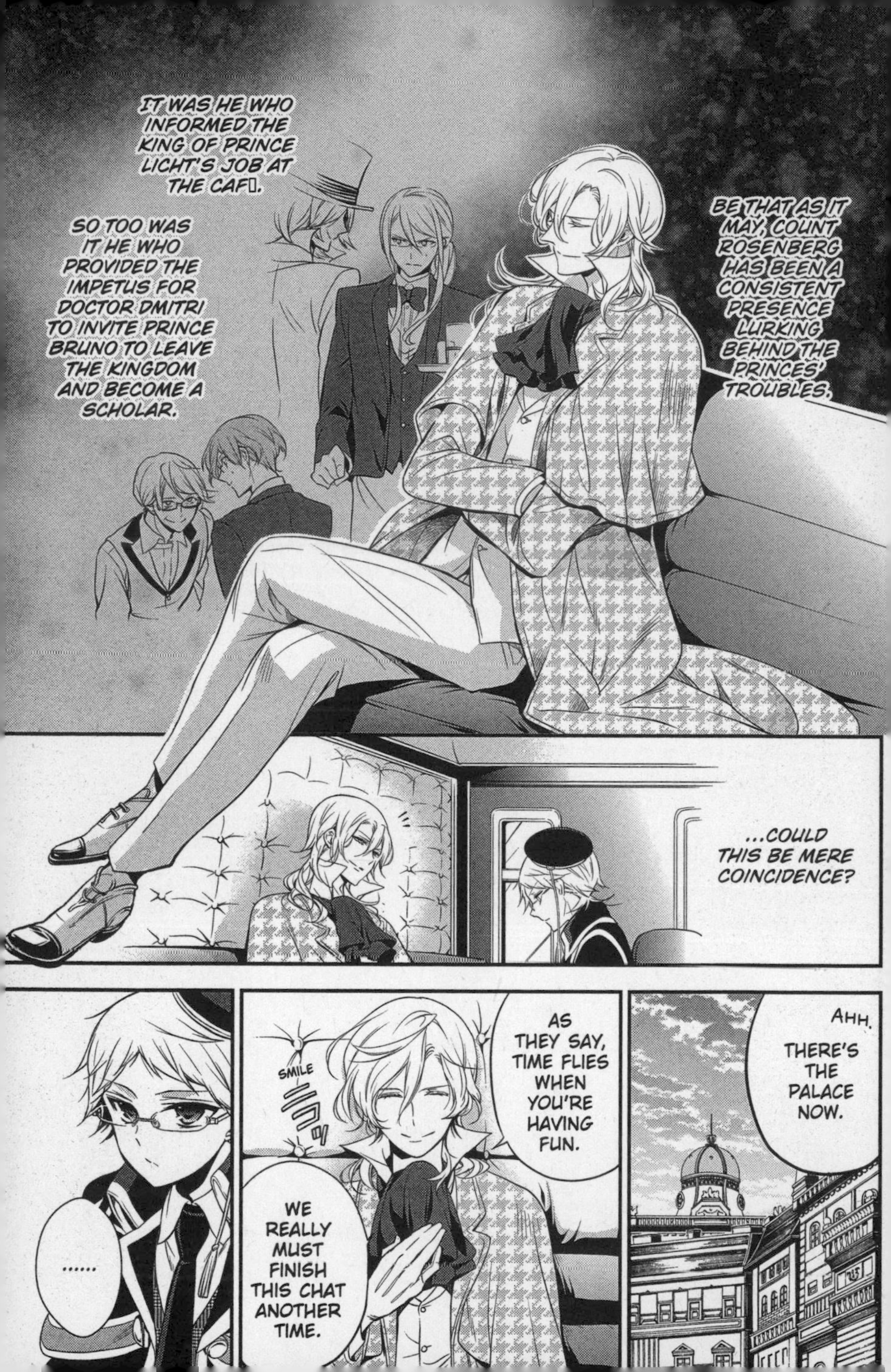

IT WAS HE WHO INFORMED THE KING OF PRINCE LICHT'S JOB AT THE CAFÉ.
SO TOO WAS IT HE WHO PROVIDED THE IMPETUS FOR DOCTOR DMITRI TO INVITE PRINCE BRUNO TO LEAVE THE KINGDOM AND BECOME A SCHOLAR.
BE THAT AS IT MAY, COUNT ROSENBERG HAS BEEN A CONSISTENT PRESENCE LURKING BEHIND THE PRINCES' TROUBLES.
...COULD THIS BE MERE COINCIDENCE?
AHH.
THERE'S THE PALACE NOW.
AS THEY SAY, TIME FLIES WHEN YOU'RE HAVING FUN.
SMILE
WE REALLY MUST FINISH THIS CHAT ANOTHER TIME.
......

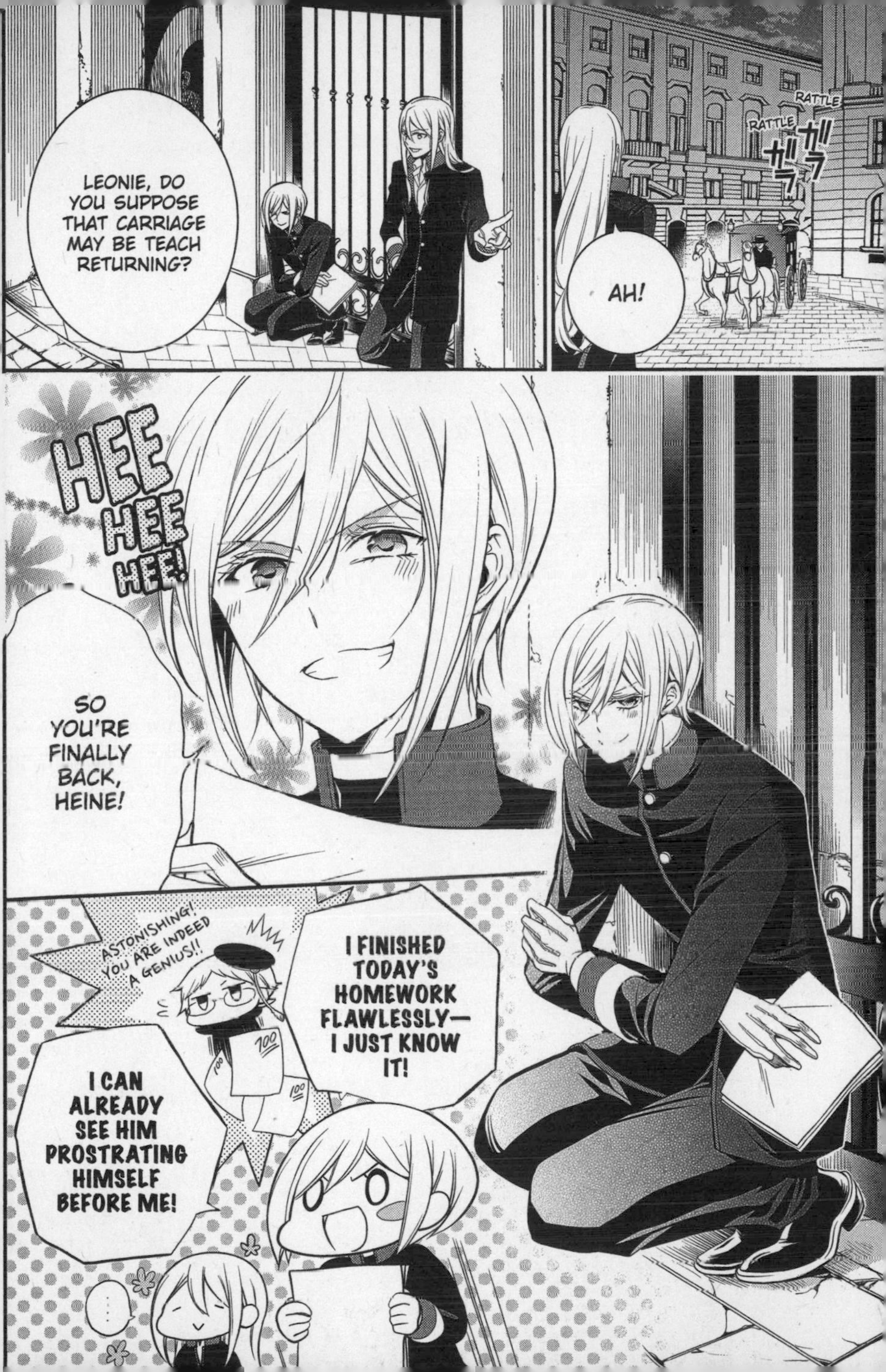
RATTLE
RATTLE
ガラ
ガラ
AH!
LEONIE, DO YOU SUPPOSE THAT CARRIAGE MAY BE TEACH RETURNING?
HEE HEE HEE!
SO YOU'RE FINALLY BACK, HEINE!
I FINISHED TODAY'S HOMEWORK FLAWLESSLY—I JUST KNOW IT!
ASTONISHING! YOU ARE INDEED A GENIUS!!
I CAN ALREADY SEE HIM PROSTRATING HIMSELF BEFORE ME!
...

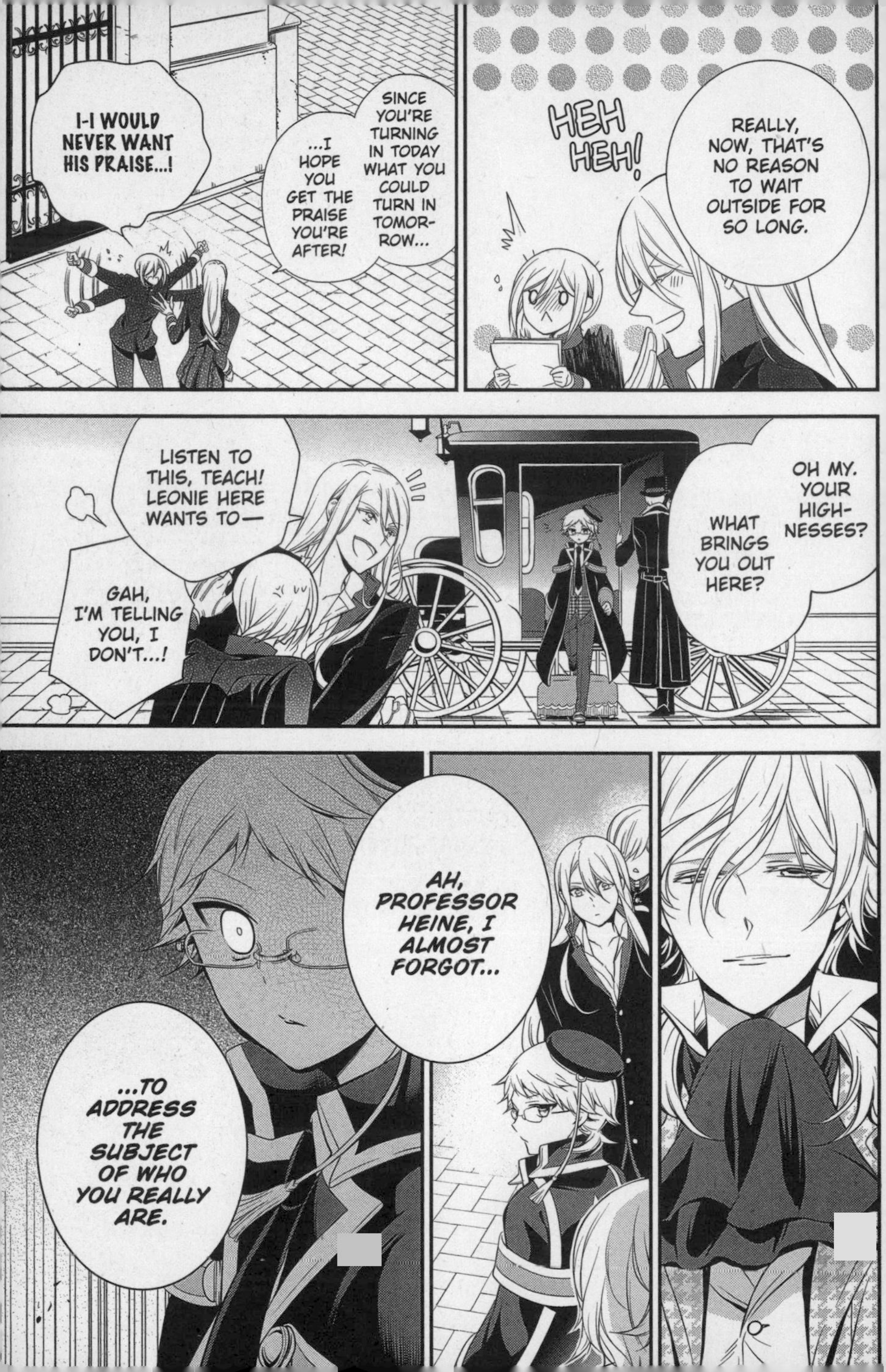
REALLY, NOW, THAT'S NO REASON TO WAIT OUTSIDE FOR SO LONG.
HEH HEH!
SINCE YOU'RE TURNING IN TODAY WHAT YOU COULD TURN IN TOMORROW...
...I HOPE YOU GET THE PRAISE YOU'RE AFTER!
I-I WOULD NEVER WANT HIS PRAISE...!
OH MY. YOUR HIGHNESSES?
WHAT BRINGS YOU OUT HERE?
LISTEN TO THIS, TEACH! LEONIE HERE WANTS TO—
GAH, I'M TELLING YOU, I DON'T...!
AH, PROFESSOR HEINE, I ALMOST FORGOT...
...TO ADDRESS THE SUBJECT OF WHO YOU REALLY ARE.

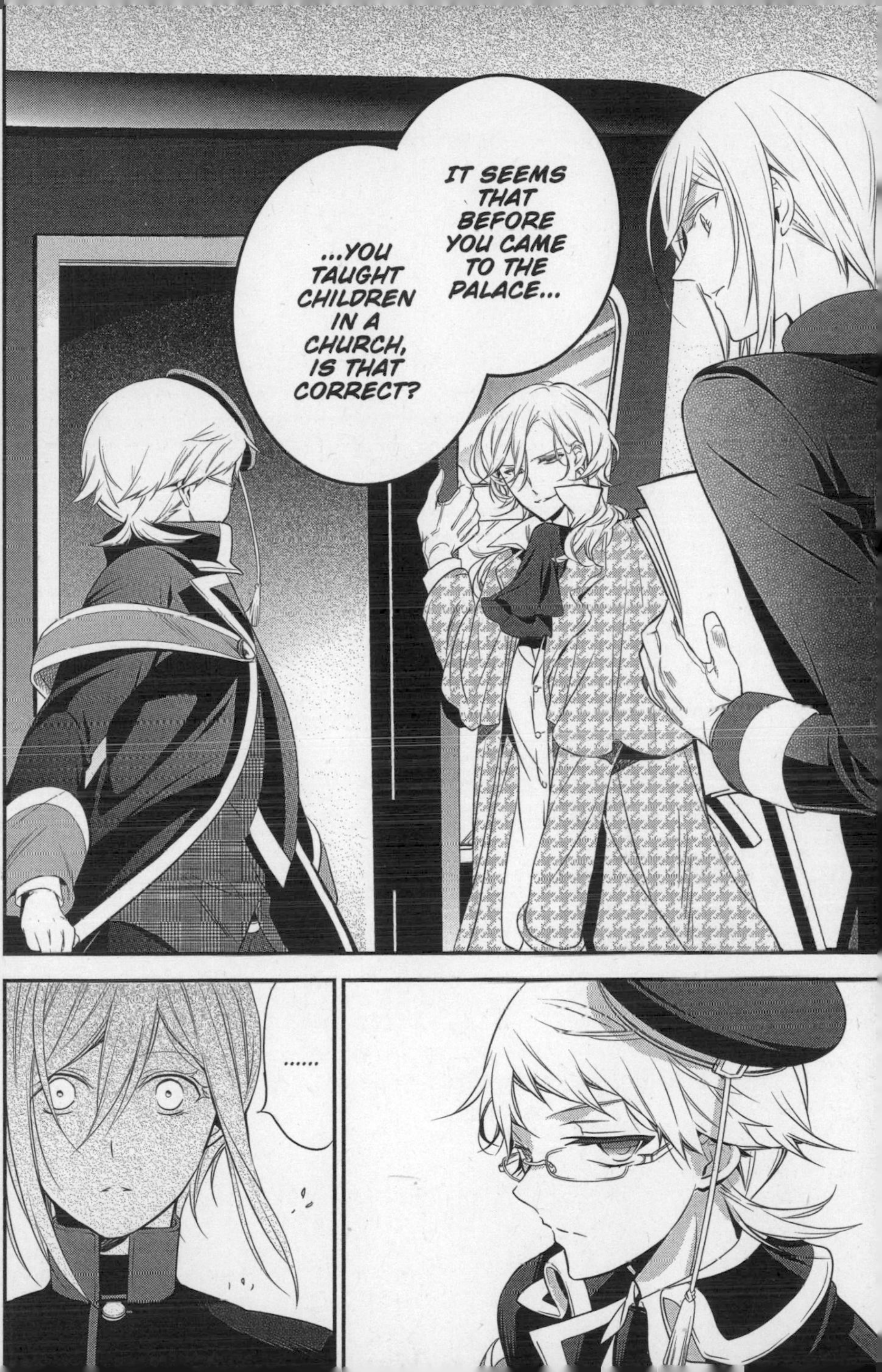
IT SEEMS THAT BEFORE YOU CAME TO THE PALACE...
...YOU TAUGHT CHILDREN IN A CHURCH, IS THAT CORRECT?
......

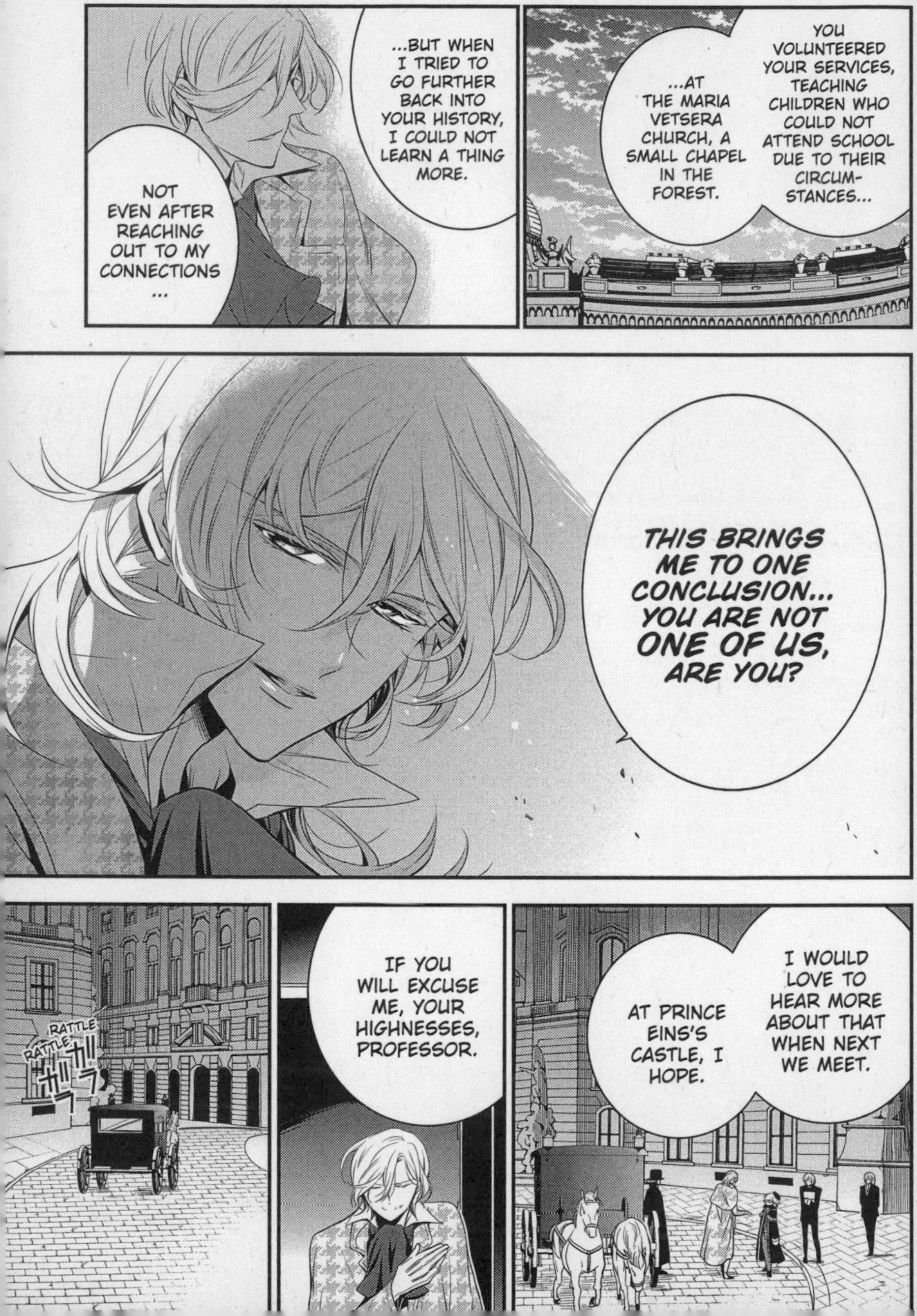
YOU VOLUNTEERED YOUR SERVICES, TEACHING CHILDREN WHO COULD NOT ATTEND SCHOOL DUE TO THEIR CIRCUM-STANCES...
...AT THE MARIA VETSERA CHURCH, A SMALL CHAPEL IN THE FOREST.
...BUT WHEN I TRIED TO GO FURTHER BACK INTO YOUR HISTORY, I COULD NOT LEARN A THING MORE.
NOT EVEN AFTER REACHING OUT TO MY CONNECTIONS ...
THIS BRINGS ME TO ONE CONCLUSION... YOU ARE NOT ONE OF US, ARE YOU?
I WOULD LOVE TO HEAR MORE ABOUT THAT WHEN NEXT WE MEET.
AT PRINCE EINS'S CASTLE, I HOPE.
IF YOU WILL EXCUSE ME, YOUR HIGHNESSES, PROFESSOR.
RATTLE RATTLE

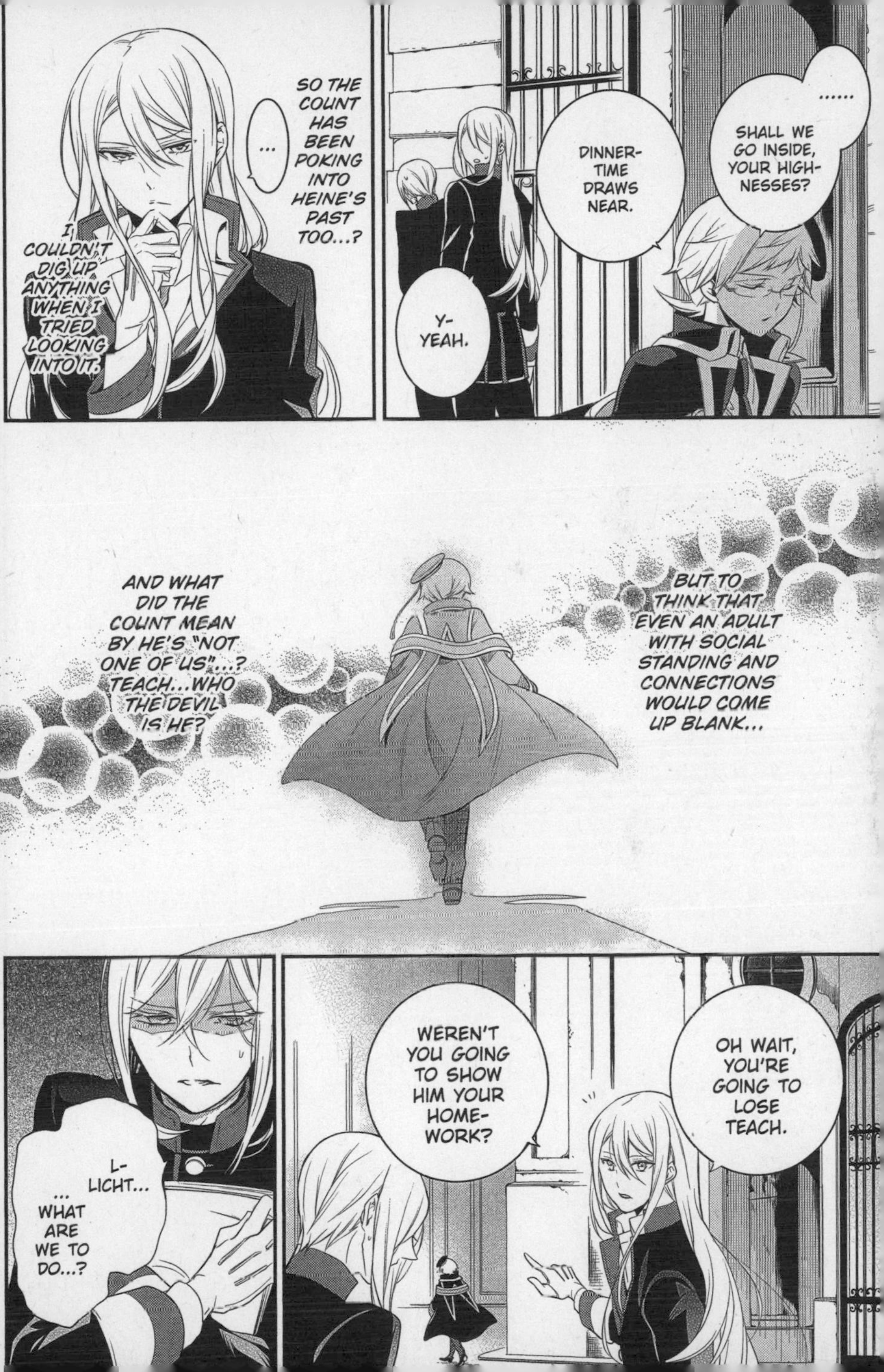
......
SHALL WE GO INSIDE, YOUR HIGHNESSES?
DINNER-TIME DRAWS NEAR.
Y-YEAH.
SO THE COUNT HAS BEEN POKING INTO HEINE'S PAST TOO...?
...
I COULDN'T DIG UP ANYTHING WHEN I TRIED LOOKING INTO IT.
BUT TO THINK THAT EVEN AN ADULT WITH SOCIAL STANDING AND CONNECTIONS WOULD COME UP BLANK...
AND WHAT DID THE COUNT MEAN BY HE'S "NOT ONE OF US"...? TEACH...WHO THE DEVIL IS HE?
OH WAIT, YOU'RE GOING TO LOSE TEACH.
WEREN'T YOU GOING TO SHOW HIM YOUR HOMEWORK?
L-LICHT...
...WHAT ARE WE TO DO...?

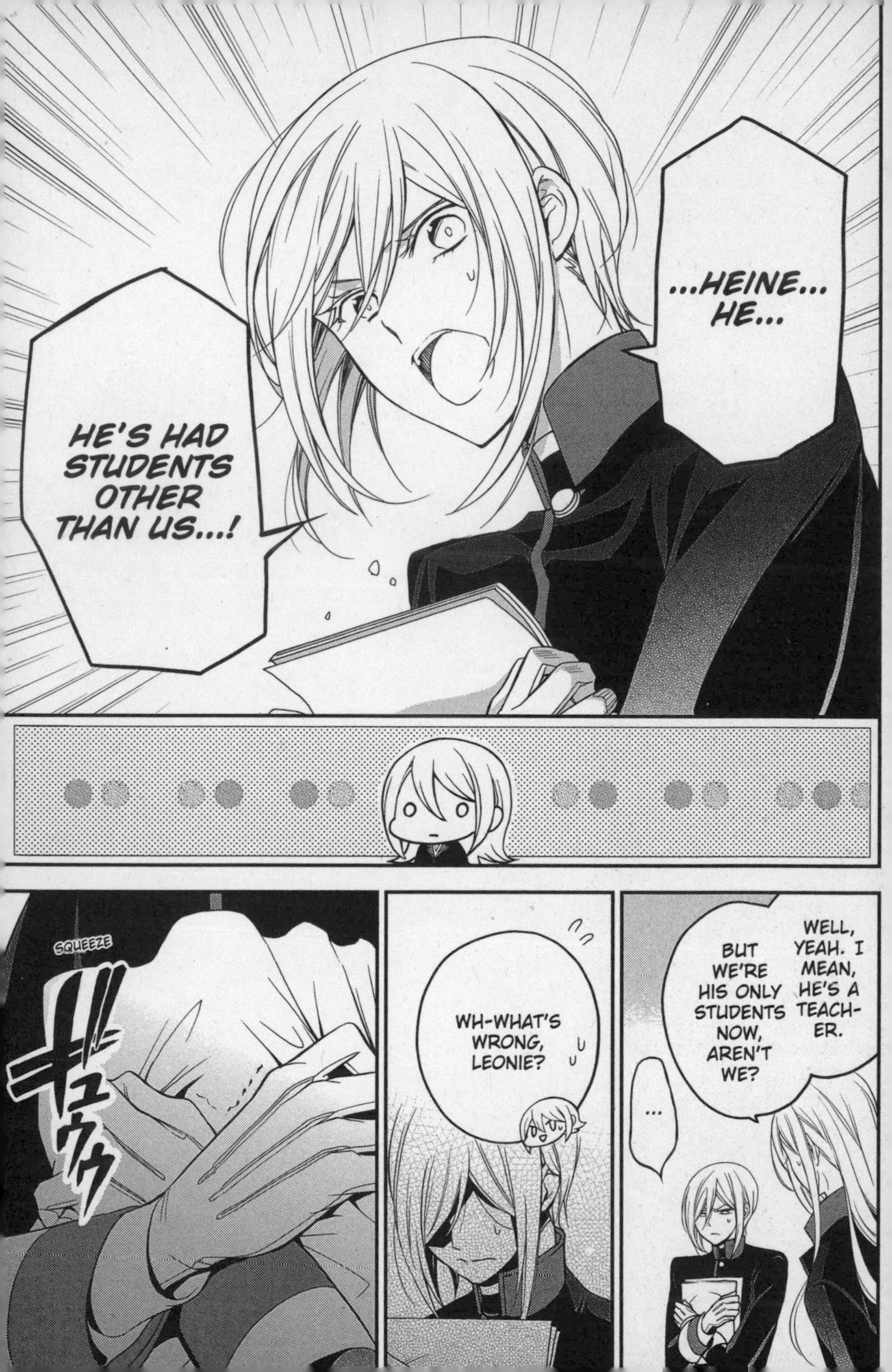
...HEINE... HE...
HE'S HAD STUDENTS OTHER THAN US...!
WELL, YEAH. I MEAN, HE'S A TEACH-ER.
BUT WE'RE HIS ONLY STUDENTS NOW, AREN'T WE?
...
WH-WHAT'S WRONG, LEONIE?
SQUEEZE

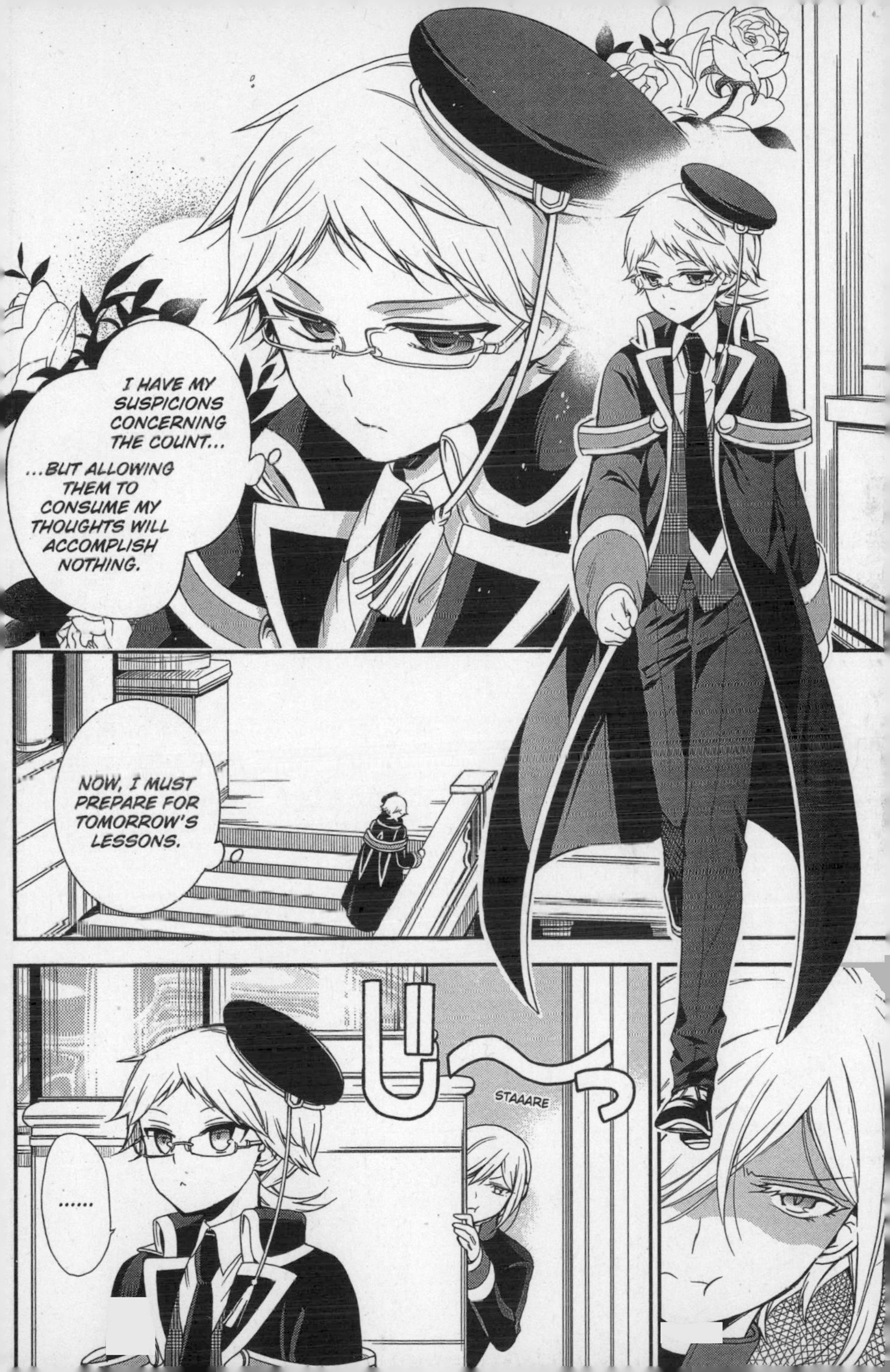
I HAVE MY SUSPICIONS CONCERNING THE COUNT...
...BUT ALLOWING THEM TO CONSUME MY THOUGHTS WILL ACCOMPLISH NOTHING.
NOW, I MUST PREPARE FOR TOMORROW'S LESSONS.
STAAARE
......

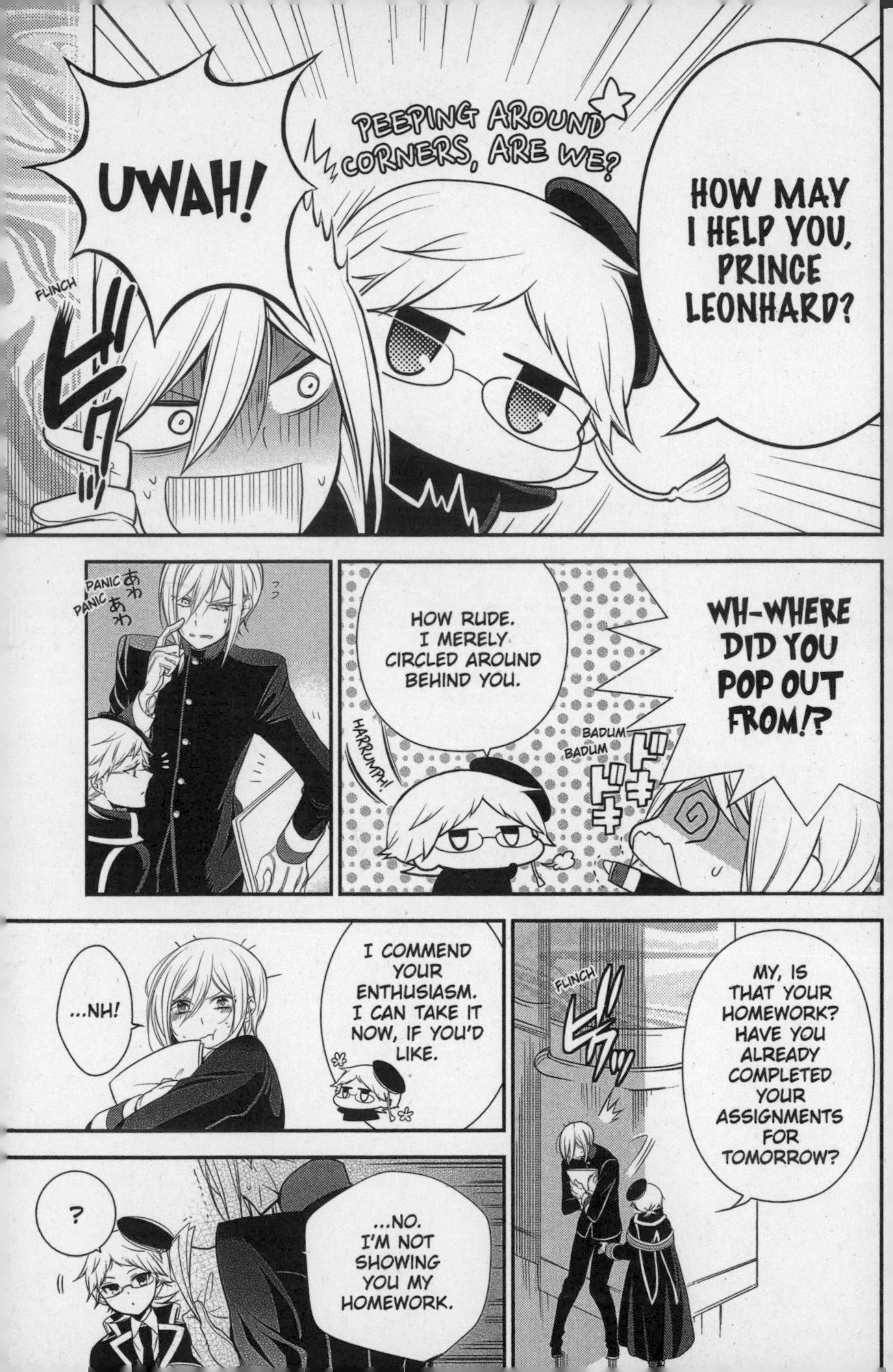
HOW MAY I HELP YOU, PRINCE LEONHARD?
PEEPING AROUND CORNERS, ARE WE?
UWAH!
FLINCH
ビクッ
WH-WHERE DID YOU POP OUT FROM!?
BADUM BADUM
ドキドキ
HOW RUDE. I MERELY CIRCLED AROUND BEHIND YOU.
HARRUMPH!
PANIC PANIC
あわあわ
MY, IS THAT YOUR HOMEWORK? HAVE YOU ALREADY COMPLETED YOUR ASSIGNMENTS FOR TOMORROW?
FLINCH
ビクッ
I COMMEND YOUR ENTHUSIASM. I CAN TAKE IT NOW, IF YOU'D LIKE.
...NH!
...NO. I'M NOT SHOWING YOU MY HOMEWORK.
?

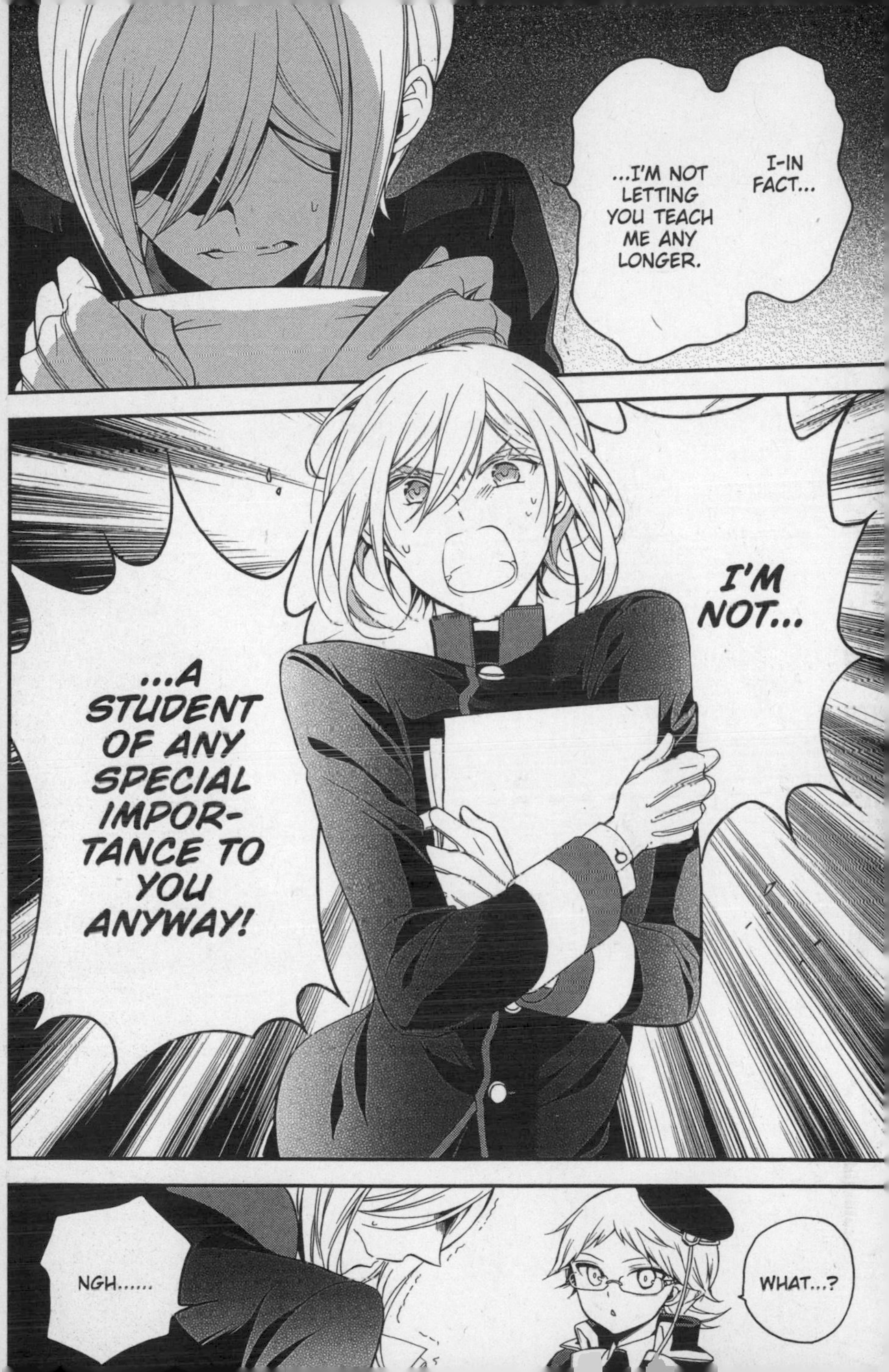
I-IN FACT...
...I'M NOT LETTING YOU TEACH ME ANY LONGER.
I'M NOT...
...A STUDENT OF ANY SPECIAL IMPORTANCE TO YOU ANYWAY!
WHAT...?
NGH......

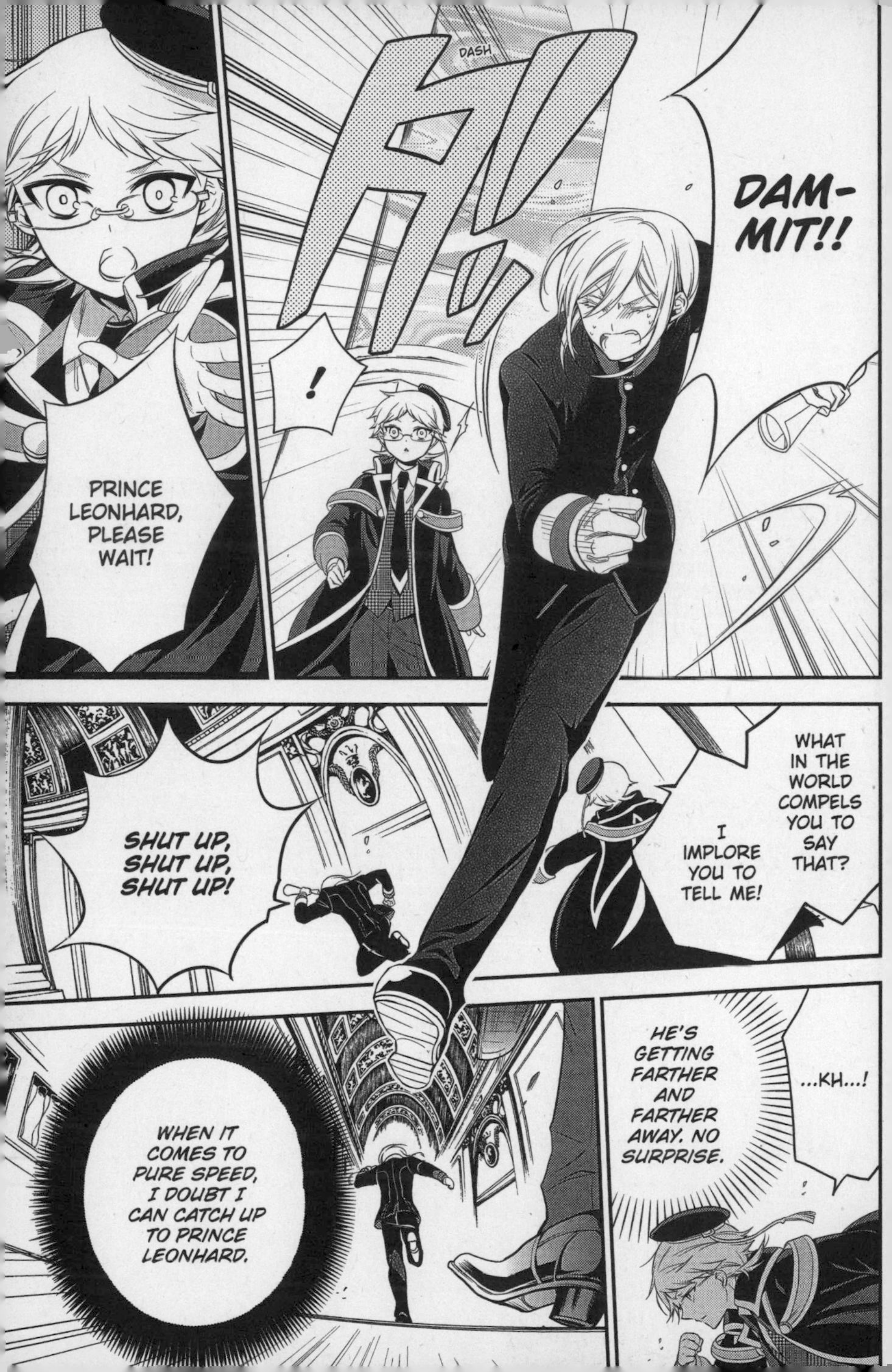
DASH
DAM-MIT!!
!
PRINCE LEONHARD, PLEASE WAIT!
WHAT IN THE WORLD COMPELS YOU TO SAY THAT?
I IMPLORE YOU TO TELL ME!
SHUT UP, SHUT UP, SHUT UP!
...KH...!
HE'S GETTING FARTHER AND FARTHER AWAY. NO SURPRISE.
WHEN IT COMES TO PURE SPEED, I DOUBT I CAN CATCH UP TO PRINCE LEONHARD.

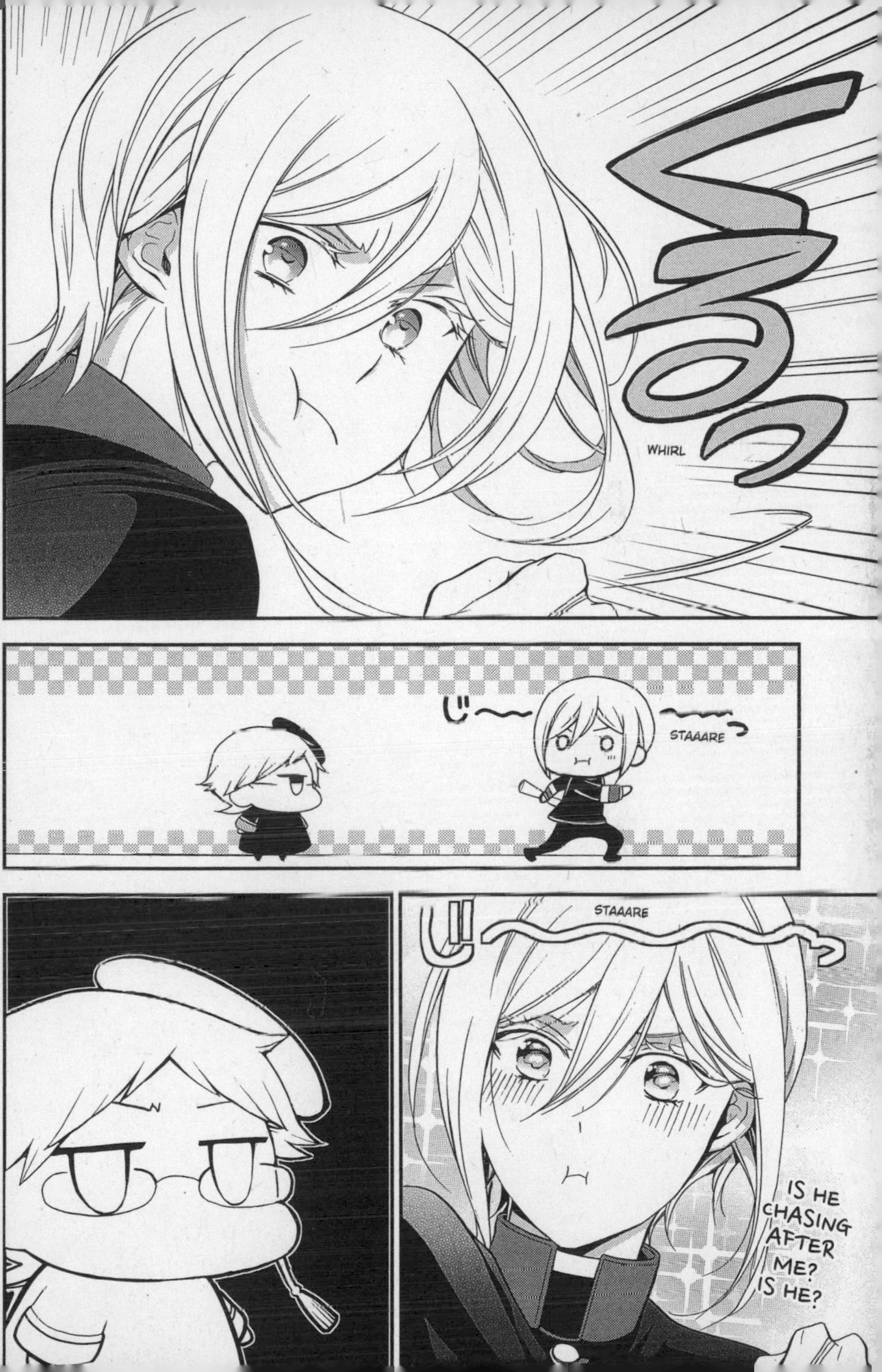
WHIRL
STAAARE
STAAARE
IS HE CHASING AFTER ME? IS HE?

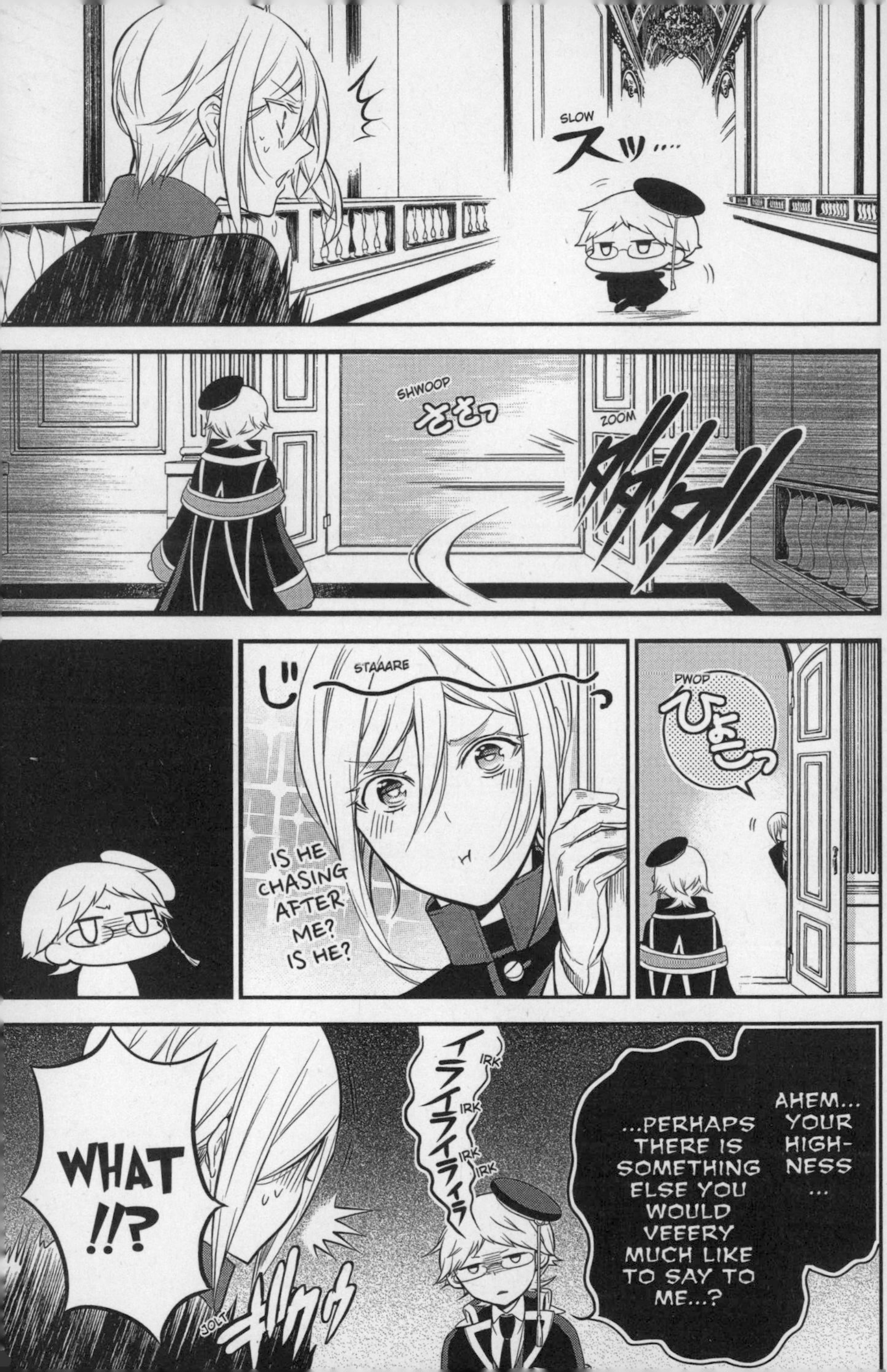
SLOW
スッ…
SHWOOP
そそっ
ZOOM
ダダダッ
PWOP
ひょこっ
STAAARE
じーっ
IS HE CHASING AFTER ME? IS HE?
AHEM... YOUR HIGHNESS...
...PERHAPS THERE IS SOMETHING ELSE YOU WOULD VEEERY MUCH LIKE TO SAY TO ME...?
IRK IRK IRK IRK
イライライラ
WHAT!!?
JOLT
ギクウ

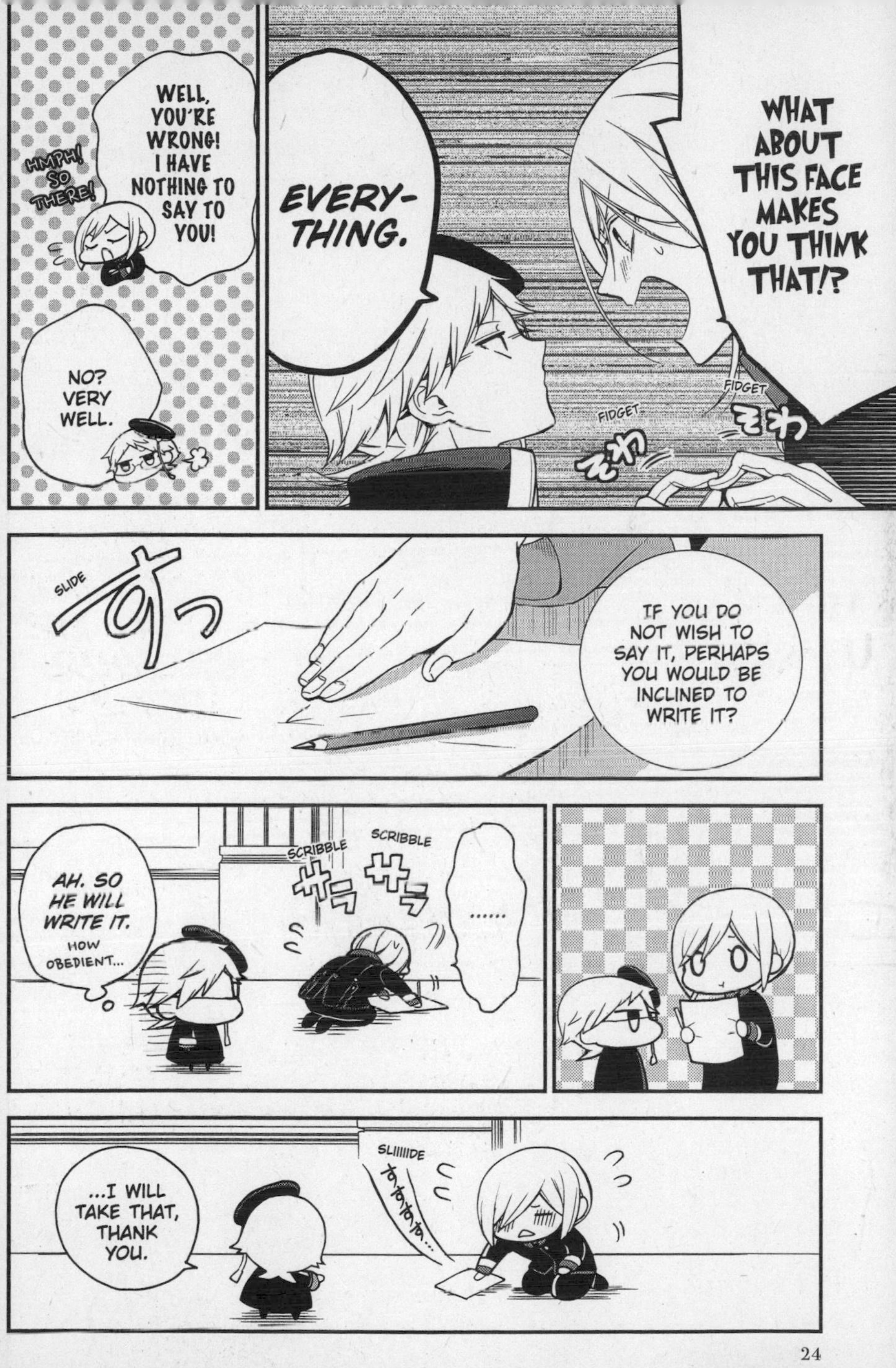
WHAT ABOUT THIS FACE MAKES YOU THINK THAT!?
EVERY-THING.
FIDGET
FIDGET
WELL, YOU'RE WRONG! I HAVE NOTHING TO SAY TO YOU!
HMPH! SO THERE!
NO? VERY WELL.
IF YOU DO NOT WISH TO SAY IT, PERHAPS YOU WOULD BE INCLINED TO WRITE IT?
SLIDE
......
SCRIBBLE
SCRIBBLE
AH. SO HE WILL WRITE IT.
HOW OBEDIENT...
SLIIIIIDE
...I WILL TAKE THAT, THANK YOU.

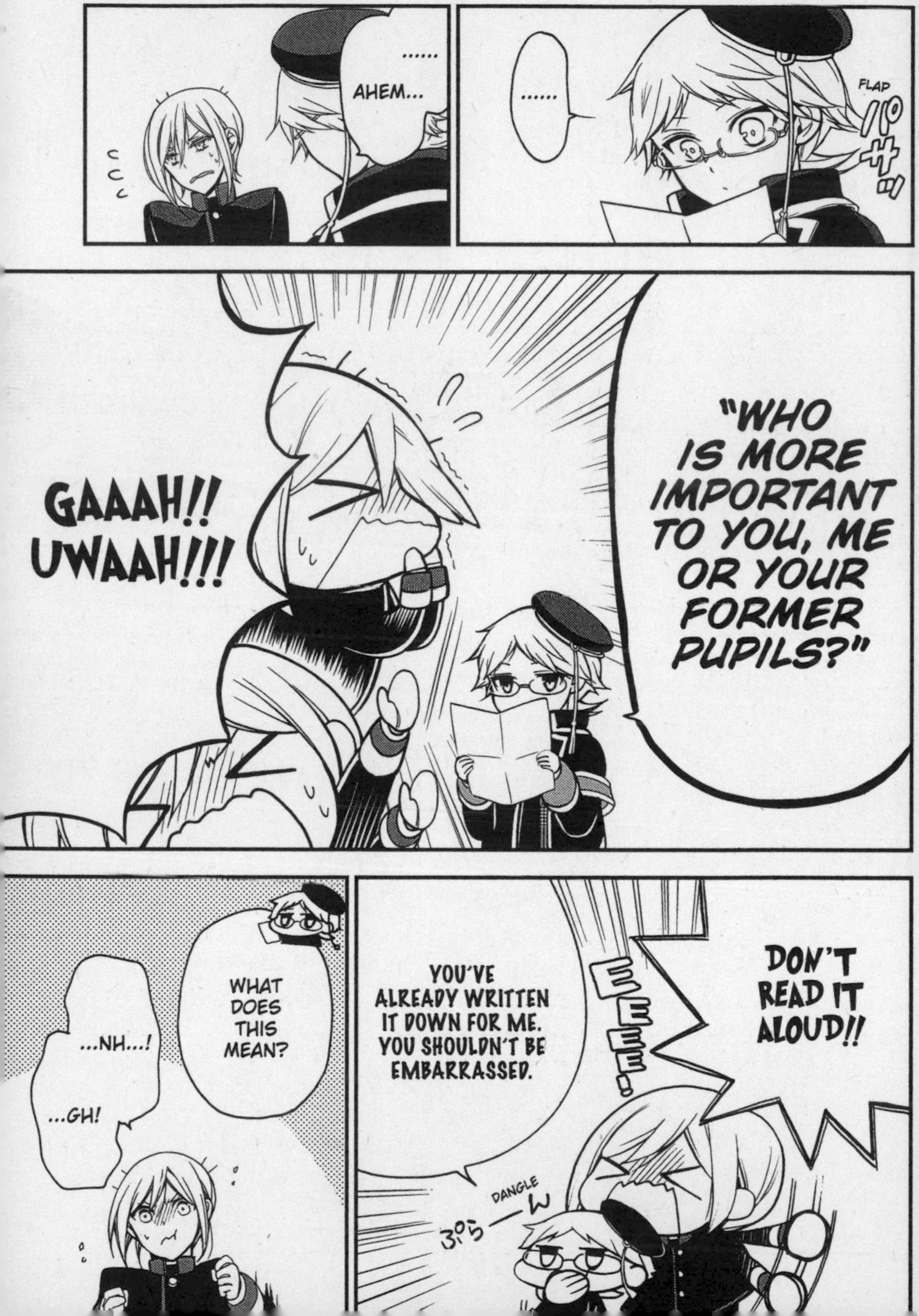
......
FLAP
パサッ
......
AHEM...
"WHO IS MORE IMPORTANT TO YOU, ME OR YOUR FORMER PUPILS?"
GAAAH!! UWAAH!!!
DON'T READ IT ALOUD!!
EEEEE!
YOU'VE ALREADY WRITTEN IT DOWN FOR ME. YOU SHOULDN'T BE EMBARRASSED.
DANGLE
ぷら—ん
WHAT DOES THIS MEAN?
...NH...!
...GH!

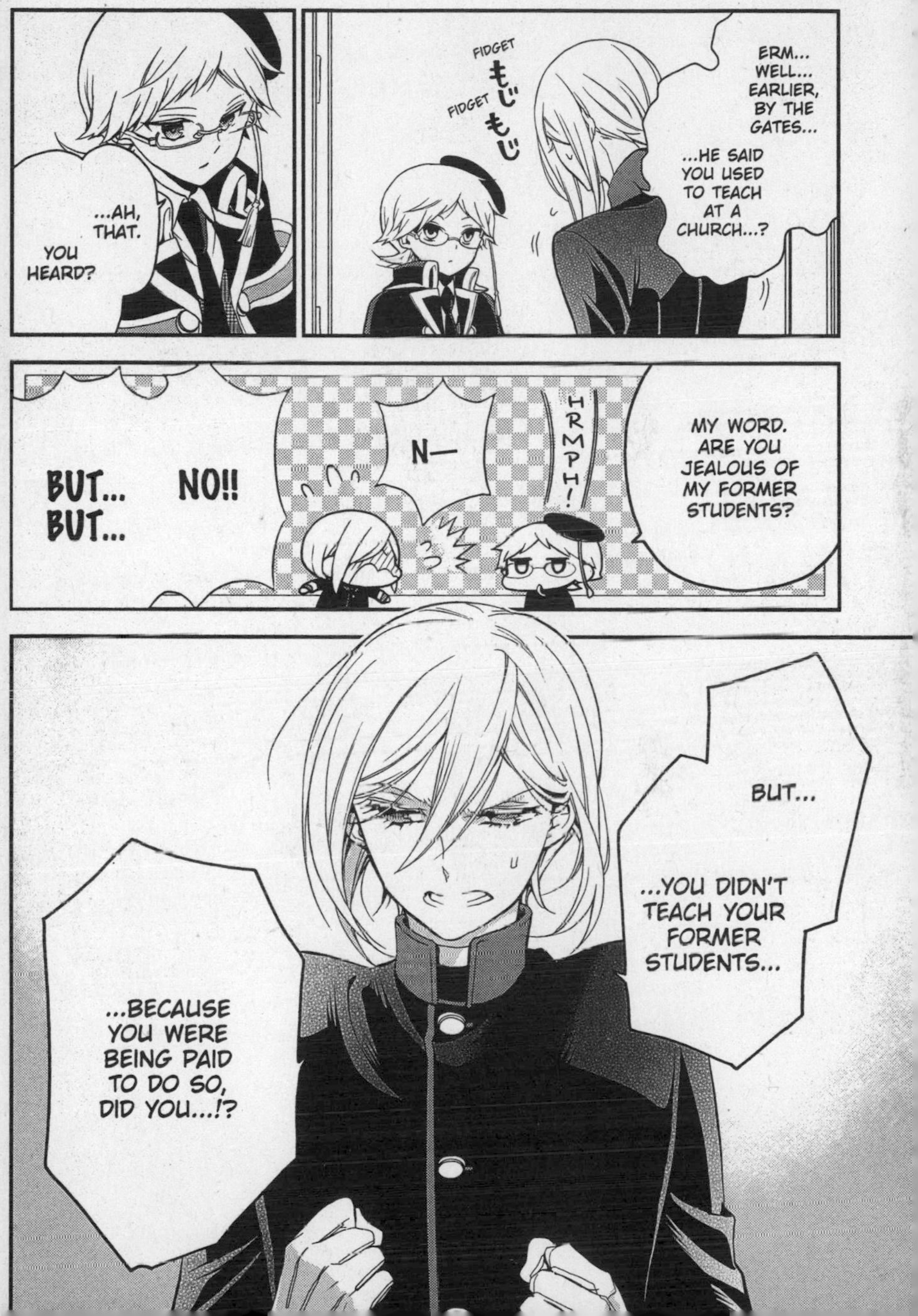
ERM... WELL... EARLIER, BY THE GATES...
...HE SAID YOU USED TO TEACH AT A CHURCH...?
FIDGET
もじ
FIDGET
もじ
...AH, THAT.
YOU HEARD?
MY WORD. ARE YOU JEALOUS OF MY FORMER STUDENTS?
HRMPH!
N—
NO!!
BUT... BUT...
BUT...
...YOU DIDN'T TEACH YOUR FORMER STUDENTS...
...BECAUSE YOU WERE BEING PAID TO DO SO, DID YOU...!?

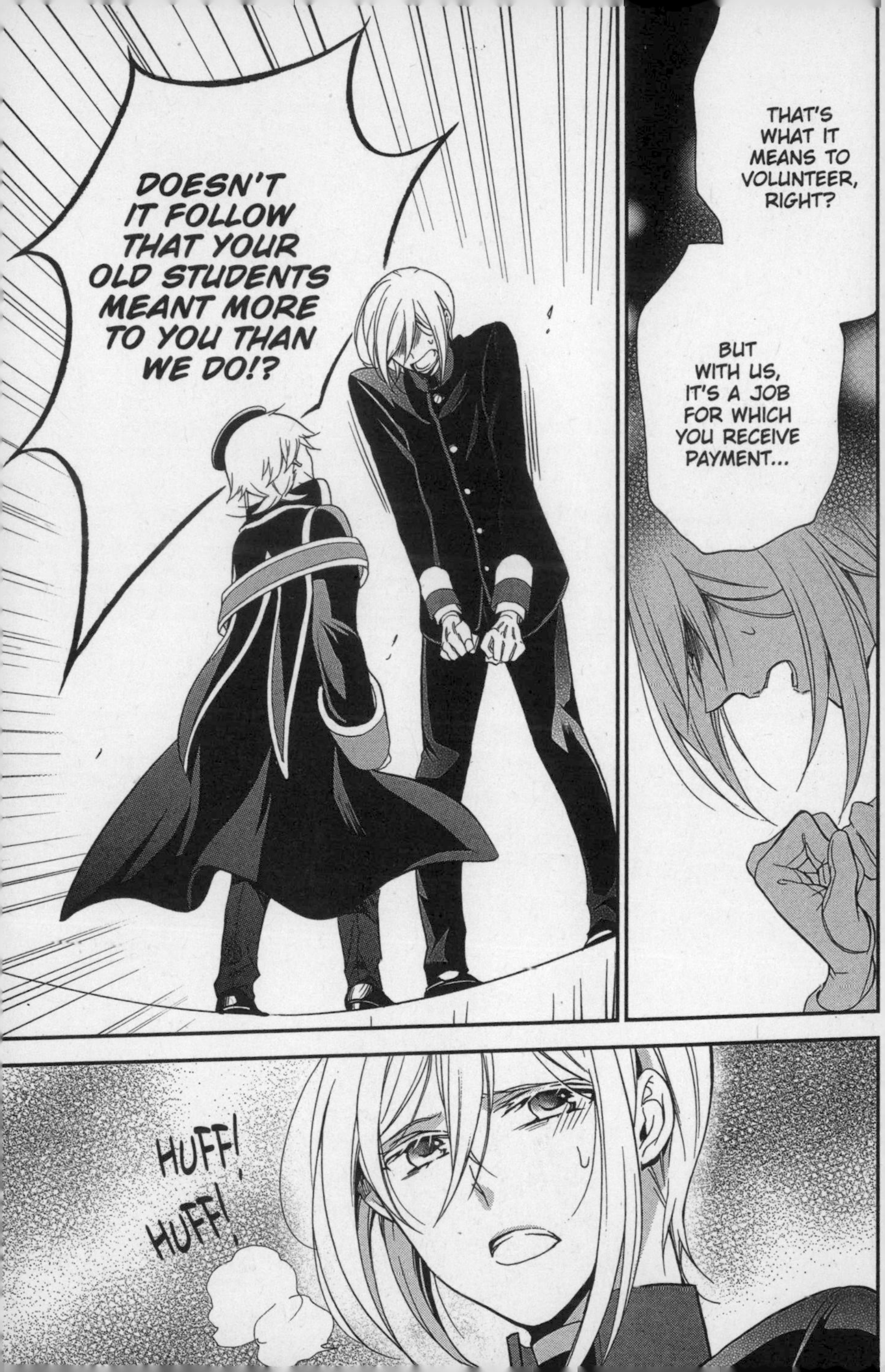
THAT'S WHAT IT MEANS TO VOLUNTEER, RIGHT?
BUT WITH US, IT'S A JOB FOR WHICH YOU RECEIVE PAYMENT...
DOESN'T IT FOLLOW THAT YOUR OLD STUDENTS MEANT MORE TO YOU THAN WE DO!?
HUFF! HUFF!

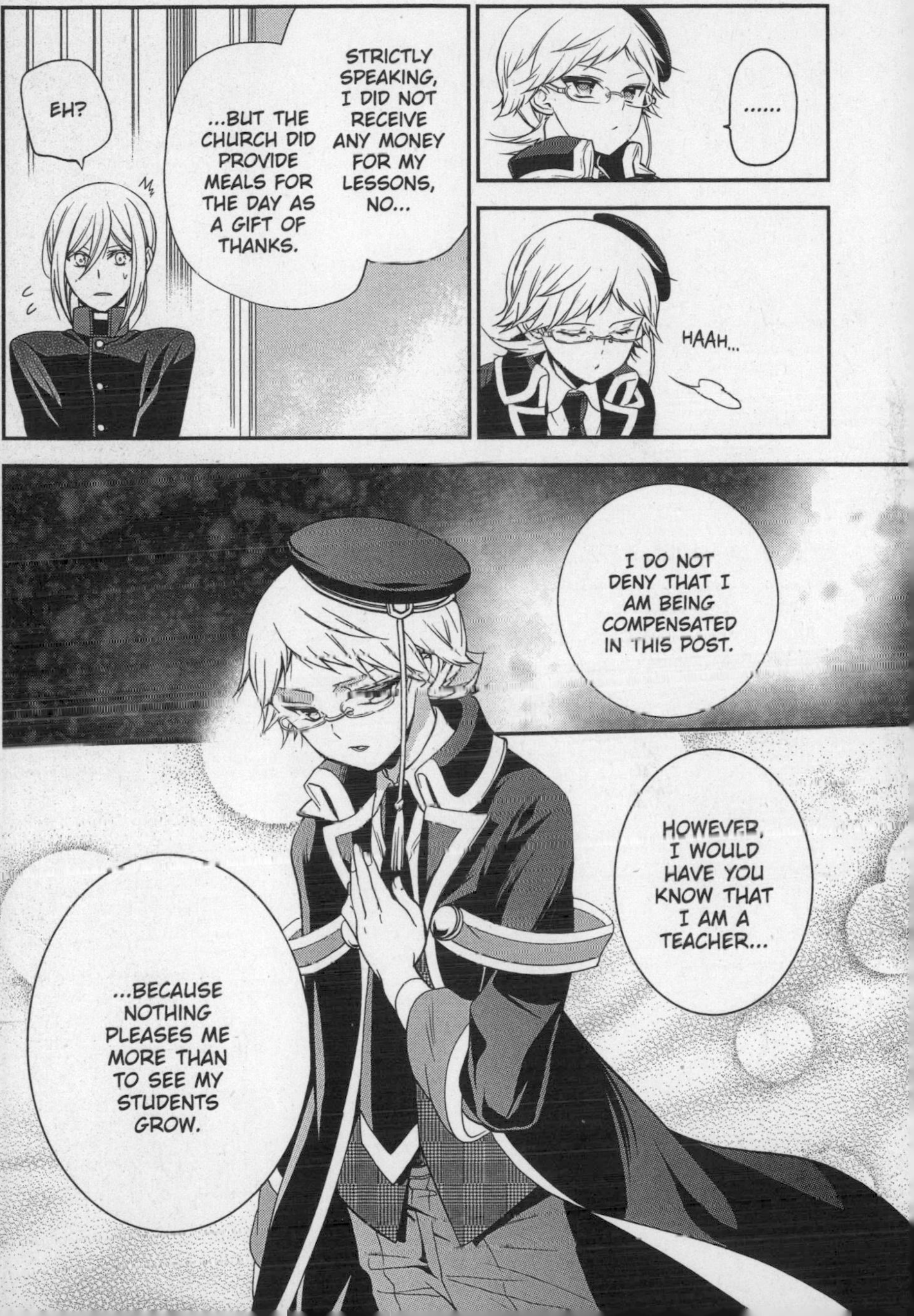
......
HAAH...
STRICTLY SPEAKING, I DID NOT RECEIVE ANY MONEY FOR MY LESSONS, NO...
...BUT THE CHURCH DID PROVIDE MEALS FOR THE DAY AS A GIFT OF THANKS.
EH?
I DO NOT DENY THAT I AM BEING COMPENSATED IN THIS POST.
HOWEVER, I WOULD HAVE YOU KNOW THAT I AM A TEACHER...
...BECAUSE NOTHING PLEASES ME MORE THAN TO SEE MY STUDENTS GROW.

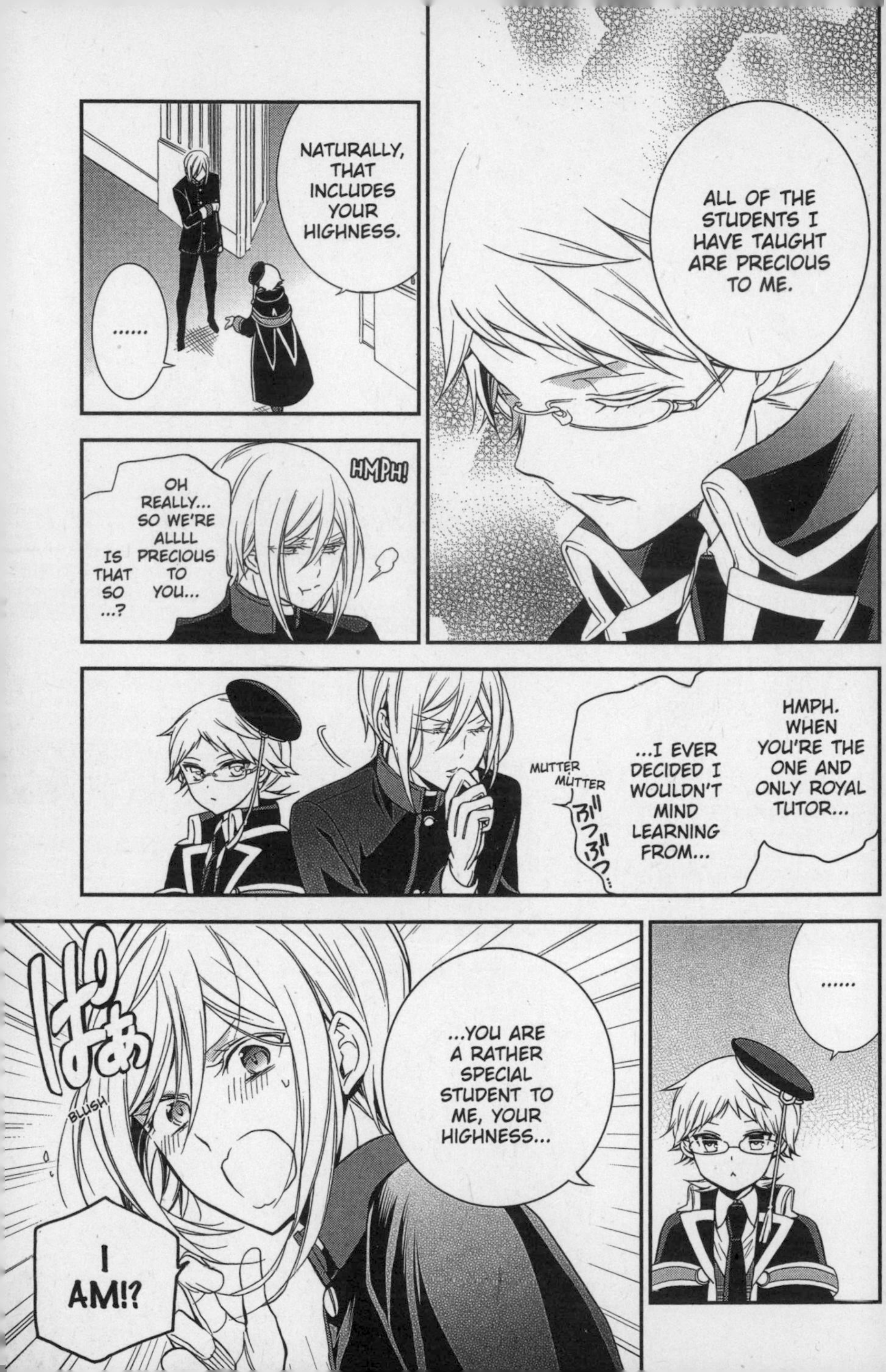
ALL OF THE STUDENTS I HAVE TAUGHT ARE PRECIOUS TO ME.
NATURALLY, THAT INCLUDES YOUR HIGHNESS.
......
HMPH!
OH REALLY... SO WE'RE ALLLL PRECIOUS TO YOU...
IS THAT SO ...?
HMPH. WHEN YOU'RE THE ONE AND ONLY ROYAL TUTOR...
...I EVER DECIDED I WOULDN'T MIND LEARNING FROM...
MUTTER MUTTER
ぶつぶつ...
......
...YOU ARE A RATHER SPECIAL STUDENT TO ME, YOUR HIGHNESS...
ぱあ
BLUSH
I AM!?

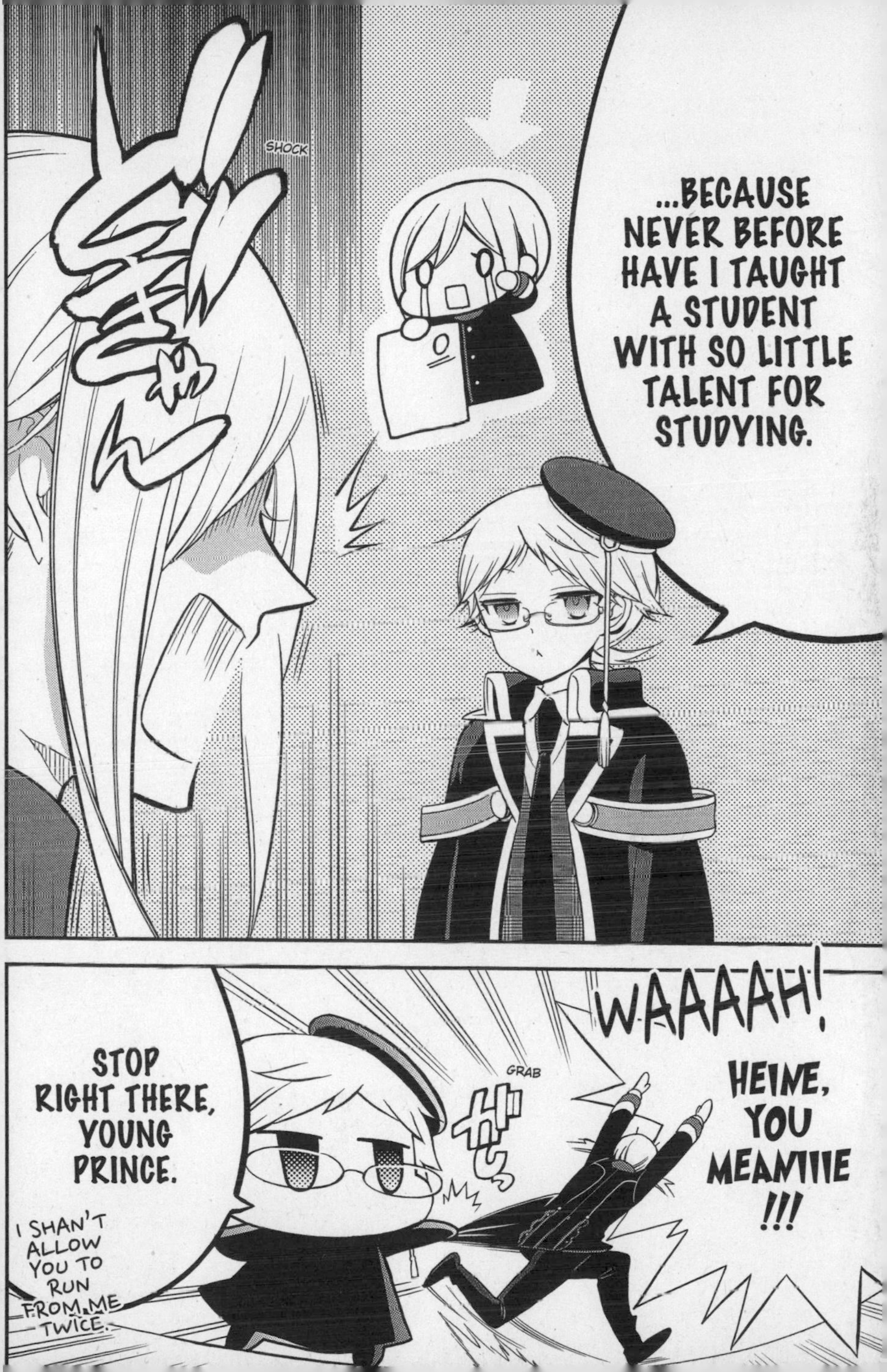
...BECAUSE NEVER BEFORE HAVE I TAUGHT A STUDENT WITH SO LITTLE TALENT FOR STUDYING.
SHOCK
WAAAAH!
HEINE, YOU MEANIIIE !!!
GRAB
STOP RIGHT THERE, YOUNG PRINCE.
I SHAN'T ALLOW YOU TO RUN FROM ME TWICE.

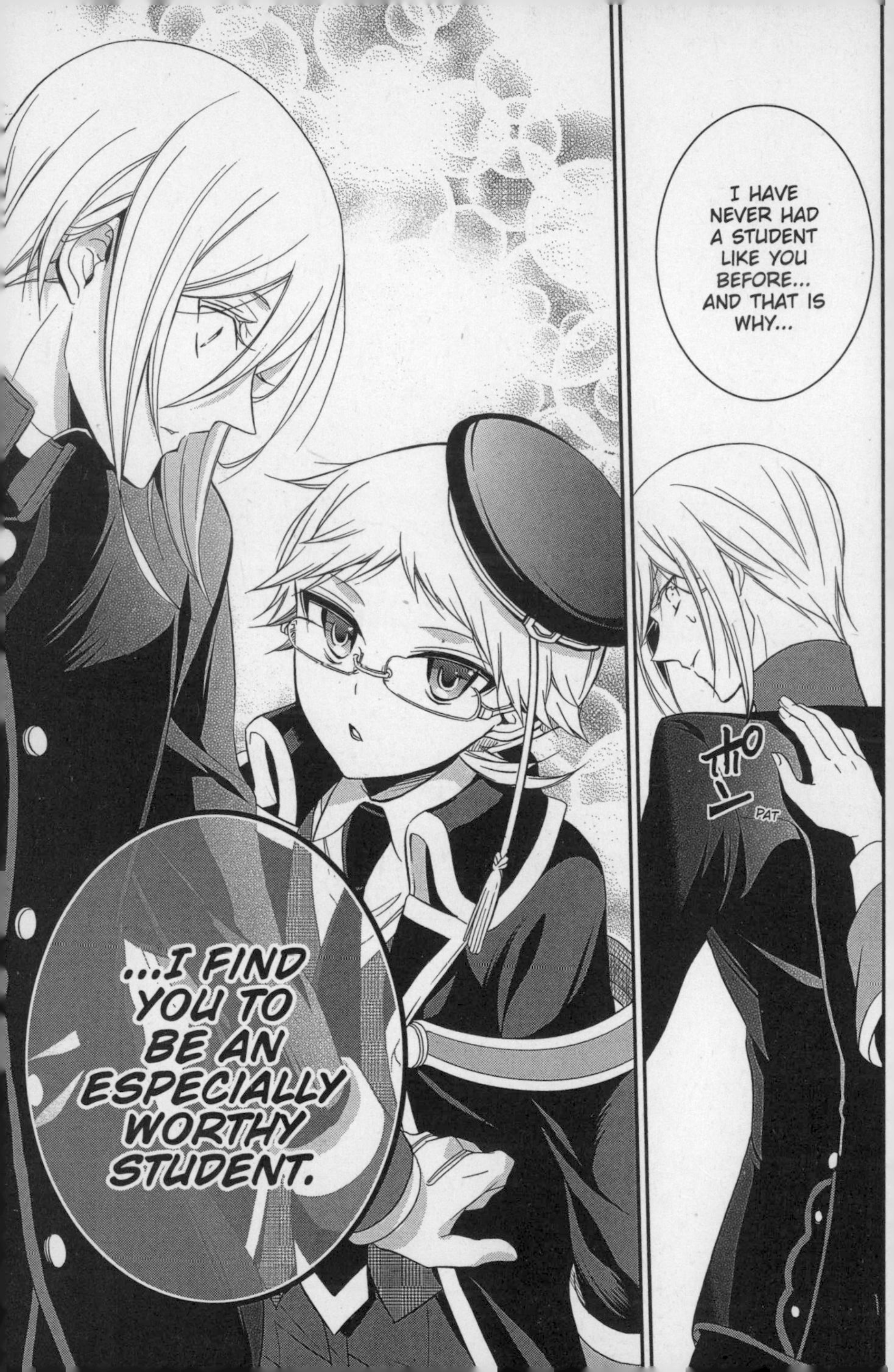
I HAVE NEVER HAD A STUDENT LIKE YOU BEFORE... AND THAT IS WHY...
PAT
...I FIND YOU TO BE AN ESPECIALLY WORTHY STUDENT.

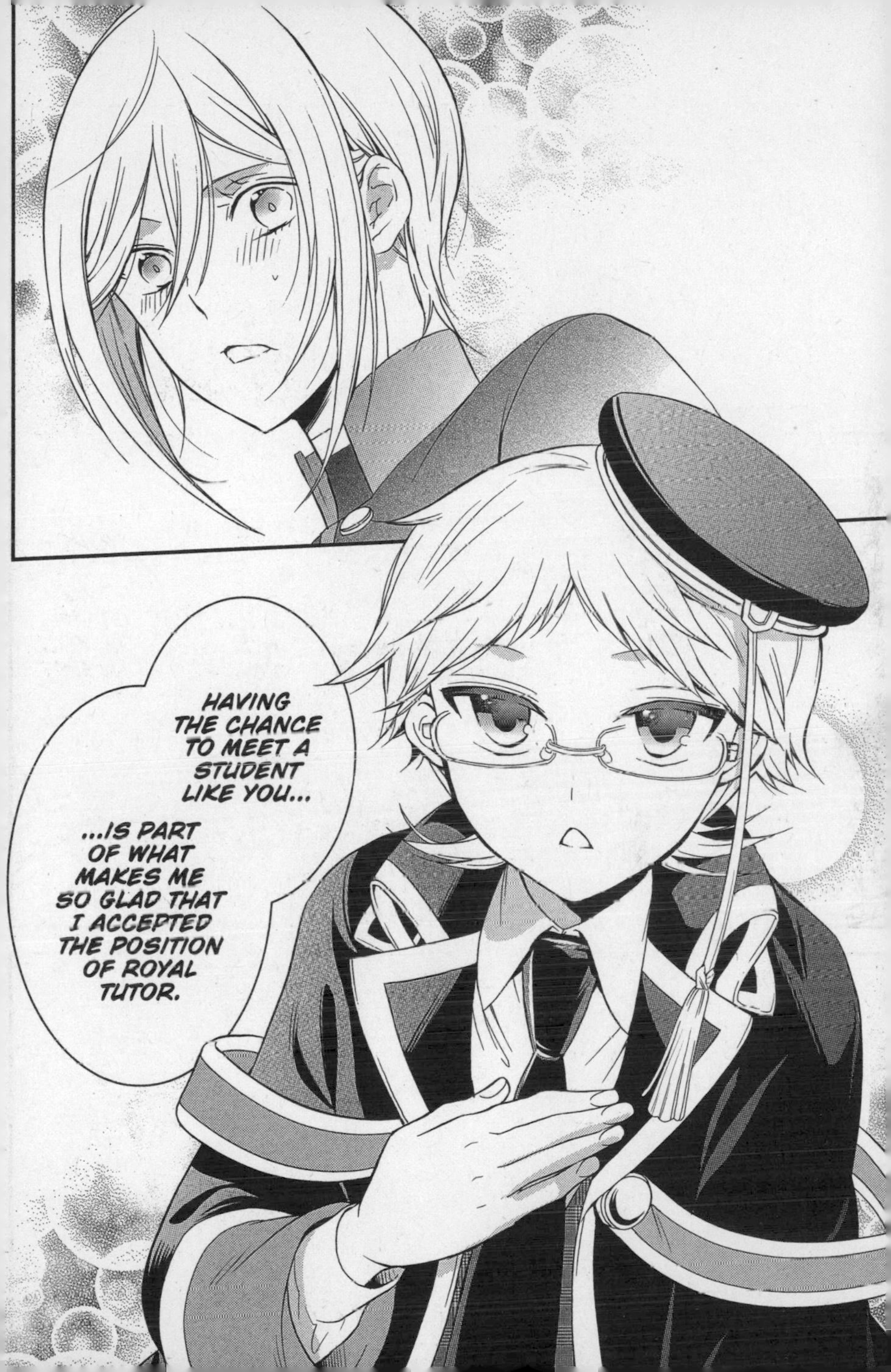
HAVING THE CHANCE TO MEET A STUDENT LIKE YOU...
...IS PART OF WHAT MAKES ME SO GLAD THAT I ACCEPTED THE POSITION OF ROYAL TUTOR.

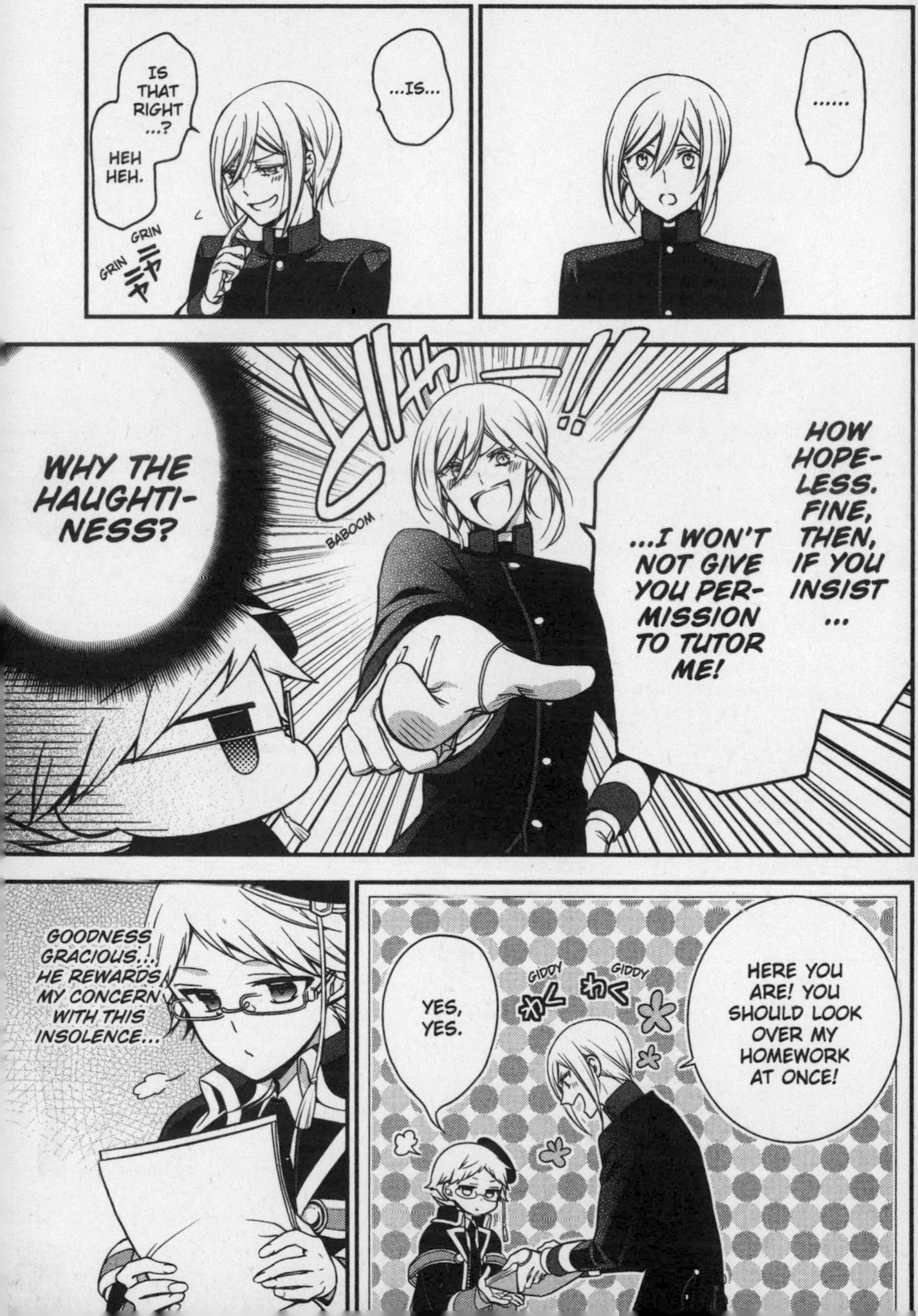
......
...IS...
IS THAT RIGHT ...?
HEH HEH.
GRIN GRIN ニヤニヤ
HOW HOPELESS. FINE, THEN, IF YOU INSIST ...
...I WON'T NOT GIVE YOU PERMISSION TO TUTOR ME!
BABOOM
WHY THE HAUGHTINESS?
HERE YOU ARE! YOU SHOULD LOOK OVER MY HOMEWORK AT ONCE!
GIDDY GIDDY わくわく
YES, YES.
GOODNESS GRACIOUS... HE REWARDS MY CONCERN WITH THIS INSOLENCE...

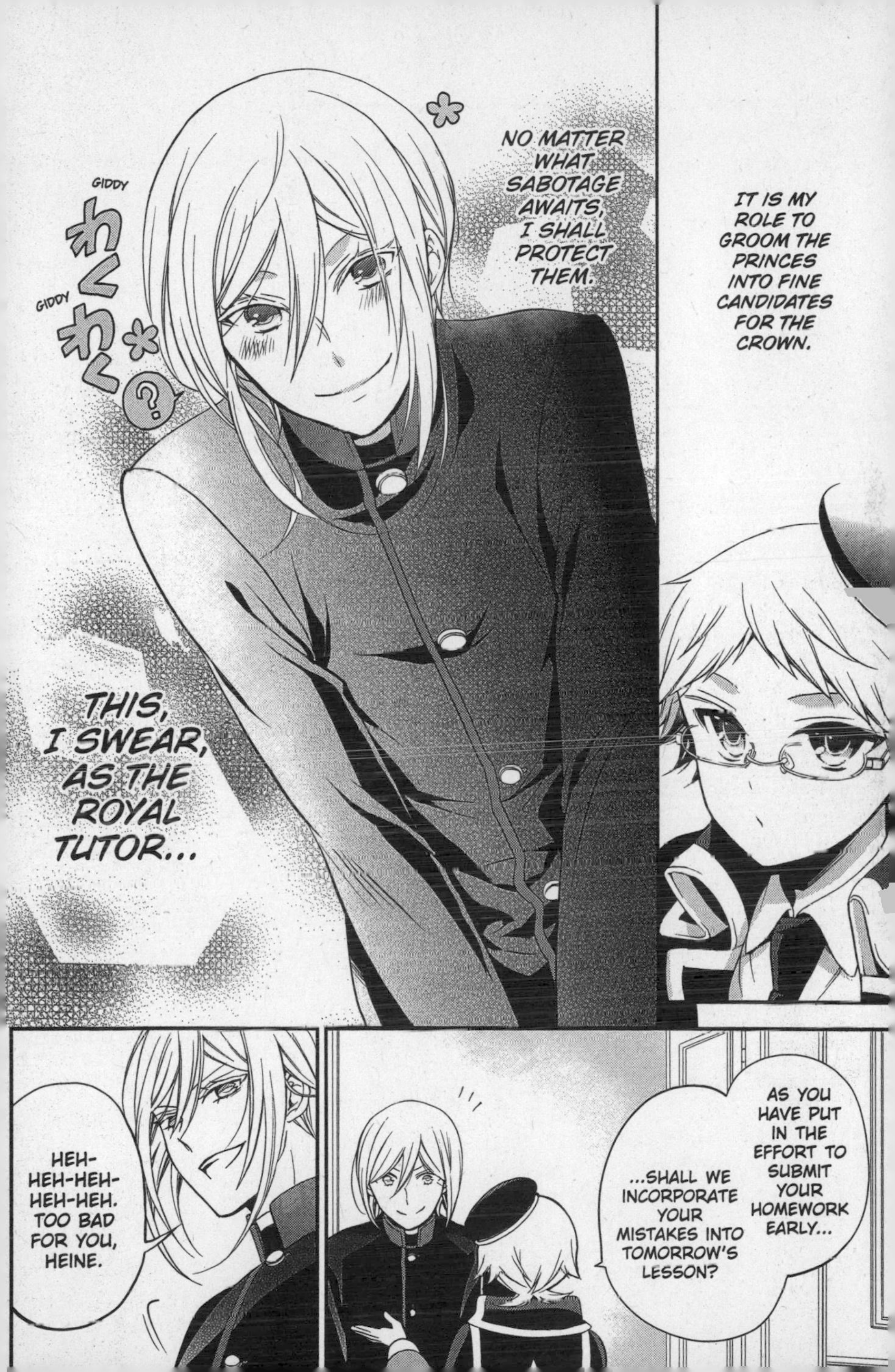

IT IS MY ROLE TO GROOM THE PRINCES INTO FINE CANDIDATES FOR THE CROWN.
NO MATTER WHAT SABOTAGE AWAITS, I SHALL PROTECT THEM.
GIDDY GIDDY
わくわく
?
THIS, I SWEAR, AS THE ROYAL TUTOR...
AS YOU HAVE PUT IN THE EFFORT TO SUBMIT YOUR HOMEWORK EARLY...
...SHALL WE INCORPORATE YOUR MISTAKES INTO TOMORROW'S LESSON?
HEH-HEH-HEH-HEH-HEH. TOO BAD FOR YOU, HEINE.

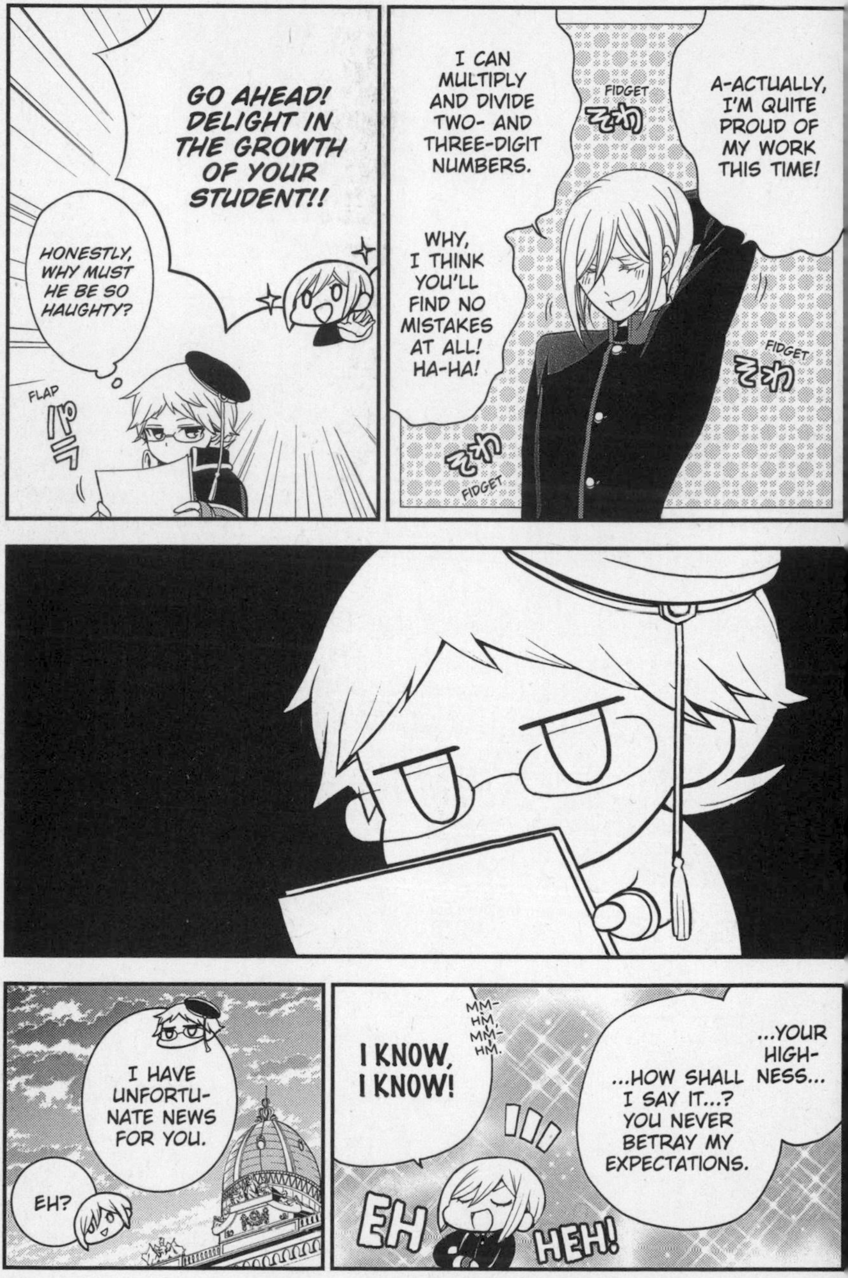
A-ACTUALLY, I'M QUITE PROUD OF MY WORK THIS TIME!
FIDGET
そわ
I CAN MULTIPLY AND DIVIDE TWO- AND THREE-DIGIT NUMBERS.
WHY, I THINK YOU'LL FIND NO MISTAKES AT ALL! HA-HA!
FIDGET
そわ
そわ
FIDGET
GO AHEAD! DELIGHT IN THE GROWTH OF YOUR STUDENT!!
HONESTLY, WHY MUST HE BE SO HAUGHTY?
FLAP
パラ
...YOUR HIGHNESS...
...HOW SHALL I SAY IT...? YOU NEVER BETRAY MY EXPECTATIONS.
MM-HM, MM-HM.
I KNOW, I KNOW!
EH HEH!
I HAVE UNFORTUNATE NEWS FOR YOU.
EH?

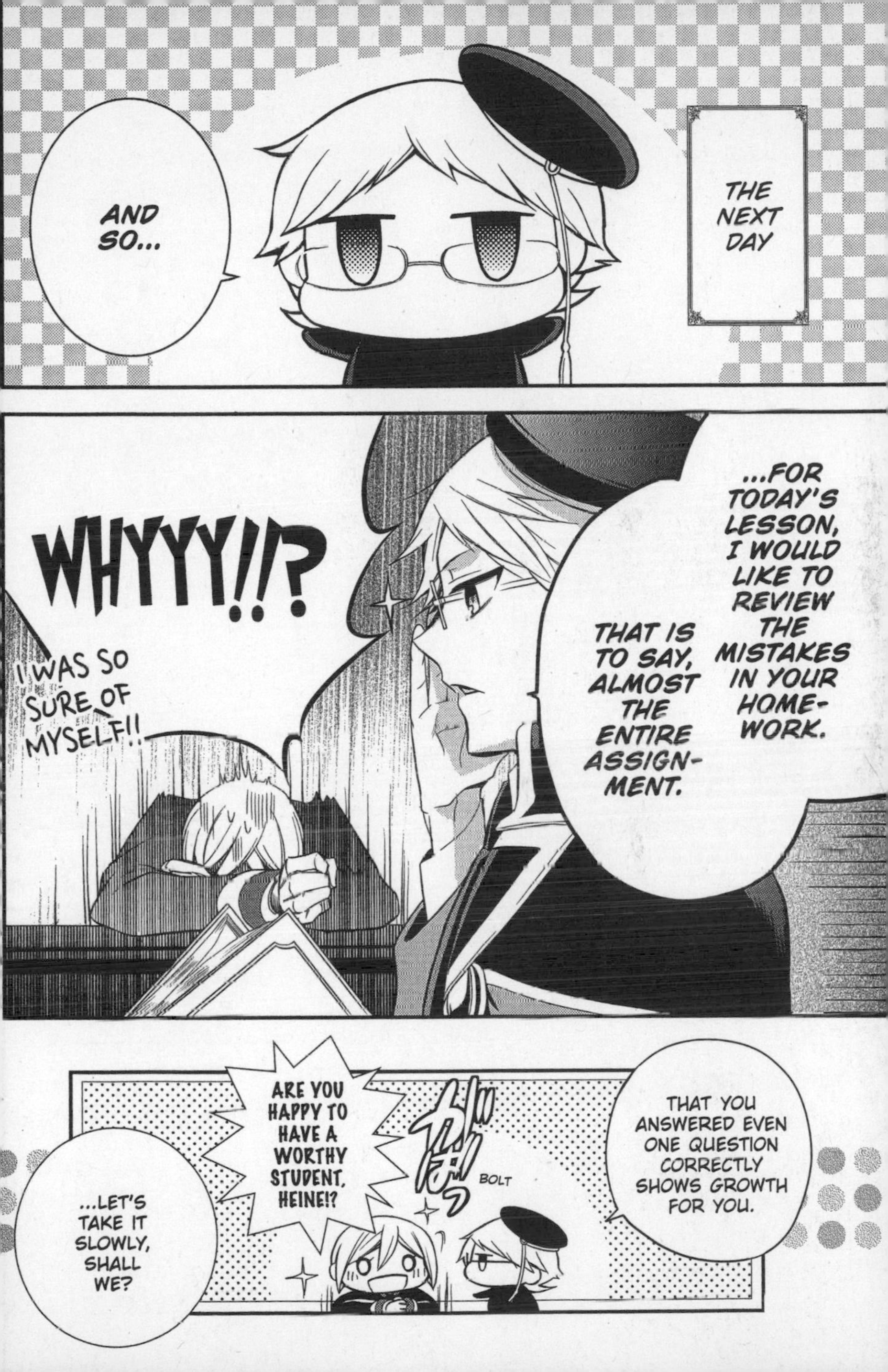
THE NEXT DAY
AND SO...
...FOR TODAY'S LESSON, I WOULD LIKE TO REVIEW THE MISTAKES IN YOUR HOMEWORK.
THAT IS TO SAY, ALMOST THE ENTIRE ASSIGNMENT.
WHYYY!!?
I WAS SO SURE OF MYSELF!!
THAT YOU ANSWERED EVEN ONE QUESTION CORRECTLY SHOWS GROWTH FOR YOU.
BOLT
ARE YOU HAPPY TO HAVE A WORTHY STUDENT, HEINE!?
...LET'S TAKE IT SLOWLY, SHALL WE?

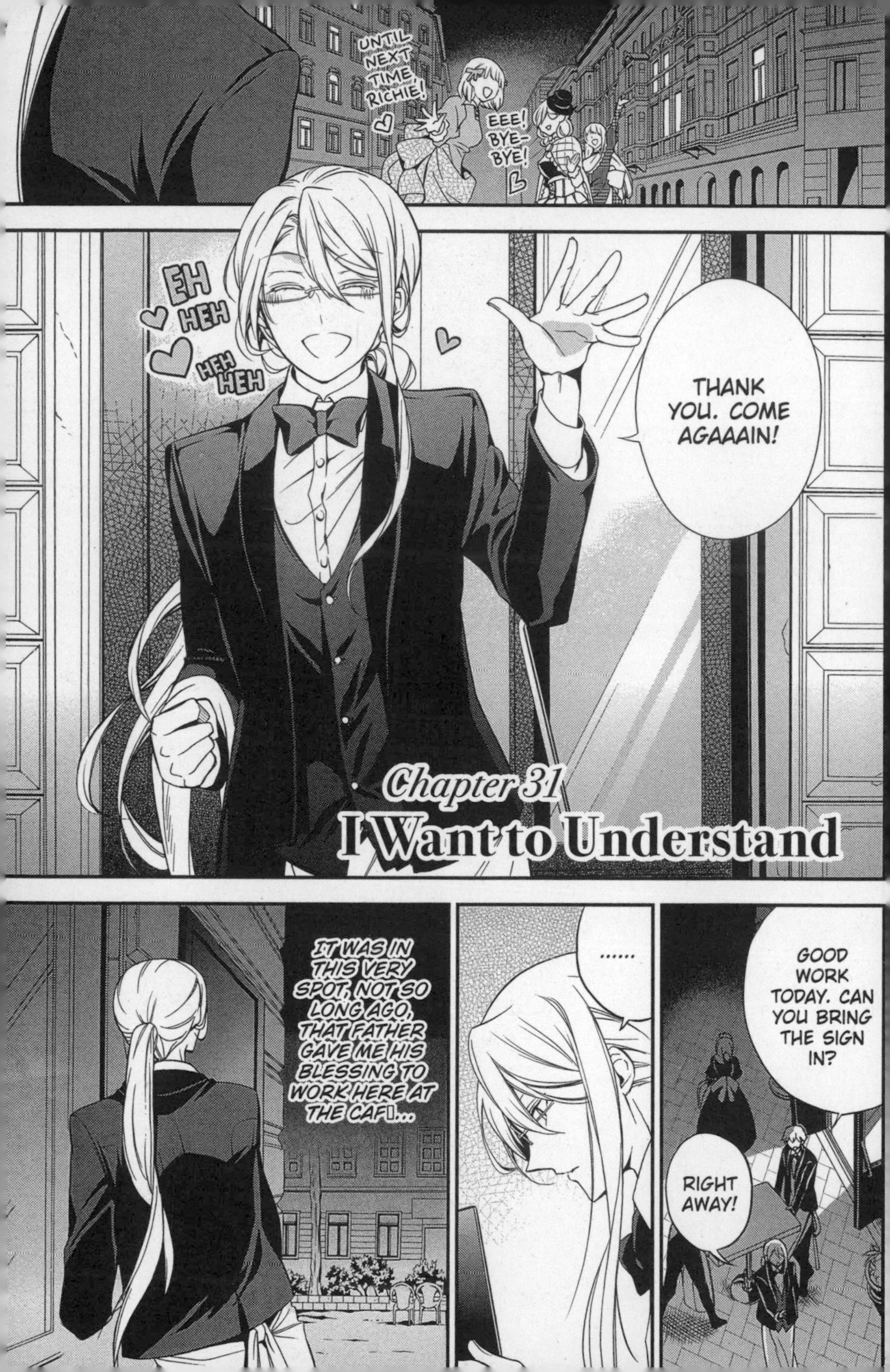
EEE! BYE-BYE! ♡
UNTIL NEXT TIME, RICHIE! ♡
THANK YOU. COME AGAAAIN!
EH HEH ♡ ♡ HEH HEH ♡
Chapter 31
I Want to Understand
GOOD WORK TODAY. CAN YOU BRING THE SIGN IN?
RIGHT AWAY!
......
IT WAS IN THIS VERY SPOT, NOT SO LONG AGO, THAT FATHER GAVE ME HIS BLESSING TO WORK HERE AT THE CAFÉ...

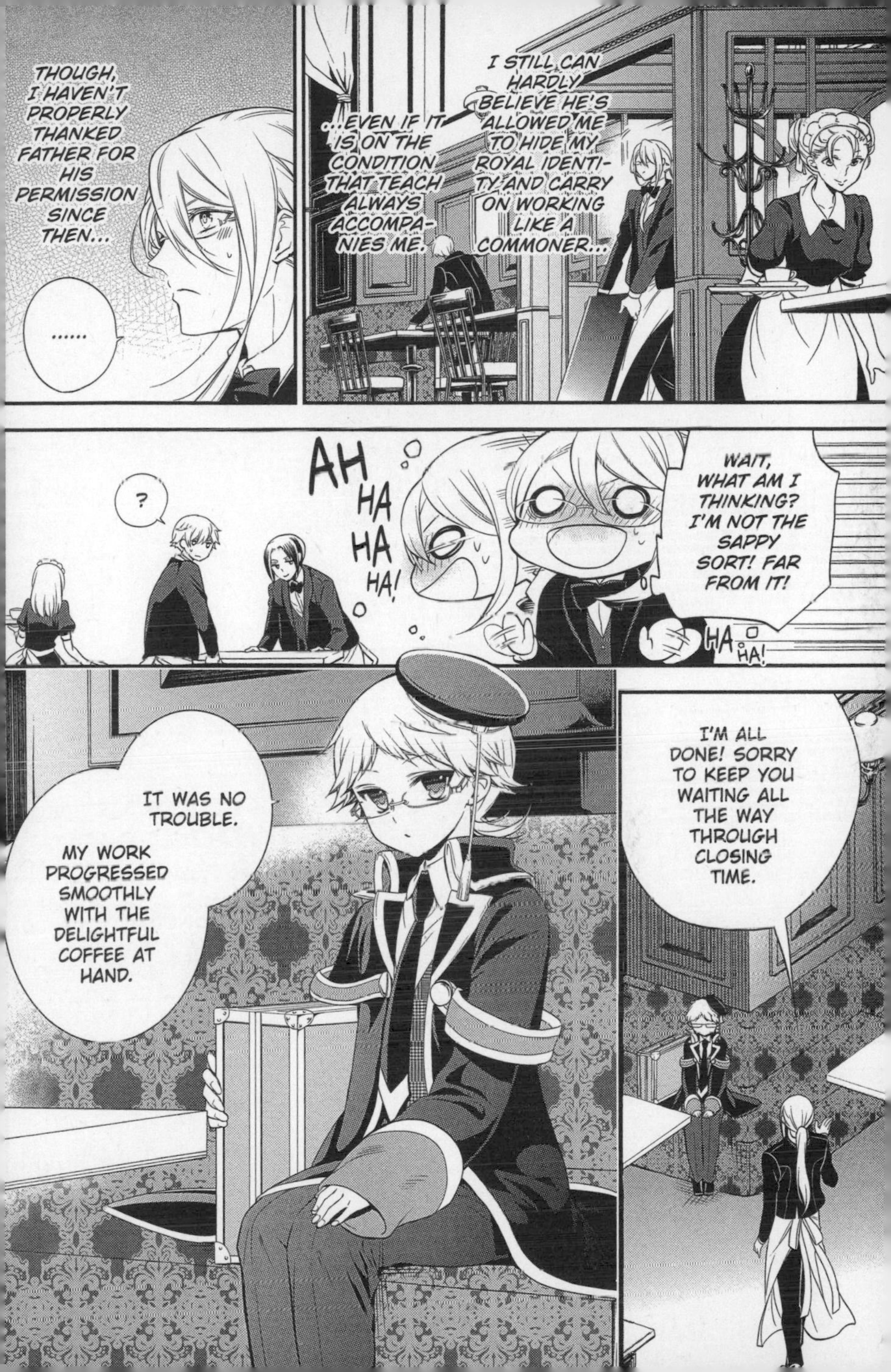
I STILL CAN HARDLY BELIEVE HE'S ALLOWED ME TO HIDE MY ROYAL IDENTITY AND CARRY ON WORKING LIKE A COMMONER...
...EVEN IF IT IS ON THE CONDITION THAT TEACH ALWAYS ACCOMPANIES ME.
THOUGH, I HAVEN'T PROPERLY THANKED FATHER FOR HIS PERMISSION SINCE THEN...
......
WAIT, WHAT AM I THINKING? I'M NOT THE SAPPY SORT! FAR FROM IT!
AH HA HA HA!
HA HA!
?
I'M ALL DONE! SORRY TO KEEP YOU WAITING ALL THE WAY THROUGH CLOSING TIME.
IT WAS NO TROUBLE.
MY WORK PROGRESSED SMOOTHLY WITH THE DELIGHTFUL COFFEE AT HAND.

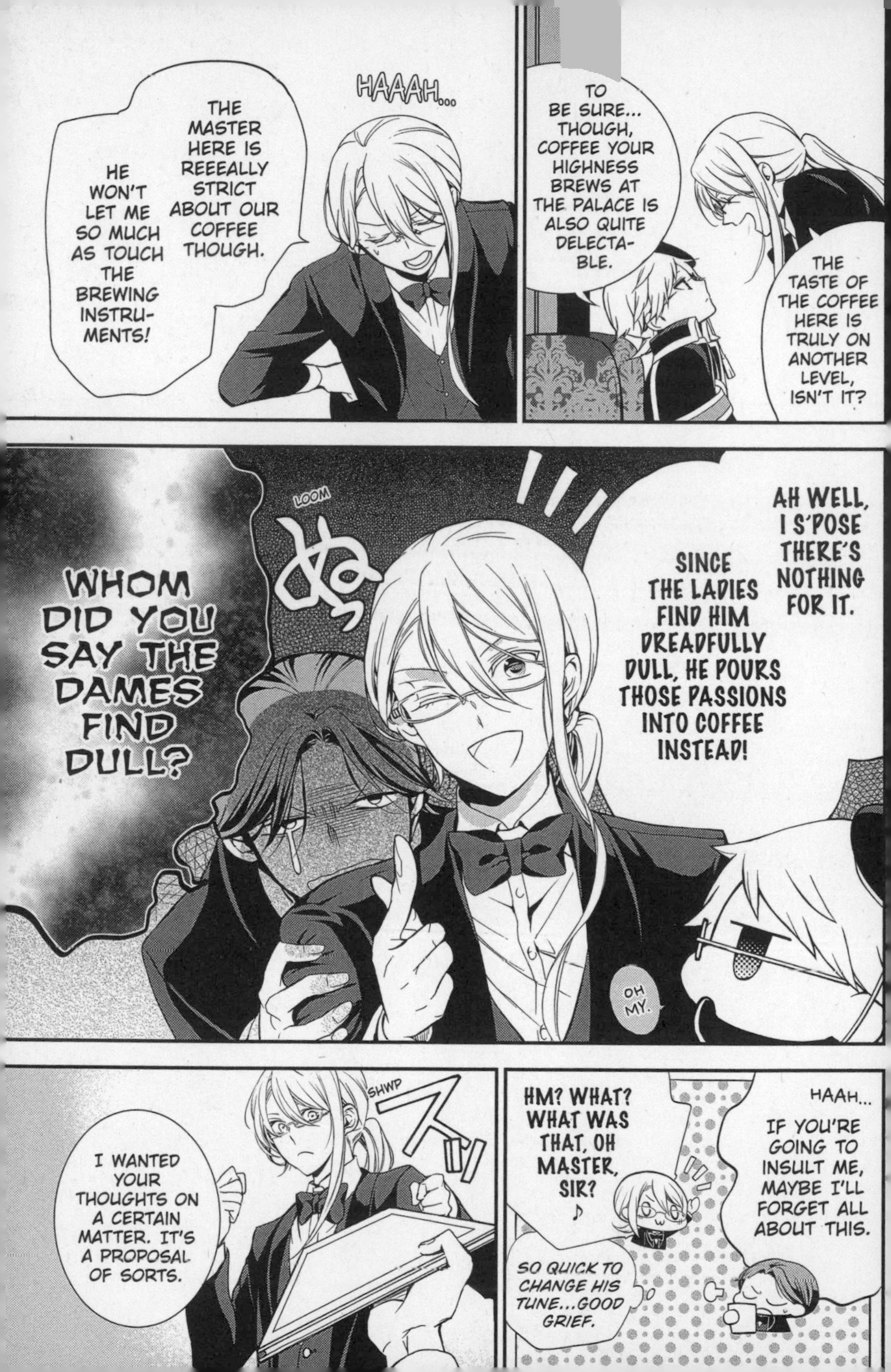
THE TASTE OF THE COFFEE HERE IS TRULY ON ANOTHER LEVEL, ISN'T IT?
TO BE SURE... THOUGH, COFFEE YOUR HIGHNESS BREWS AT THE PALACE IS ALSO QUITE DELECTA-BLE.
HAAAH...
THE MASTER HERE IS REEEALLY STRICT ABOUT OUR COFFEE THOUGH.
HE WON'T LET ME SO MUCH AS TOUCH THE BREWING INSTRU-MENTS!
AH WELL, I S'POSE THERE'S NOTHING FOR IT.
SINCE THE LADIES FIND HIM DREADFULLY DULL, HE POURS THOSE PASSIONS INTO COFFEE INSTEAD!
LOOM
WHOM DID YOU SAY THE DAMES FIND DULL?
OH MY.
HAAH...
IF YOU'RE GOING TO INSULT ME, MAYBE I'LL FORGET ALL ABOUT THIS.
HM? WHAT? WHAT WAS THAT, OH MASTER, SIR? ♪
SO QUICK TO CHANGE HIS TUNE...GOOD GRIEF.
SHWP
I WANTED YOUR THOUGHTS ON A CERTAIN MATTER. IT'S A PROPOSAL OF SORTS.

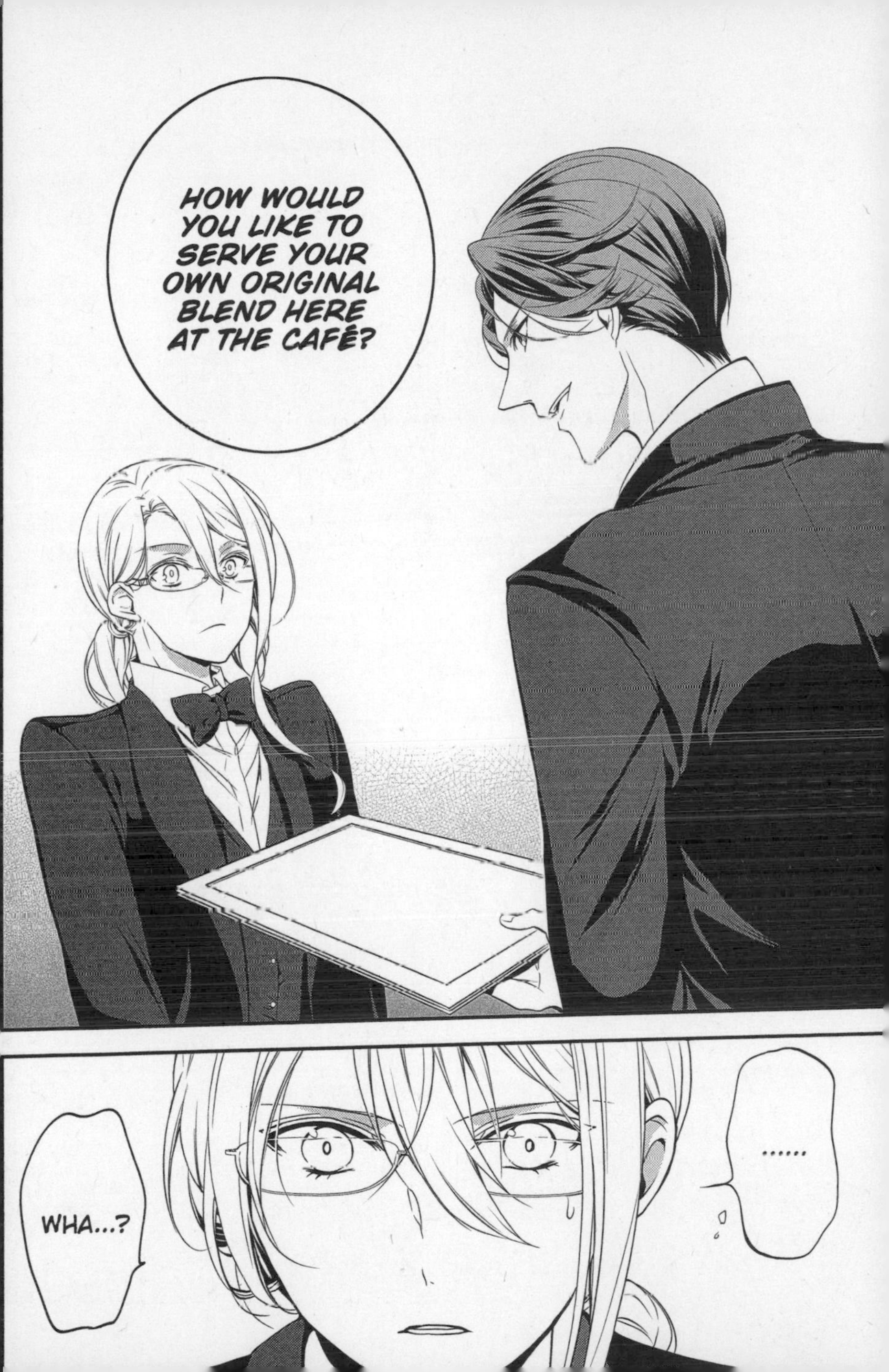
HOW WOULD YOU LIKE TO SERVE YOUR OWN ORIGINAL BLEND HERE AT THE CAFÉ?
......
WHA...?

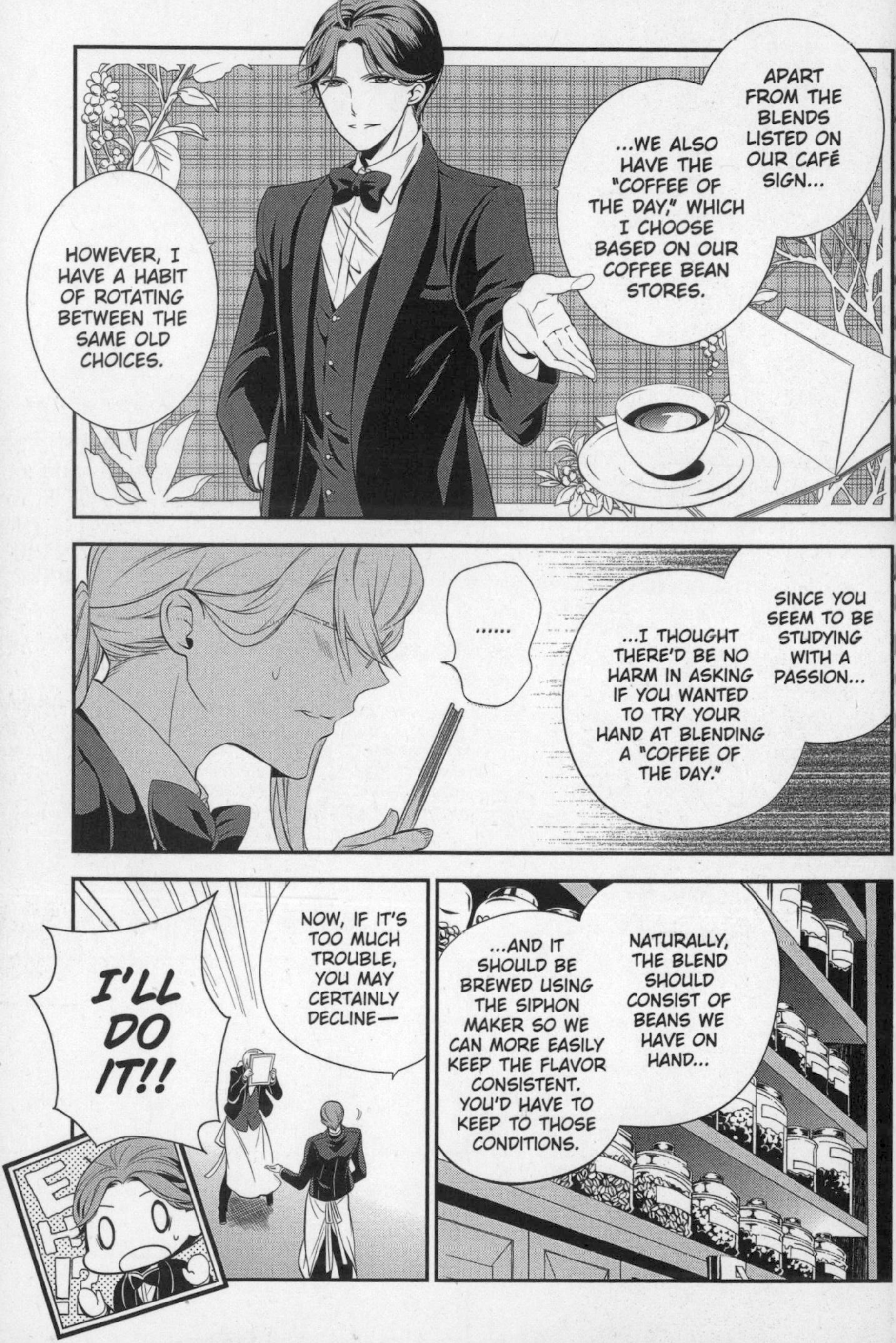
APART FROM THE BLENDS LISTED ON OUR CAFÉ SIGN...
...WE ALSO HAVE THE "COFFEE OF THE DAY," WHICH I CHOOSE BASED ON OUR COFFEE BEAN STORES.
HOWEVER, I HAVE A HABIT OF ROTATING BETWEEN THE SAME OLD CHOICES.
SINCE YOU SEEM TO BE STUDYING WITH A PASSION...
...I THOUGHT THERE'D BE NO HARM IN ASKING IF YOU WANTED TO TRY YOUR HAND AT BLENDING A "COFFEE OF THE DAY."
......
NATURALLY, THE BLEND SHOULD CONSIST OF BEANS WE HAVE ON HAND...
...AND IT SHOULD BE BREWED USING THE SIPHON MAKER SO WE CAN MORE EASILY KEEP THE FLAVOR CONSISTENT. YOU'D HAVE TO KEEP TO THOSE CONDITIONS.
NOW, IF IT'S TOO MUCH TROUBLE, YOU MAY CERTAINLY DECLINE—
I'LL DO IT!!

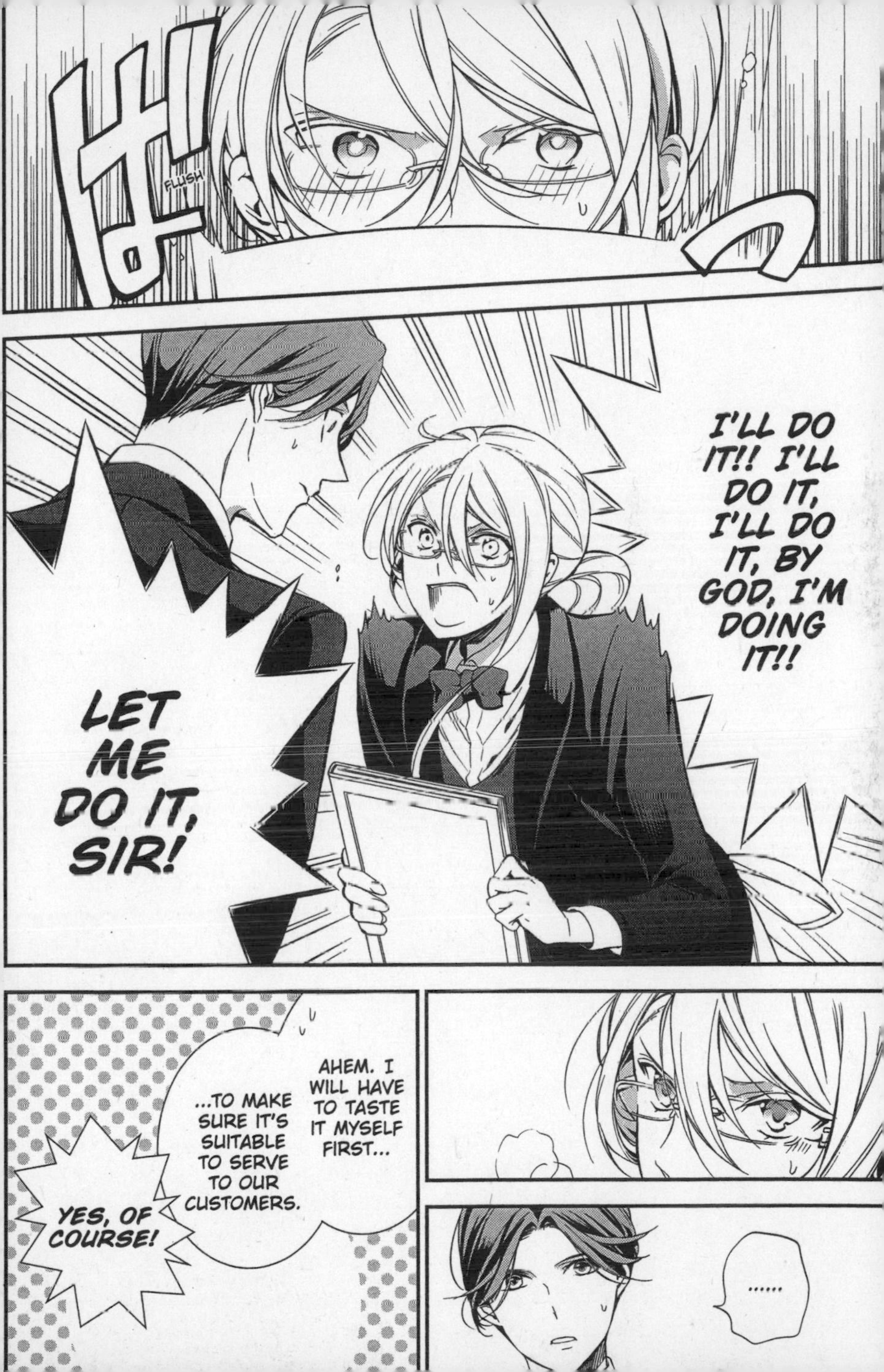
は!
FLUSH
っ
I'LL DO IT!! I'LL DO IT, I'LL DO IT, BY GOD, I'M DOING IT!!
LET ME DO IT, SIR!
......
AHEM. I WILL HAVE TO TASTE IT MYSELF FIRST...
...TO MAKE SURE IT'S SUITABLE TO SERVE TO OUR CUSTOMERS.
YES, OF COURSE!

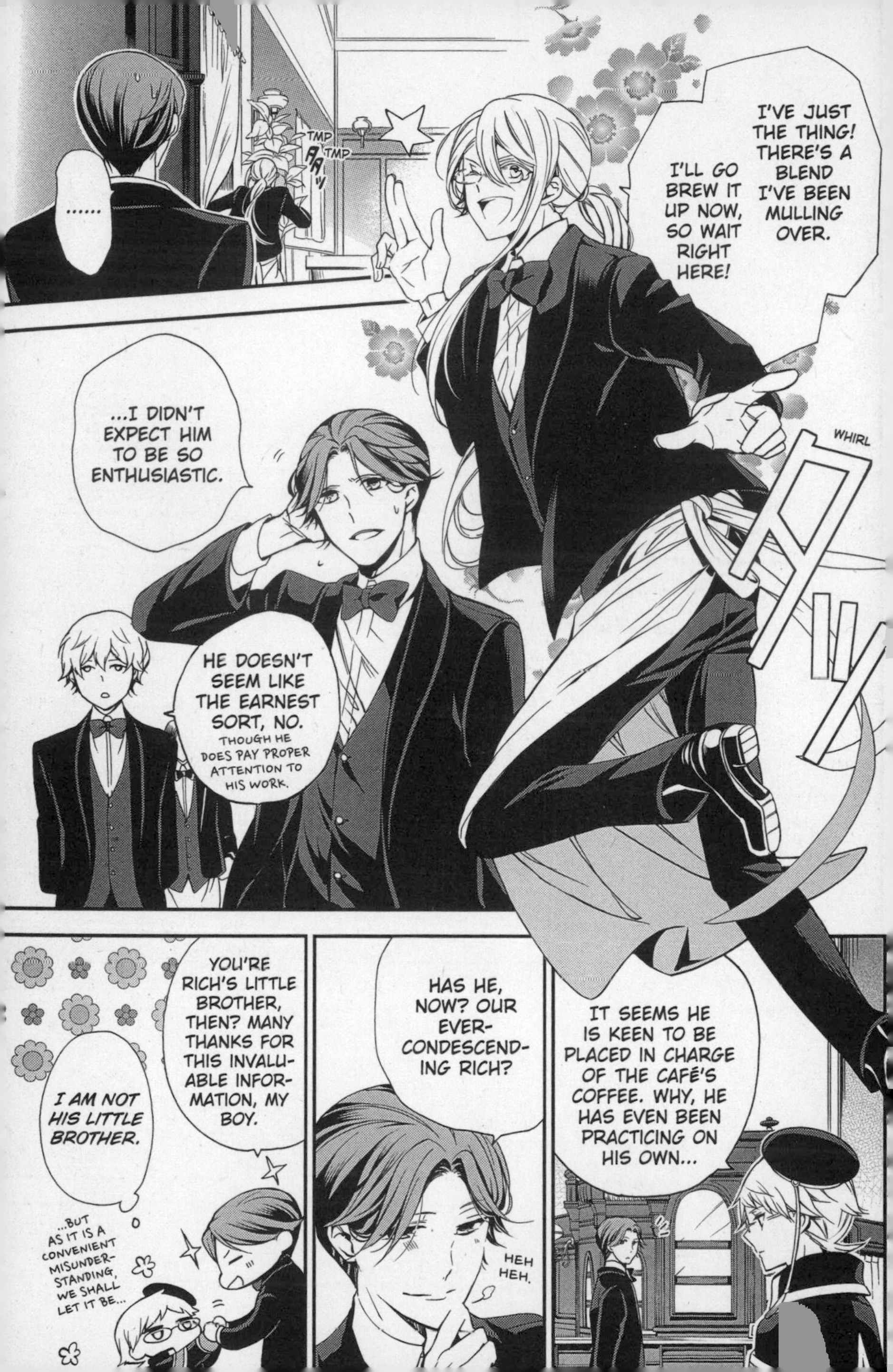
I'VE JUST THE THING! THERE'S A BLEND I'VE BEEN MULLING OVER.
I'LL GO BREW IT UP NOW, SO WAIT RIGHT HERE!
WHIRL
TMP TMP
......
...I DIDN'T EXPECT HIM TO BE SO ENTHUSIASTIC.
HE DOESN'T SEEM LIKE THE EARNEST SORT, NO.
THOUGH HE DOES PAY PROPER ATTENTION TO HIS WORK.
IT SEEMS HE IS KEEN TO BE PLACED IN CHARGE OF THE CAFÉ'S COFFEE. WHY, HE HAS EVEN BEEN PRACTICING ON HIS OWN...
HAS HE, NOW? OUR EVER-CONDESCENDING RICH?
HEH HEH.
YOU'RE RICH'S LITTLE BROTHER, THEN? MANY THANKS FOR THIS INVALUABLE INFORMATION, MY BOY.
I AM NOT HIS LITTLE BROTHER.
...BUT AS IT IS A CONVENIENT MISUNDERSTANDING, WE SHALL LET IT BE...

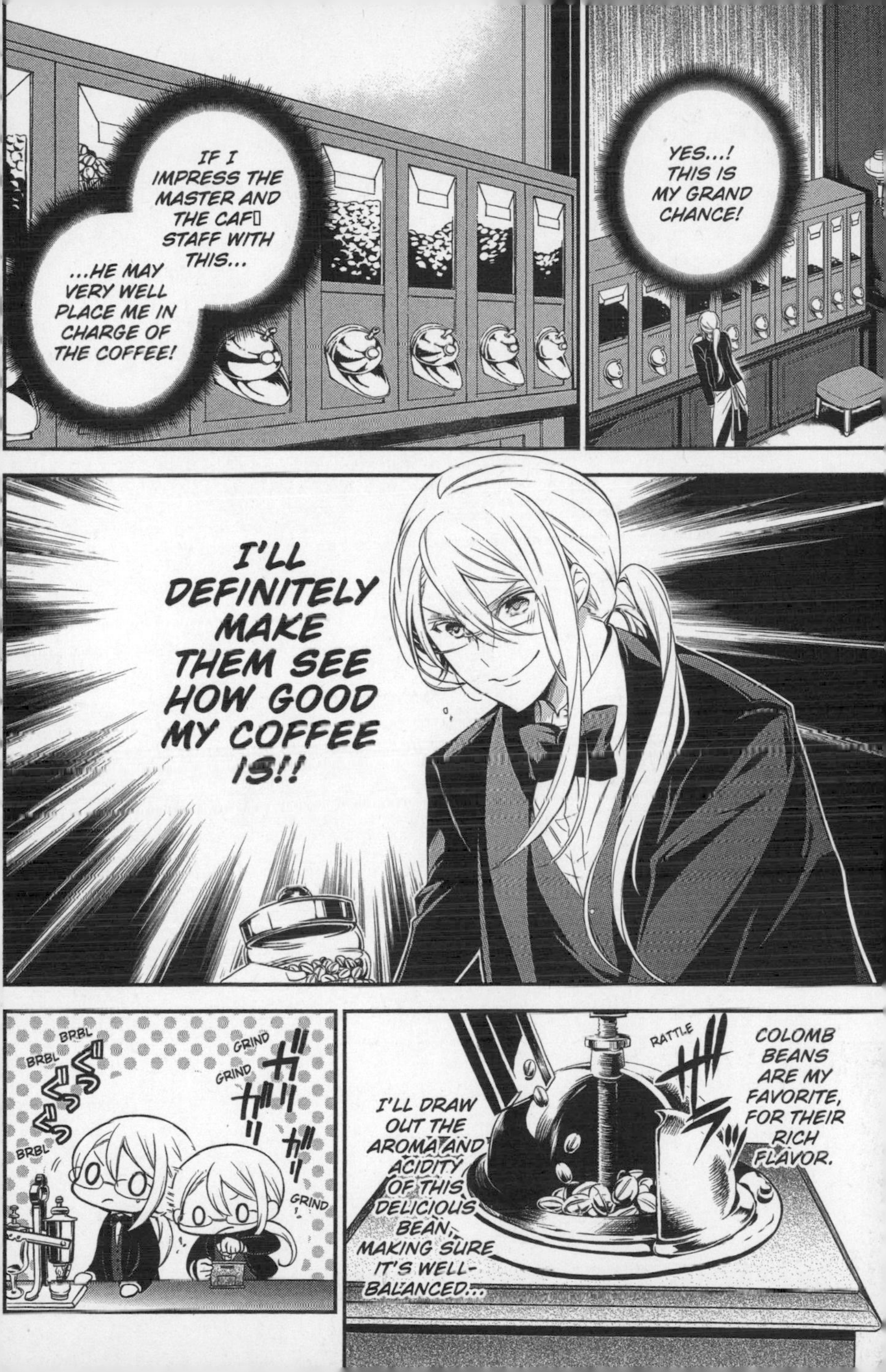
YES...! THIS IS MY GRAND CHANCE!
IF I IMPRESS THE MASTER AND THE CAFÉ STAFF WITH THIS...
...HE MAY VERY WELL PLACE ME IN CHARGE OF THE COFFEE!
I'LL DEFINITELY MAKE THEM SEE HOW GOOD MY COFFEE IS!!
COLOMB BEANS ARE MY FAVORITE, FOR THEIR RICH FLAVOR.
RATTLE
I'LL DRAW OUT THE AROMA AND ACIDITY OF THIS DELICIOUS BEAN, MAKING SURE IT'S WELL-BALANCED...
GRIND
GRIND
GRIND
BRBL
BRBL
BRBL

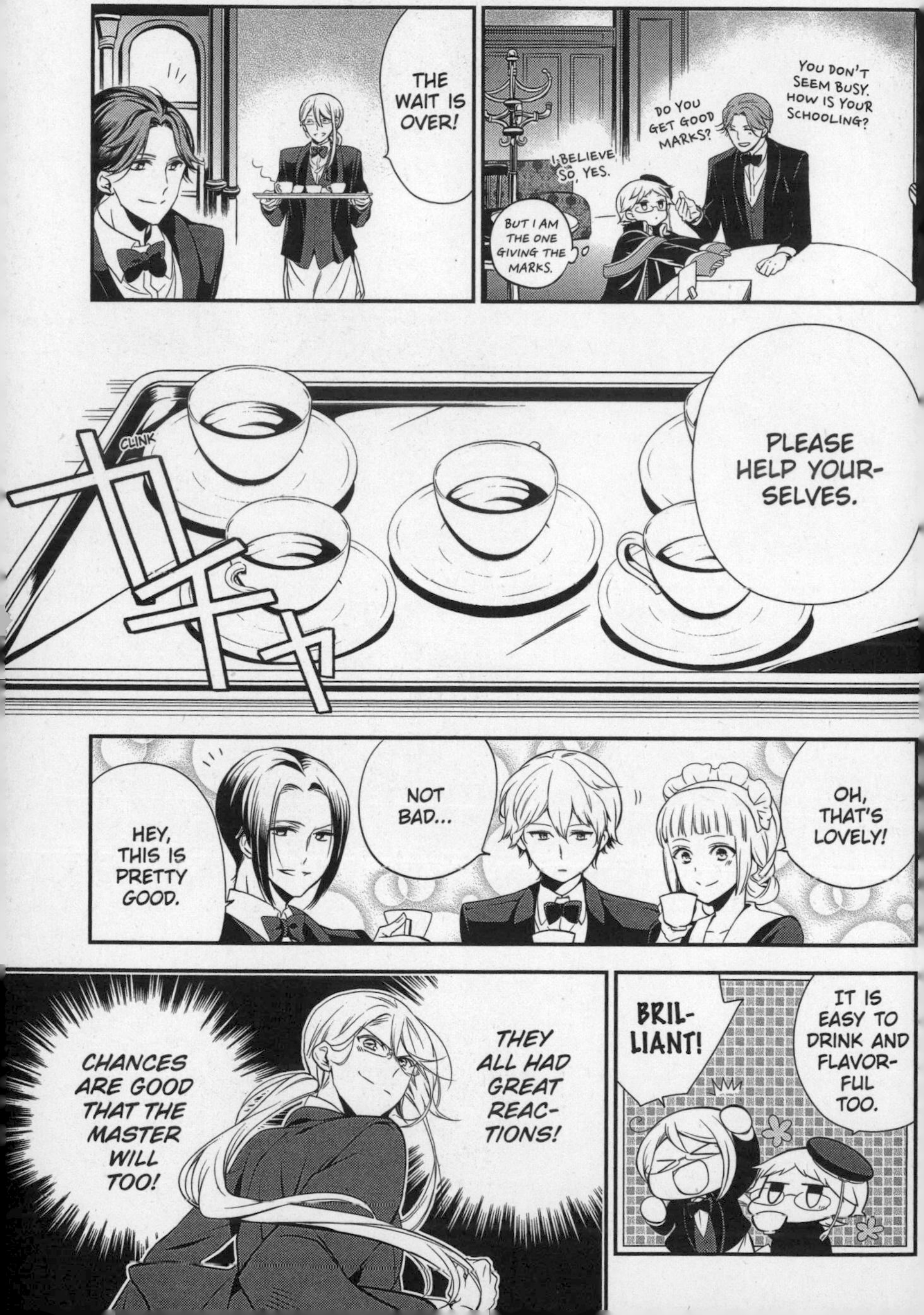
YOU DON'T SEEM BUSY. HOW IS YOUR SCHOOLING?
DO YOU GET GOOD MARKS?
I BELIEVE SO, YES.
BUT I AM THE ONE GIVING THE MARKS.
THE WAIT IS OVER!
PLEASE HELP YOUR-SELVES.
CLINK
OH, THAT'S LOVELY!
NOT BAD...
HEY, THIS IS PRETTY GOOD.
IT IS EASY TO DRINK AND FLAVOR-FUL TOO.
BRIL-LIANT!
THEY ALL HAD GREAT REAC-TIONS!
CHANCES ARE GOOD THAT THE MASTER WILL TOO!

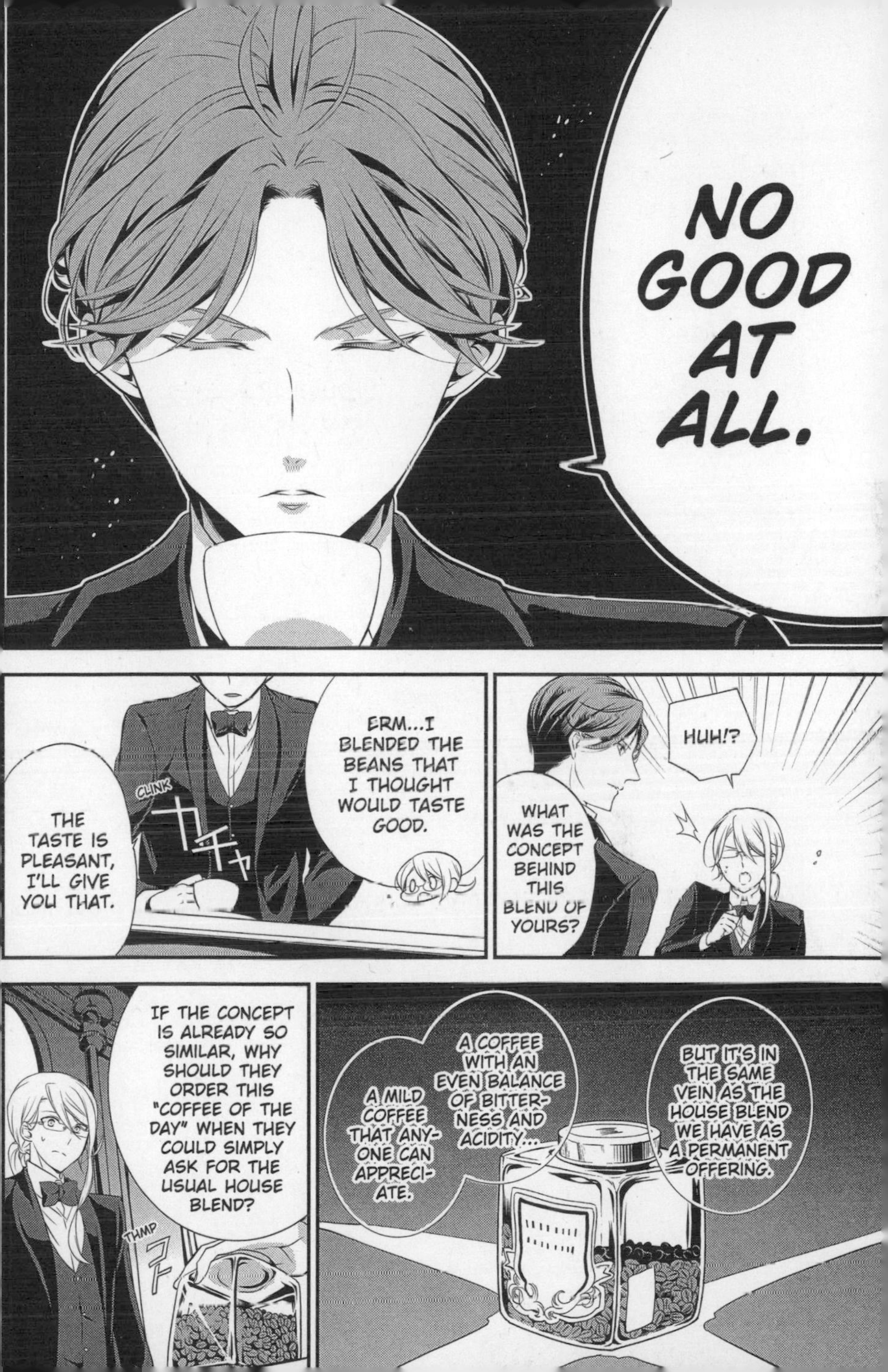
NO GOOD AT ALL.
HUH!?
WHAT WAS THE CONCEPT BEHIND THIS BLEND OF YOURS?
ERM...I BLENDED THE BEANS THAT I THOUGHT WOULD TASTE GOOD.
CLINK
カチャ
THE TASTE IS PLEASANT, I'LL GIVE YOU THAT.
BUT IT'S IN THE SAME VEIN AS THE HOUSE BLEND WE HAVE AS A PERMANENT OFFERING.
A COFFEE WITH AN EVEN BALANCE OF BITTER-NESS AND ACIDITY...
A MILD COFFEE THAT ANY-ONE CAN APPRECI-ATE.
IF THE CONCEPT IS ALREADY SO SIMILAR, WHY SHOULD THEY ORDER THIS "COFFEE OF THE DAY" WHEN THEY COULD SIMPLY ASK FOR THE USUAL HOUSE BLEND?
THMP

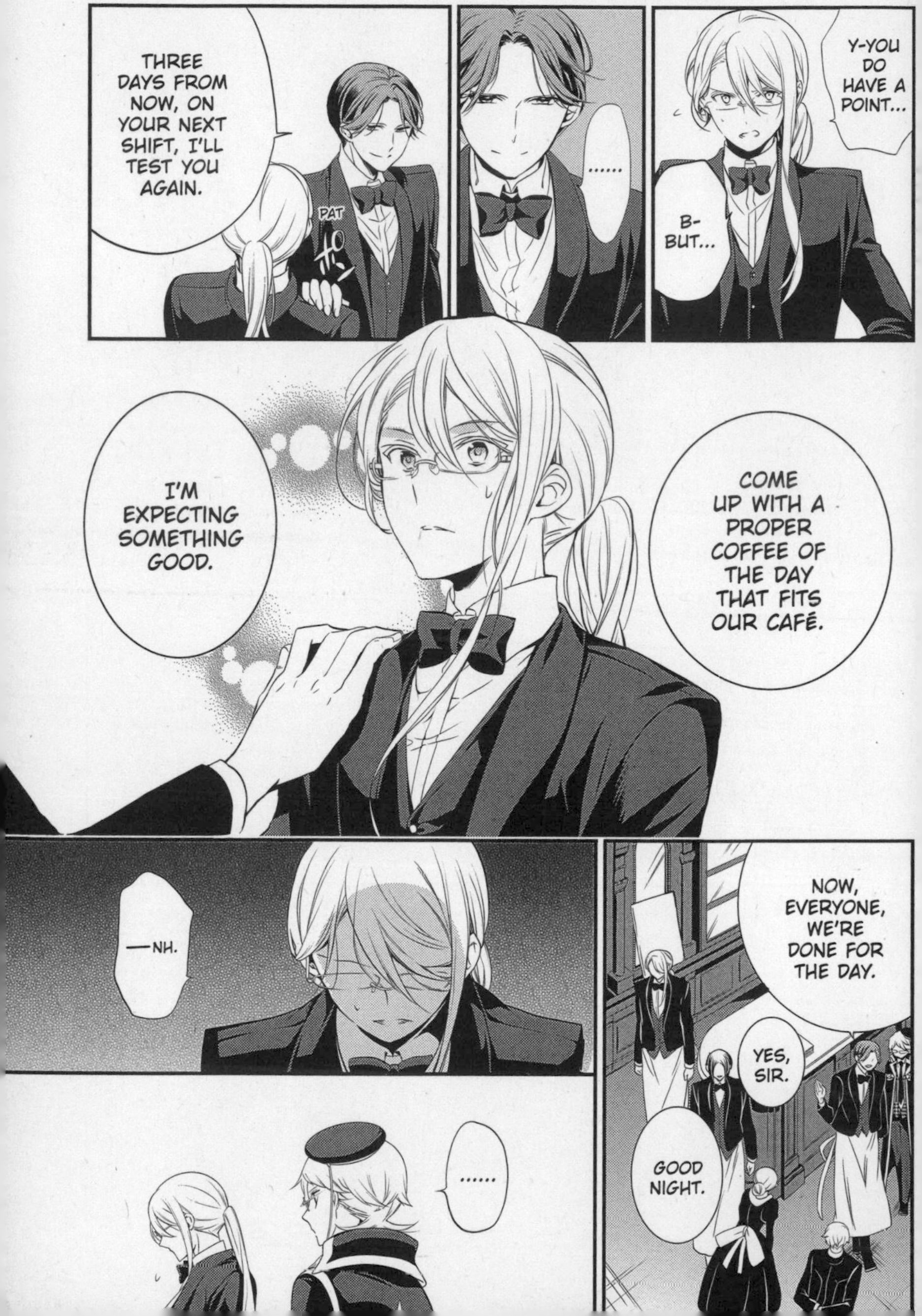
Y-YOU DO HAVE A POINT...
B-BUT...
......
THREE DAYS FROM NOW, ON YOUR NEXT SHIFT, I'LL TEST YOU AGAIN.
PAT
COME UP WITH A PROPER COFFEE OF THE DAY THAT FITS OUR CAFÉ.
I'M EXPECTING SOMETHING GOOD.
NOW, EVERYONE, WE'RE DONE FOR THE DAY.
YES, SIR.
GOOD NIGHT.
—NH.
......

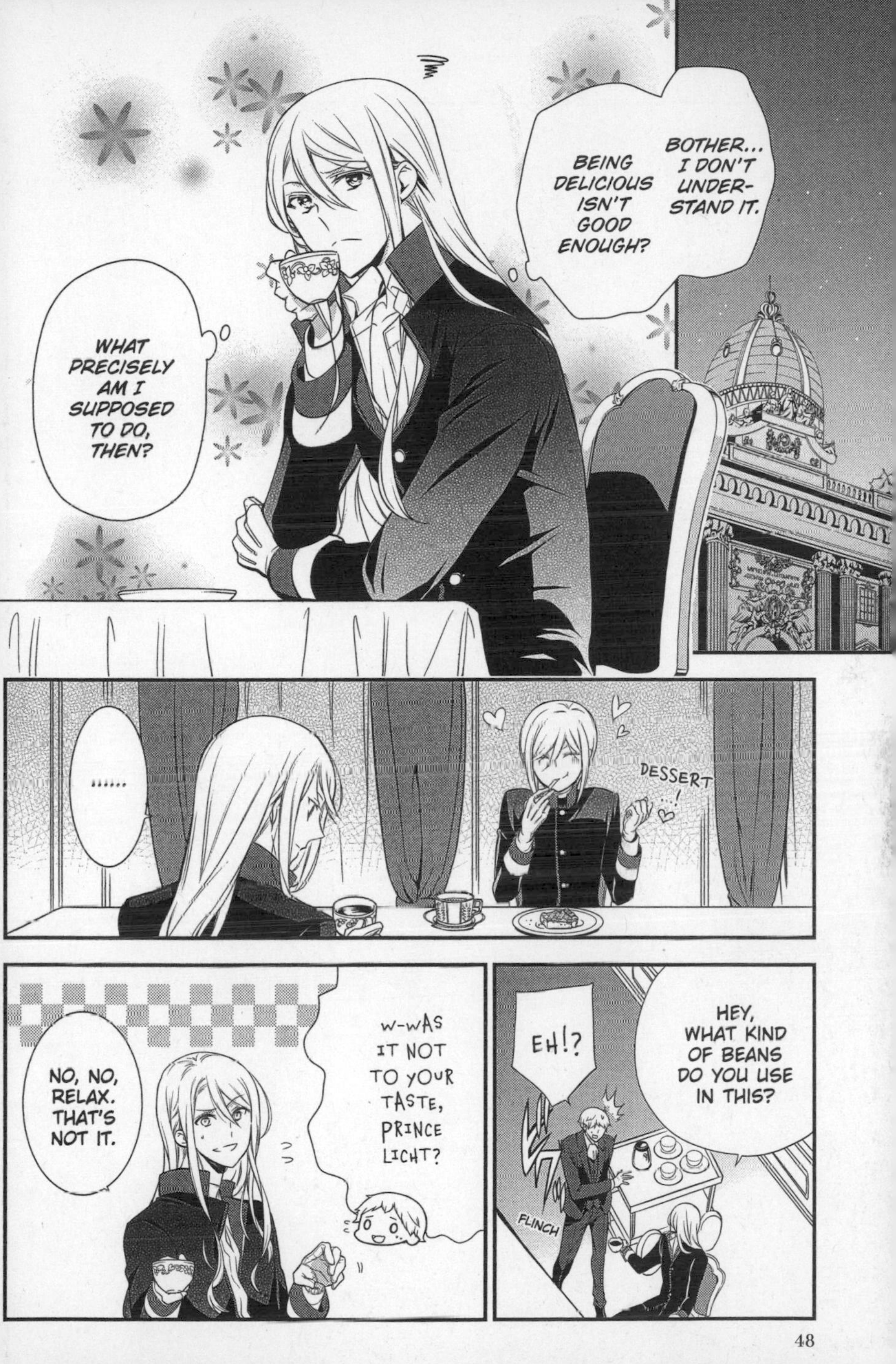
BOTHER... I DON'T UNDER-STAND IT.
BEING DELICIOUS ISN'T GOOD ENOUGH?
WHAT PRECISELY AM I SUPPOSED TO DO, THEN?
DESSERT...!
......
HEY, WHAT KIND OF BEANS DO YOU USE IN THIS?
EH!?
FLINCH
W-WAS IT NOT TO YOUR TASTE, PRINCE LICHT?
NO, NO, RELAX. THAT'S NOT IT.

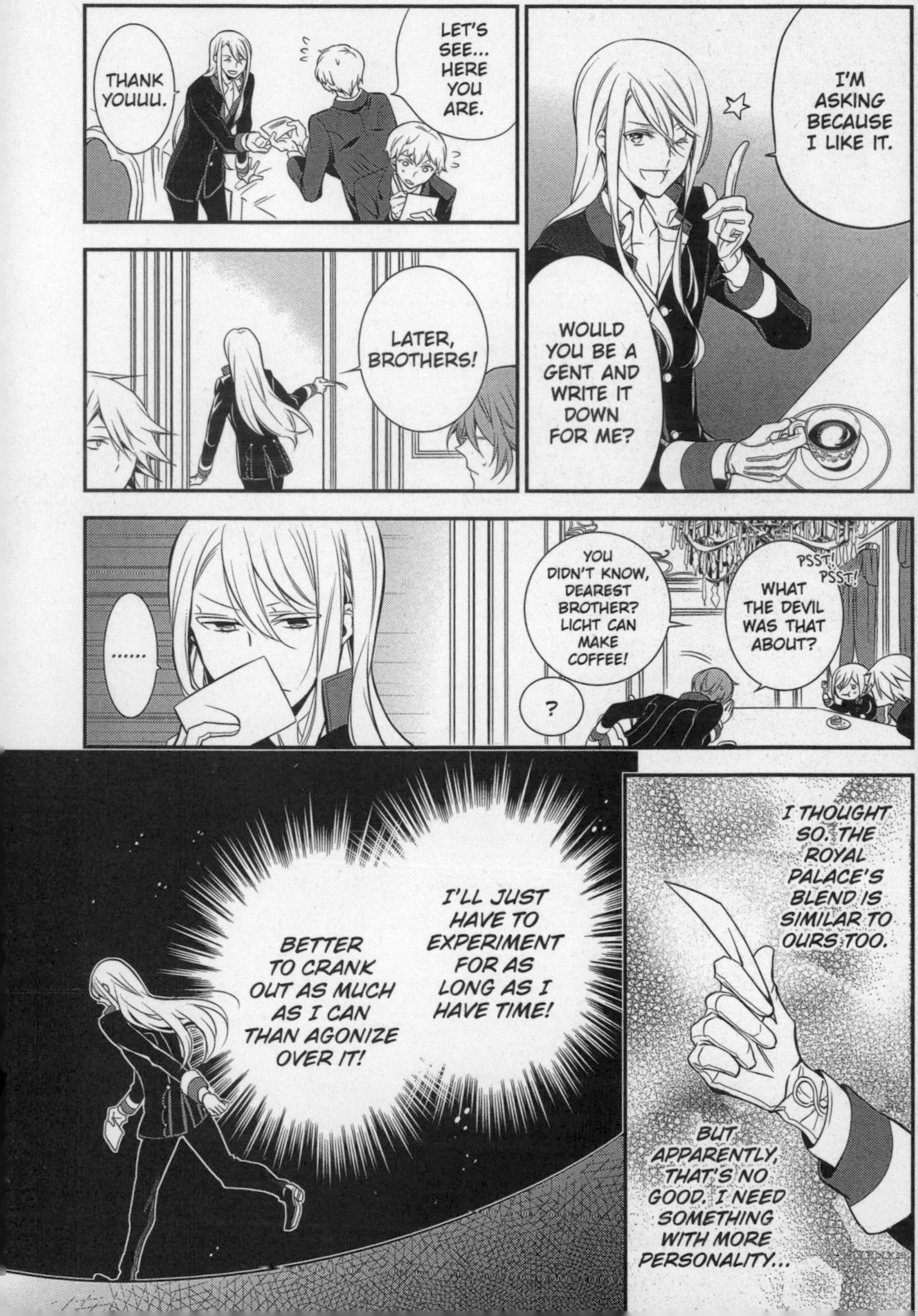
I'M ASKING BECAUSE I LIKE IT.
WOULD YOU BE A GENT AND WRITE IT DOWN FOR ME?
LET'S SEE... HERE YOU ARE.
THANK YOUUU.
LATER, BROTHERS!
PSST! PSST!
WHAT THE DEVIL WAS THAT ABOUT?
YOU DIDN'T KNOW, DEAREST BROTHER? LICHT CAN MAKE COFFEE!
?
......
I THOUGHT SO. THE ROYAL PALACE'S BLEND IS SIMILAR TO OURS TOO.
BUT APPARENTLY, THAT'S NO GOOD. I NEED SOMETHING WITH MORE PERSONALITY...
I'LL JUST HAVE TO EXPERIMENT FOR AS LONG AS I HAVE TIME!
BETTER TO CRANK OUT AS MUCH AS I CAN THAN AGONIZE OVER IT!

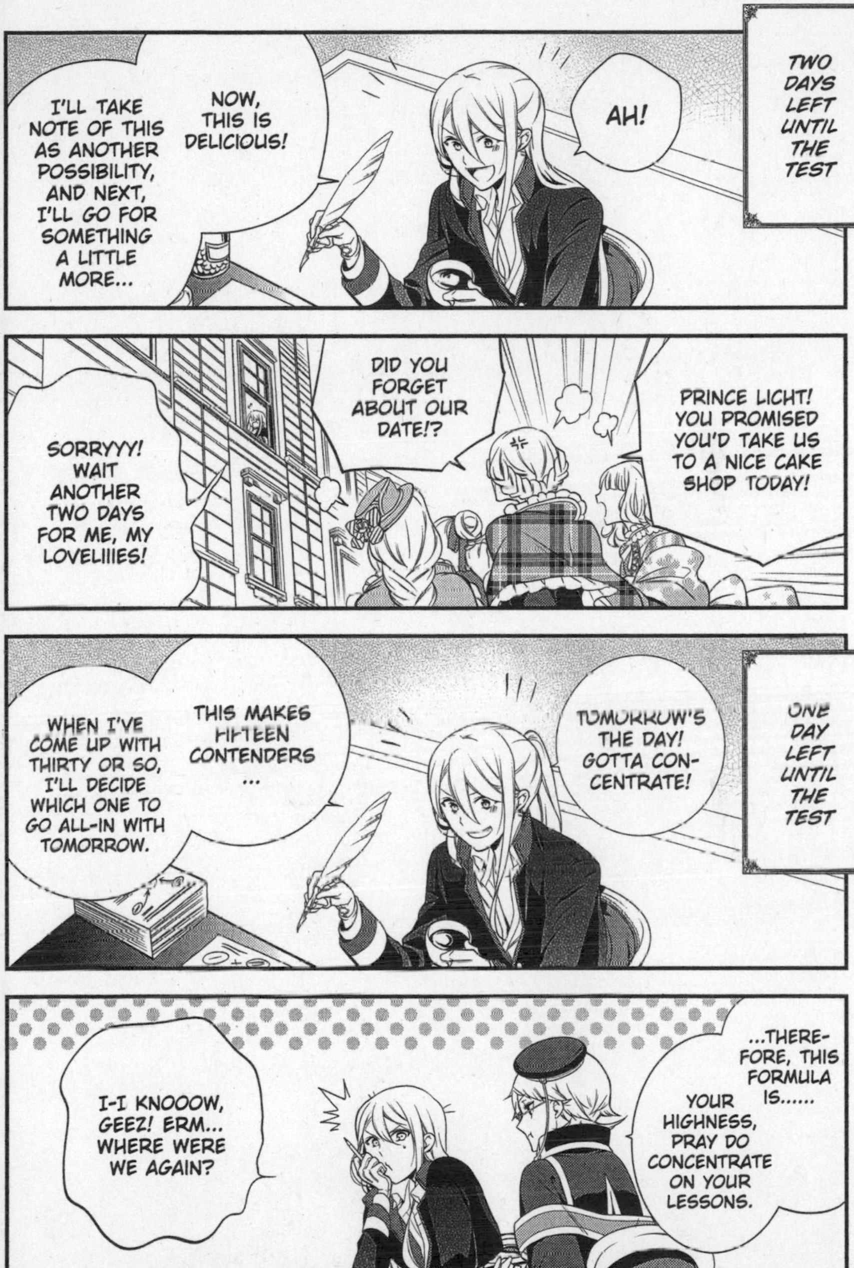
TWO DAYS LEFT UNTIL THE TEST
AH!
NOW, THIS IS DELICIOUS!
I'LL TAKE NOTE OF THIS AS ANOTHER POSSIBILITY, AND NEXT, I'LL GO FOR SOMETHING A LITTLE MORE...
PRINCE LICHT! YOU PROMISED YOU'D TAKE US TO A NICE CAKE SHOP TODAY!
DID YOU FORGET ABOUT OUR DATE!?
SORRYYY! WAIT ANOTHER TWO DAYS FOR ME, MY LOVELIIIES!
ONE DAY LEFT UNTIL THE TEST
TOMORROW'S THE DAY! GOTTA CON-CENTRATE!
THIS MAKES FIFTEEN CONTENDERS ...
WHEN I'VE COME UP WITH THIRTY OR SO, I'LL DECIDE WHICH ONE TO GO ALL-IN WITH TOMORROW.
...THERE-FORE, THIS FORMULA IS......
YOUR HIGHNESS, PRAY DO CONCENTRATE ON YOUR LESSONS.
I-I KNOOOW, GEEZ! ERM... WHERE WERE WE AGAIN?

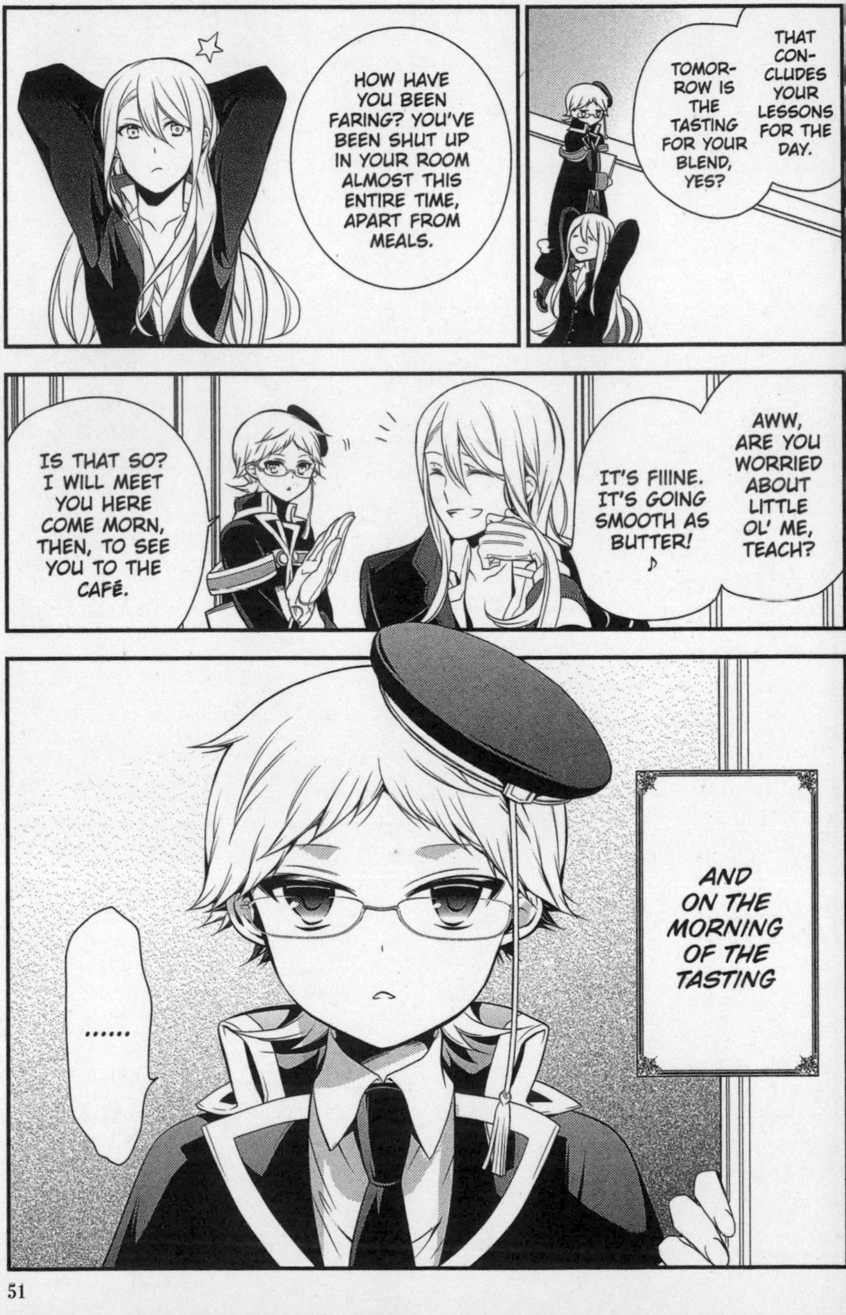
THAT CONCLUDES YOUR LESSONS FOR THE DAY.
TOMORROW IS THE TASTING FOR YOUR BLEND, YES?
HOW HAVE YOU BEEN FARING? YOU'VE BEEN SHUT UP IN YOUR ROOM ALMOST THIS ENTIRE TIME, APART FROM MEALS.
AWW, ARE YOU WORRIED ABOUT LITTLE OL' ME, TEACH?
IT'S FIIINE. IT'S GOING SMOOTH AS BUTTER! ♪
IS THAT SO? I WILL MEET YOU HERE COME MORN, THEN, TO SEE YOU TO THE CAFÉ.
AND ON THE MORNING OF THE TASTING
......

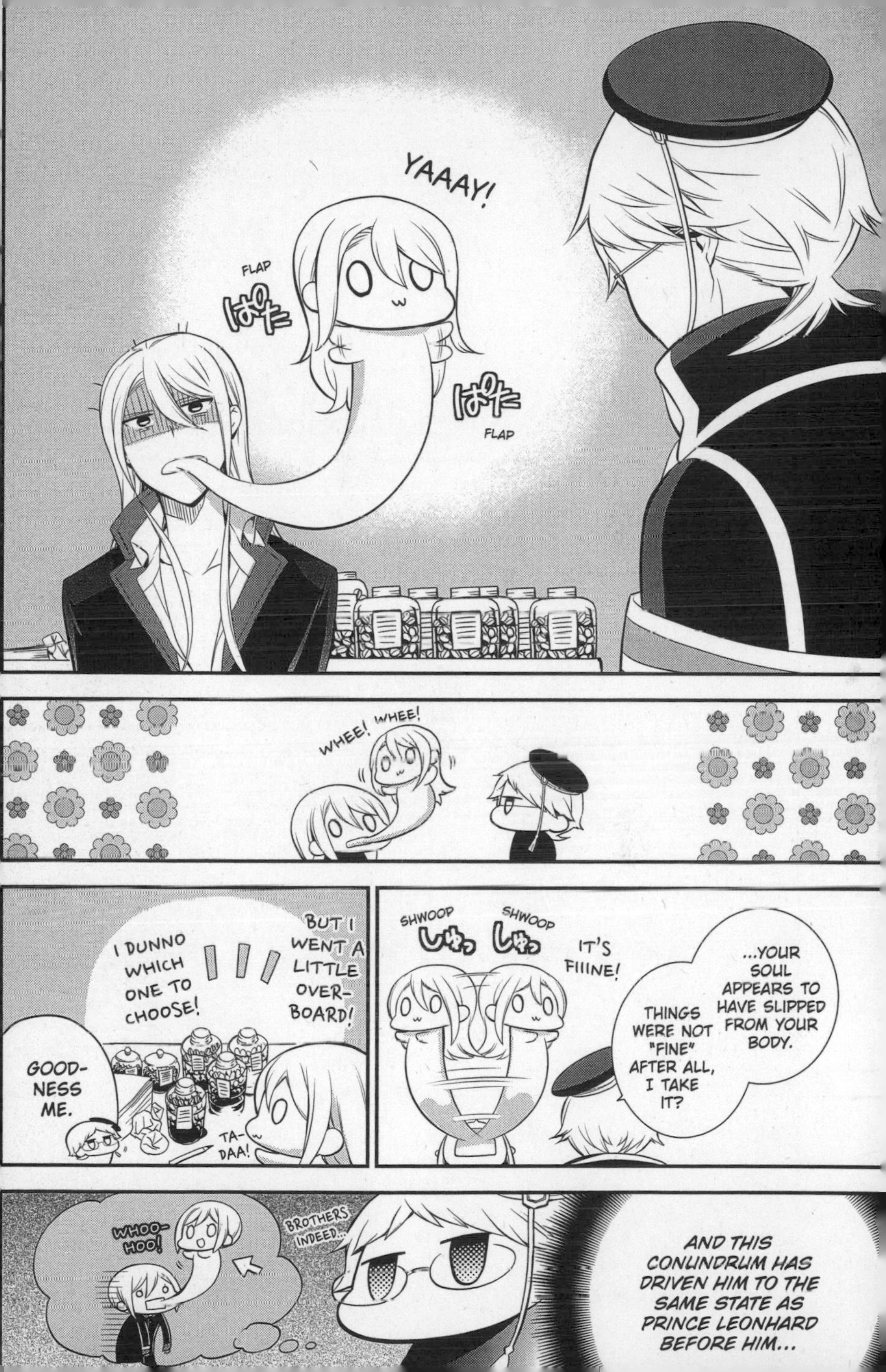
YAAAY!
FLAP
ぱた
ぱた
FLAP
WHEE! WHEE!
SHWOOP
しゅっ
SHWOOP
しゅっ
IT'S FIIINE!
...YOUR SOUL APPEARS TO HAVE SLIPPED FROM YOUR BODY.
THINGS WERE NOT "FINE" AFTER ALL, I TAKE IT?
BUT I WENT A LITTLE OVER-BOARD!
I DUNNO WHICH ONE TO CHOOSE!
GOOD-NESS ME.
TA-DAA!
AND THIS CONUNDRUM HAS DRIVEN HIM TO THE SAME STATE AS PRINCE LEONHARD BEFORE HIM...
BROTHERS INDEED...
WHOO-HOO!

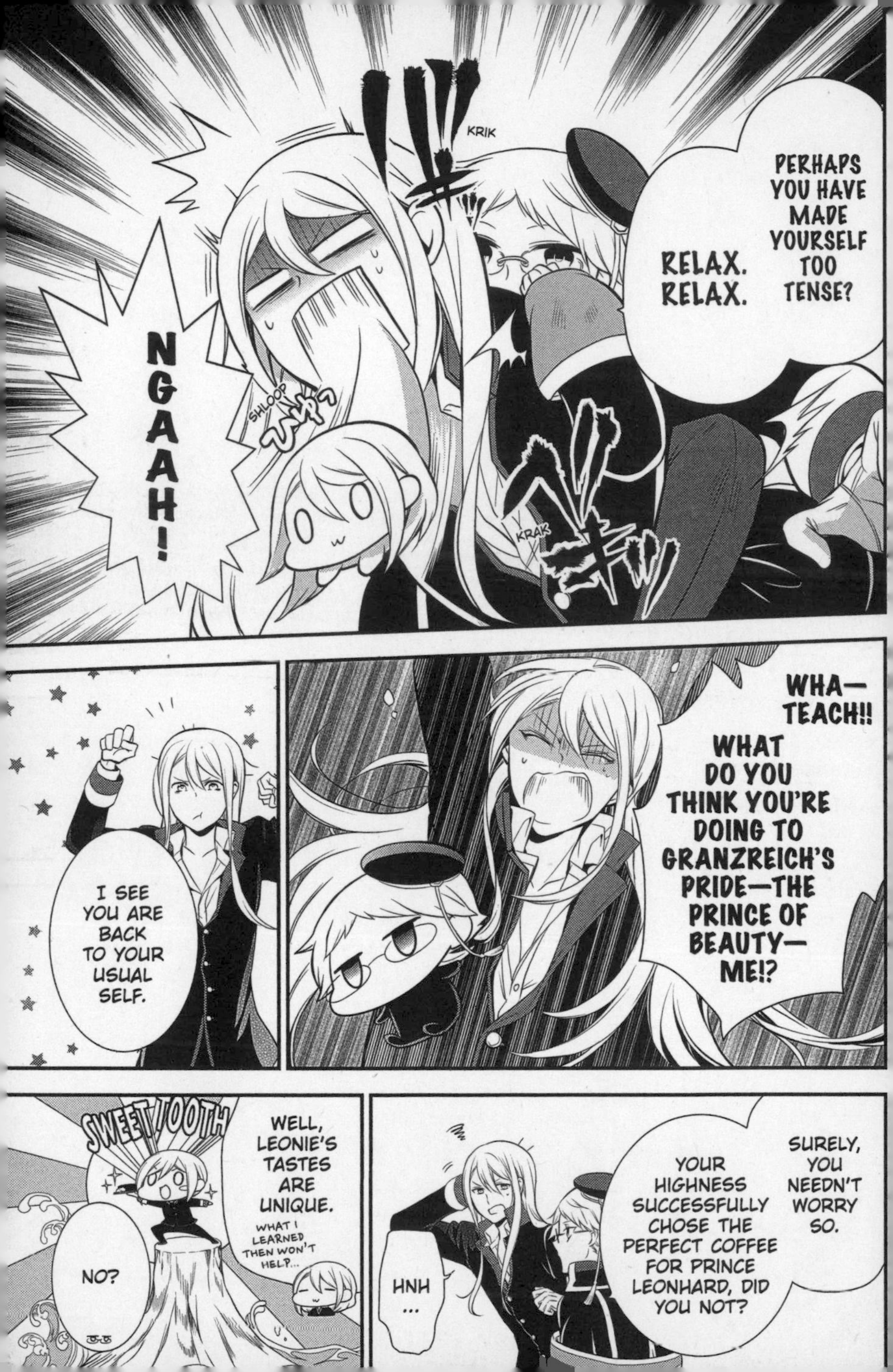
PERHAPS YOU HAVE MADE YOURSELF TOO TENSE?
RELAX. RELAX.
KRIK
NGAAH!
SHLOOP
KRAK
WHA— TEACH!!
WHAT DO YOU THINK YOU'RE DOING TO GRANZREICH'S PRIDE—THE PRINCE OF BEAUTY—ME!?
I SEE YOU ARE BACK TO YOUR USUAL SELF.
SURELY, YOU NEEDN'T WORRY SO.
YOUR HIGHNESS SUCCESSFULLY CHOSE THE PERFECT COFFEE FOR PRINCE LEONHARD, DID YOU NOT?
HNH ...
WELL, LEONIE'S TASTES ARE UNIQUE.
SWEET TOOTH
NO?
WHAT I LEARNED THEN WON'T HELP...

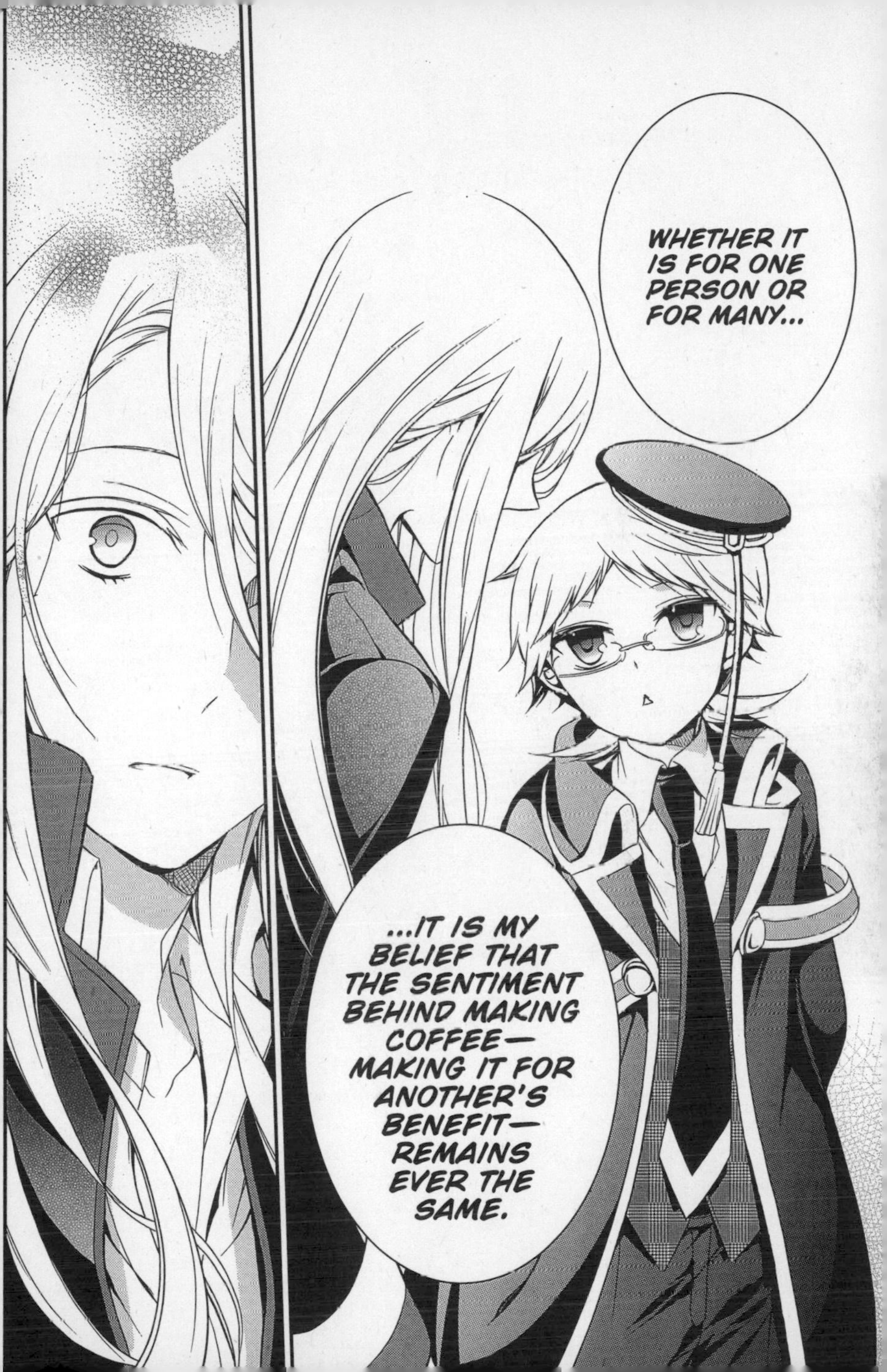
WHETHER IT IS FOR ONE PERSON OR FOR MANY...
...IT IS MY BELIEF THAT THE SENTIMENT BEHIND MAKING COFFEE—MAKING IT FOR ANOTHER'S BENEFIT—REMAINS EVER THE SAME.

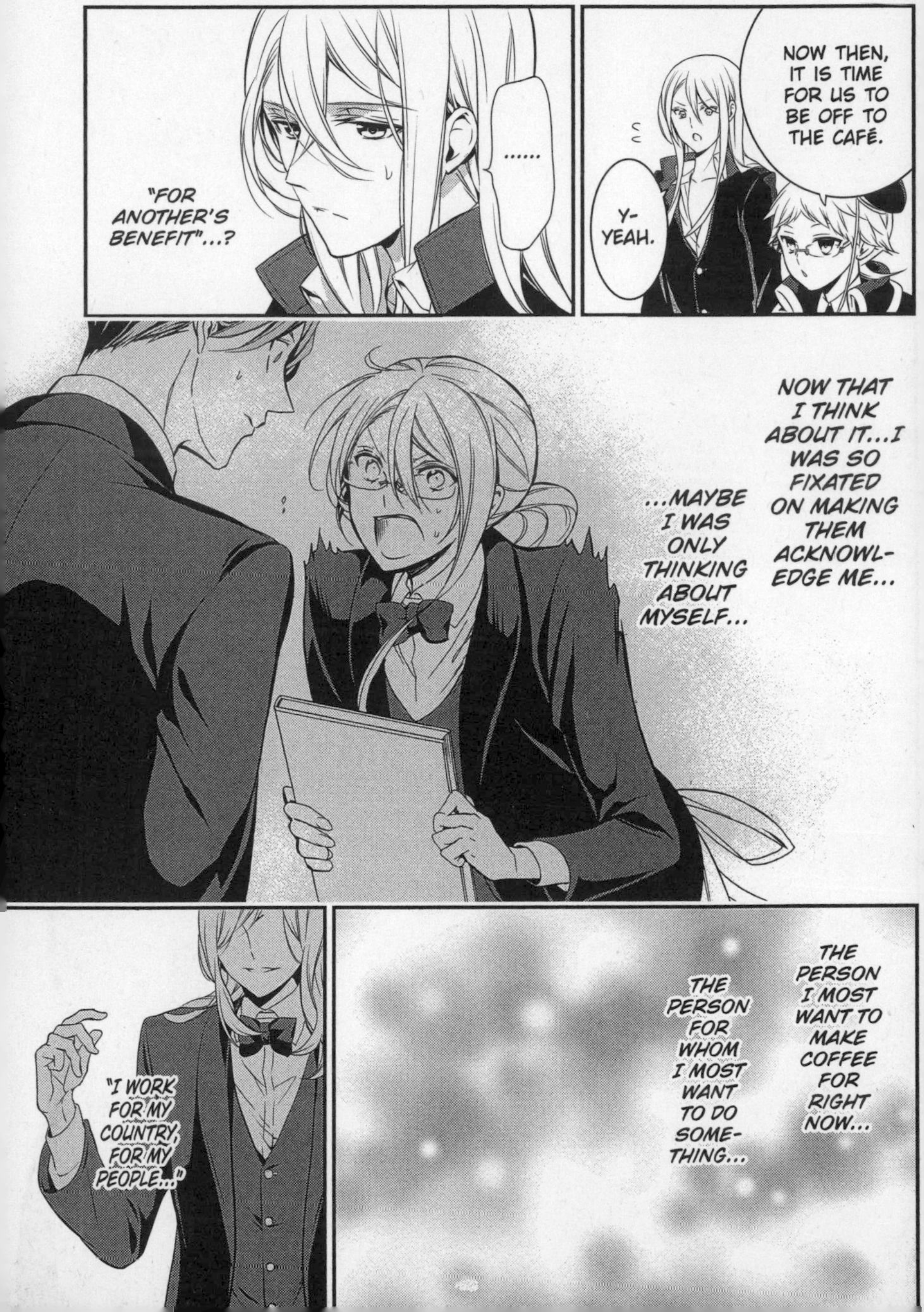
NOW THEN, IT IS TIME FOR US TO BE OFF TO THE CAFÉ.
Y-YEAH.
......
"FOR ANOTHER'S BENEFIT"...?
NOW THAT I THINK ABOUT IT...I WAS SO FIXATED ON MAKING THEM ACKNOWL-EDGE ME...
...MAYBE I WAS ONLY THINKING ABOUT MYSELF...
THE PERSON I MOST WANT TO MAKE COFFEE FOR RIGHT NOW...
THE PERSON FOR WHOM I MOST WANT TO DO SOME-THING...
"I WORK FOR MY COUNTRY, FOR MY PEOPLE..."

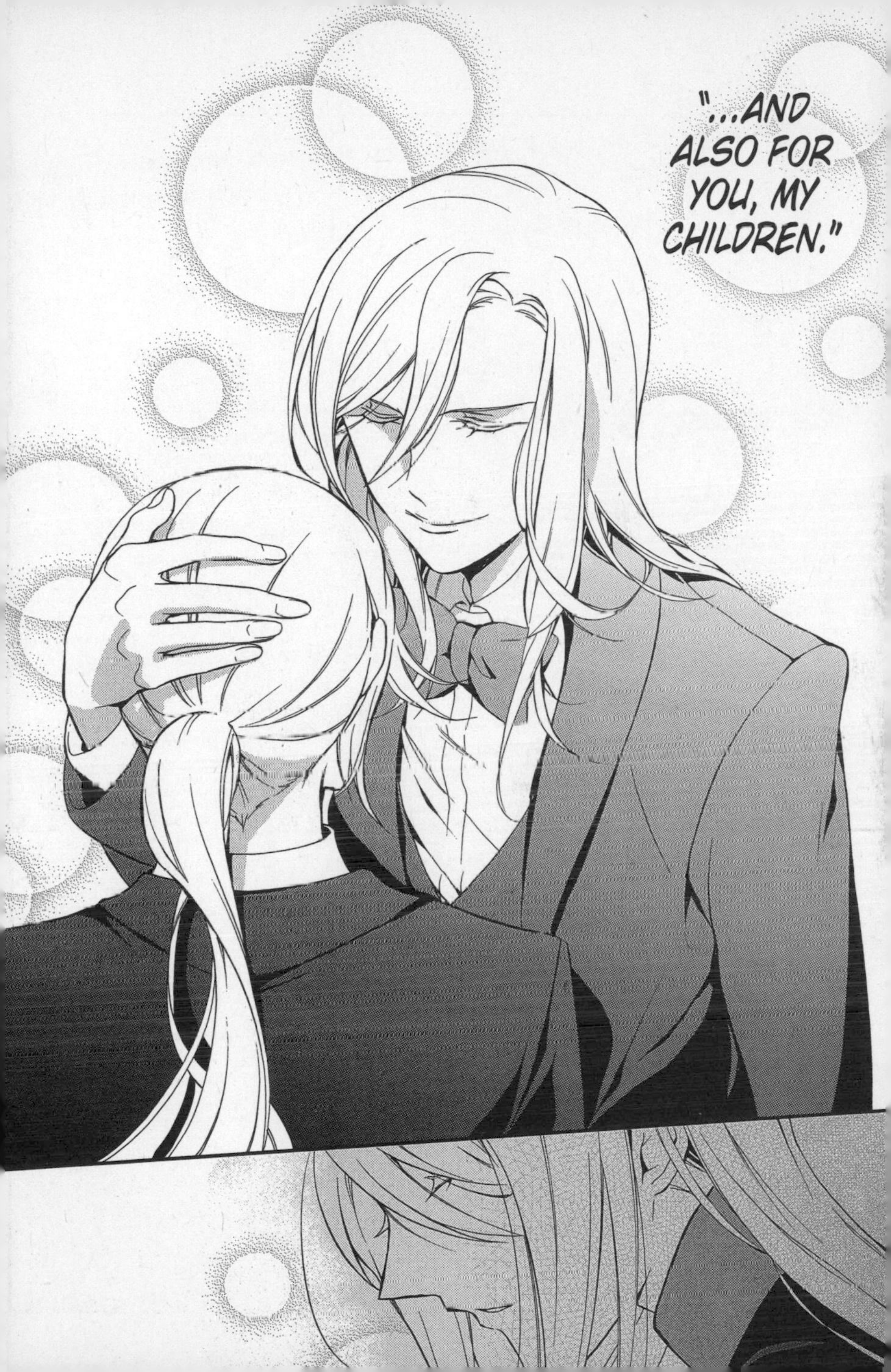
"...AND ALSO FOR YOU, MY CHILDREN."

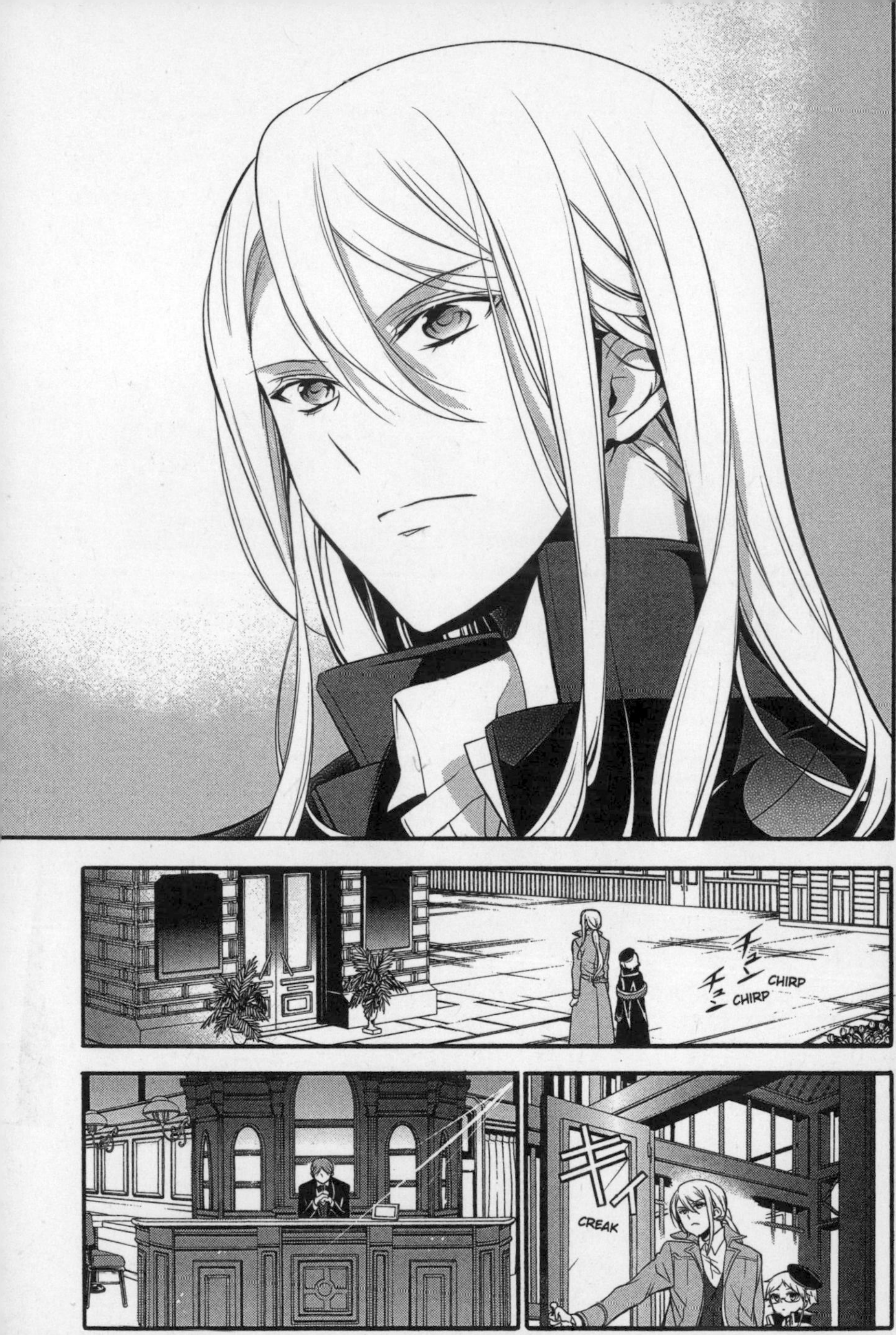
チュン
CHIRP
チュン
CHIRP
キイ
CREAK

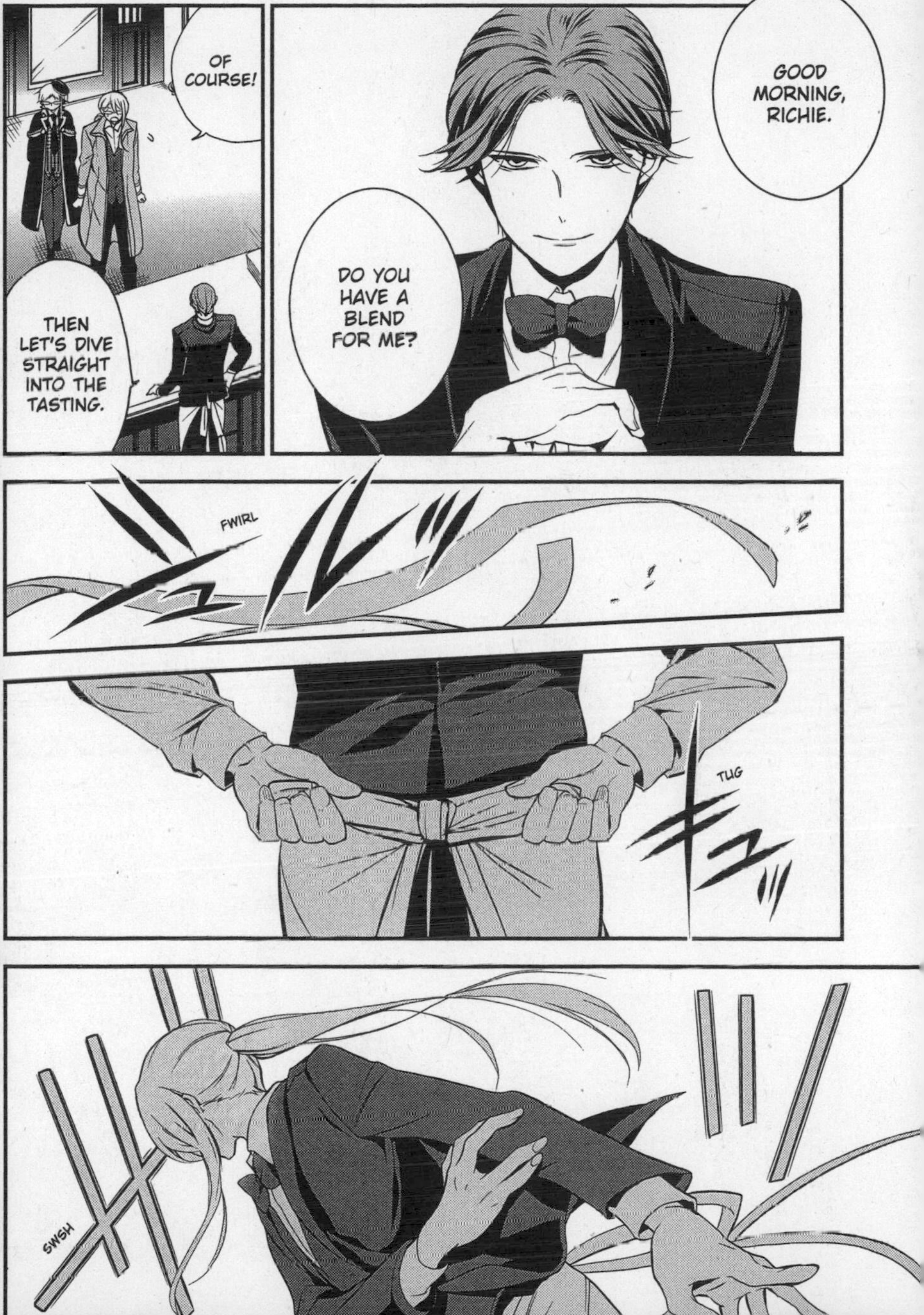
GOOD MORNING, RICHIE.
DO YOU HAVE A BLEND FOR ME?
OF COURSE!
THEN LET'S DIVE STRAIGHT INTO THE TASTING.
FWIRL
TUG
SWSH

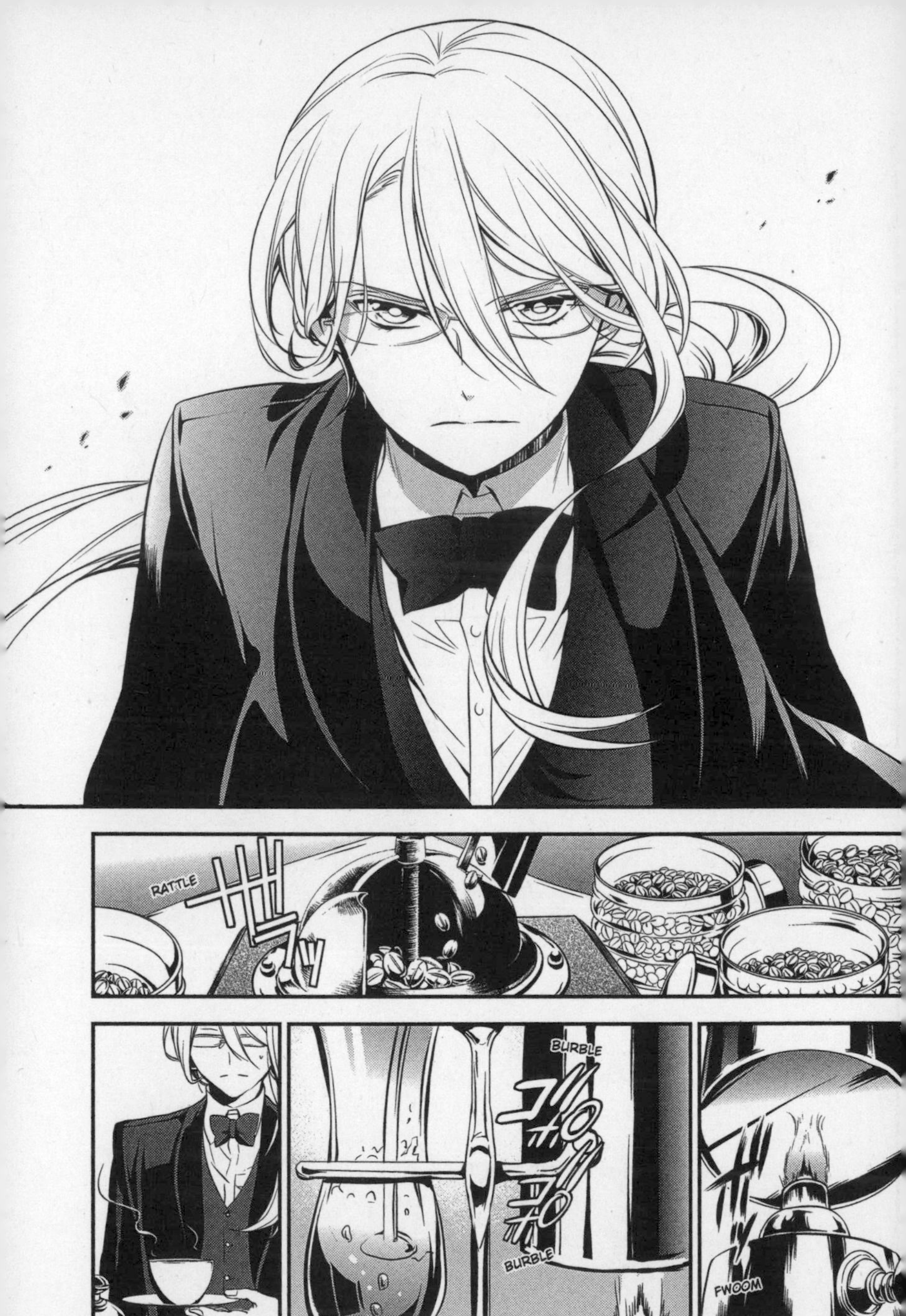
RATTLE
FWOOM
BURBLE
BURBLE

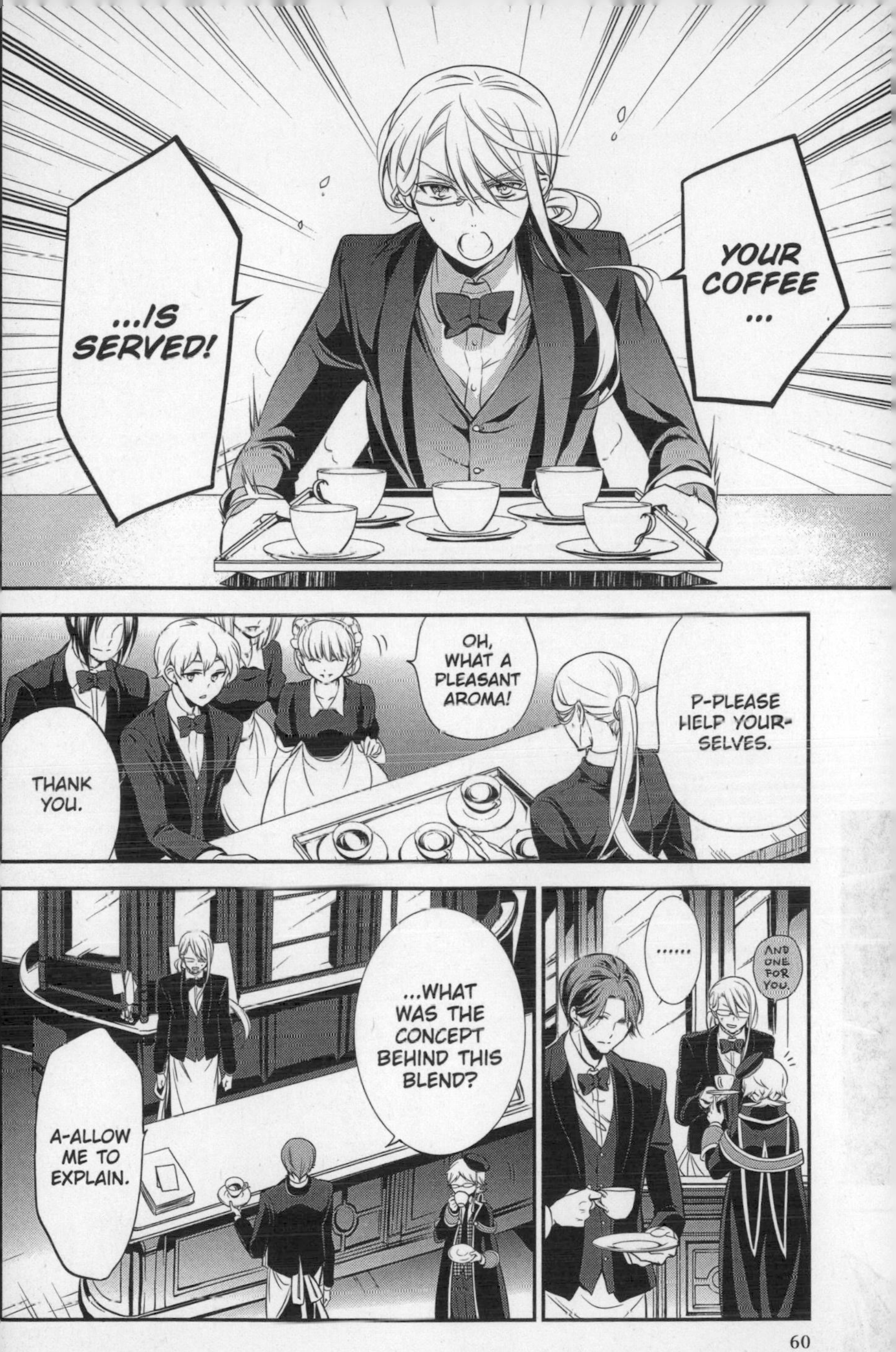
YOUR COFFEE ...
...IS SERVED!
P-PLEASE HELP YOUR-SELVES.
OH, WHAT A PLEASANT AROMA!
THANK YOU.
AND ONE FOR YOU.
......
...WHAT WAS THE CONCEPT BEHIND THIS BLEND?
A-ALLOW ME TO EXPLAIN.

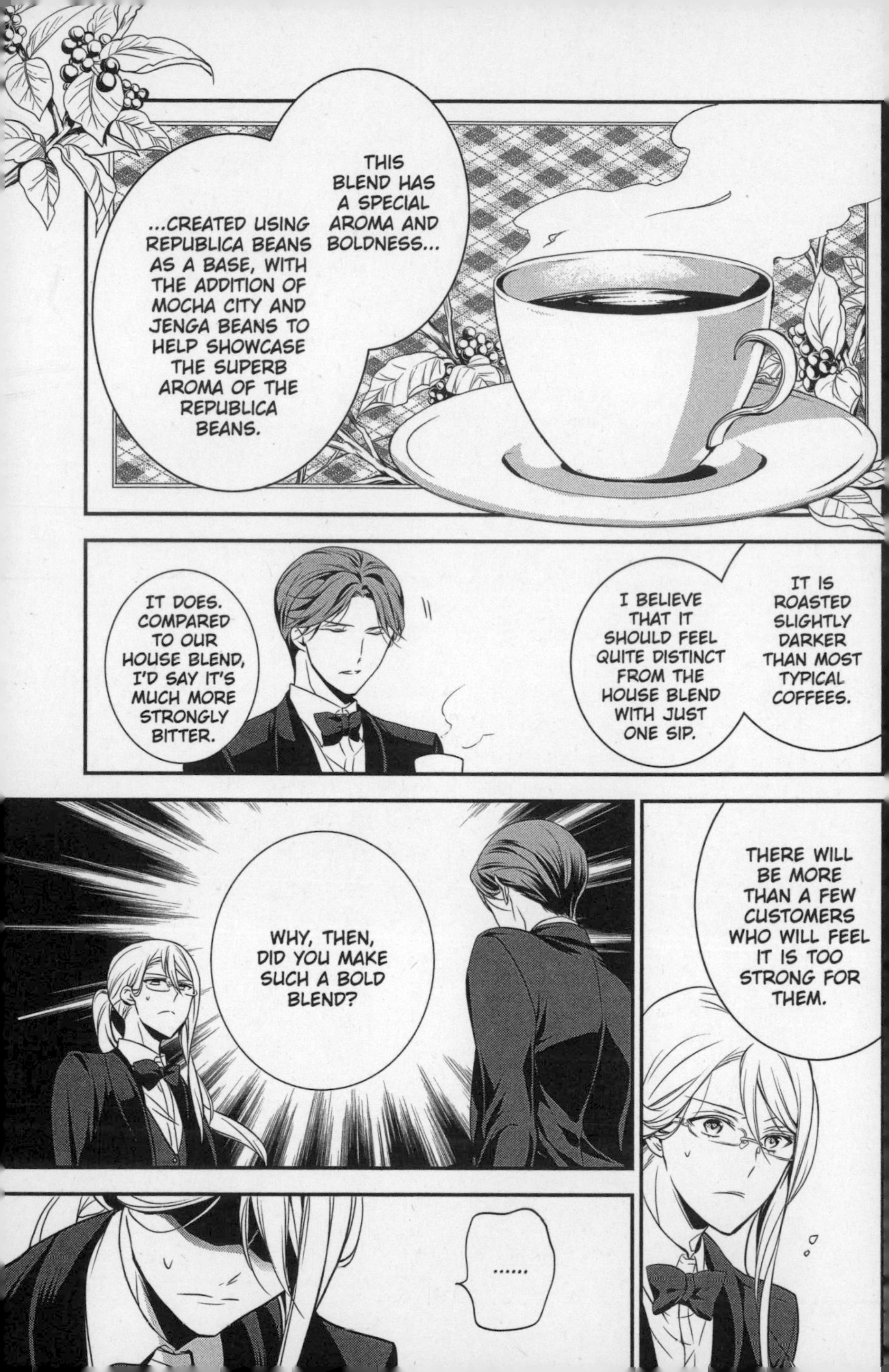
THIS BLEND HAS A SPECIAL AROMA AND BOLDNESS...
...CREATED USING REPUBLICA BEANS AS A BASE, WITH THE ADDITION OF MOCHA CITY AND JENGA BEANS TO HELP SHOWCASE THE SUPERB AROMA OF THE REPUBLICA BEANS.
IT IS ROASTED SLIGHTLY DARKER THAN MOST TYPICAL COFFEES.
I BELIEVE THAT IT SHOULD FEEL QUITE DISTINCT FROM THE HOUSE BLEND WITH JUST ONE SIP.
IT DOES. COMPARED TO OUR HOUSE BLEND, I'D SAY IT'S MUCH MORE STRONGLY BITTER.
THERE WILL BE MORE THAN A FEW CUSTOMERS WHO WILL FEEL IT IS TOO STRONG FOR THEM.
WHY, THEN, DID YOU MAKE SUCH A BOLD BLEND?
......

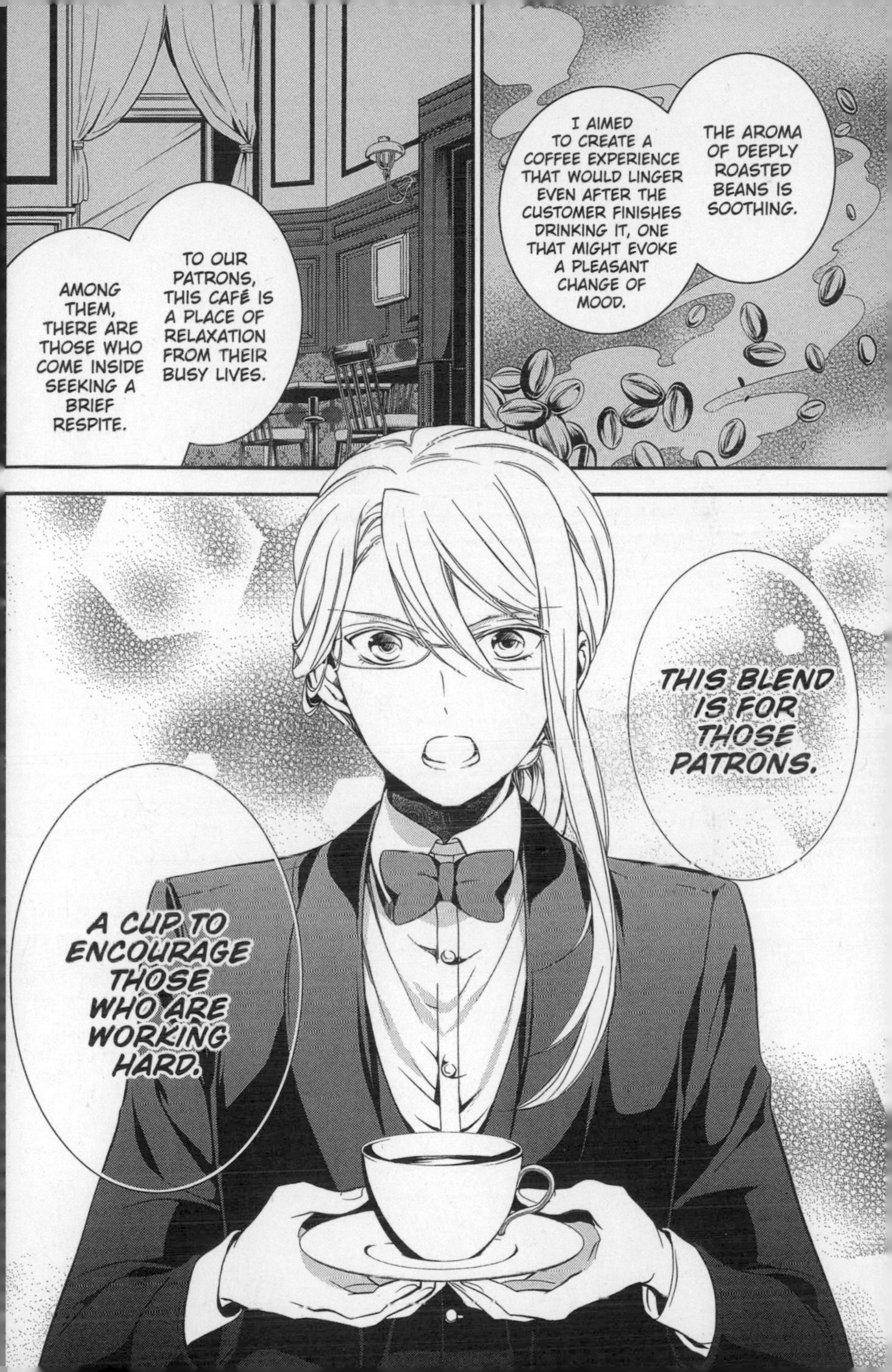
THE AROMA OF DEEPLY ROASTED BEANS IS SOOTHING.
I AIMED TO CREATE A COFFEE EXPERIENCE THAT WOULD LINGER EVEN AFTER THE CUSTOMER FINISHES DRINKING IT, ONE THAT MIGHT EVOKE A PLEASANT CHANGE OF MOOD.
TO OUR PATRONS, THIS CAFÉ IS A PLACE OF RELAXATION FROM THEIR BUSY LIVES.
AMONG THEM, THERE ARE THOSE WHO COME INSIDE SEEKING A BRIEF RESPITE.
THIS BLEND IS FOR THOSE PATRONS.
A CUP TO ENCOURAGE THOSE WHO ARE WORKING HARD.

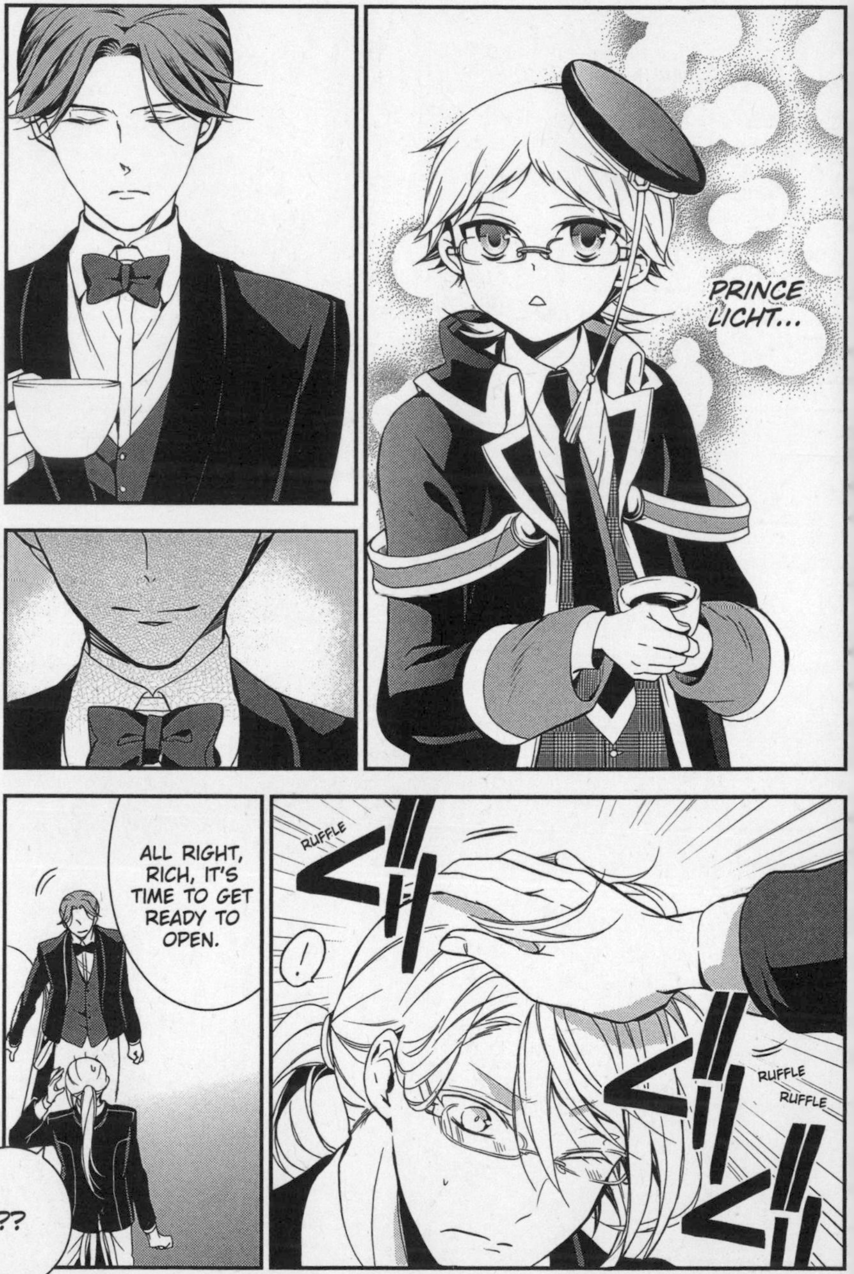
PRINCE LICHT...
RUFFLE
!
RUFFLE
RUFFLE
ALL RIGHT, RICH, IT'S TIME TO GET READY TO OPEN.
??

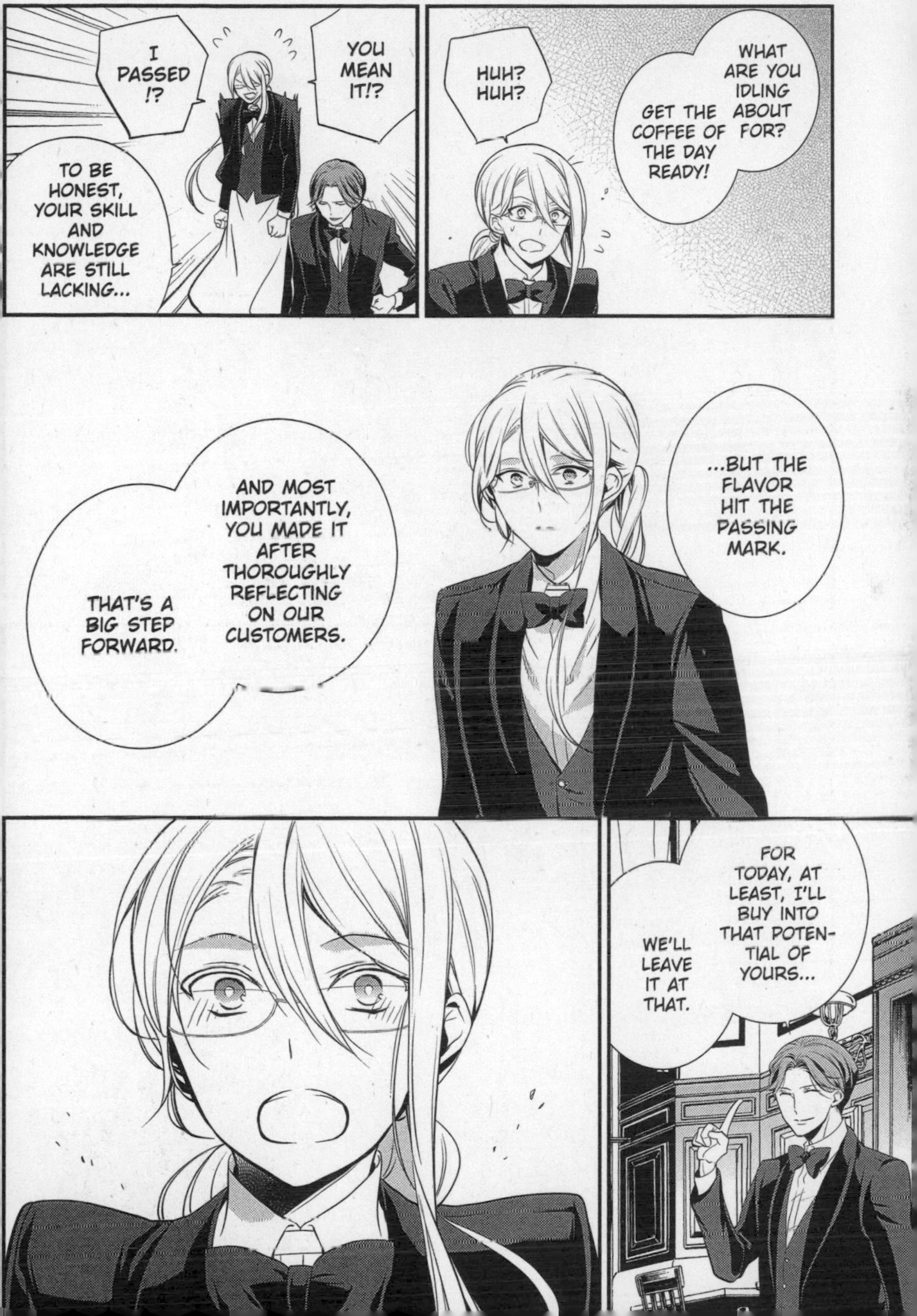
WHAT ARE YOU IDLING ABOUT FOR?
GET THE COFFEE OF THE DAY READY!
HUH? HUH?
YOU MEAN IT!?
I PASSED !?
TO BE HONEST, YOUR SKILL AND KNOWLEDGE ARE STILL LACKING...
...BUT THE FLAVOR HIT THE PASSING MARK.
AND MOST IMPORTANTLY, YOU MADE IT AFTER THOROUGHLY REFLECTING ON OUR CUSTOMERS.
THAT'S A BIG STEP FORWARD.
FOR TODAY, AT LEAST, I'LL BUY INTO THAT POTEN-TIAL OF YOURS...
WE'LL LEAVE IT AT THAT.

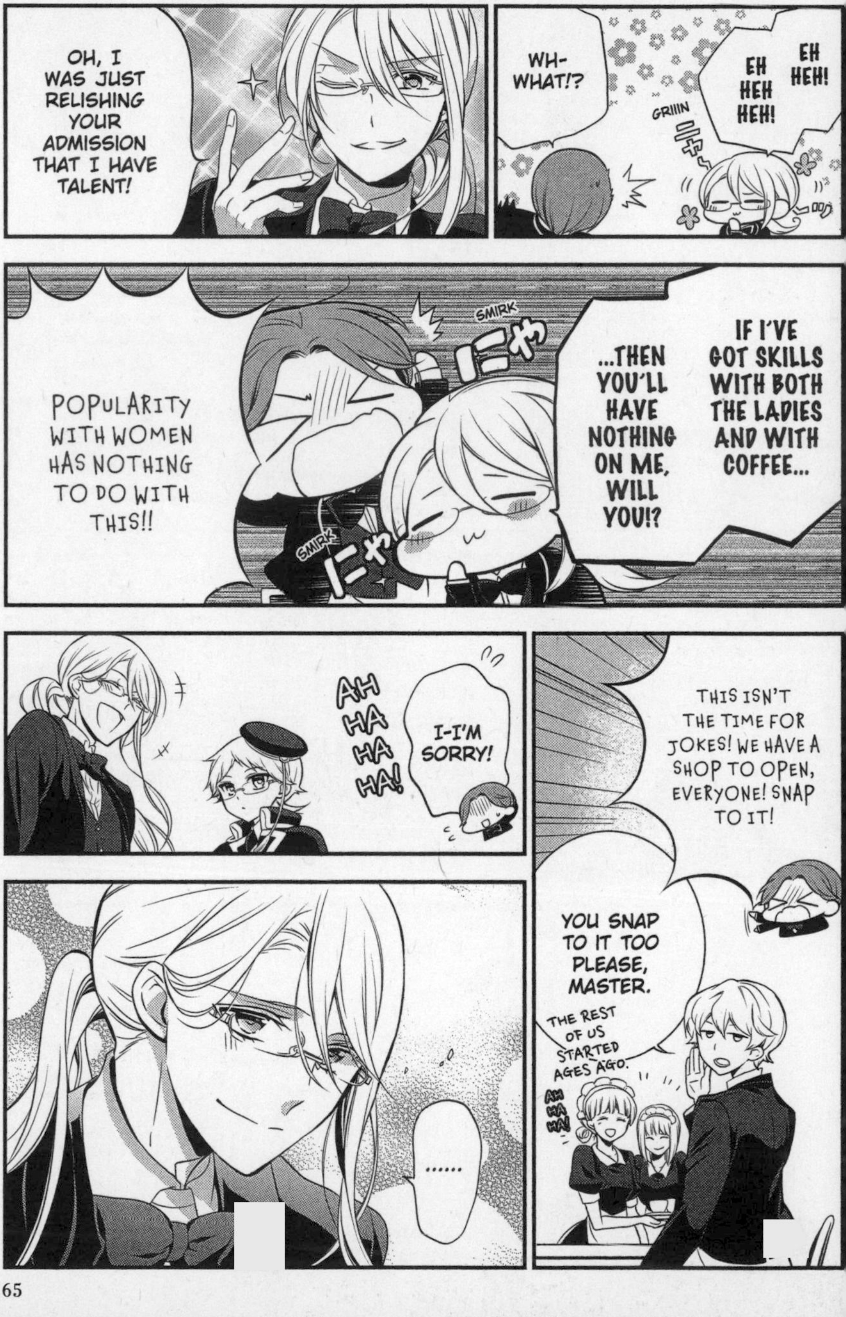
EH HEH!
EH HEH HEH!
WH-WHAT!?
GRIIIN
OH, I WAS JUST RELISHING YOUR ADMISSION THAT I HAVE TALENT!
IF I'VE GOT SKILLS WITH BOTH THE LADIES AND WITH COFFEE...
...THEN YOU'LL HAVE NOTHING ON ME, WILL YOU!?
SMIRK
SMIRK
POPULARITY WITH WOMEN HAS NOTHING TO DO WITH THIS!!
THIS ISN'T THE TIME FOR JOKES! WE HAVE A SHOP TO OPEN, EVERYONE! SNAP TO IT!
YOU SNAP TO IT TOO PLEASE, MASTER.
THE REST OF US STARTED AGES AGO.
AH HA HA!
I-I'M SORRY!
AH HA HA HA!
......

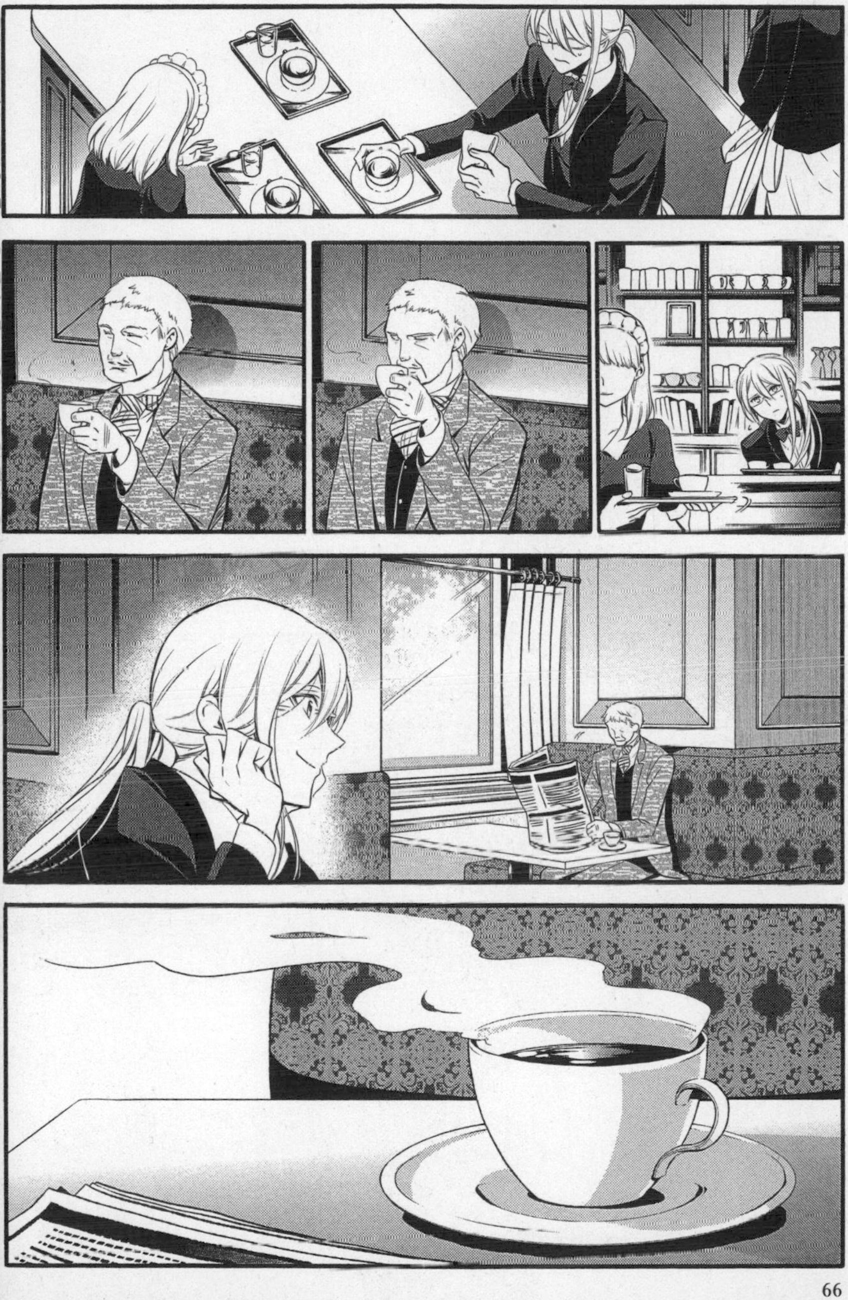

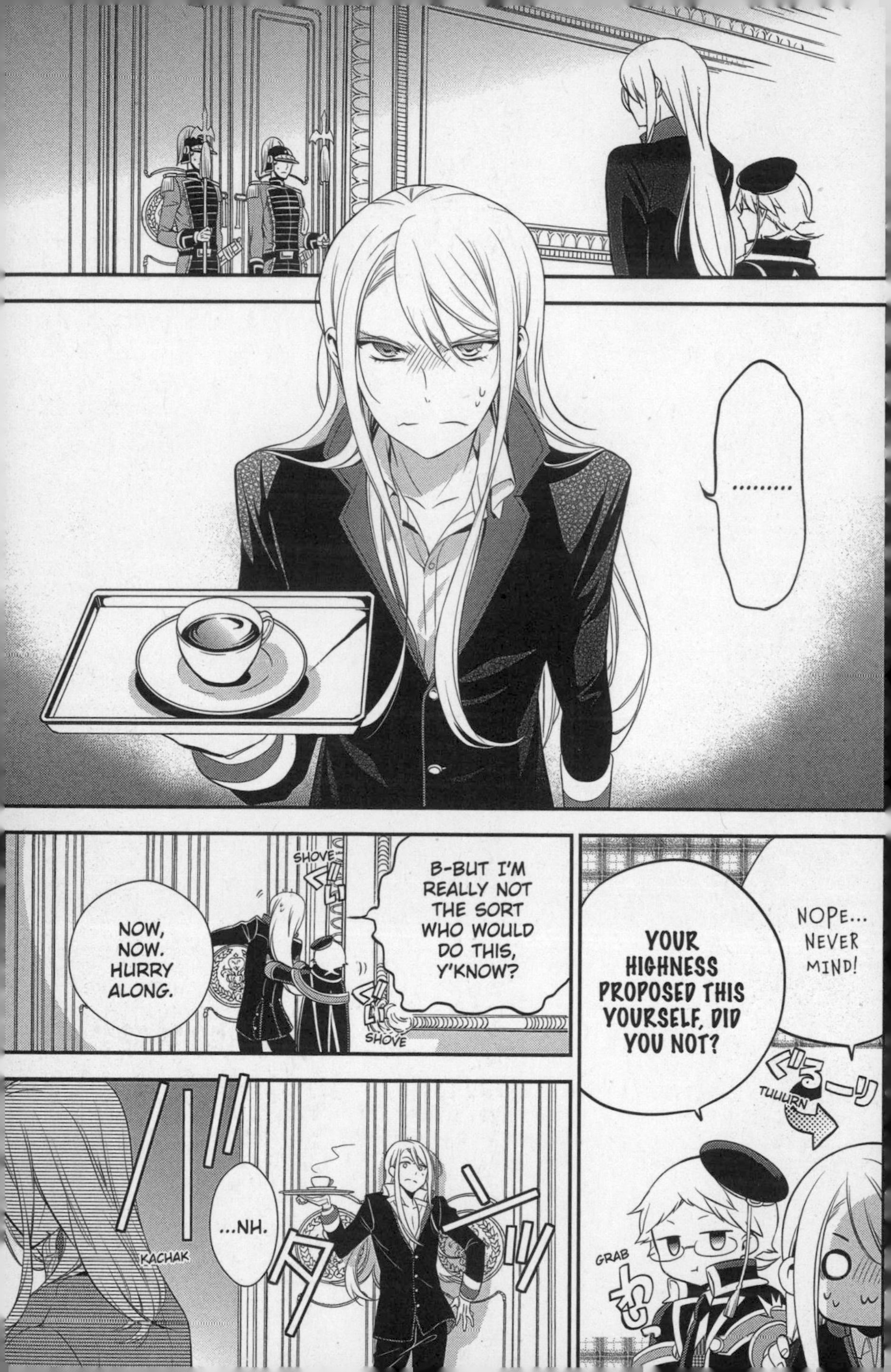

....
NOPE... NEVER MIND!
YOUR HIGHNESS PROPOSED THIS YOURSELF, DID YOU NOT?
ぐるーり
TUUURN
GRAB
B-BUT I'M REALLY NOT THE SORT WHO WOULD DO THIS, Y'KNOW?
SHOVE
NOW, NOW. HURRY ALONG.
SHOVE
...NH.
KACHAK

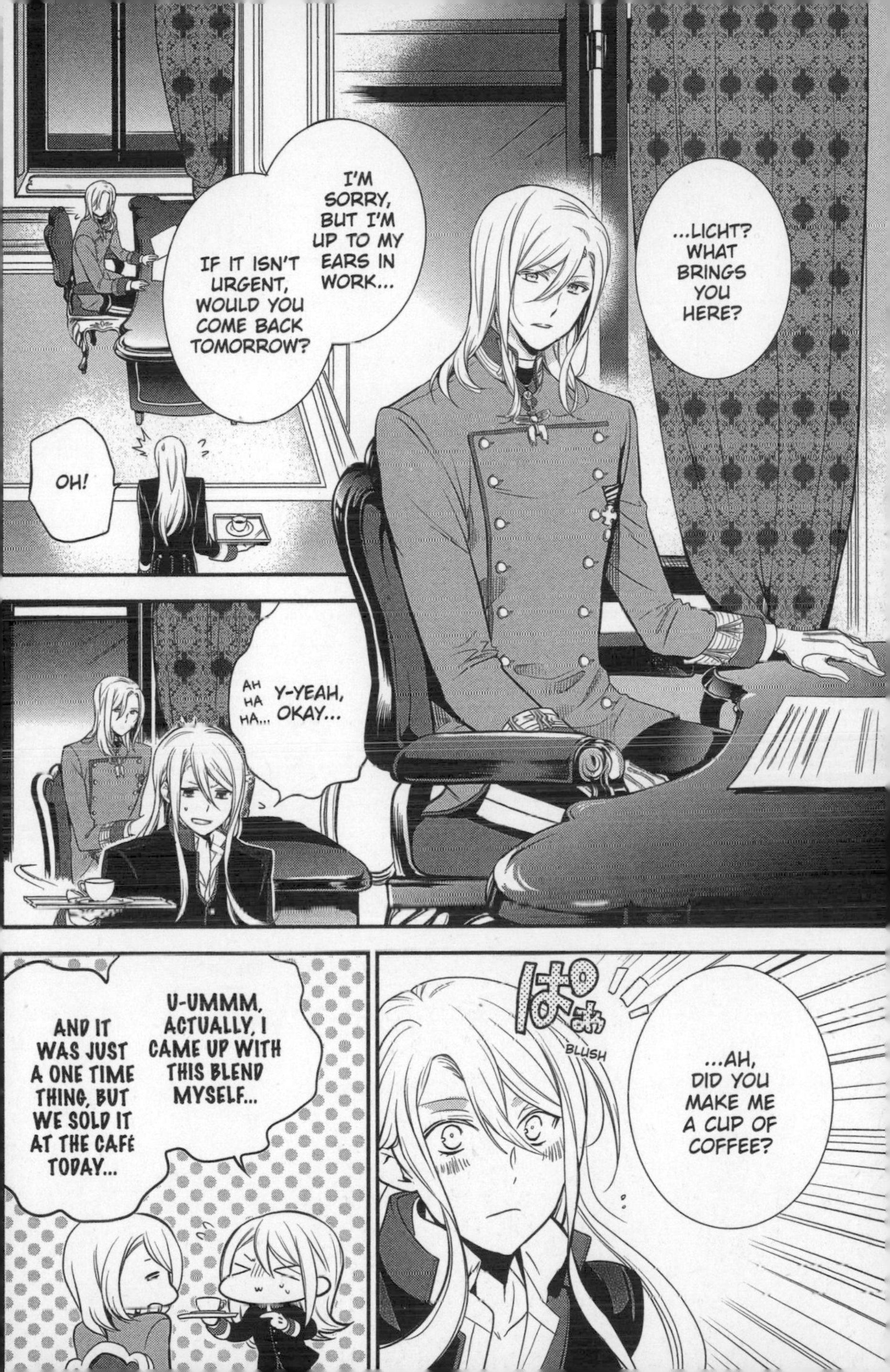

...LICHT? WHAT BRINGS YOU HERE?
I'M SORRY, BUT I'M UP TO MY EARS IN WORK...
IF IT ISN'T URGENT, WOULD YOU COME BACK TOMORROW?
OH!
AH HA HA...
Y-YEAH, OKAY...
ぱぁ
BLUSH
...AH, DID YOU MAKE ME A CUP OF COFFEE?
U-UMMM, ACTUALLY, I CAME UP WITH THIS BLEND MYSELF...
AND IT WAS JUST A ONE TIME THING, BUT WE SOLD IT AT THE CAFÉ TODAY...

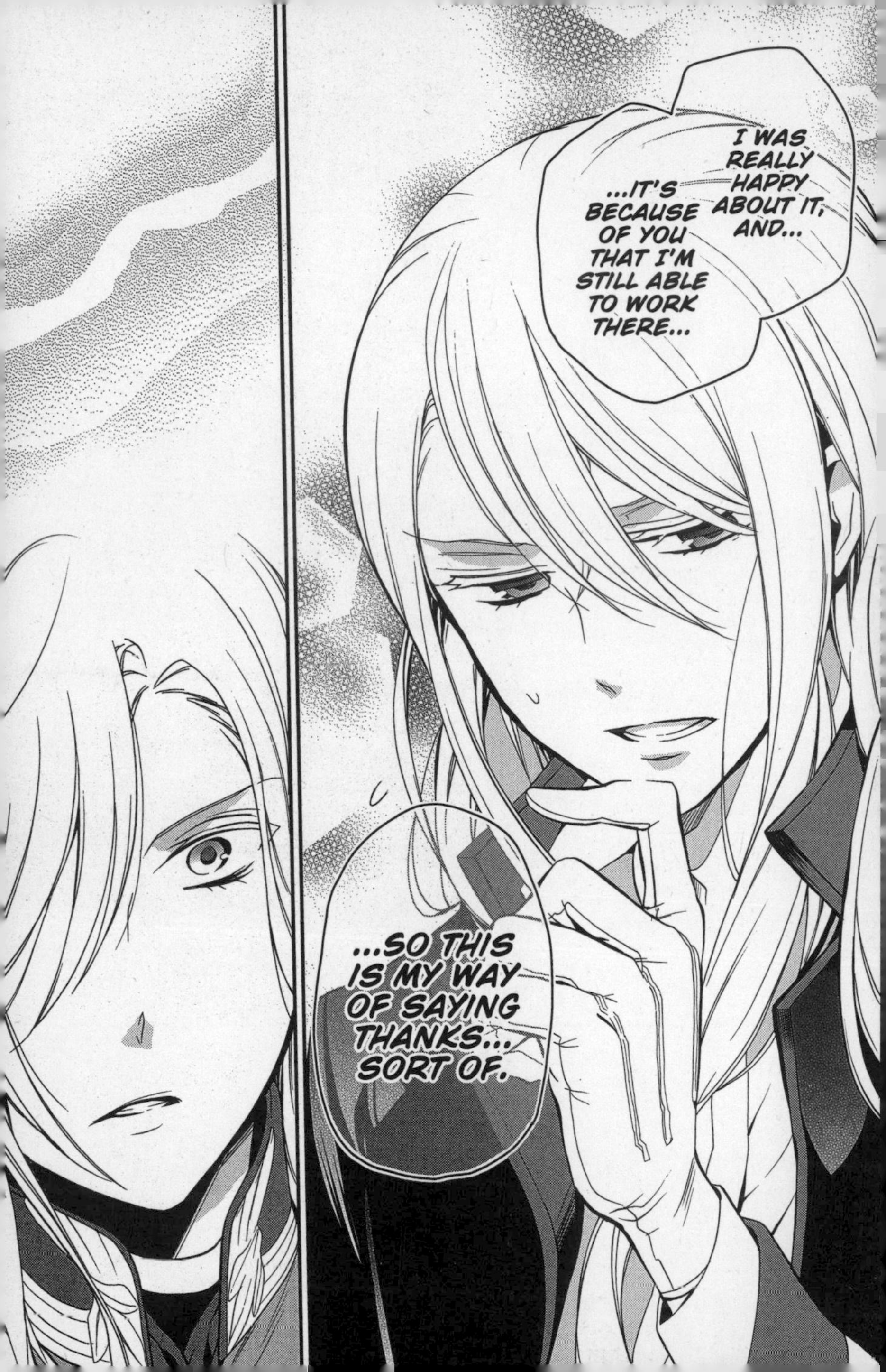
I WAS REALLY HAPPY ABOUT IT, AND...
...IT'S BECAUSE OF YOU THAT I'M STILL ABLE TO WORK THERE...
...SO THIS IS MY WAY OF SAYING THANKS... SORT OF.

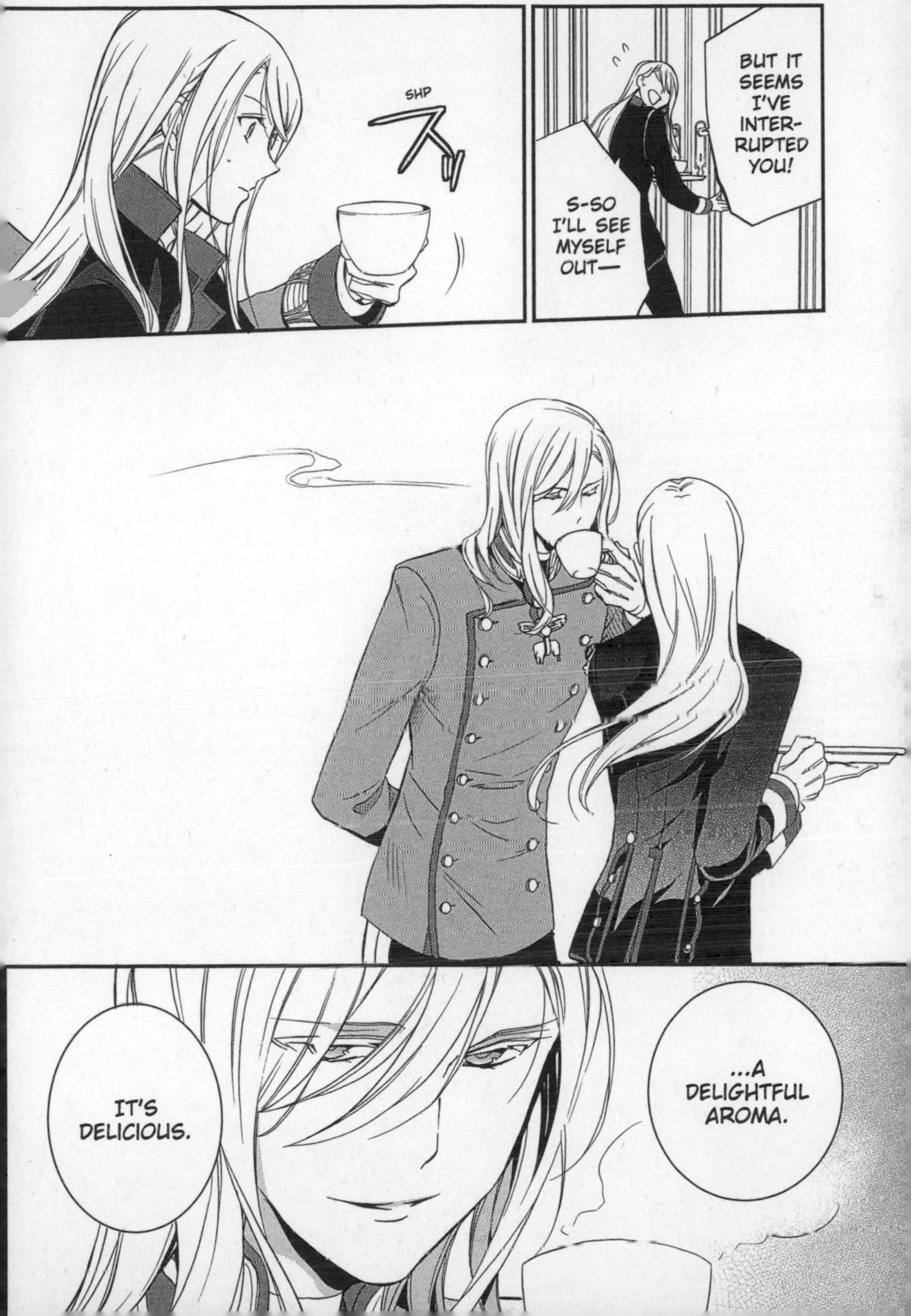
BUT IT SEEMS I'VE INTER-RUPTED YOU!
S-SO I'LL SEE MYSELF OUT—
SHP
...A DELIGHTFUL AROMA.
IT'S DELICIOUS.

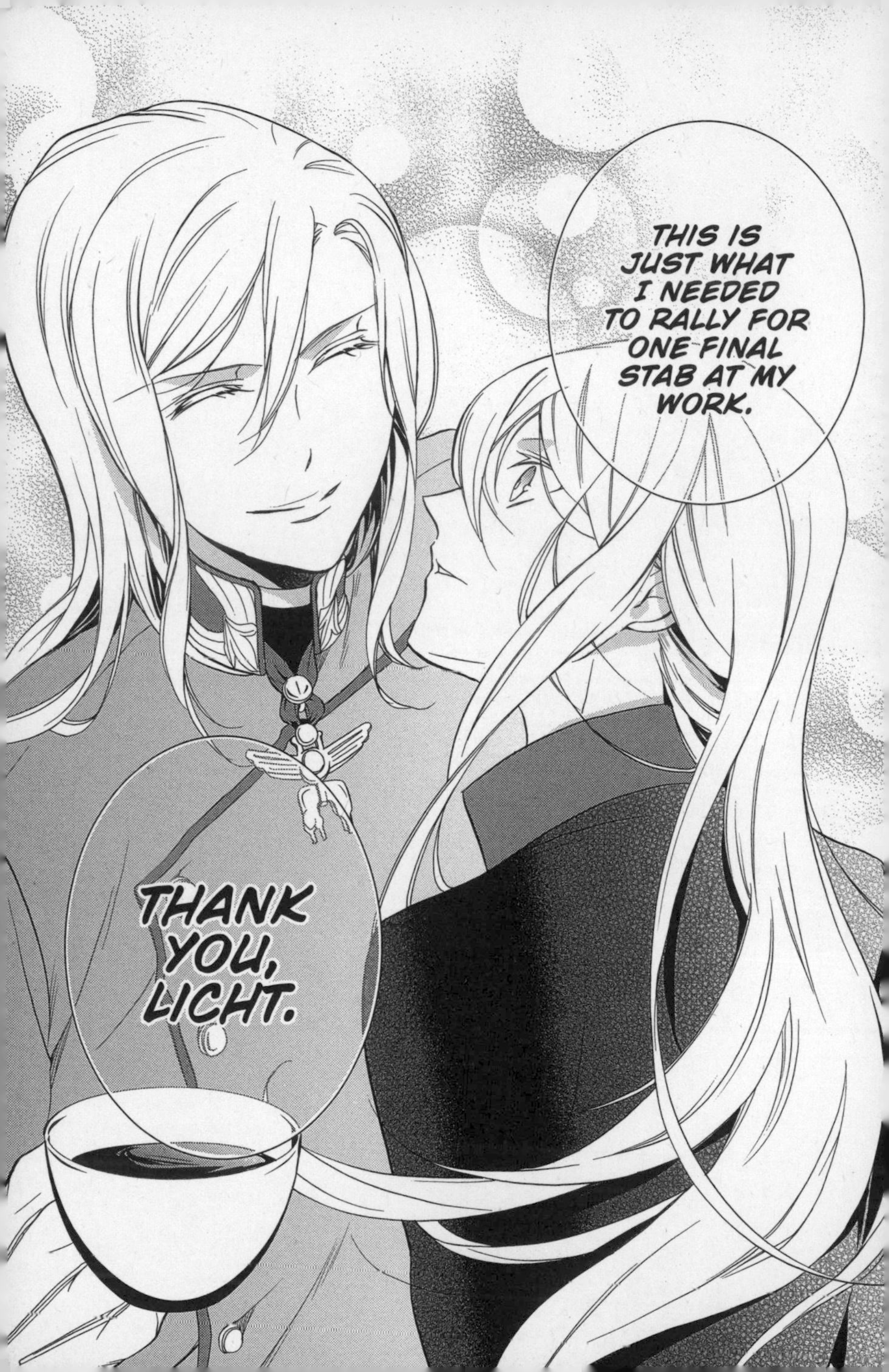
THIS IS JUST WHAT I NEEDED TO RALLY FOR ONE FINAL STAB AT MY WORK.
THANK YOU, LICHT.

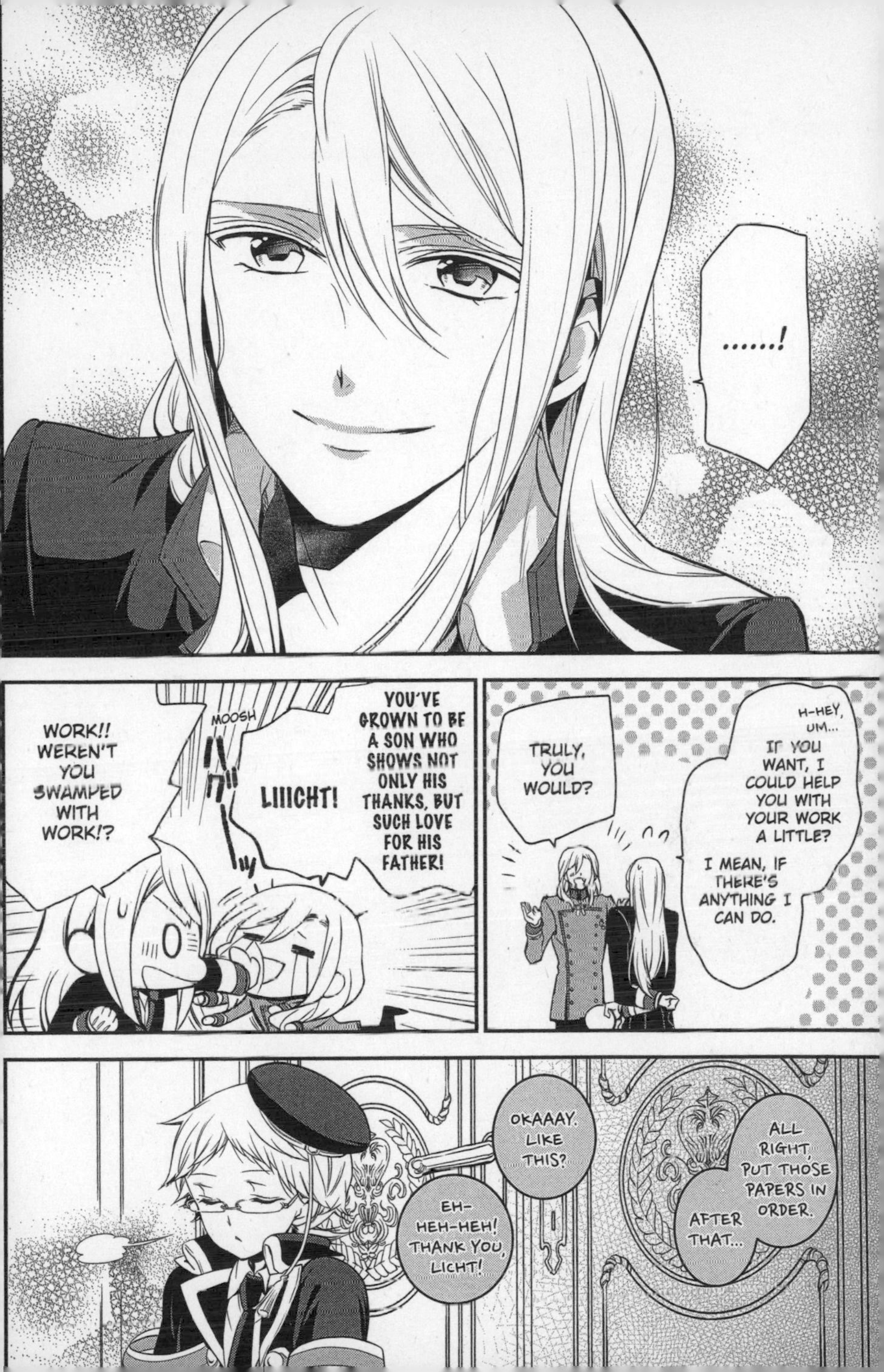
......!
H-HEY, UM... IF YOU WANT, I COULD HELP YOU WITH YOUR WORK A LITTLE?
I MEAN, IF THERE'S ANYTHING I CAN DO.
TRULY, YOU WOULD?
YOU'VE GROWN TO BE A SON WHO SHOWS NOT ONLY HIS THANKS, BUT SUCH LOVE FOR HIS FATHER!
LIIICHT!
MOOSH
WORK!! WEREN'T YOU SWAMPED WITH WORK!?
ALL RIGHT, PUT THOSE PAPERS IN ORDER.
AFTER THAT...
OKAAAY. LIKE THIS?
EH-HEH-HEH! THANK YOU, LICHT!

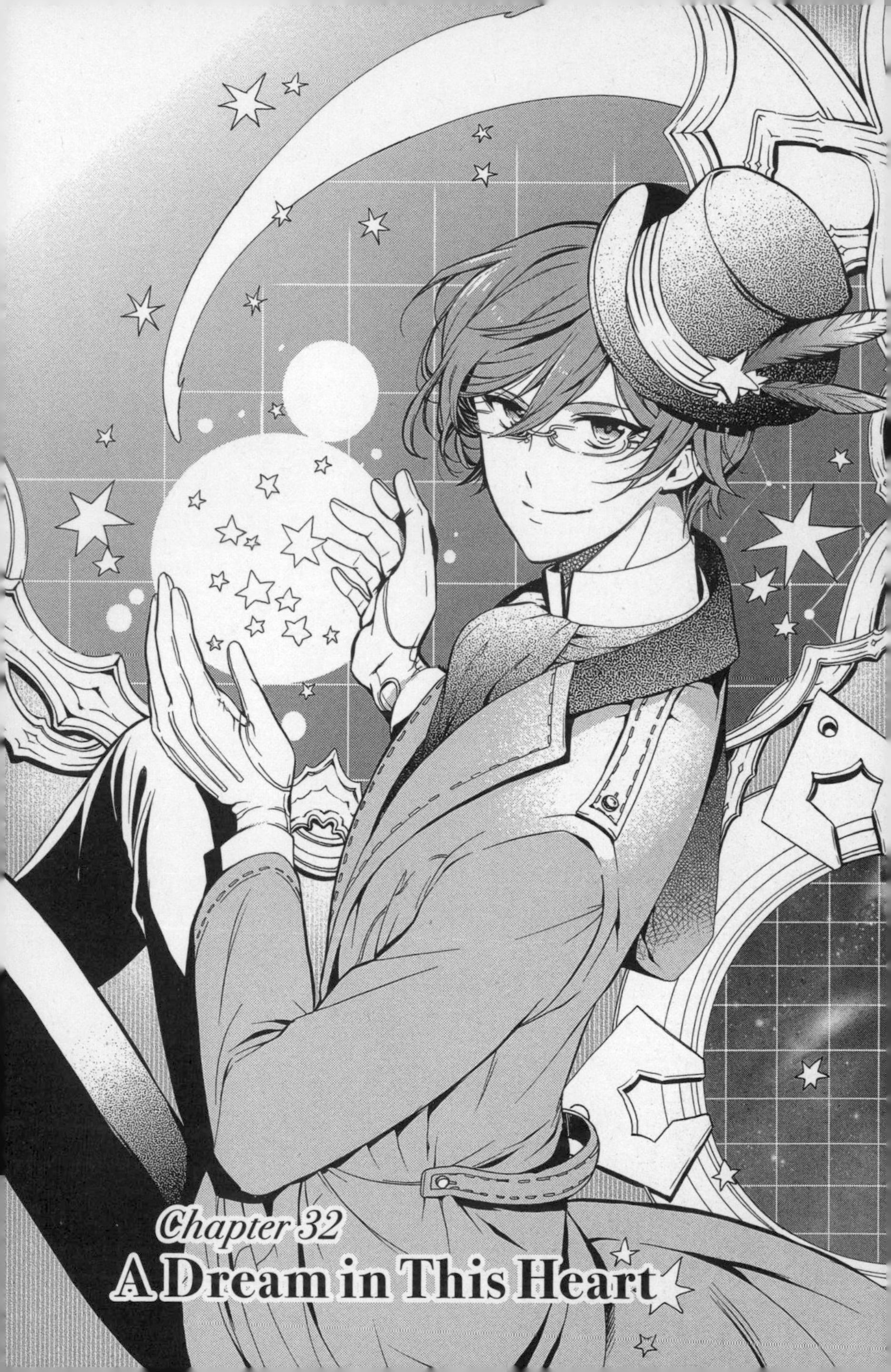
Chapter 32
A Dream in This Heart

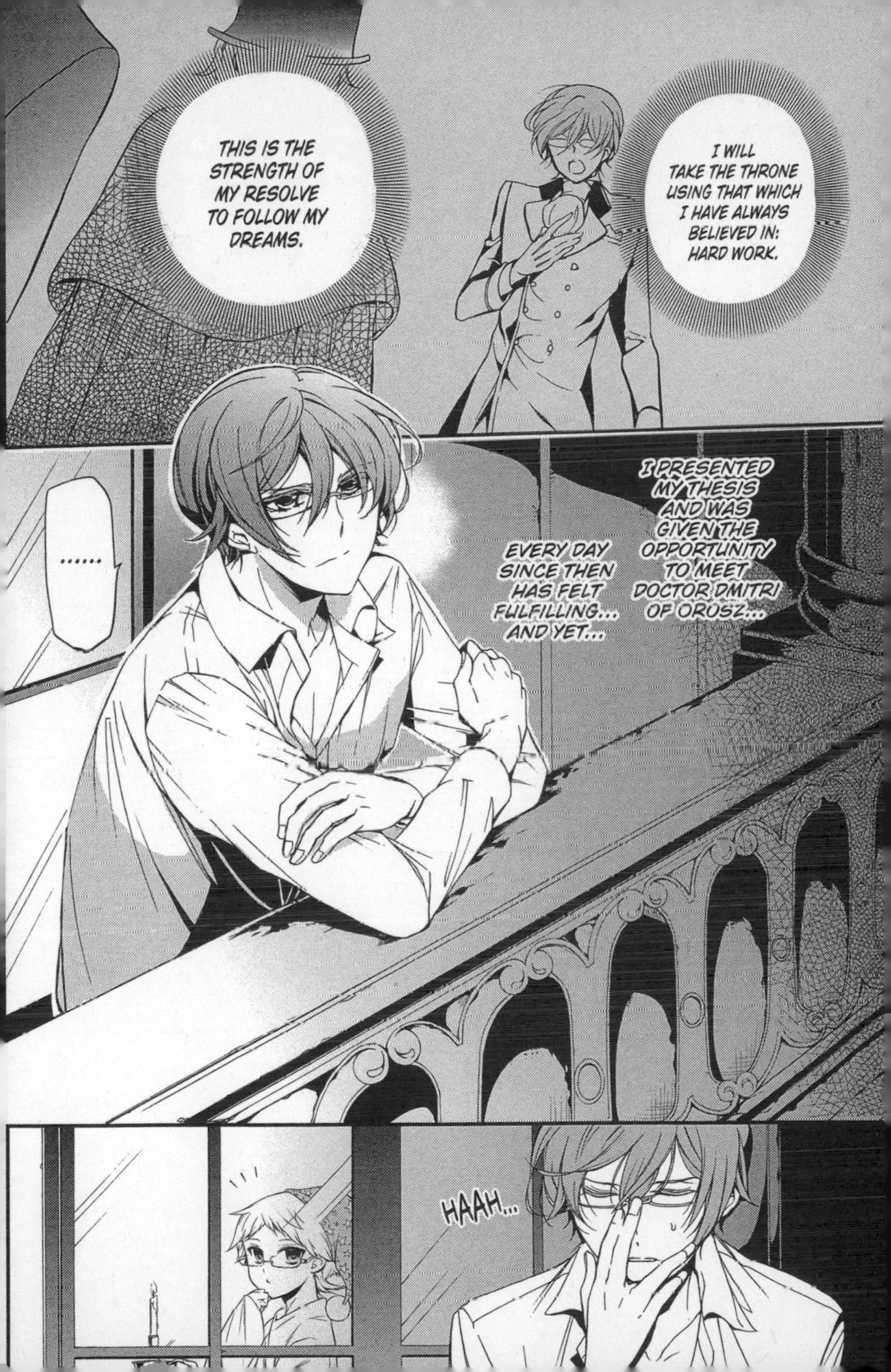
I WILL TAKE THE THRONE USING THAT WHICH I HAVE ALWAYS BELIEVED IN: HARD WORK.
THIS IS THE STRENGTH OF MY RESOLVE TO FOLLOW MY DREAMS.
I PRESENTED MY THESIS AND WAS GIVEN THE OPPORTUNITY TO MEET DOCTOR DMITRI OF OROSZ...
EVERY DAY SINCE THEN HAS FELT FULFILLING... AND YET...
......
HAAH...

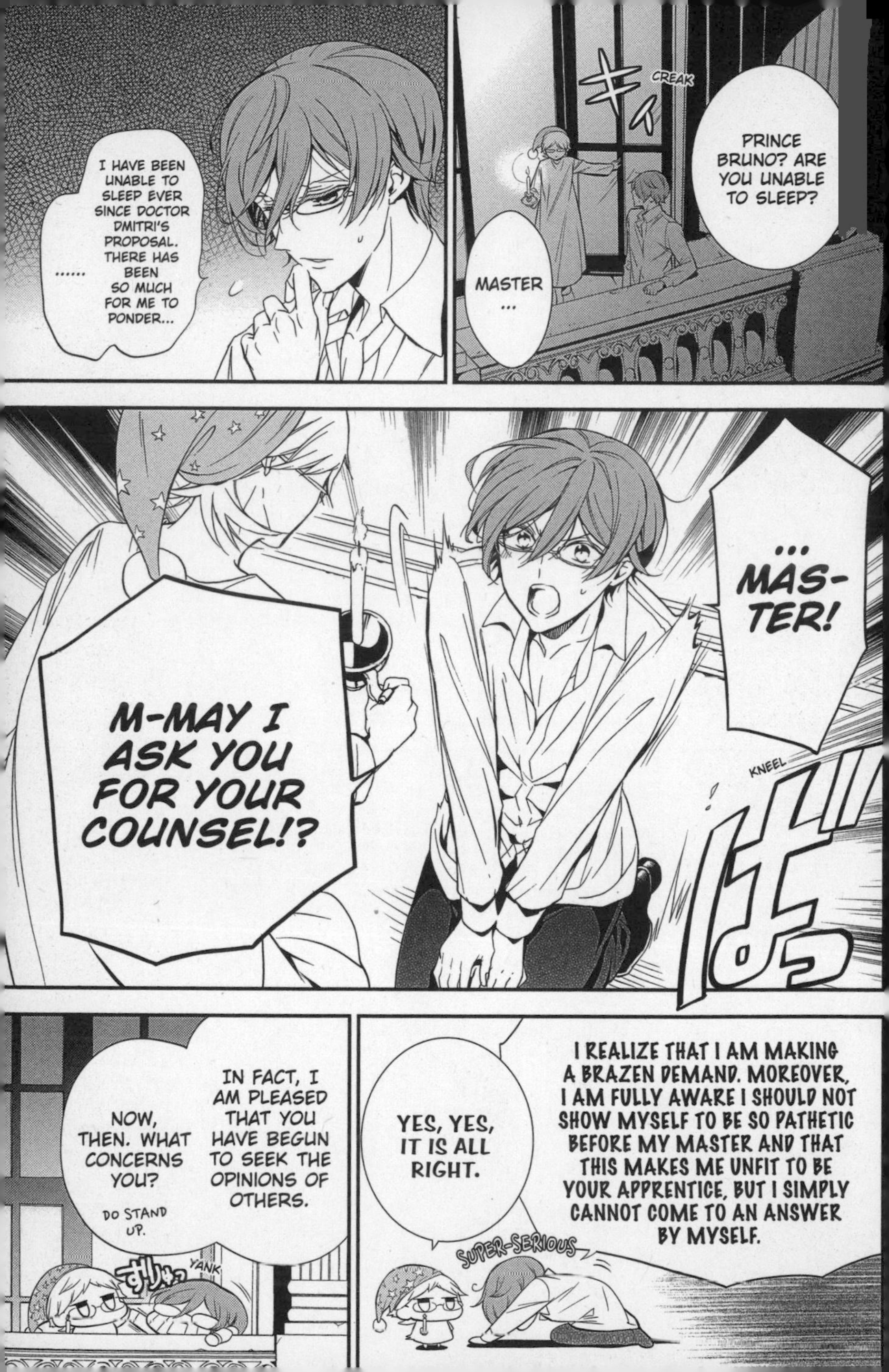
CREAK
PRINCE BRUNO? ARE YOU UNABLE TO SLEEP?
MASTER ...
I HAVE BEEN UNABLE TO SLEEP EVER SINCE DOCTOR DMITRI'S PROPOSAL. THERE HAS BEEN SO MUCH FOR ME TO PONDER...
......
... MÄS-TER!
KNEEL
M-MAY I ASK YOU FOR YOUR COUNSEL!?
I REALIZE THAT I AM MAKING A BRAZEN DEMAND. MOREOVER, I AM FULLY AWARE I SHOULD NOT SHOW MYSELF TO BE SO PATHETIC BEFORE MY MASTER AND THAT THIS MAKES ME UNFIT TO BE YOUR APPRENTICE, BUT I SIMPLY CANNOT COME TO AN ANSWER BY MYSELF.
YES, YES, IT IS ALL RIGHT.
SUPER-SERIOUS
IN FACT, I AM PLEASED THAT YOU HAVE BEGUN TO SEEK THE OPINIONS OF OTHERS.
NOW, THEN. WHAT CONCERNS YOU?
DO STAND UP.
YANK

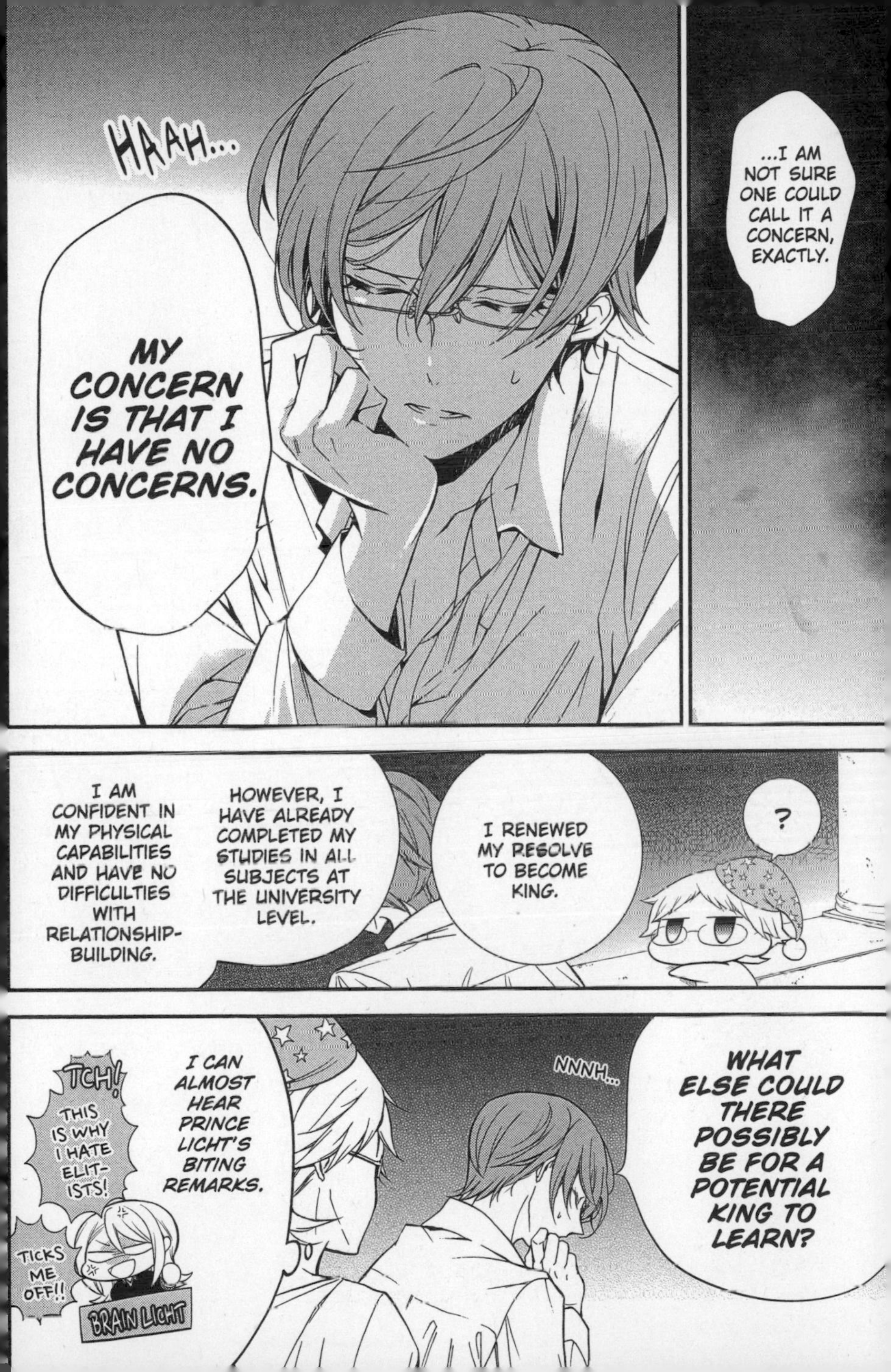
...I AM NOT SURE ONE COULD CALL IT A CONCERN, EXACTLY.
HAAH...
MY CONCERN IS THAT I HAVE NO CONCERNS.
?
I RENEWED MY RESOLVE TO BECOME KING.
HOWEVER, I HAVE ALREADY COMPLETED MY STUDIES IN ALL SUBJECTS AT THE UNIVERSITY LEVEL.
I AM CONFIDENT IN MY PHYSICAL CAPABILITIES AND HAVE NO DIFFICULTIES WITH RELATIONSHIP-BUILDING.
WHAT ELSE COULD THERE POSSIBLY BE FOR A POTENTIAL KING TO LEARN?
NNNH...
I CAN ALMOST HEAR PRINCE LICHT'S BITING REMARKS.
TCH!
THIS IS WHY I HATE ELIT-ISTS!
TICKS ME OFF!!
BRAIN LICHT

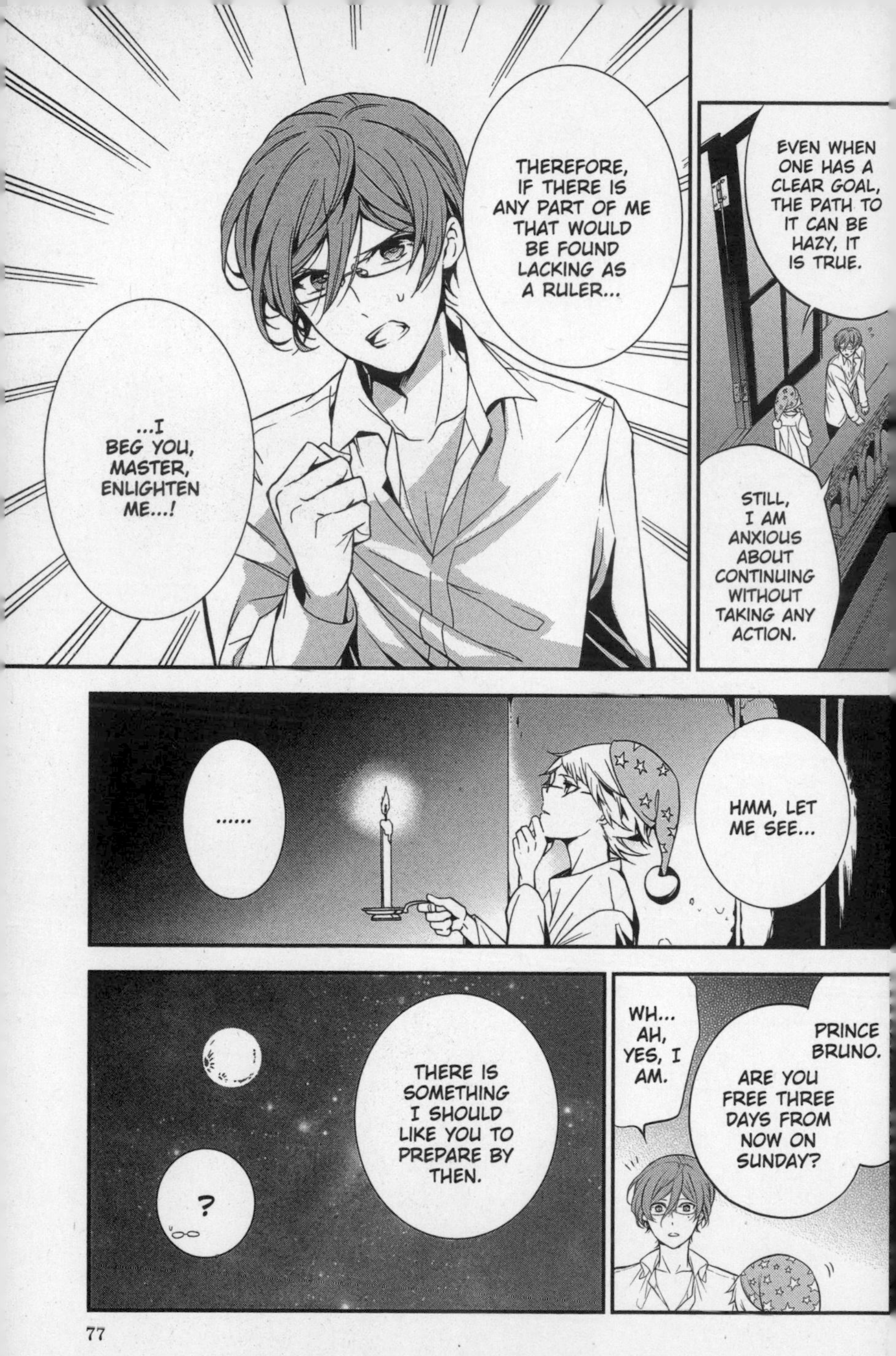
EVEN WHEN ONE HAS A CLEAR GOAL, THE PATH TO IT CAN BE HAZY, IT IS TRUE.
STILL, I AM ANXIOUS ABOUT CONTINUING WITHOUT TAKING ANY ACTION.
THEREFORE, IF THERE IS ANY PART OF ME THAT WOULD BE FOUND LACKING AS A RULER...
...I BEG YOU, MASTER, ENLIGHTEN ME...!
HMM, LET ME SEE...
......
PRINCE BRUNO.
ARE YOU FREE THREE DAYS FROM NOW ON SUNDAY?
WH... AH, YES, I AM.
THERE IS SOMETHING I SHOULD LIKE YOU TO PREPARE BY THEN.
?

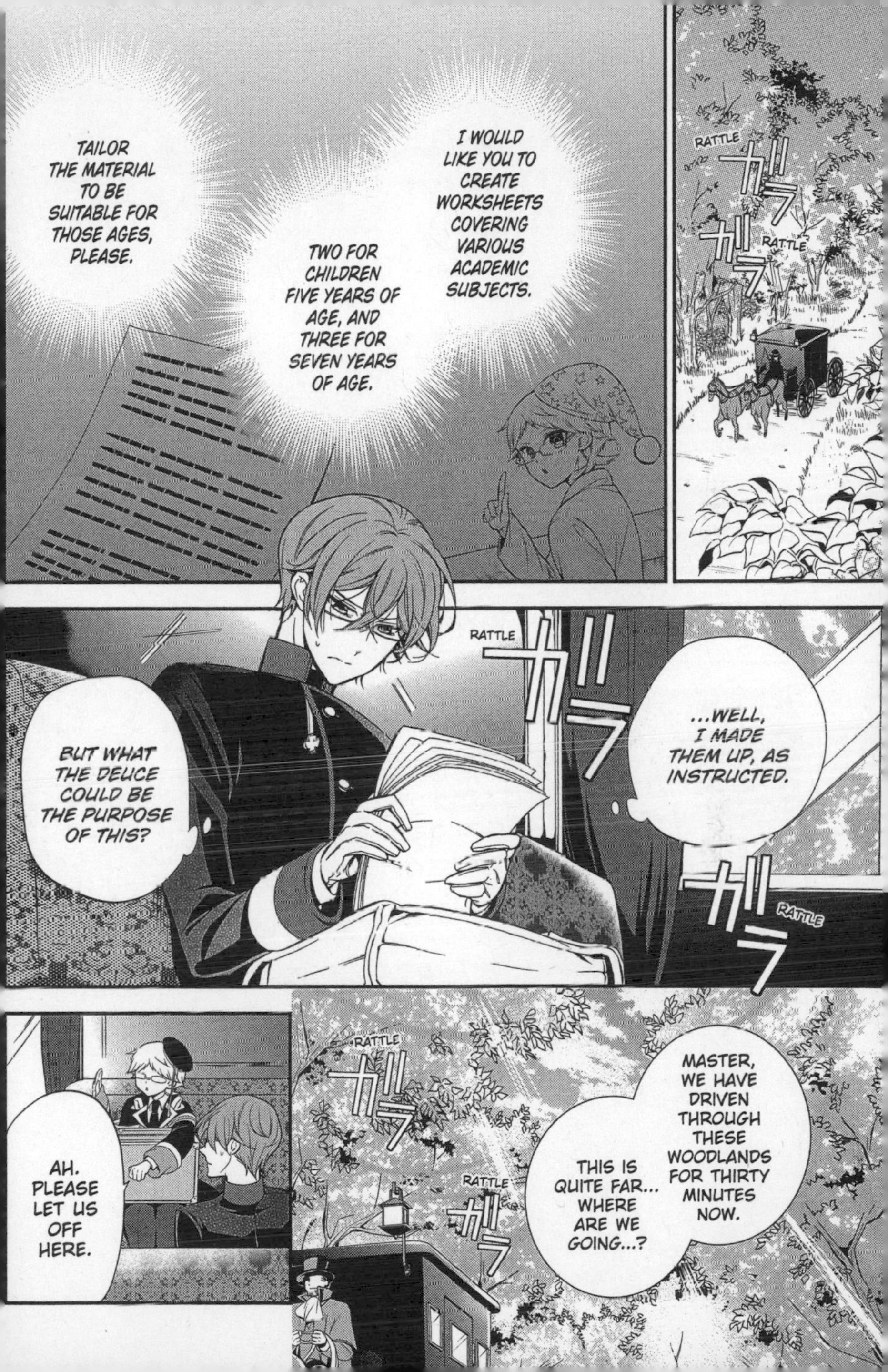
RATTLE
ガラ
RATTLE
ガラ
I WOULD LIKE YOU TO CREATE WORKSHEETS COVERING VARIOUS ACADEMIC SUBJECTS.
TWO FOR CHILDREN FIVE YEARS OF AGE, AND THREE FOR SEVEN YEARS OF AGE.
TAILOR THE MATERIAL TO BE SUITABLE FOR THOSE AGES, PLEASE.
RATTLE
ガラ
...WELL, I MADE THEM UP, AS INSTRUCTED.
RATTLE
ガラ
BUT WHAT THE DEUCE COULD BE THE PURPOSE OF THIS?
MASTER, WE HAVE DRIVEN THROUGH THESE WOODLANDS FOR THIRTY MINUTES NOW.
THIS IS QUITE FAR... WHERE ARE WE GOING...?
RATTLE
ガラ
RATTLE
ガラ
AH. PLEASE LET US OFF HERE.

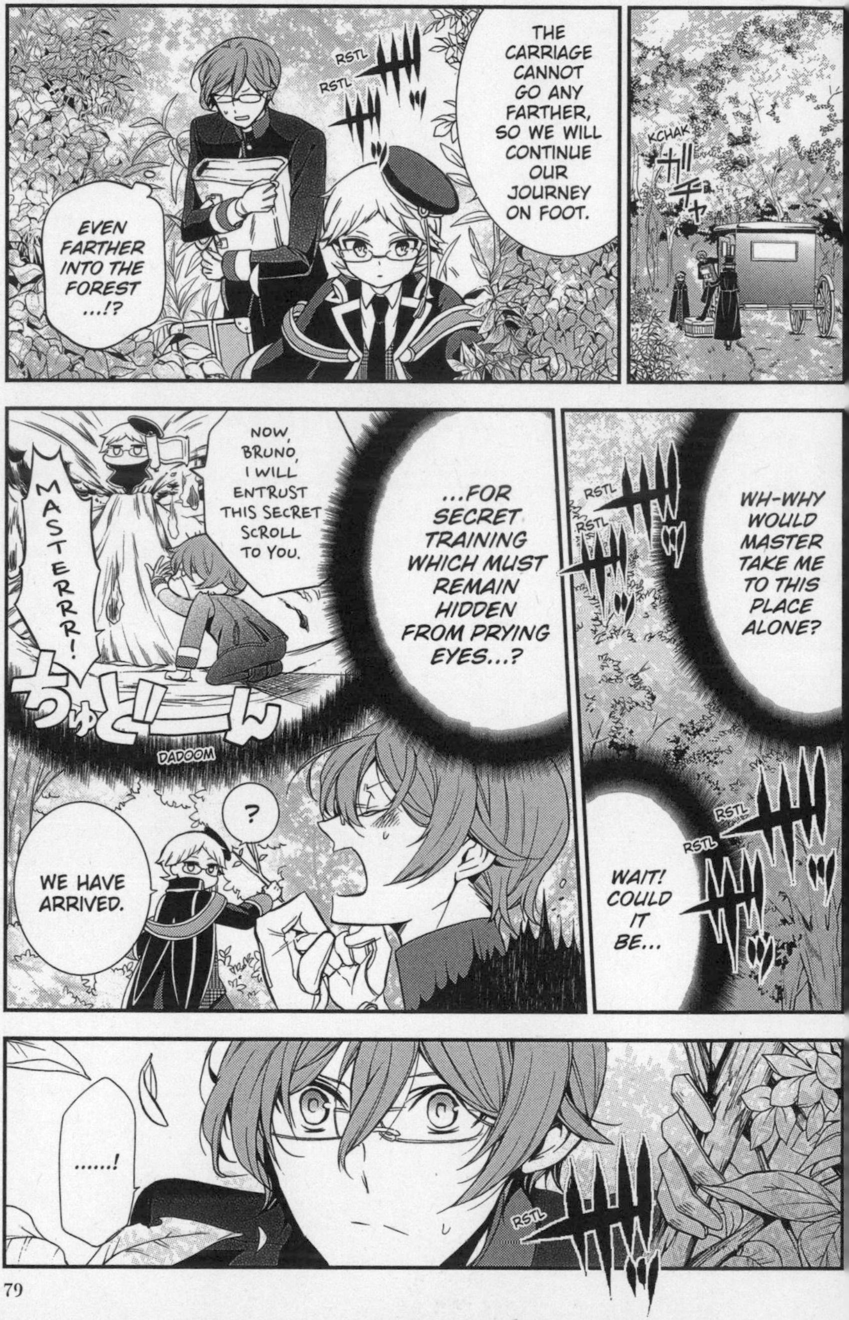
KCHAK
ガチャ
THE CARRIAGE CANNOT GO ANY FARTHER, SO WE WILL CONTINUE OUR JOURNEY ON FOOT.
RSTL
RSTL
EVEN FARTHER INTO THE FOREST ...!?
WH-WHY WOULD MASTER TAKE ME TO THIS PLACE ALONE?
RSTL
RSTL
WAIT! COULD IT BE...
RSTL
RSTL
...FOR SECRET TRAINING WHICH MUST REMAIN HIDDEN FROM PRYING EYES...?
NOW, BRUNO, I WILL ENTRUST THIS SECRET SCROLL TO YOU.
MASTERRR!
ちゅどーーん
DADOOM
?
WE HAVE ARRIVED.
......!
RSTL

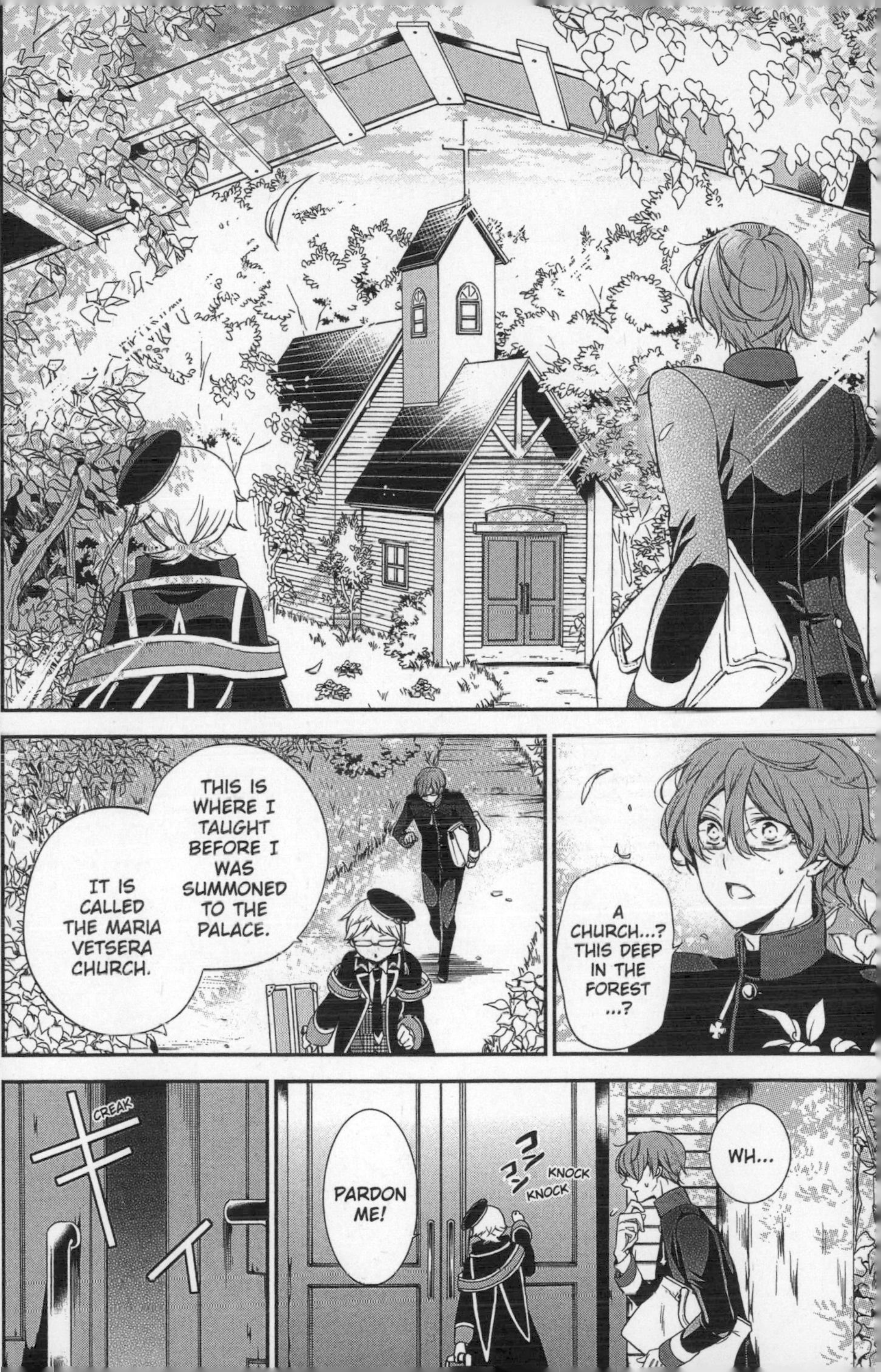
A CHURCH...? THIS DEEP IN THE FOREST ...?
THIS IS WHERE I TAUGHT BEFORE I WAS SUMMONED TO THE PALACE.
IT IS CALLED THE MARIA VETSERA CHURCH.
WH...
コン コン
KNOCK KNOCK
PARDON ME!
キイ
CREAK

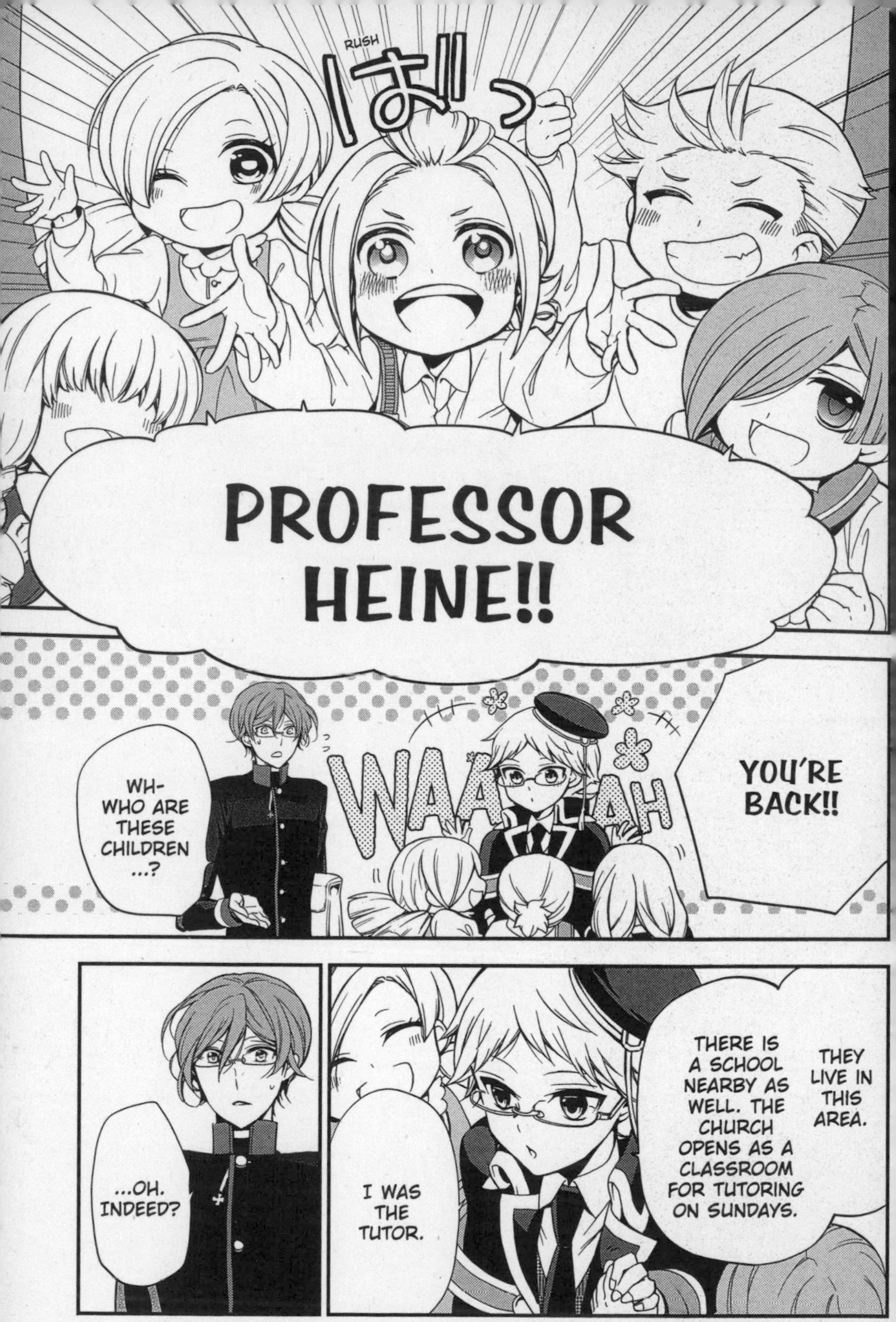
RUSH
ばっ
PROFESSOR HEINE!!
YOU'RE BACK!!
WAA AH
WH- WHO ARE THESE CHILDREN ...?
THEY LIVE IN THIS AREA.
THERE IS A SCHOOL NEARBY AS WELL. THE CHURCH OPENS AS A CLASSROOM FOR TUTORING ON SUNDAYS.
I WAS THE TUTOR.
...OH. INDEED?

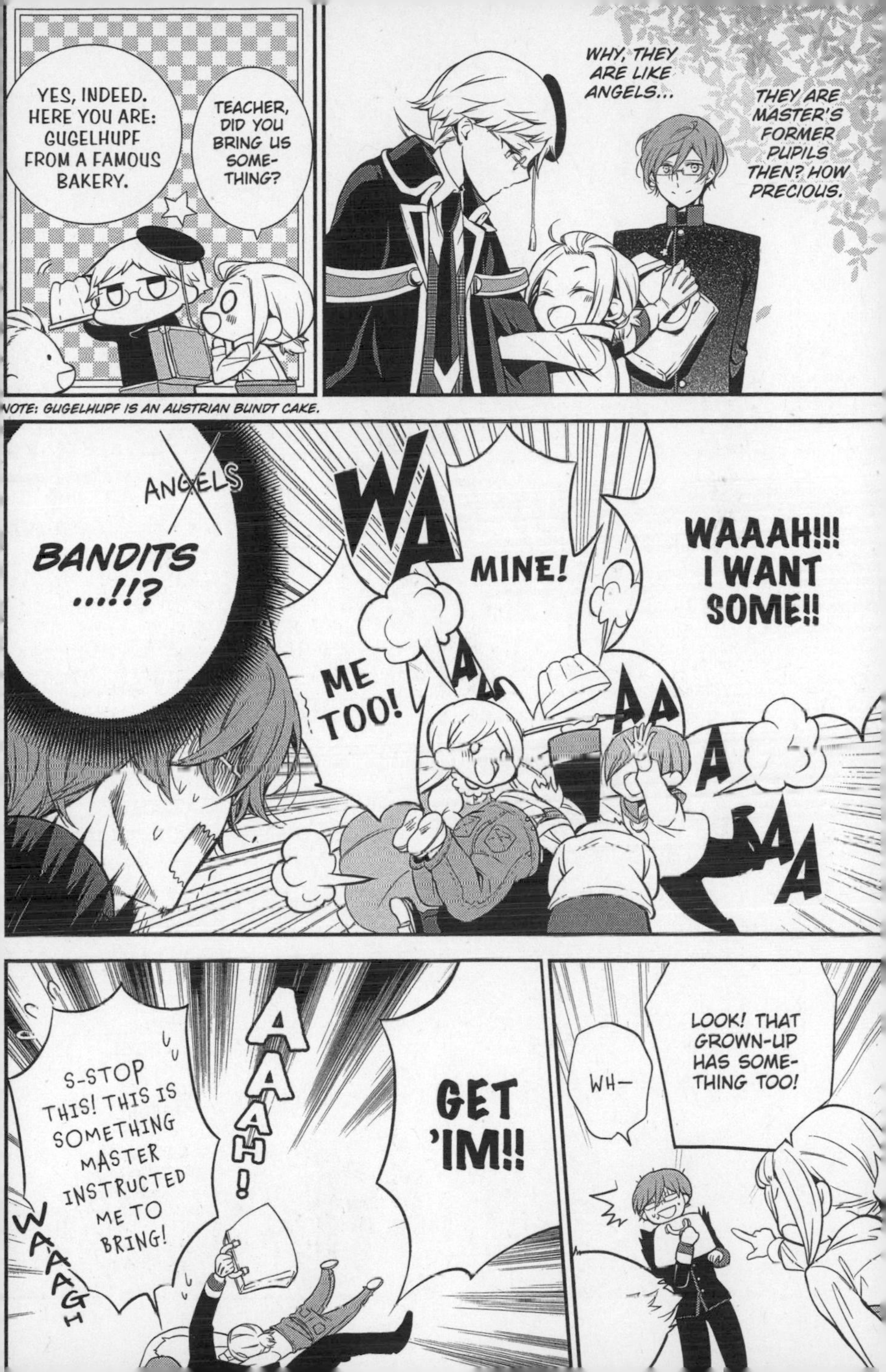
WHY, THEY ARE LIKE ANGELS...
THEY ARE MASTER'S FORMER PUPILS THEN? HOW PRECIOUS.
TEACHER, DID YOU BRING US SOME-THING?
YES, INDEED. HERE YOU ARE: GUGELHUPF FROM A FAMOUS BAKERY.
NOTE: GUGELHUPF IS AN AUSTRIAN BUNDT CAKE.
WAAAH!!! I WANT SOME!!
MINE!
WA
ANGELS
BANDITS ...!!?
ME TOO!
AAAAA
LOOK! THAT GROWN-UP HAS SOME-THING TOO!
WH—
GET 'IM!!
AAAAH!
S-STOP THIS! THIS IS SOMETHING MASTER INSTRUCTED ME TO BRING!
WAAAGH

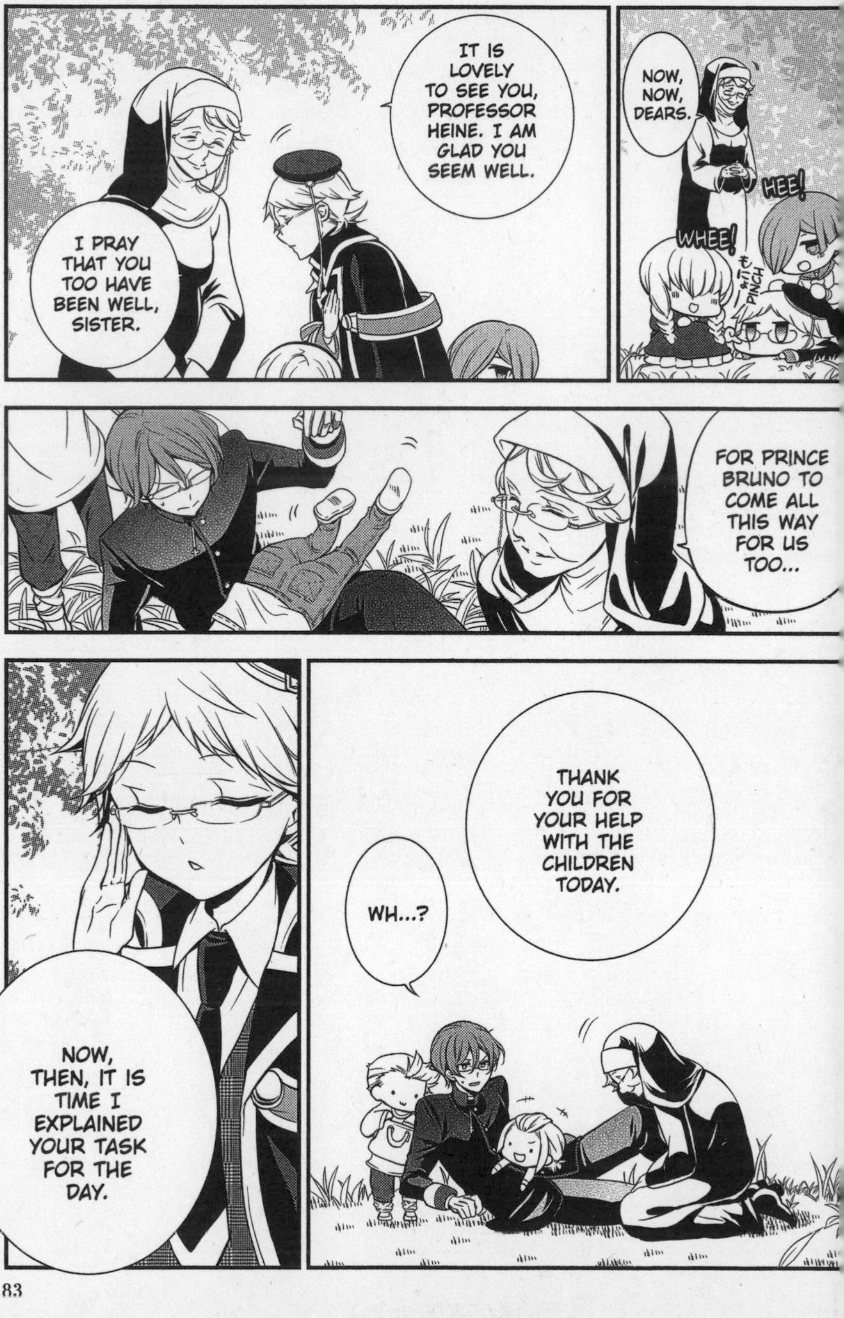
NOW, NOW, DEARS.
HEE!
WHEE!
PINCH
IT IS LOVELY TO SEE YOU, PROFESSOR HEINE. I AM GLAD YOU SEEM WELL.
I PRAY THAT YOU TOO HAVE BEEN WELL, SISTER.
FOR PRINCE BRUNO TO COME ALL THIS WAY FOR US TOO...
THANK YOU FOR YOUR HELP WITH THE CHILDREN TODAY.
WH...?
NOW, THEN, IT IS TIME I EXPLAINED YOUR TASK FOR THE DAY.

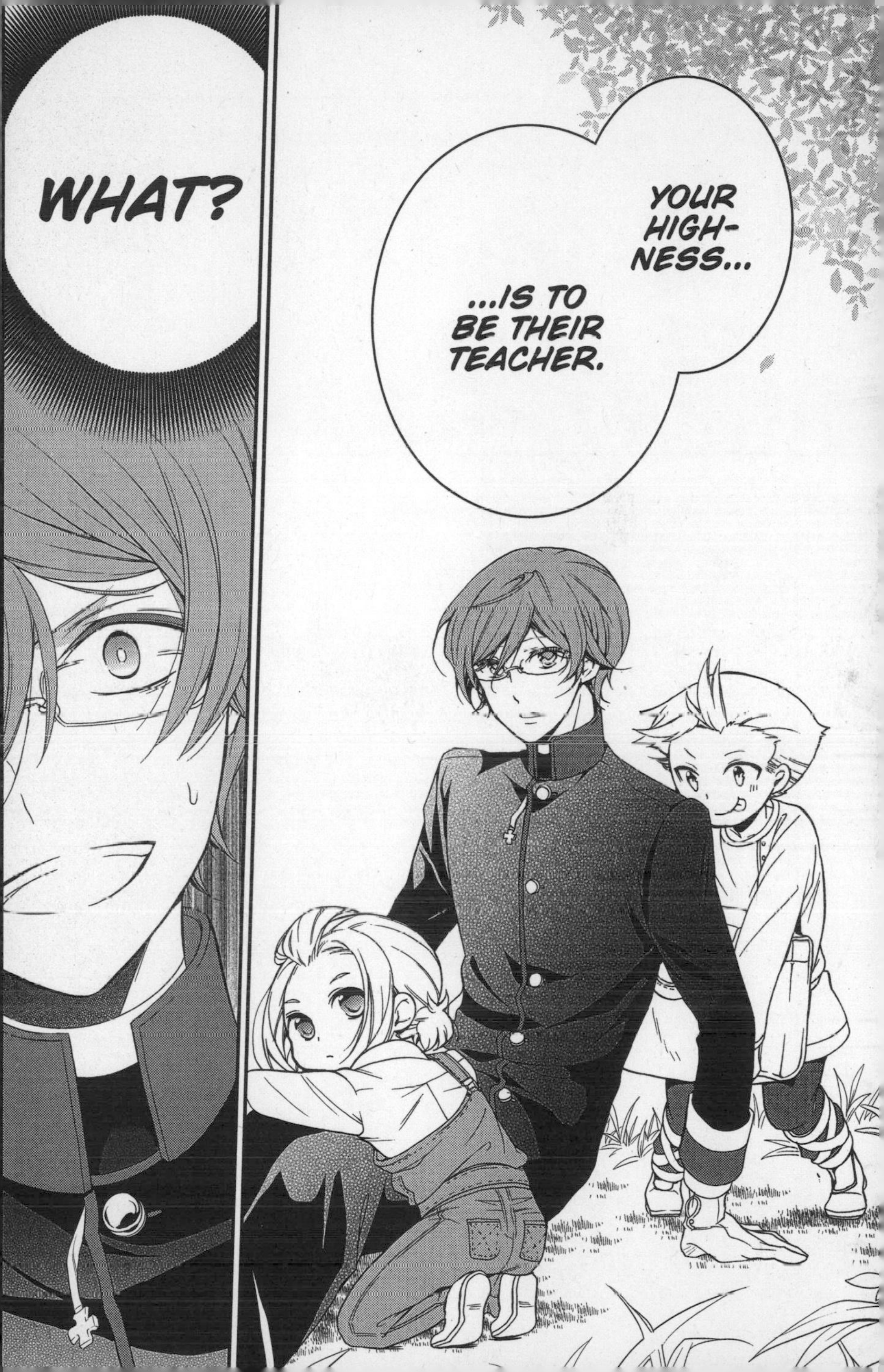
YOUR HIGH-NESS...
...IS TO BE THEIR TEACHER.
WHAT?

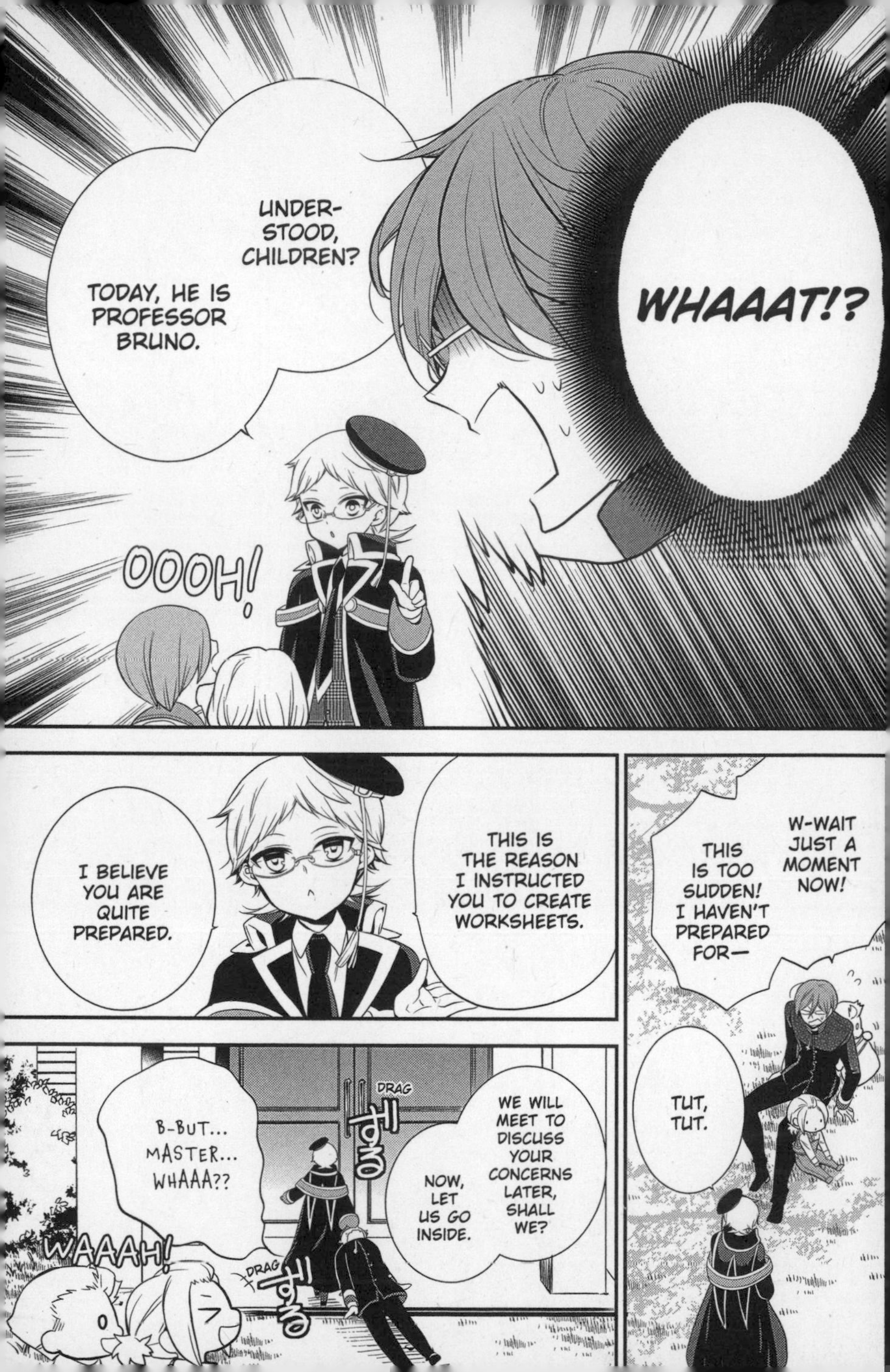
WHAAAT!?
UNDER-STOOD, CHILDREN?
TODAY, HE IS PROFESSOR BRUNO.
OOOH!
W-WAIT JUST A MOMENT NOW!
THIS IS TOO SUDDEN! I HAVEN'T PREPARED FOR—
TUT, TUT.
THIS IS THE REASON I INSTRUCTED YOU TO CREATE WORKSHEETS.
I BELIEVE YOU ARE QUITE PREPARED.
WE WILL MEET TO DISCUSS YOUR CONCERNS LATER, SHALL WE?
NOW, LET US GO INSIDE.
DRAG
DRAG
B-BUT... MASTER... WHAAA??
WAAAH!

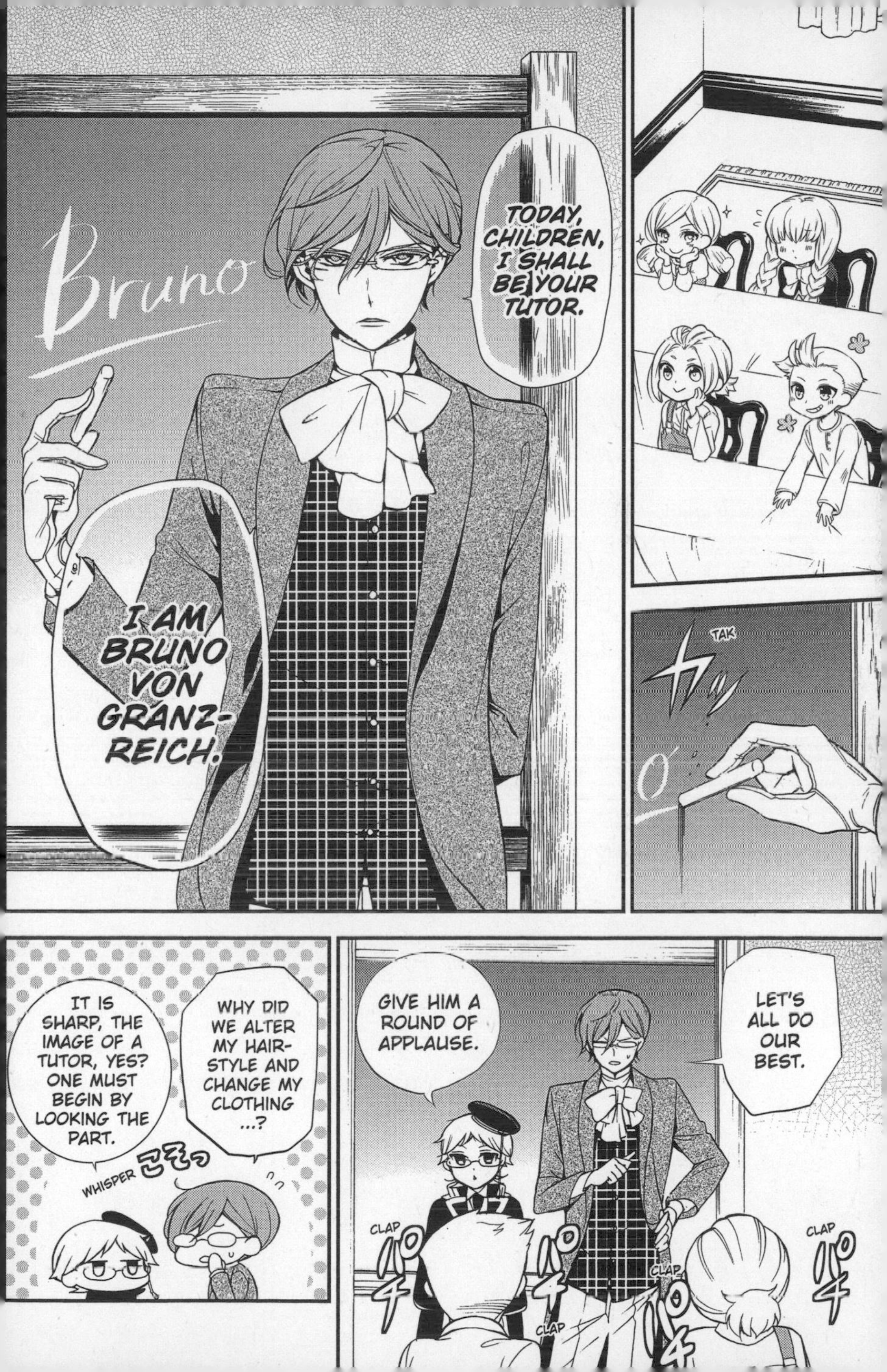
TAK
Bruno
TODAY, CHILDREN, I SHALL BE YOUR TUTOR.
I AM BRUNO VON GRANZREICH.
LET'S ALL DO OUR BEST.
GIVE HIM A ROUND OF APPLAUSE.
CLAP
CLAP
CLAP
CLAP
WHY DID WE ALTER MY HAIRSTYLE AND CHANGE MY CLOTHING ...?
IT IS SHARP, THE IMAGE OF A TUTOR, YES? ONE MUST BEGIN BY LOOKING THE PART.
WHISPER

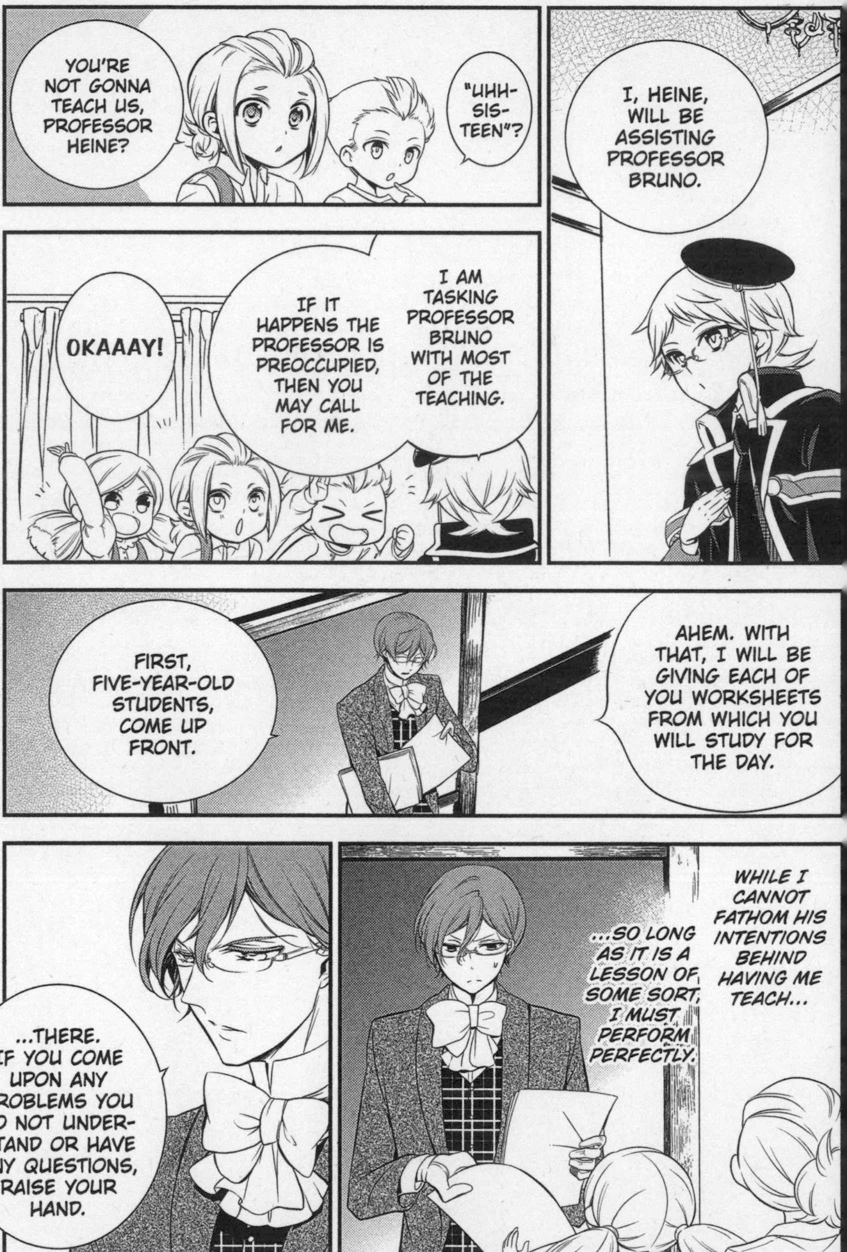
I, HEINE, WILL BE ASSISTING PROFESSOR BRUNO.
"UHH-SIS-TEEN"?
YOU'RE NOT GONNA TEACH US, PROFESSOR HEINE?
I AM TASKING PROFESSOR BRUNO WITH MOST OF THE TEACHING.
IF IT HAPPENS THE PROFESSOR IS PREOCCUPIED, THEN YOU MAY CALL FOR ME.
OKAAAY!
AHEM. WITH THAT, I WILL BE GIVING EACH OF YOU WORKSHEETS FROM WHICH YOU WILL STUDY FOR THE DAY.
FIRST, FIVE-YEAR-OLD STUDENTS, COME UP FRONT.
WHILE I CANNOT FATHOM HIS INTENTIONS BEHIND HAVING ME TEACH...
...SO LONG AS IT IS A LESSON OF SOME SORT, I MUST PERFORM PERFECTLY.
...THERE. IF YOU COME UPON ANY PROBLEMS YOU DO NOT UNDERSTAND OR HAVE ANY QUESTIONS, RAISE YOUR HAND.

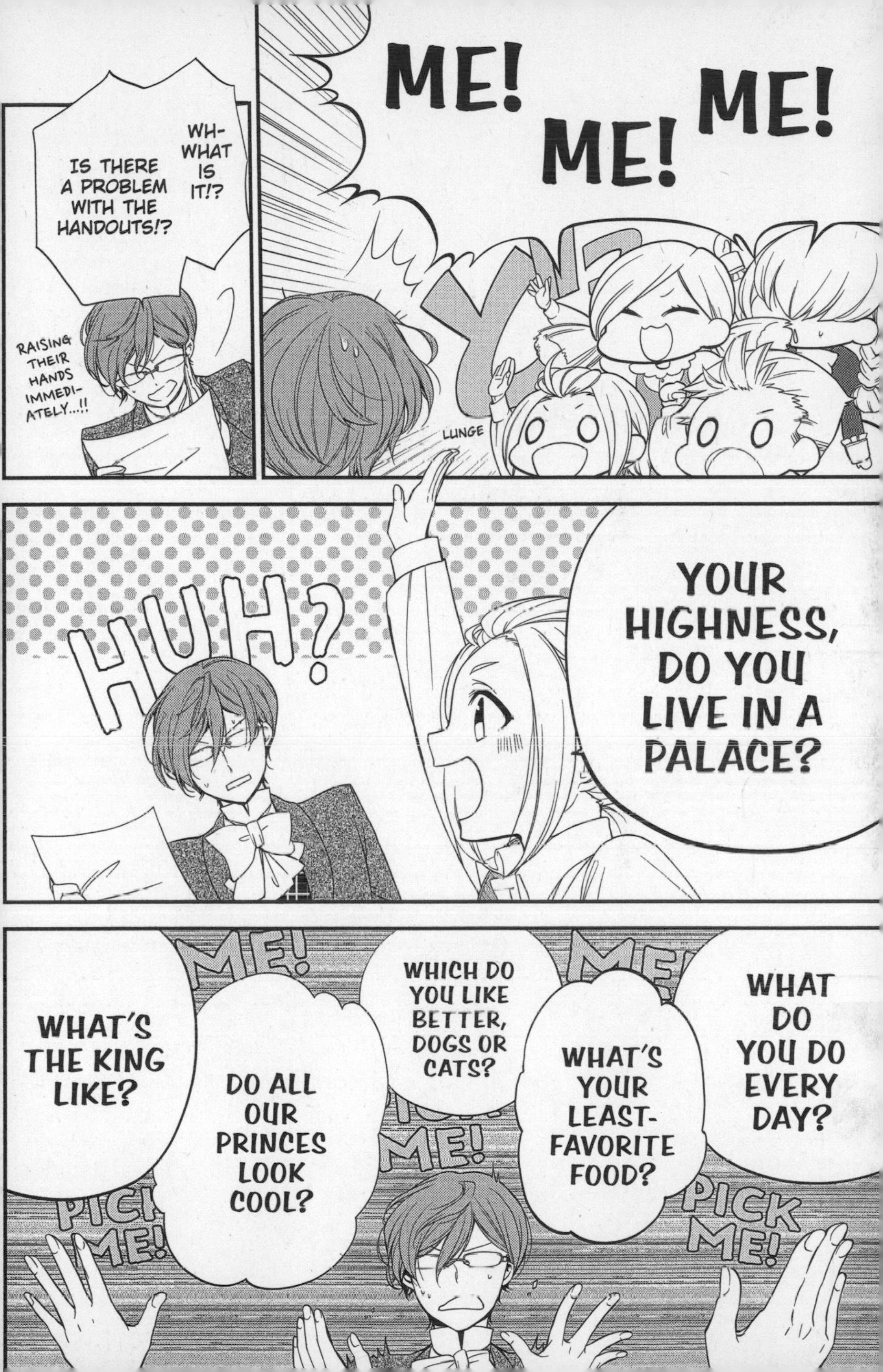
ME!
ME!
ME!
LUNGE
WH- WHAT IS IT!?
IS THERE A PROBLEM WITH THE HANDOUTS!?
RAISING THEIR HANDS IMMEDI- ATELY...!!
YOUR HIGHNESS, DO YOU LIVE IN A PALACE?
HUH?
ME!
PICK ME!
WHAT DO YOU DO EVERY DAY?
WHAT'S YOUR LEAST- FAVORITE FOOD?
WHICH DO YOU LIKE BETTER, DOGS OR CATS?
ME!
ME!
DO ALL OUR PRINCES LOOK COOL?
WHAT'S THE KING LIKE?
PICK ME!

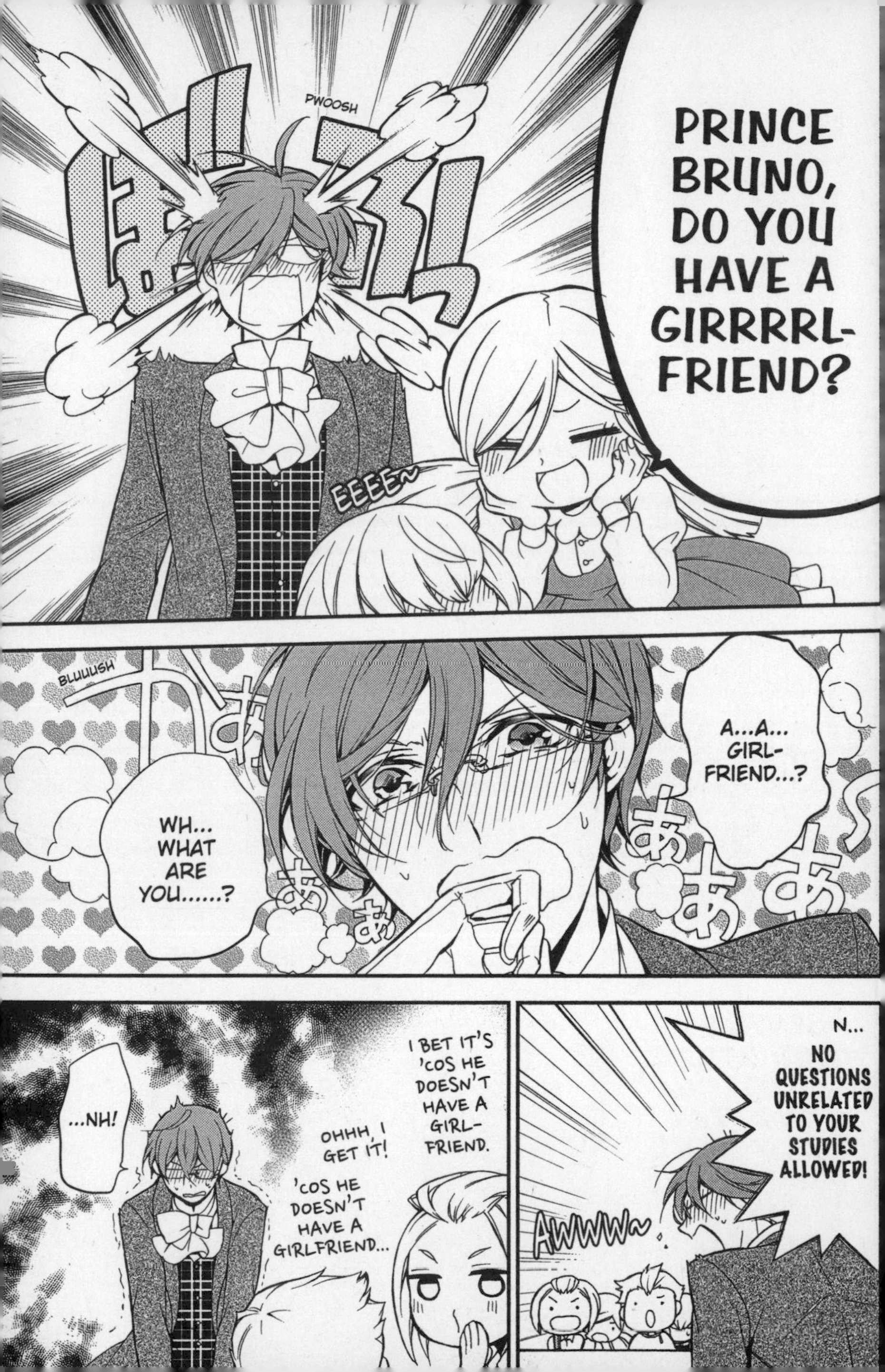
PRINCE BRUNO, DO YOU HAVE A GIRRRRL-FRIEND?
PWOOSH
EEEE~
A...A... GIRL-FRIEND...?
BLUUUSH
WH... WHAT ARE YOU......?
N... NO QUESTIONS UNRELATED TO YOUR STUDIES ALLOWED!
AWWW~
I BET IT'S 'COS HE DOESN'T HAVE A GIRL-FRIEND.
OHHH, I GET IT!
'COS HE DOESN'T HAVE A GIRLFRIEND...
...NH!

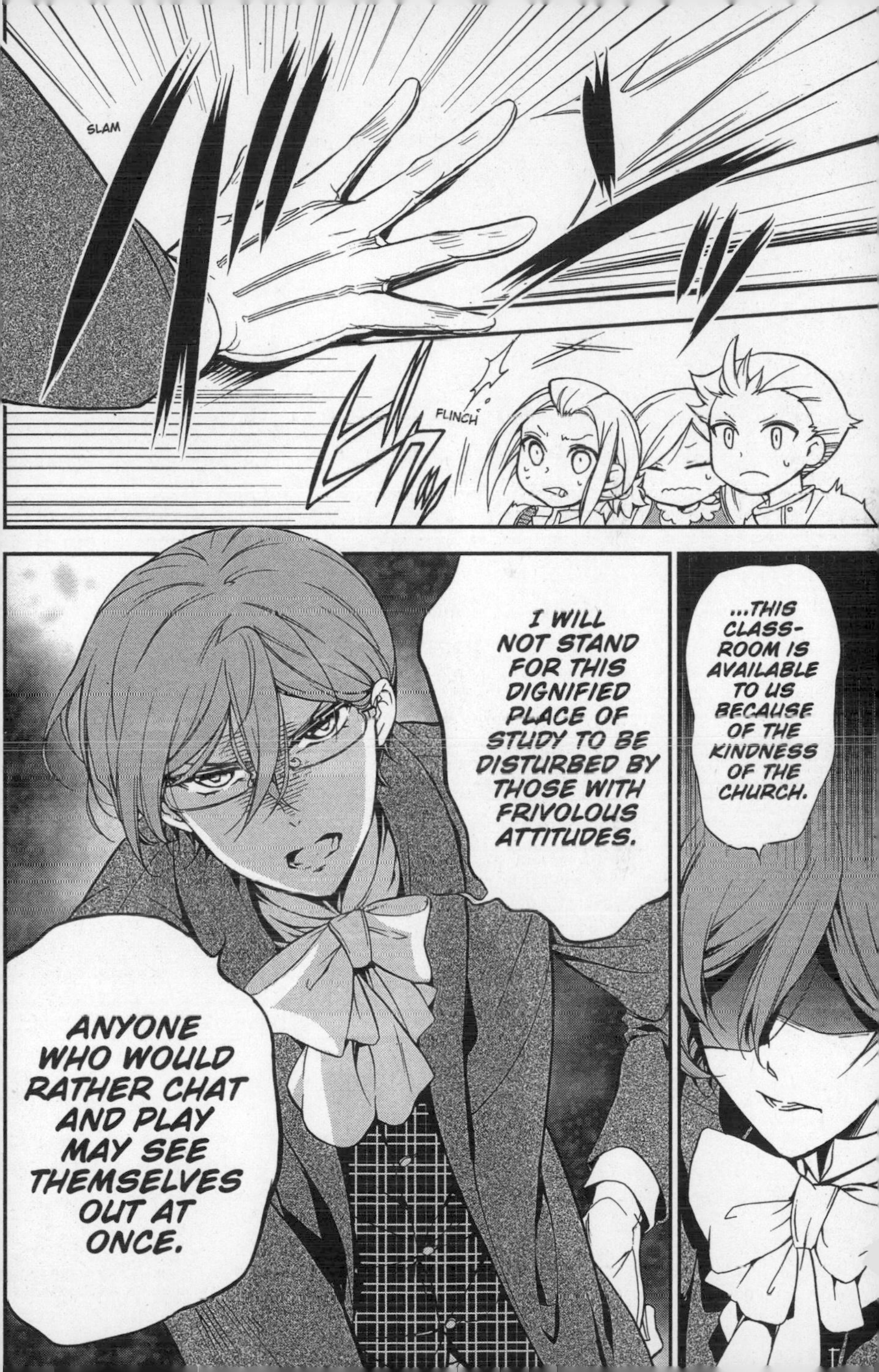
SLAM
FLINCH
...THIS CLASS-ROOM IS AVAILABLE TO US BECAUSE OF THE KINDNESS OF THE CHURCH.
I WILL NOT STAND FOR THIS DIGNIFIED PLACE OF STUDY TO BE DISTURBED BY THOSE WITH FRIVOLOUS ATTITUDES.
ANYONE WHO WOULD RATHER CHAT AND PLAY MAY SEE THEMSELVES OUT AT ONCE.

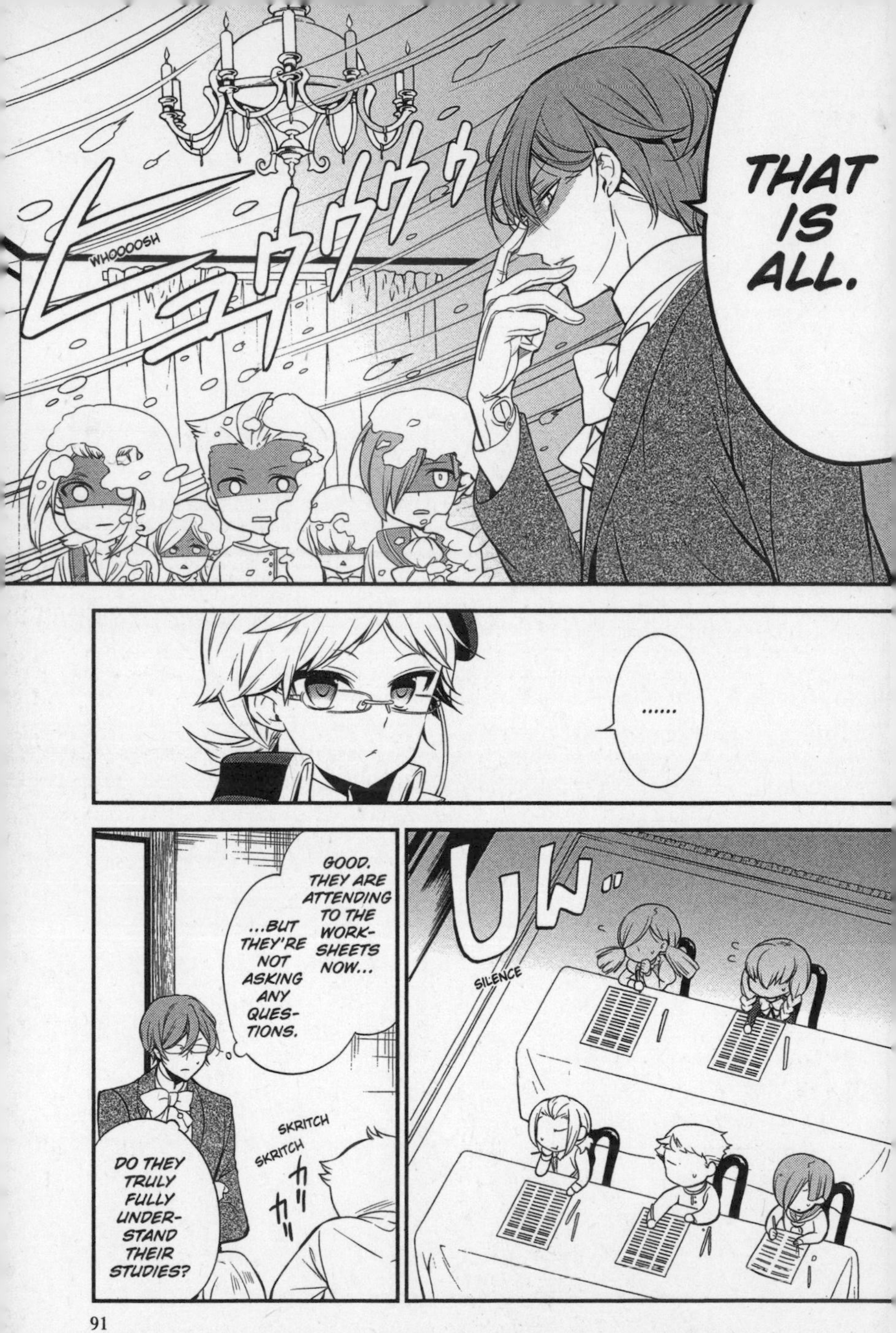
THAT IS ALL.
ヒュウウウウゥ
WHOOOOSH
......
しーん
SILENCE
GOOD. THEY ARE ATTENDING TO THE WORKSHEETS NOW...
...BUT THEY'RE NOT ASKING ANY QUESTIONS.
DO THEY TRULY FULLY UNDERSTAND THEIR STUDIES?
カリ
カリ
SKRITCH
SKRITCH

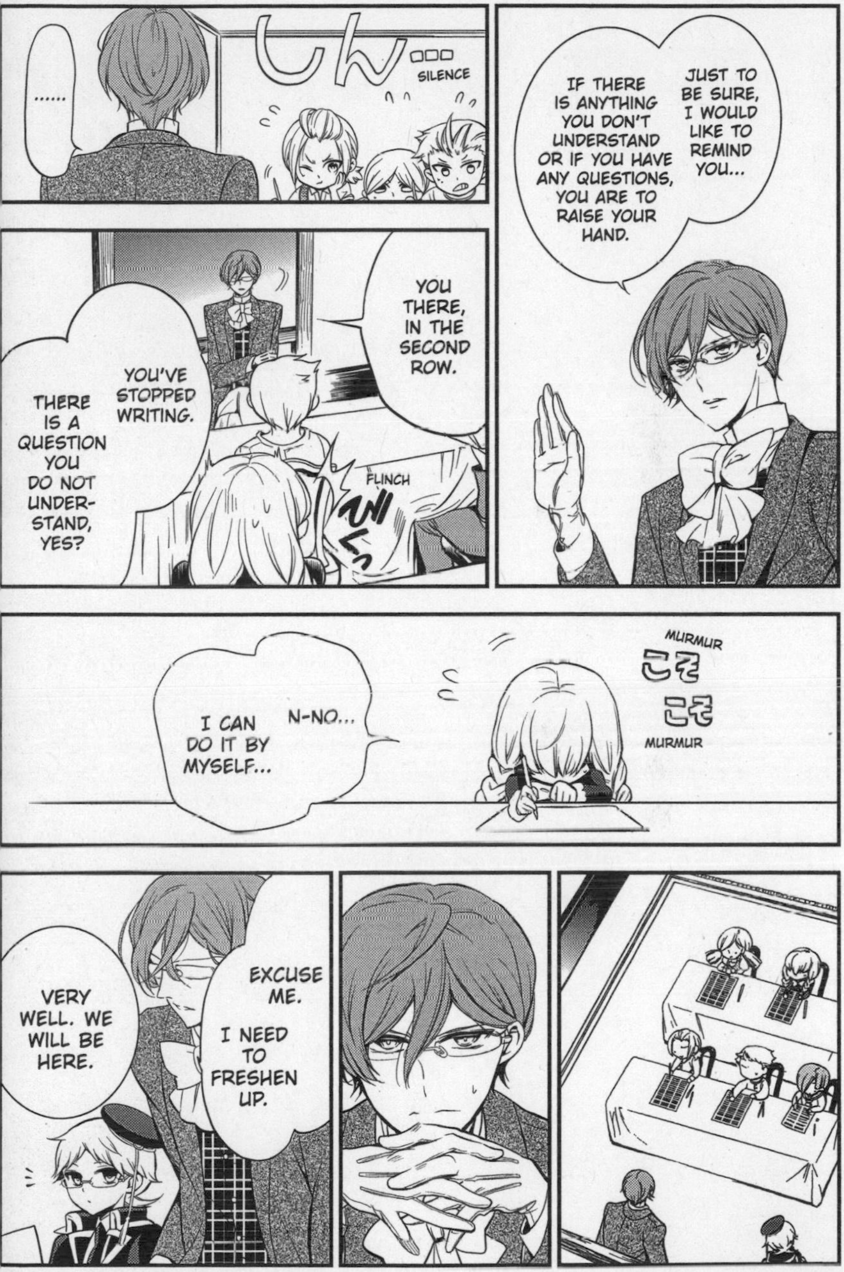
JUST TO BE SURE, I WOULD LIKE TO REMIND YOU...
IF THERE IS ANYTHING YOU DON'T UNDERSTAND OR IF YOU HAVE ANY QUESTIONS, YOU ARE TO RAISE YOUR HAND.
しん
SILENCE
......
YOU THERE, IN THE SECOND ROW.
YOU'VE STOPPED WRITING.
THERE IS A QUESTION YOU DO NOT UNDER-STAND, YES?
FLINCH
MURMUR
こそ
こそ
MURMUR
N-NO...
I CAN DO IT BY MYSELF...
EXCUSE ME.
I NEED TO FRESHEN UP.
VERY WELL. WE WILL BE HERE.

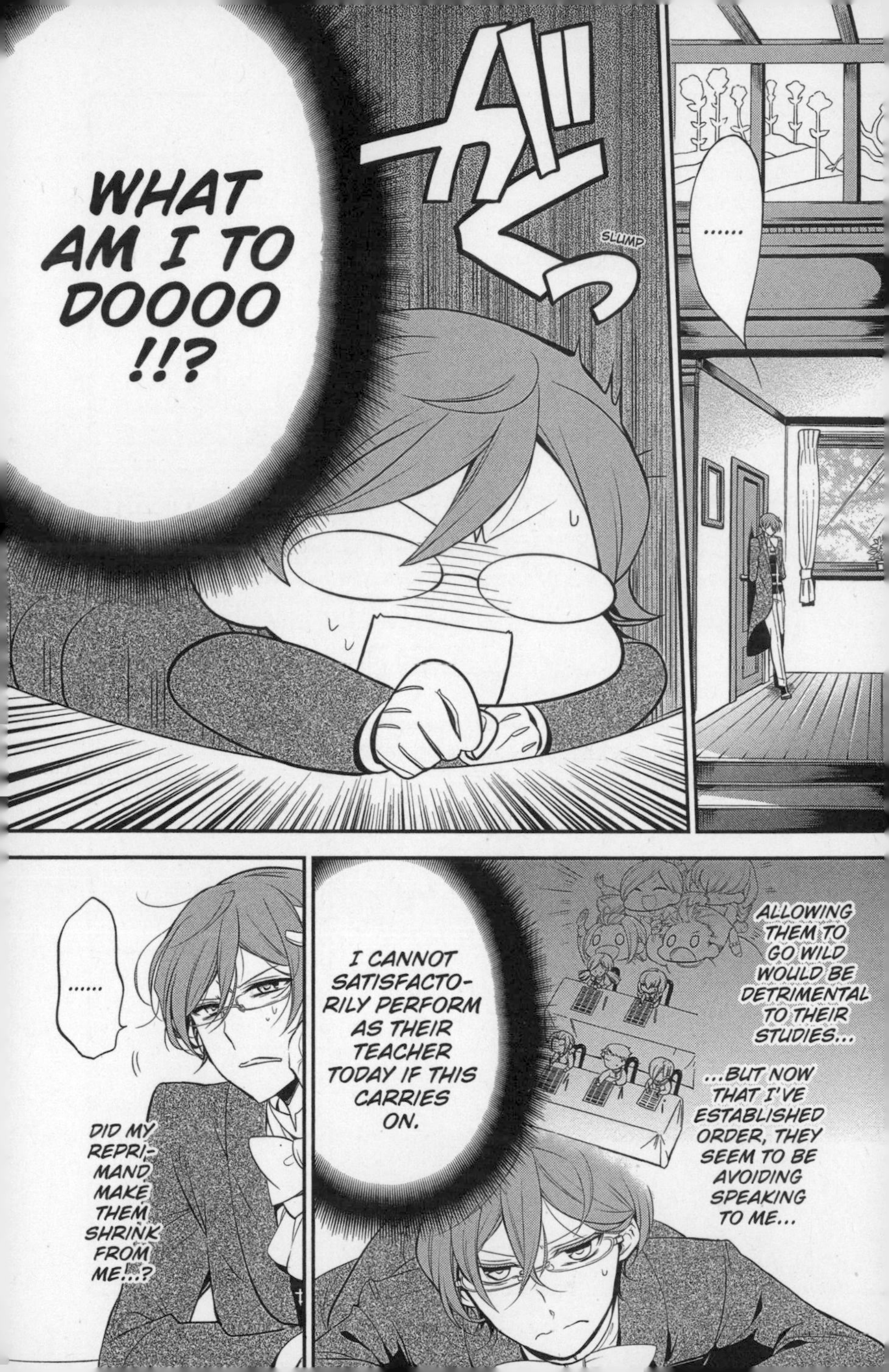
......
SLUMP
WHAT AM I TO DOOOO!!?
ALLOWING THEM TO GO WILD WOULD BE DETRIMENTAL TO THEIR STUDIES...
...BUT NOW THAT I'VE ESTABLISHED ORDER, THEY SEEM TO BE AVOIDING SPEAKING TO ME...
I CANNOT SATISFACTO-RILY PERFORM AS THEIR TEACHER TODAY IF THIS CARRIES ON.
......
DID MY REPRI-MAND MAKE THEM SHRINK FROM ME...?

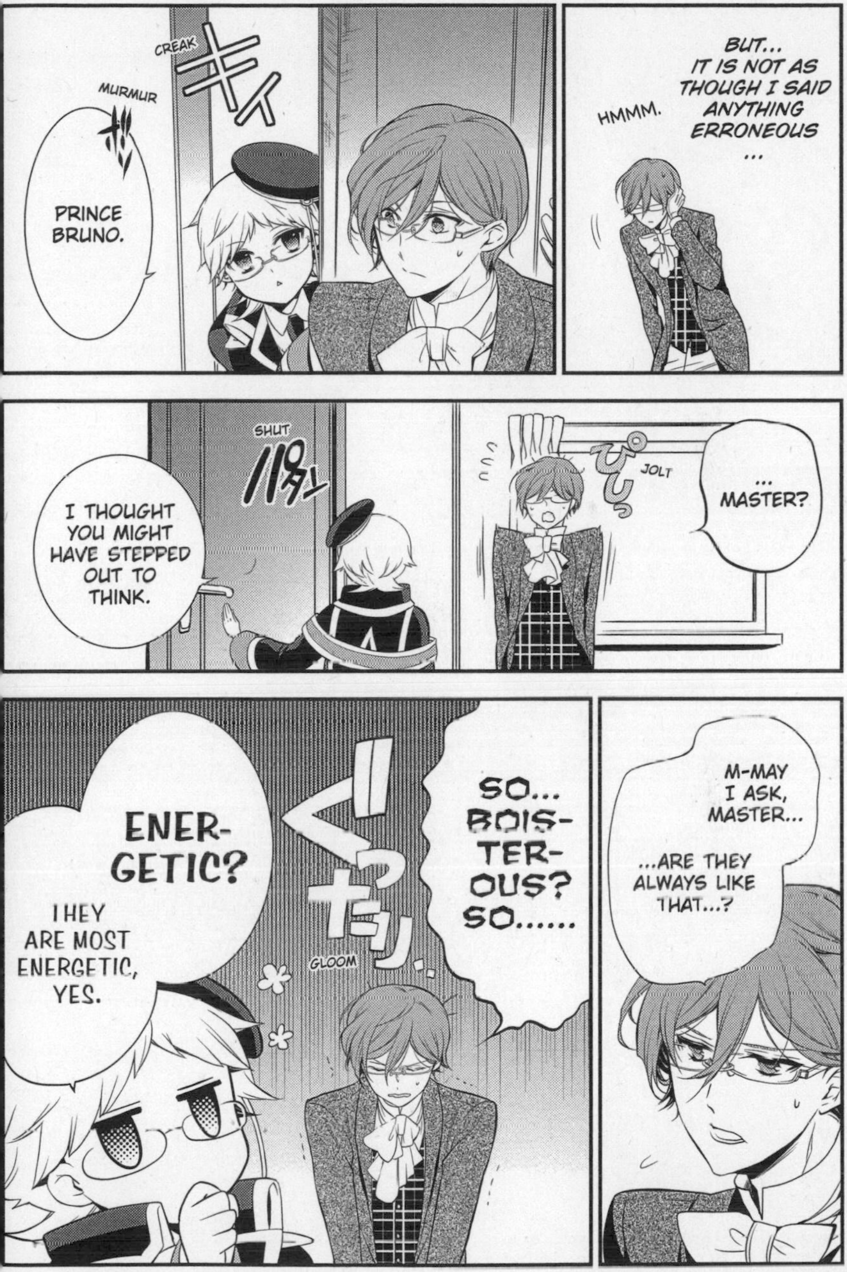
HMMM.
BUT... IT IS NOT AS THOUGH I SAID ANYTHING ERRONEOUS ...
CREAK
MURMUR
PRINCE BRUNO.
JOLT
... MASTER?
SHUT
I THOUGHT YOU MIGHT HAVE STEPPED OUT TO THINK.
M-MAY I ASK, MASTER...
...ARE THEY ALWAYS LIKE THAT...?
SO... BOIS-TER-OUS? SO......
GLOOM
ENER-GETIC?
THEY ARE MOST ENERGETIC, YES.

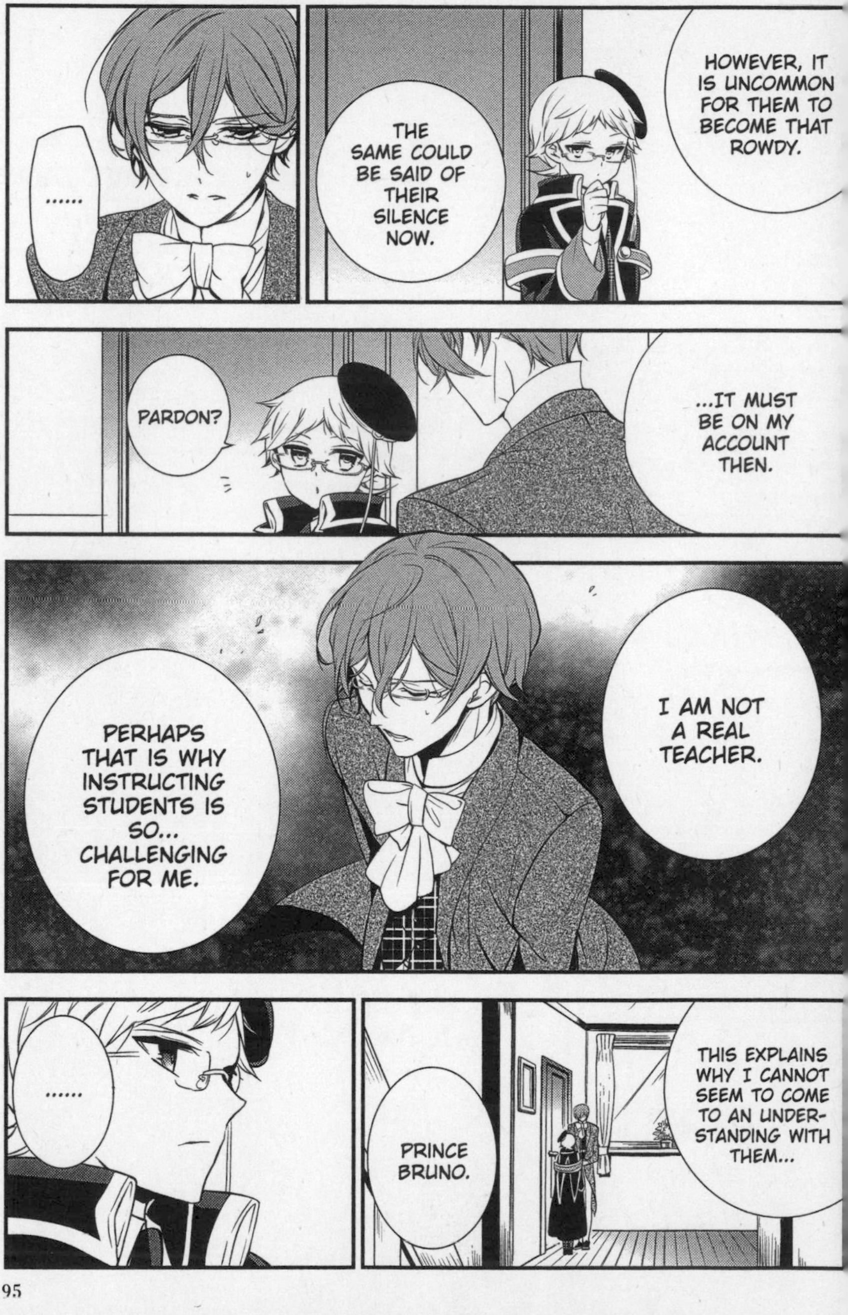
HOWEVER, IT IS UNCOMMON FOR THEM TO BECOME THAT ROWDY.
THE SAME COULD BE SAID OF THEIR SILENCE NOW.
......
...IT MUST BE ON MY ACCOUNT THEN.
PARDON?
I AM NOT A REAL TEACHER.
PERHAPS THAT IS WHY INSTRUCTING STUDENTS IS SO... CHALLENGING FOR ME.
THIS EXPLAINS WHY I CANNOT SEEM TO COME TO AN UNDER-STANDING WITH THEM...
PRINCE BRUNO.
......

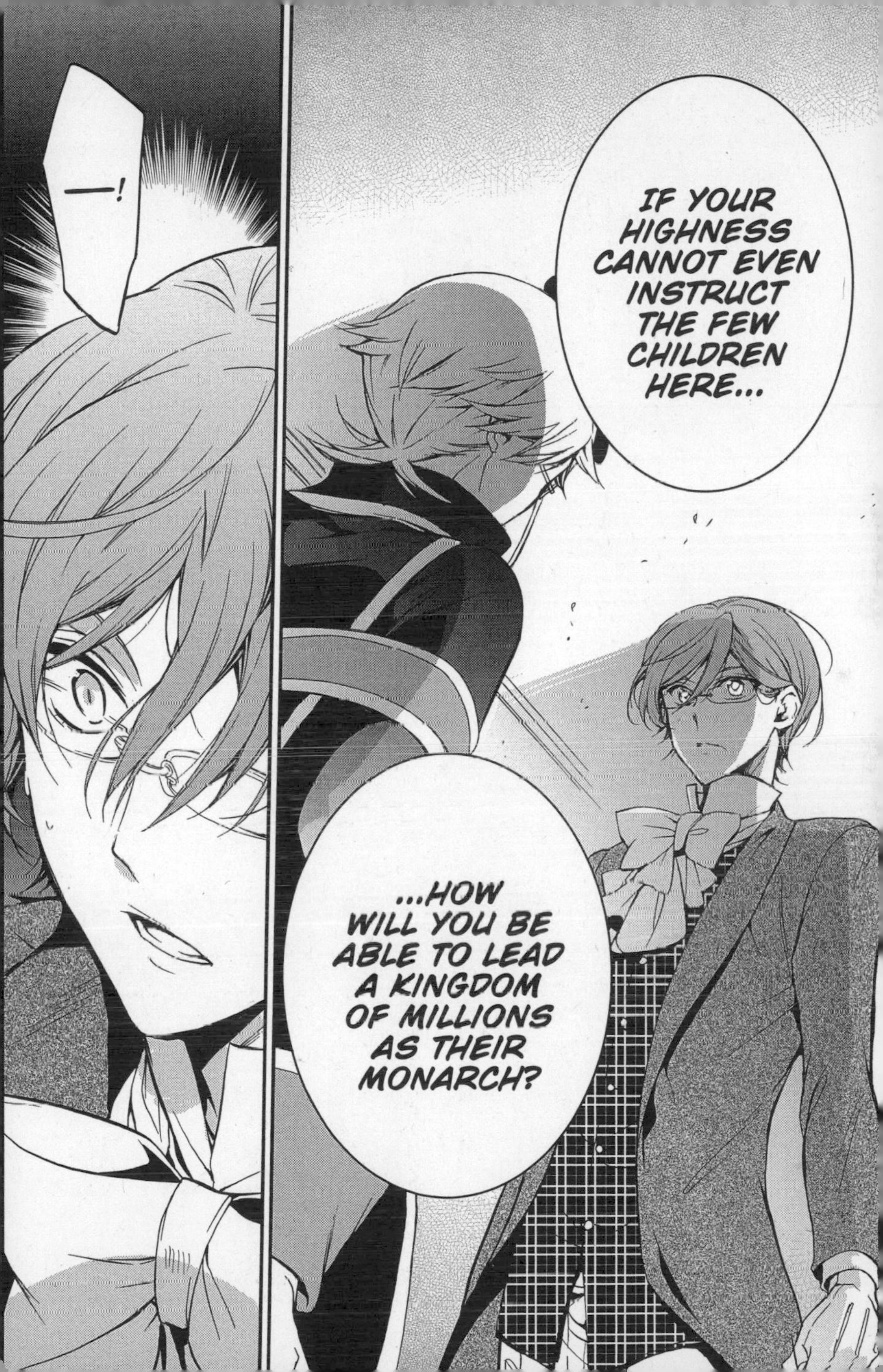
IF YOUR HIGHNESS CANNOT EVEN INSTRUCT THE FEW CHILDREN HERE...
...HOW WILL YOU BE ABLE TO LEAD A KINGDOM OF MILLIONS AS THEIR MONARCH?
—!

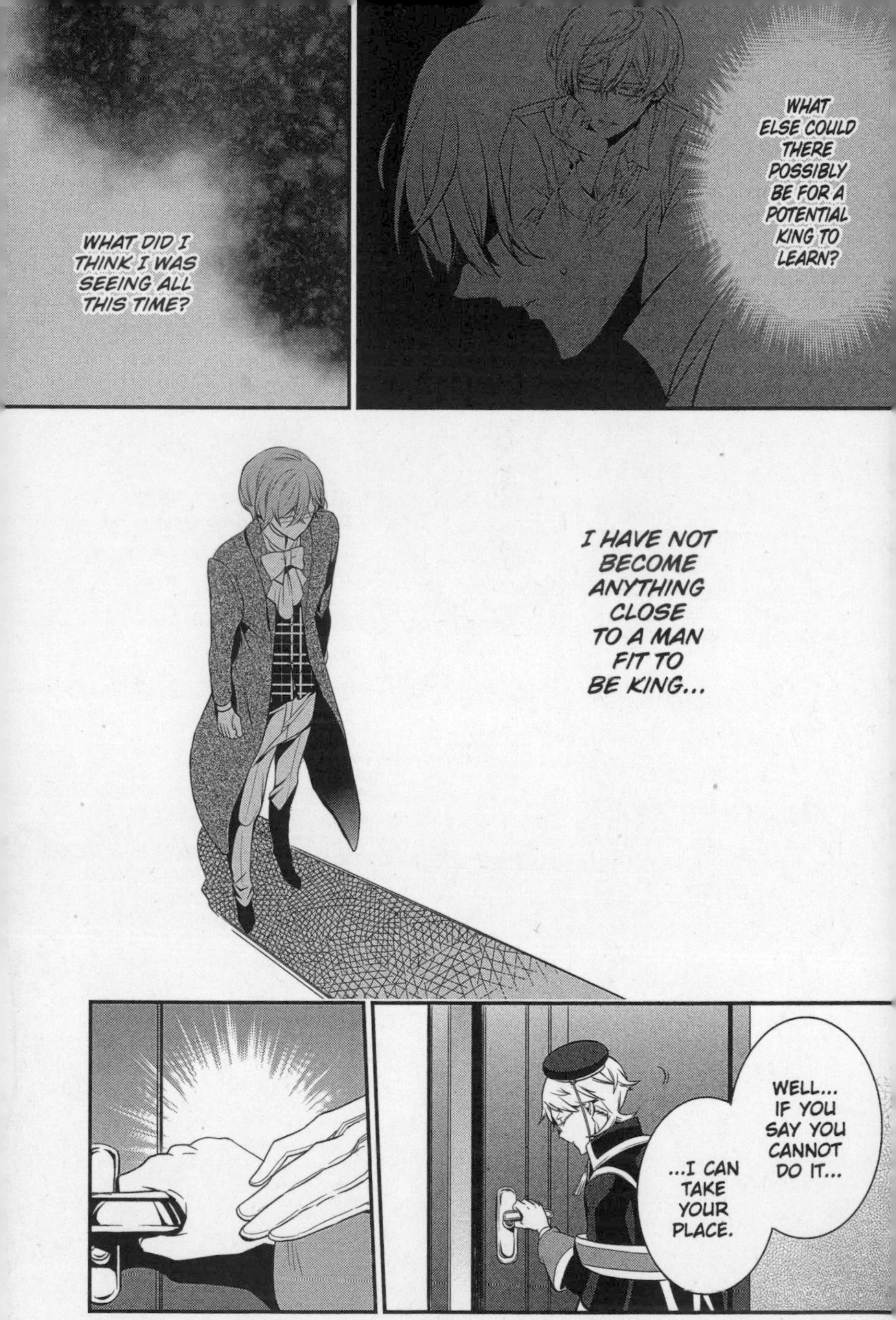
WHAT ELSE COULD THERE POSSIBLY BE FOR A POTENTIAL KING TO LEARN?
WHAT DID I THINK I WAS SEEING ALL THIS TIME?
I HAVE NOT BECOME ANYTHING CLOSE TO A MAN FIT TO BE KING...
WELL... IF YOU SAY YOU CANNOT DO IT...
...I CAN TAKE YOUR PLACE.

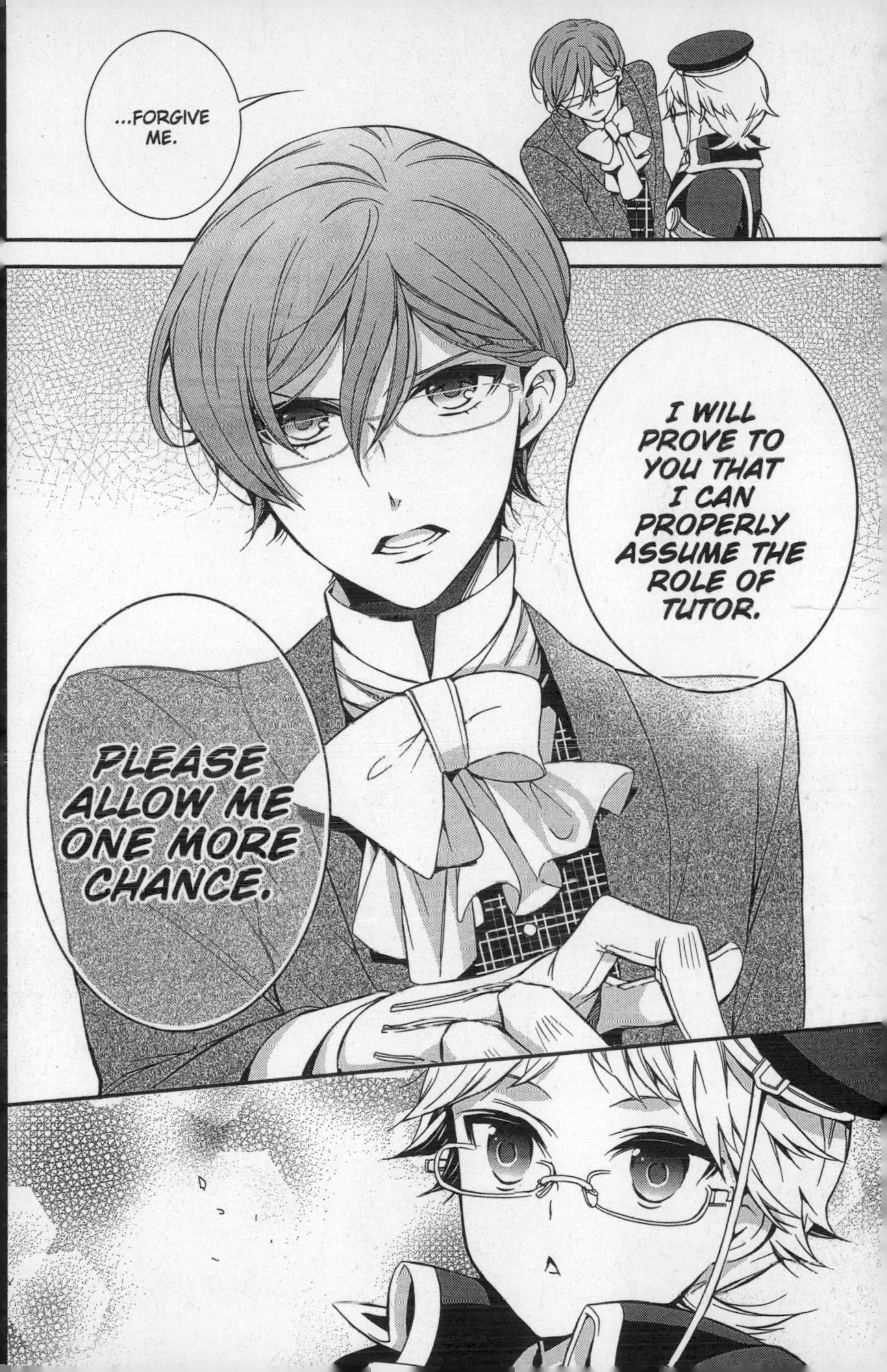
...FORGIVE ME.
I WILL PROVE TO YOU THAT I CAN PROPERLY ASSUME THE ROLE OF TUTOR.
PLEASE ALLOW ME ONE MORE CHANCE.

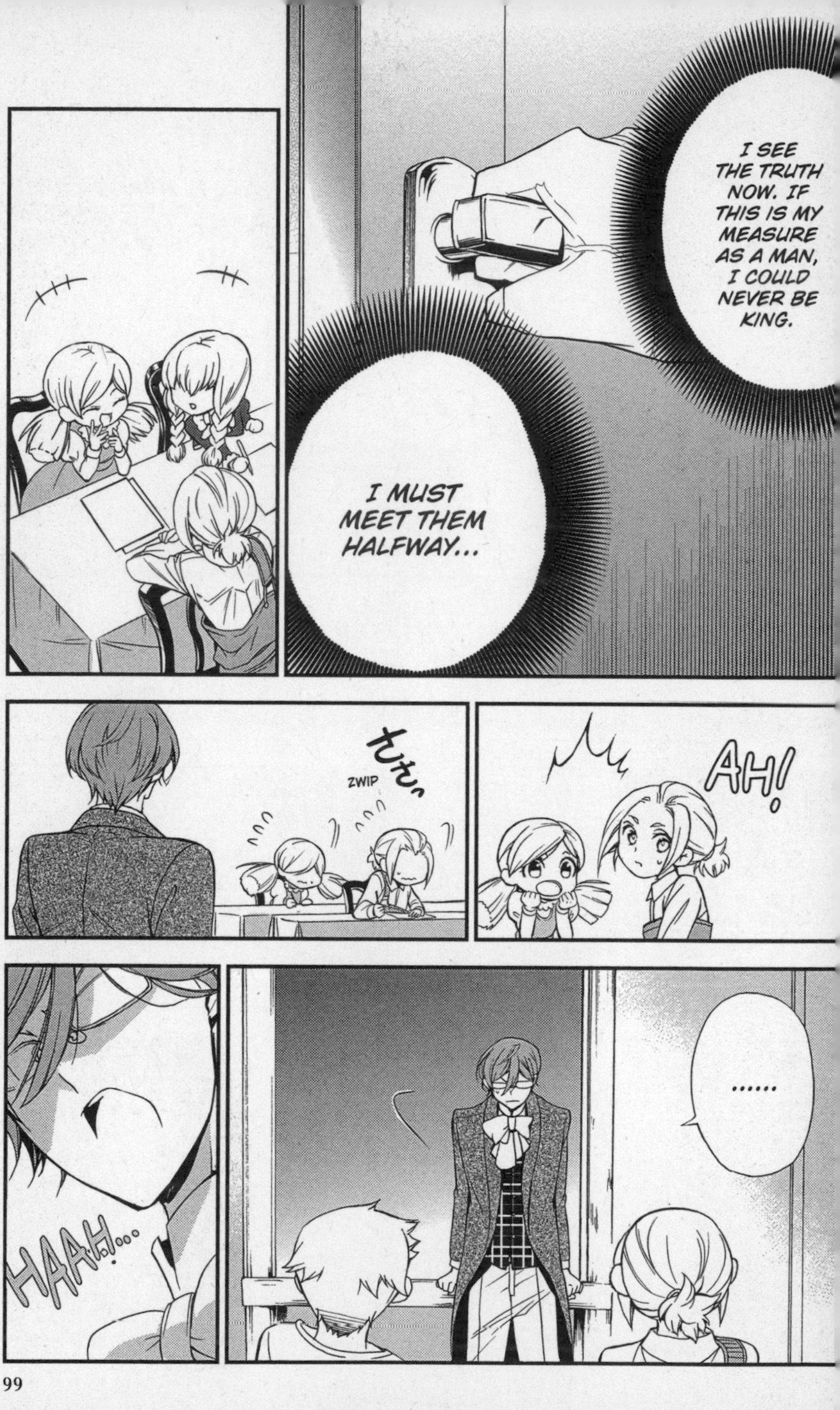
I SEE THE TRUTH NOW. IF THIS IS MY MEASURE AS A MAN, I COULD NEVER BE KING.
I MUST MEET THEM HALFWAY...
AH!
さっ
ZWIP
......
HAAH...

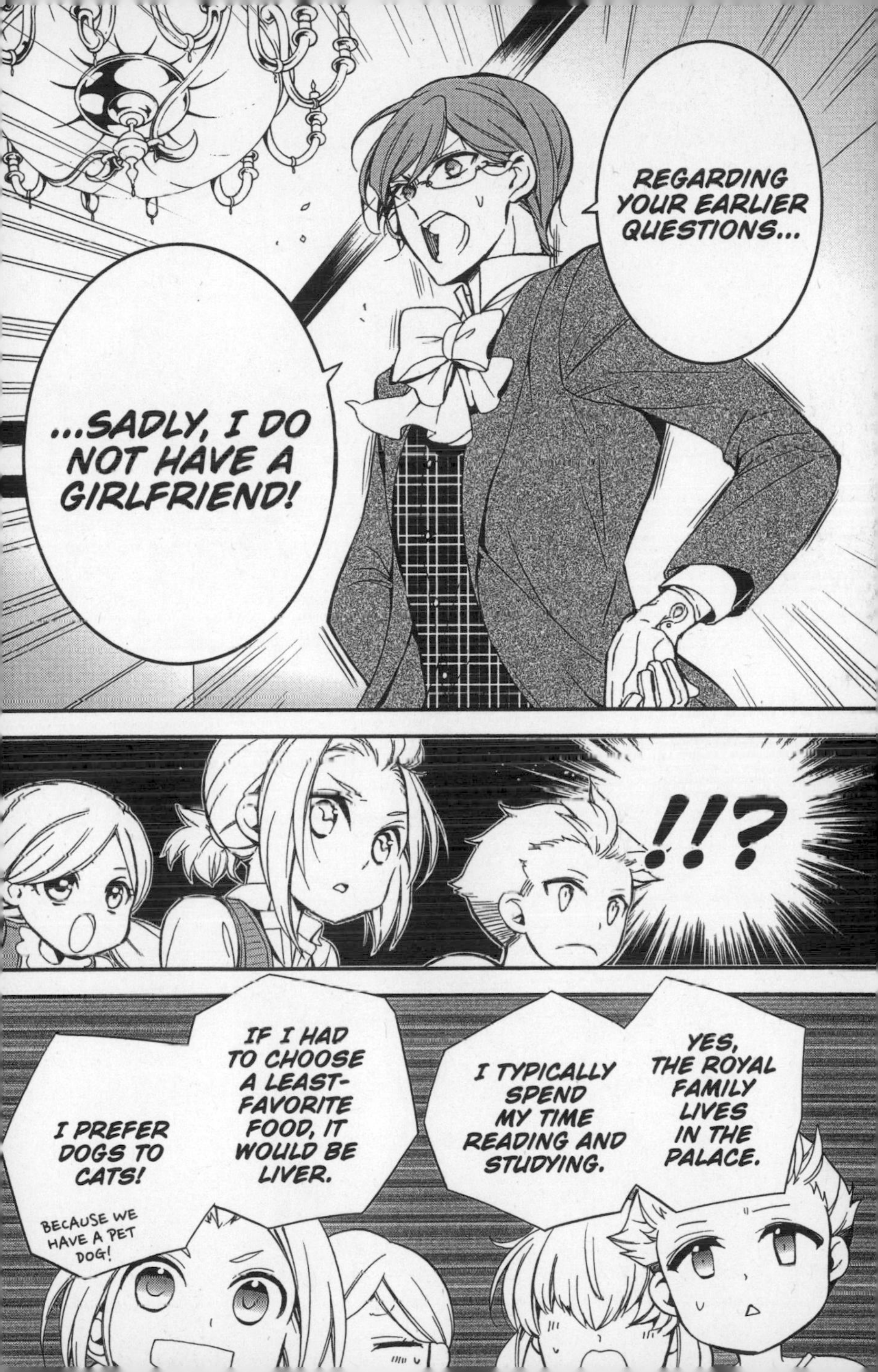
REGARDING YOUR EARLIER QUESTIONS...
...SADLY, I DO NOT HAVE A GIRLFRIEND!
!!?
YES, THE ROYAL FAMILY LIVES IN THE PALACE.
I TYPICALLY SPEND MY TIME READING AND STUDYING.
IF I HAD TO CHOOSE A LEAST-FAVORITE FOOD, IT WOULD BE LIVER.
I PREFER DOGS TO CATS!
BECAUSE WE HAVE A PET DOG!

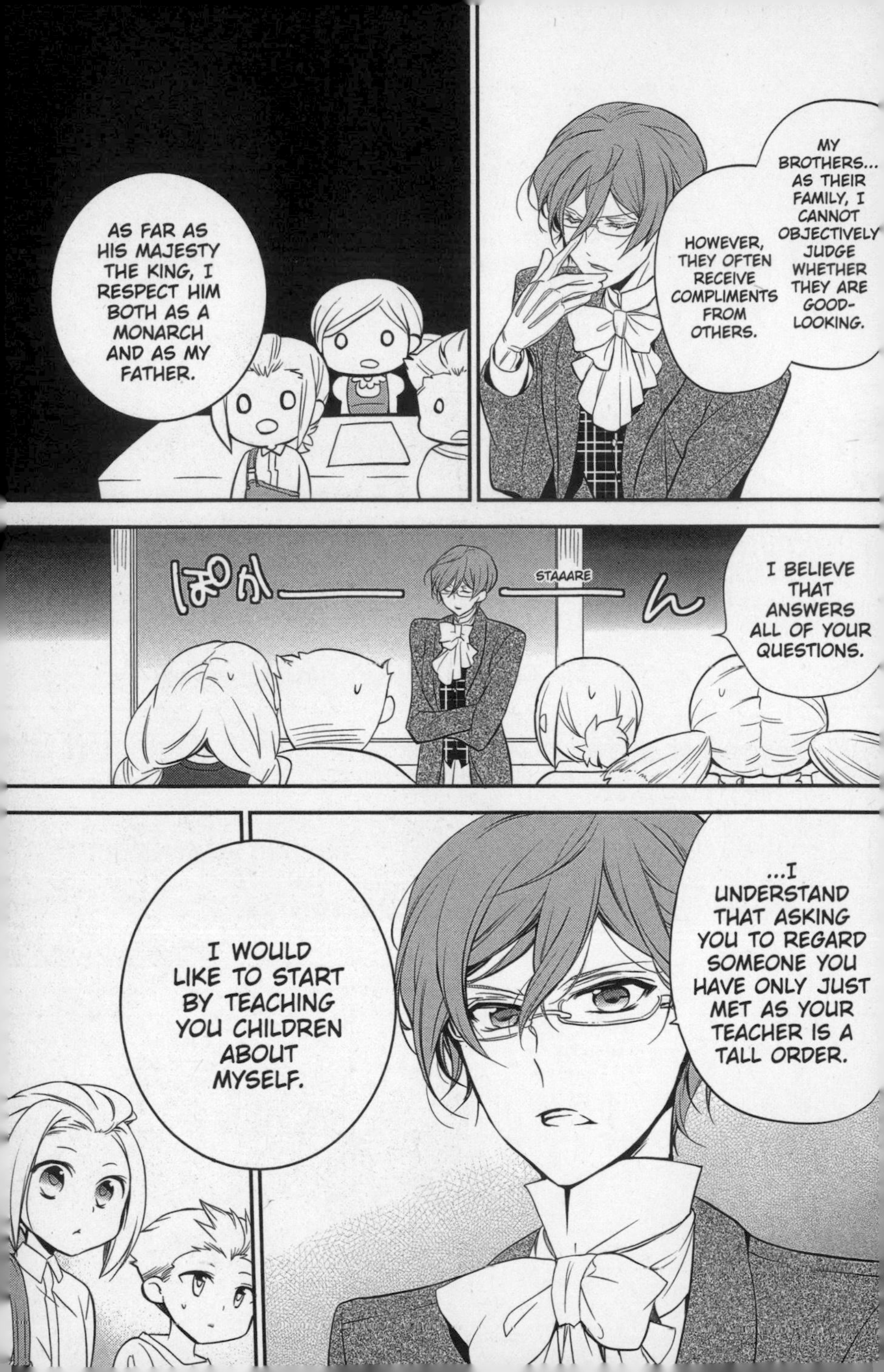

MY BROTHERS... AS THEIR FAMILY, I CANNOT OBJECTIVELY JUDGE WHETHER THEY ARE GOOD-LOOKING.
HOWEVER, THEY OFTEN RECEIVE COMPLIMENTS FROM OTHERS.
AS FAR AS HIS MAJESTY THE KING, I RESPECT HIM BOTH AS A MONARCH AND AS MY FATHER.
I BELIEVE THAT ANSWERS ALL OF YOUR QUESTIONS.
STAAARE
ぽかーーーーん
...I UNDERSTAND THAT ASKING YOU TO REGARD SOMEONE YOU HAVE ONLY JUST MET AS YOUR TEACHER IS A TALL ORDER.
I WOULD LIKE TO START BY TEACHING YOU CHILDREN ABOUT MYSELF.

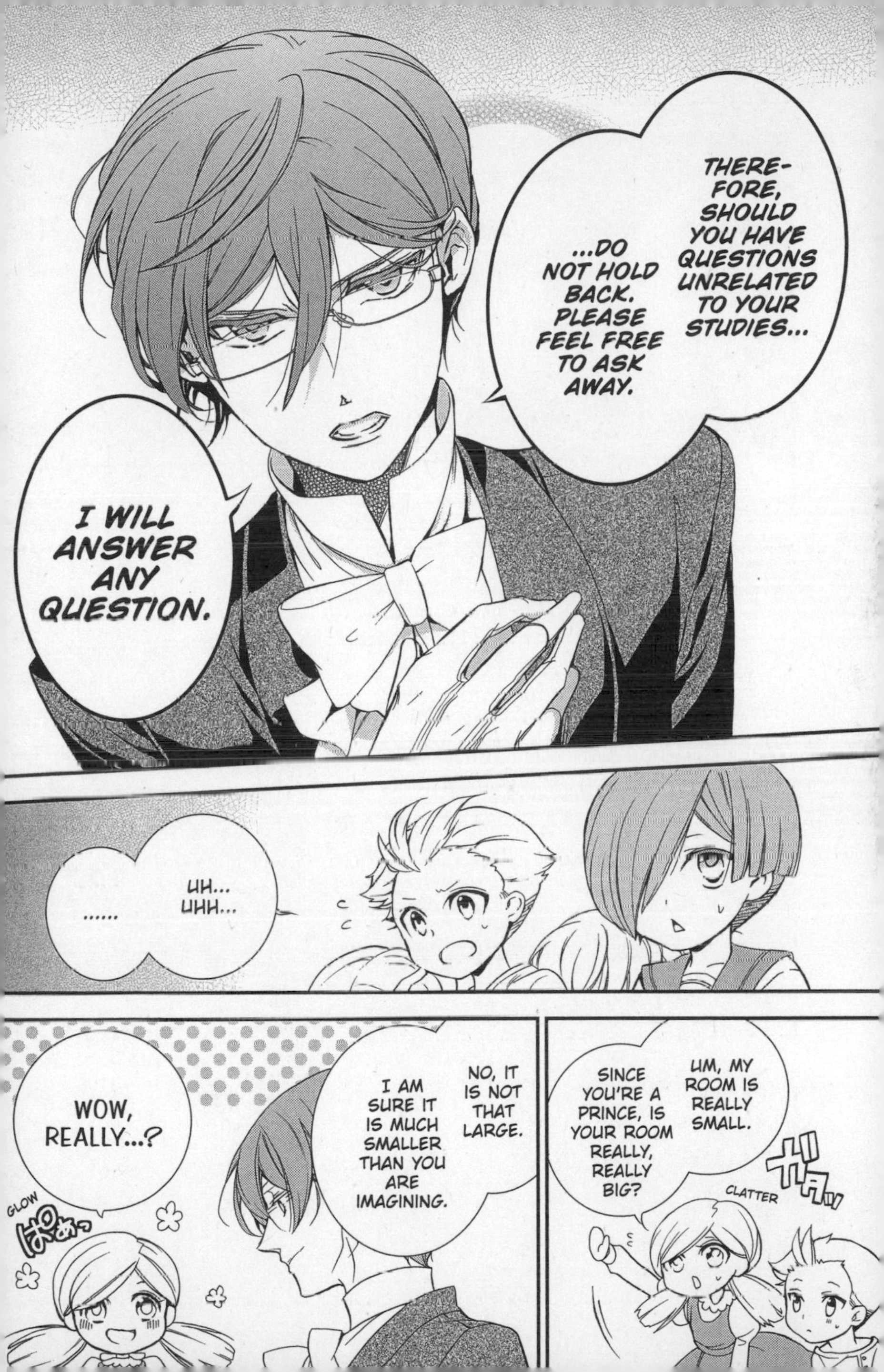
THERE-FORE, SHOULD YOU HAVE QUESTIONS UNRELATED TO YOUR STUDIES...
...DO NOT HOLD BACK. PLEASE FEEL FREE TO ASK AWAY.
I WILL ANSWER ANY QUESTION.
UH... UHH...
......
UM, MY ROOM IS REALLY SMALL.
SINCE YOU'RE A PRINCE, IS YOUR ROOM REALLY, REALLY BIG?
CLATTER
NO, IT IS NOT THAT LARGE.
I AM SURE IT IS MUCH SMALLER THAN YOU ARE IMAGINING.
WOW, REALLY...?
GLOW

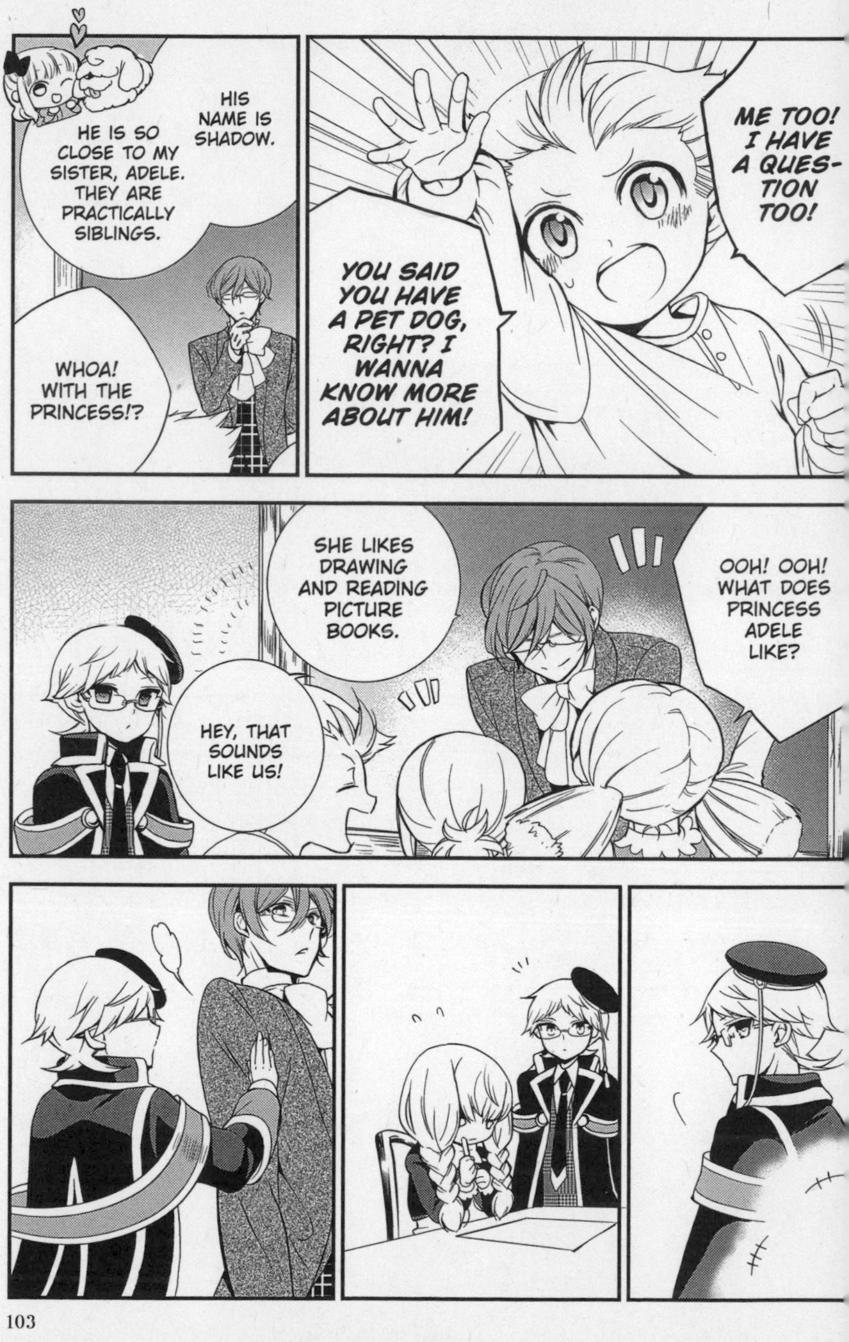
ME TOO! I HAVE A QUES-TION TOO!
YOU SAID YOU HAVE A PET DOG, RIGHT? I WANNA KNOW MORE ABOUT HIM!
HIS NAME IS SHADOW.
HE IS SO CLOSE TO MY SISTER, ADELE. THEY ARE PRACTICALLY SIBLINGS.
WHOA! WITH THE PRINCESS!?
OOH! OOH! WHAT DOES PRINCESS ADELE LIKE?
SHE LIKES DRAWING AND READING PICTURE BOOKS.
HEY, THAT SOUNDS LIKE US!

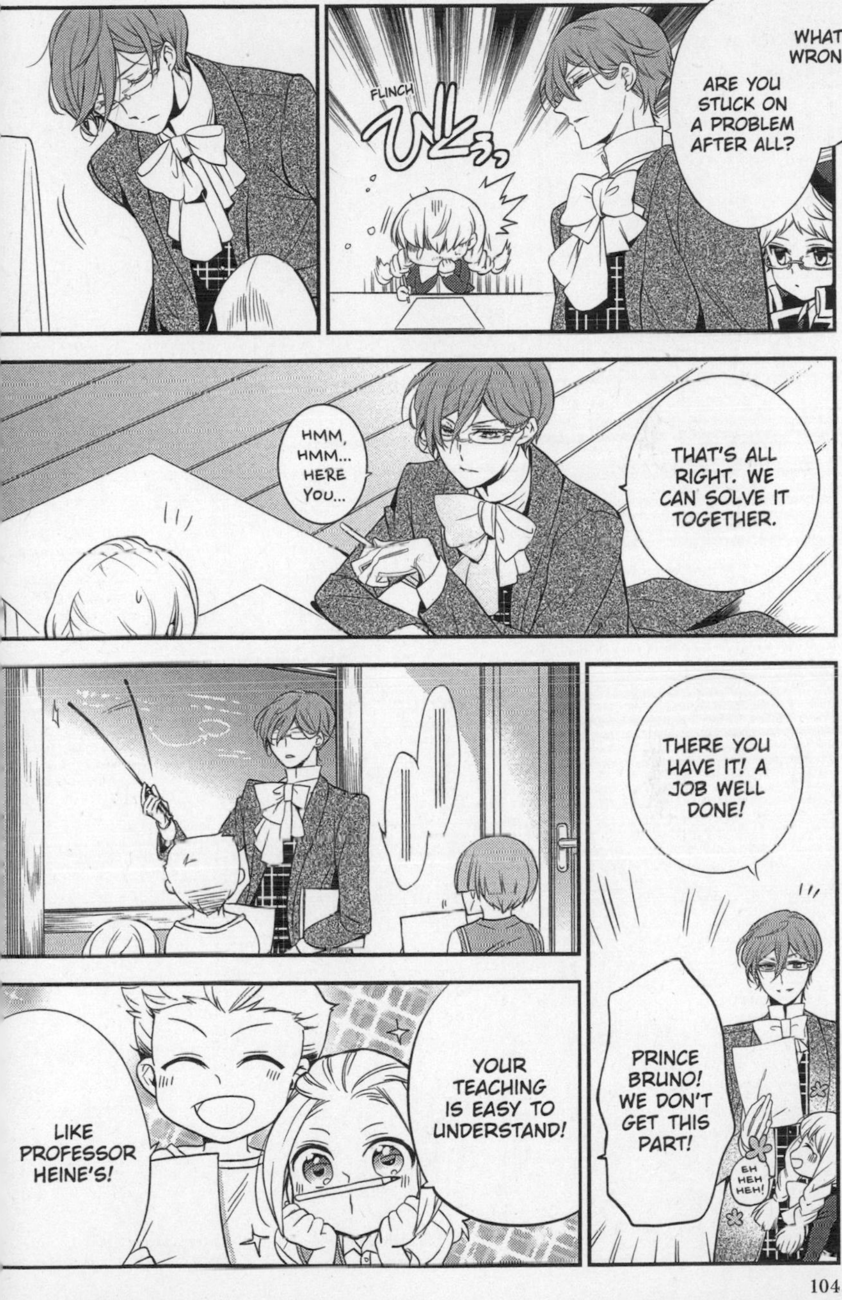
WHAT'S WRONG?
ARE YOU STUCK ON A PROBLEM AFTER ALL?
FLINCH
THAT'S ALL RIGHT. WE CAN SOLVE IT TOGETHER.
HMM, HMM... HERE YOU...
THERE YOU HAVE IT! A JOB WELL DONE!
PRINCE BRUNO! WE DON'T GET THIS PART!
EH HEH HEH!
YOUR TEACHING IS EASY TO UNDERSTAND!
LIKE PROFESSOR HEINE'S!

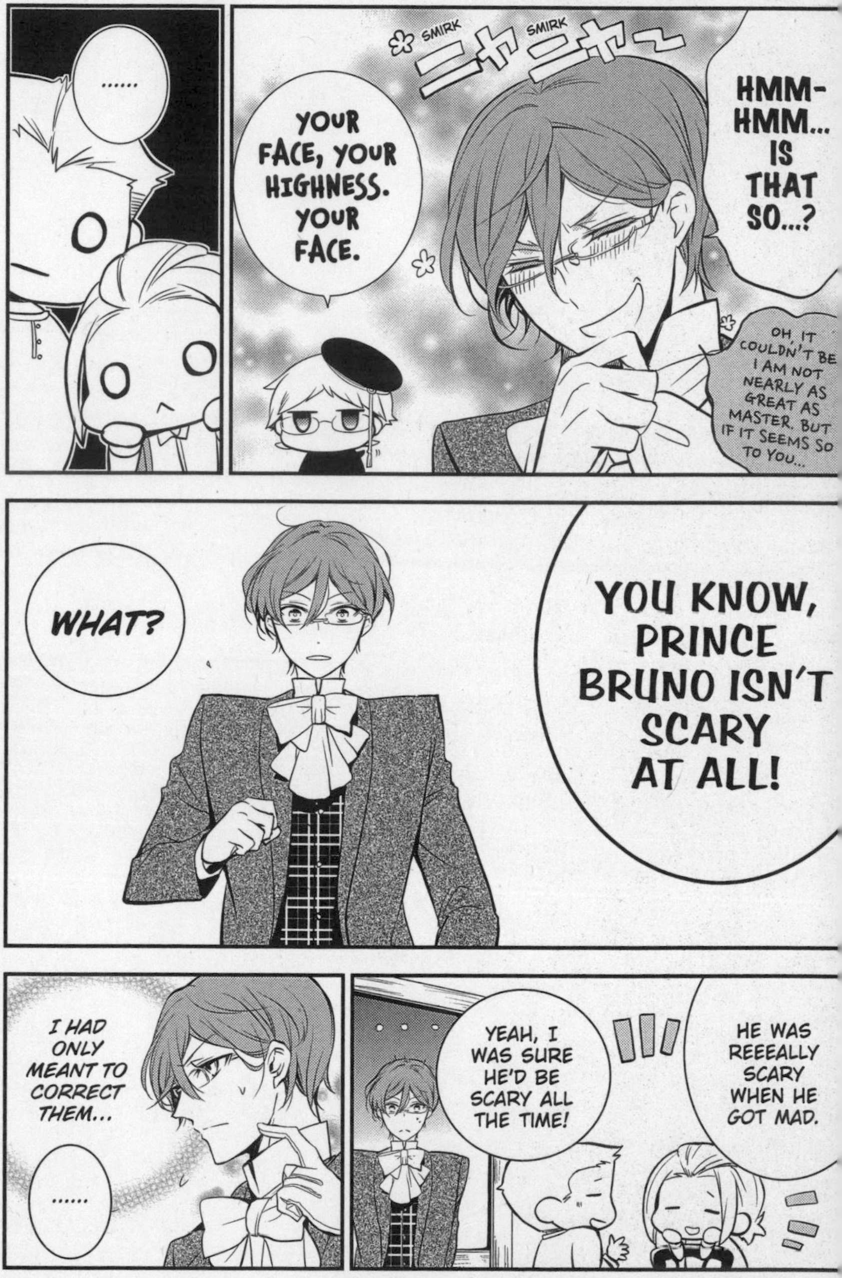
HMM-HMM... IS THAT SO...?
OH IT COULDN'T BE I AM NOT NEARLY AS GREAT AS MASTER. BUT IF IT SEEMS SO TO YOU...
SMIRK SMIRK
ニヤニヤ
YOUR FACE, YOUR HIGHNESS. YOUR FACE.
......
YOU KNOW, PRINCE BRUNO ISN'T SCARY AT ALL!
WHAT?
HE WAS REEEALLY SCARY WHEN HE GOT MAD.
YEAH, I WAS SURE HE'D BE SCARY ALL THE TIME!
I HAD ONLY MEANT TO CORRECT THEM...
......

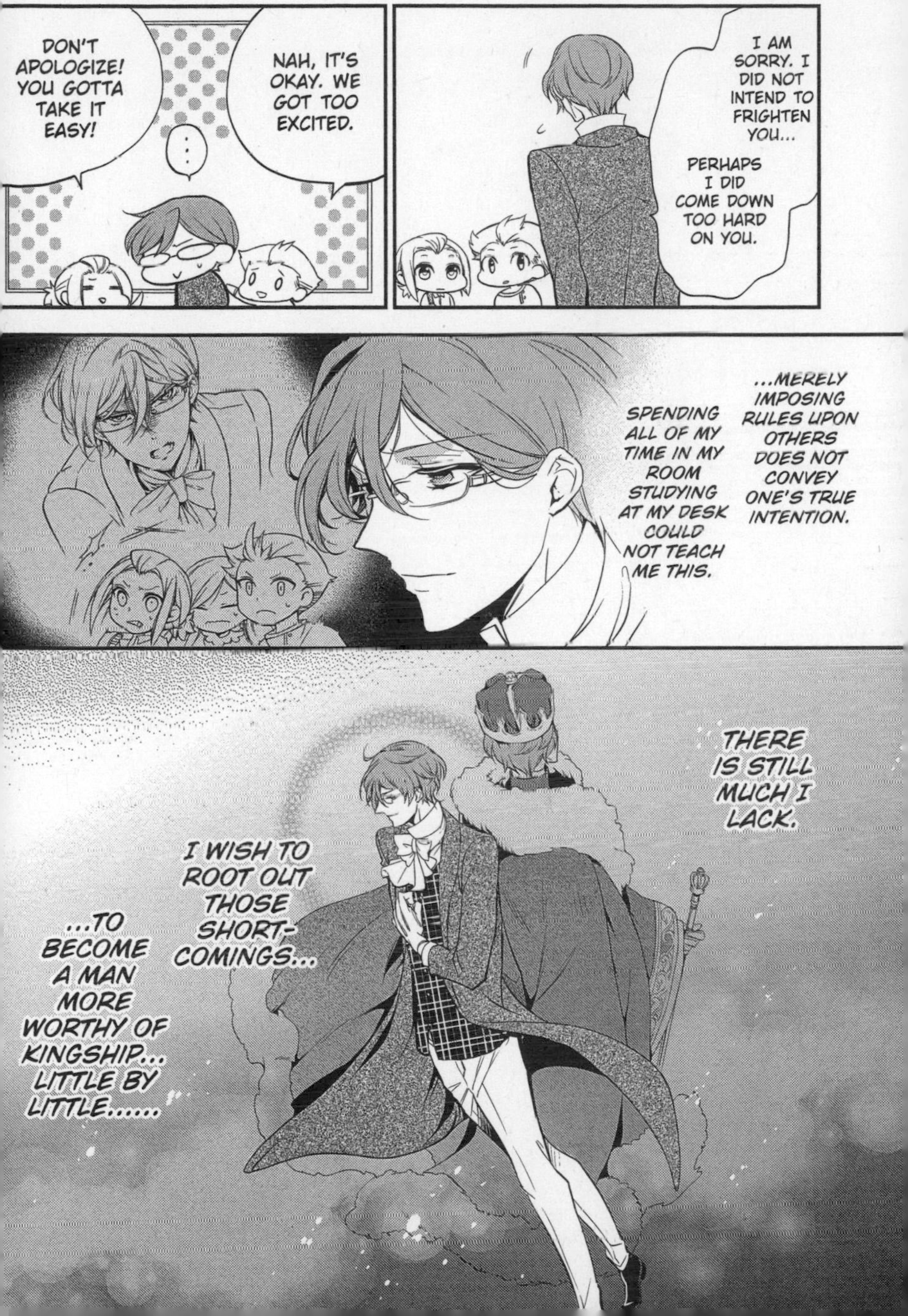
I AM SORRY. I DID NOT INTEND TO FRIGHTEN YOU...
PERHAPS I DID COME DOWN TOO HARD ON YOU.
NAH, IT'S OKAY. WE GOT TOO EXCITED.
DON'T APOLOGIZE! YOU GOTTA TAKE IT EASY!
...
...MERELY IMPOSING RULES UPON OTHERS DOES NOT CONVEY ONE'S TRUE INTENTION.
SPENDING ALL OF MY TIME IN MY ROOM STUDYING AT MY DESK COULD NOT TEACH ME THIS.
THERE IS STILL MUCH I LACK.
I WISH TO ROOT OUT THOSE SHORT-COMINGS...
...TO BECOME A MAN MORE WORTHY OF KINGSHIP... LITTLE BY LITTLE......

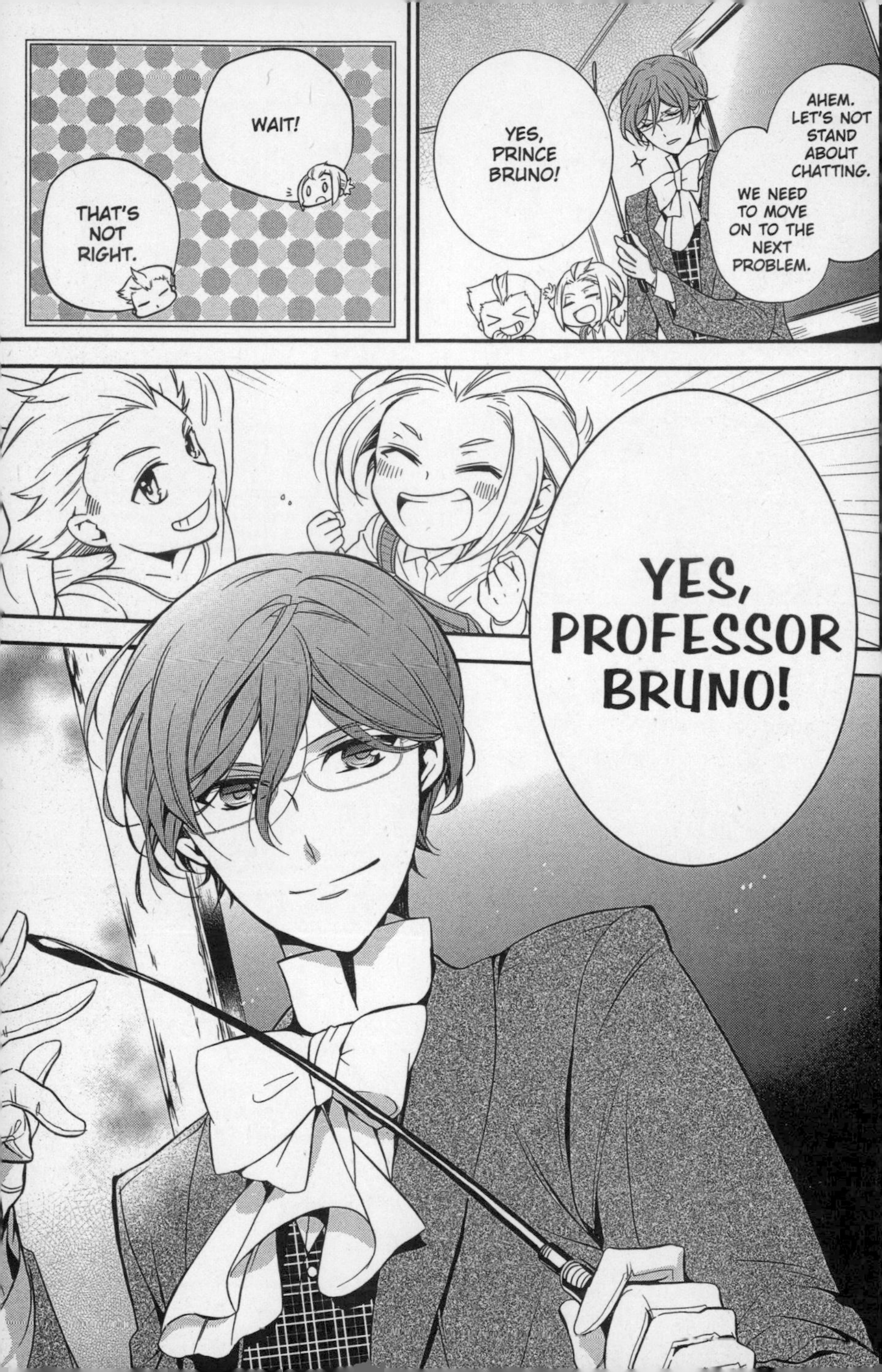
AHEM. LET'S NOT STAND ABOUT CHATTING.
WE NEED TO MOVE ON TO THE NEXT PROBLEM.
YES, PRINCE BRUNO!
WAIT!
THAT'S NOT RIGHT.
YES, PROFESSOR BRUNO!

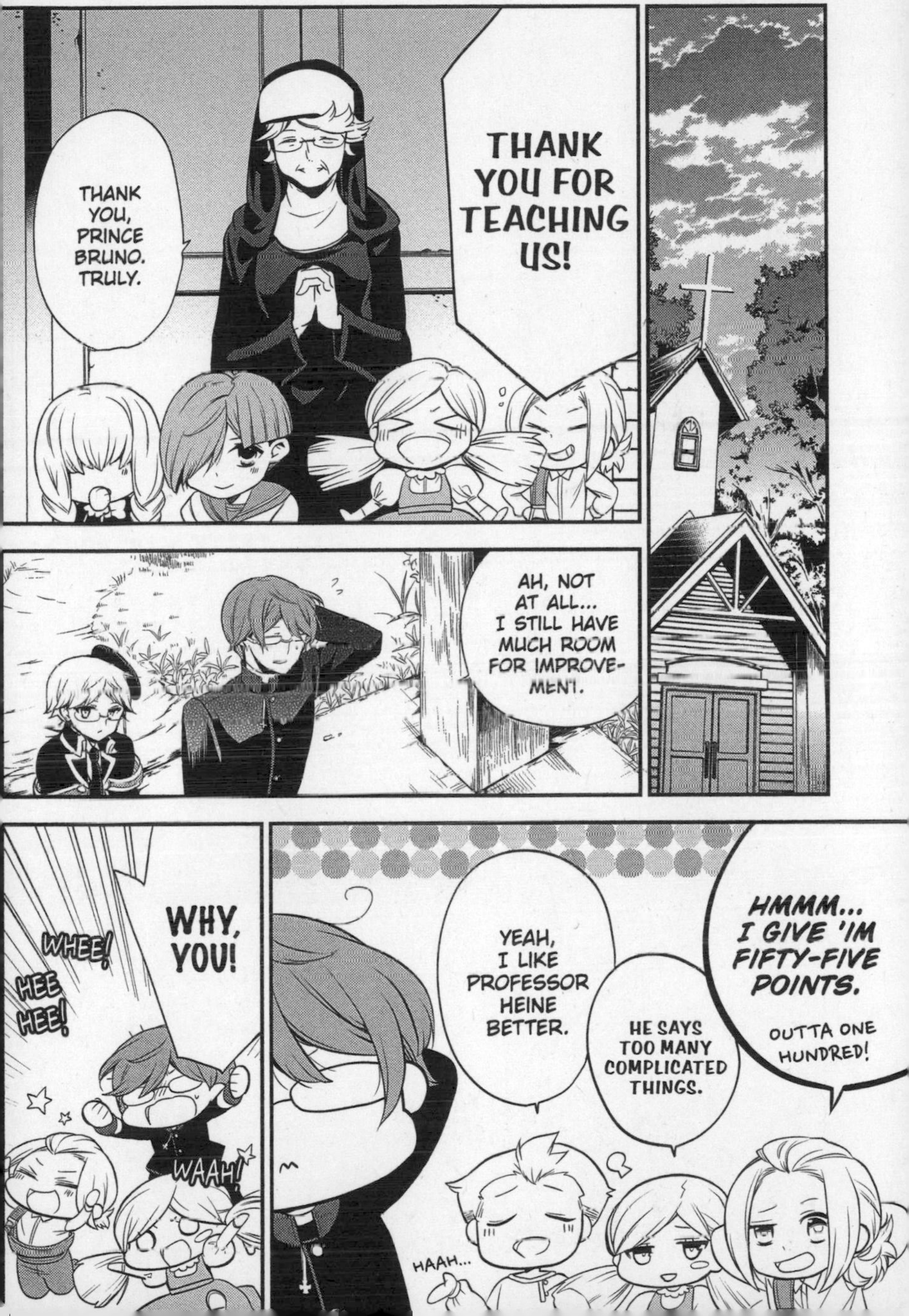
THANK YOU FOR TEACHING US!
THANK YOU, PRINCE BRUNO. TRULY.
AH, NOT AT ALL... I STILL HAVE MUCH ROOM FOR IMPROVE-MENT.
HMMM... I GIVE 'IM FIFTY-FIVE POINTS.
OUTTA ONE HUNDRED!
YEAH, I LIKE PROFESSOR HEINE BETTER.
HE SAYS TOO MANY COMPLICATED THINGS.
HAAH...
WHY, YOU!
WHEE!
HEE HEE!
WAAH!

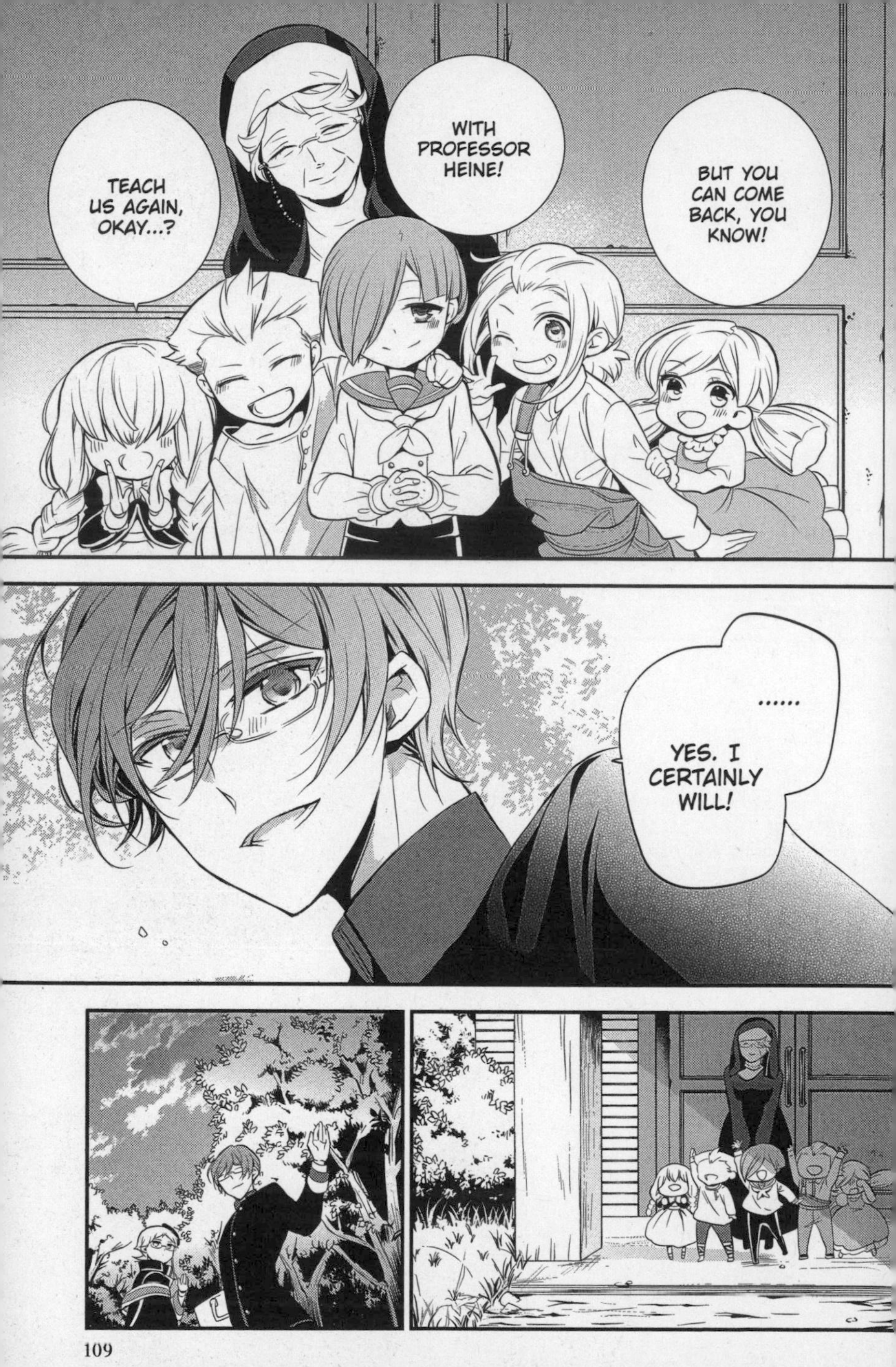
BUT YOU CAN COME BACK, YOU KNOW!
WITH PROFESSOR HEINE!
TEACH US AGAIN, OKAY...?
......
YES. I CERTAINLY WILL!

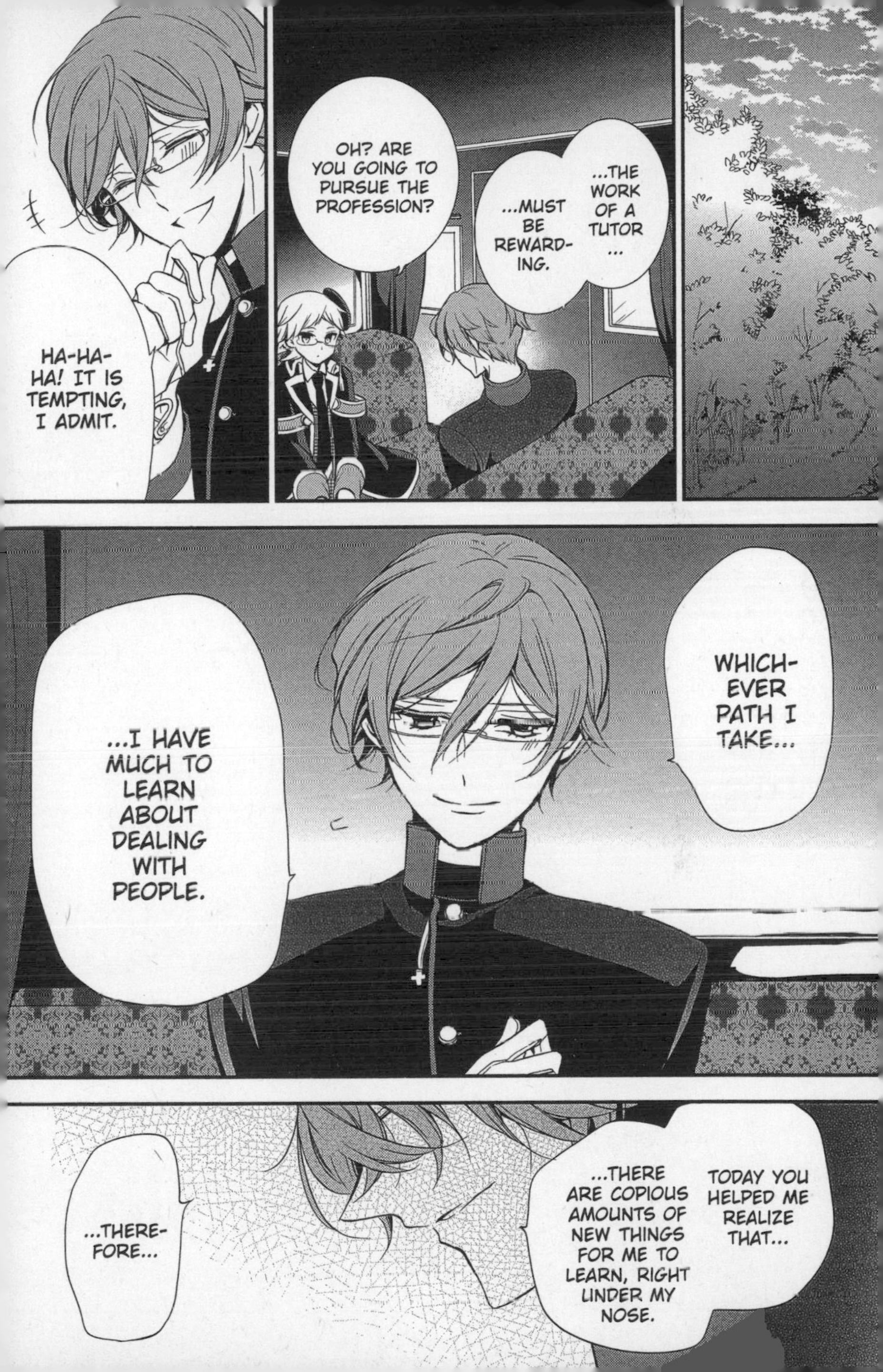
...THE WORK OF A TUTOR ...
...MUST BE REWARDING.
OH? ARE YOU GOING TO PURSUE THE PROFESSION?
HA-HA-HA! IT IS TEMPTING, I ADMIT.
WHICH-EVER PATH I TAKE...
...I HAVE MUCH TO LEARN ABOUT DEALING WITH PEOPLE.
TODAY YOU HELPED ME REALIZE THAT...
...THERE ARE COPIOUS AMOUNTS OF NEW THINGS FOR ME TO LEARN, RIGHT UNDER MY NOSE.
...THERE-FORE...

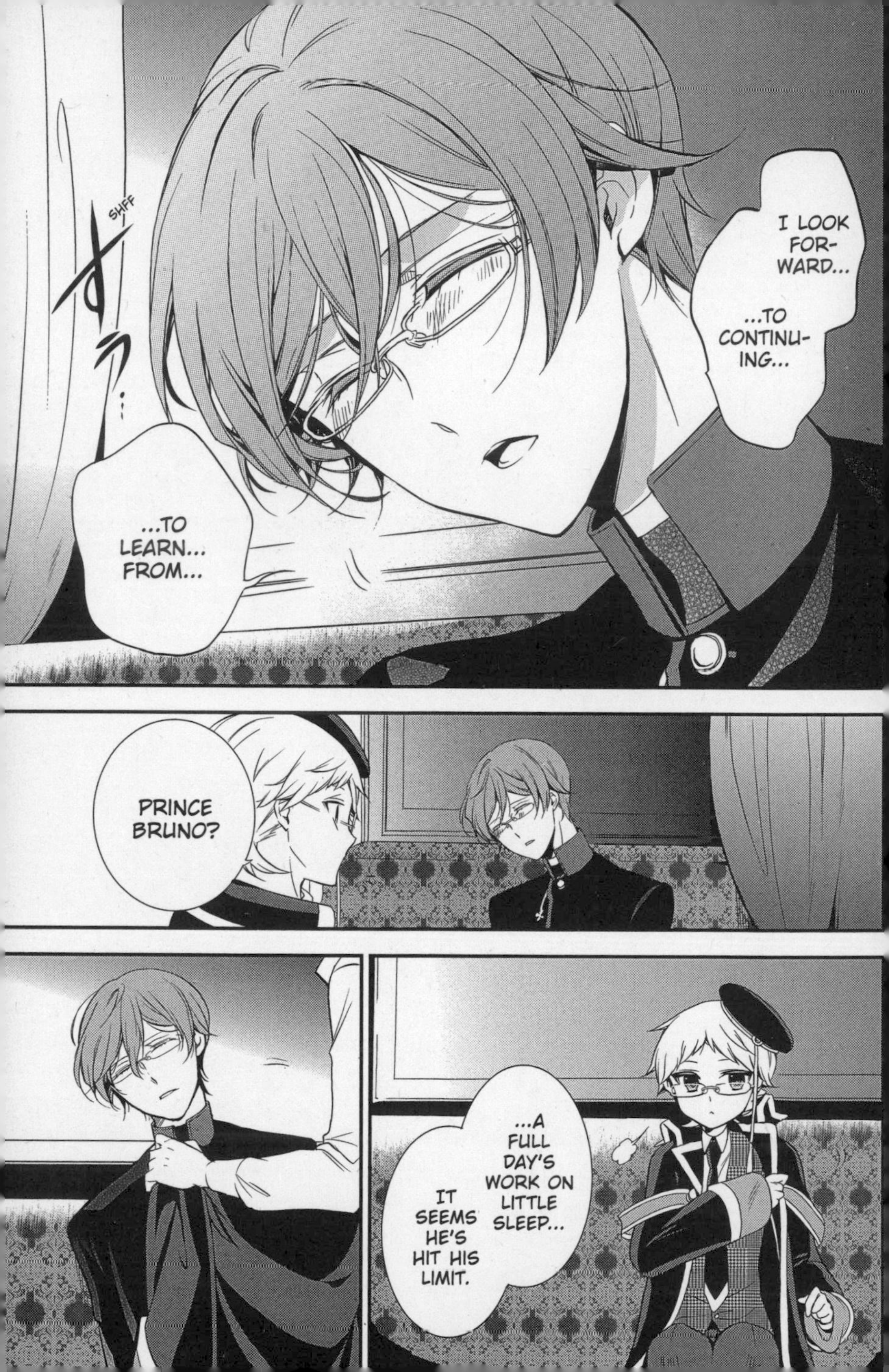
I LOOK FORWARD...
...TO CONTINUING...
SHFF
...TO LEARN... FROM...
PRINCE BRUNO?
...A FULL DAY'S WORK ON LITTLE SLEEP...
IT SEEMS HE'S HIT HIS LIMIT.

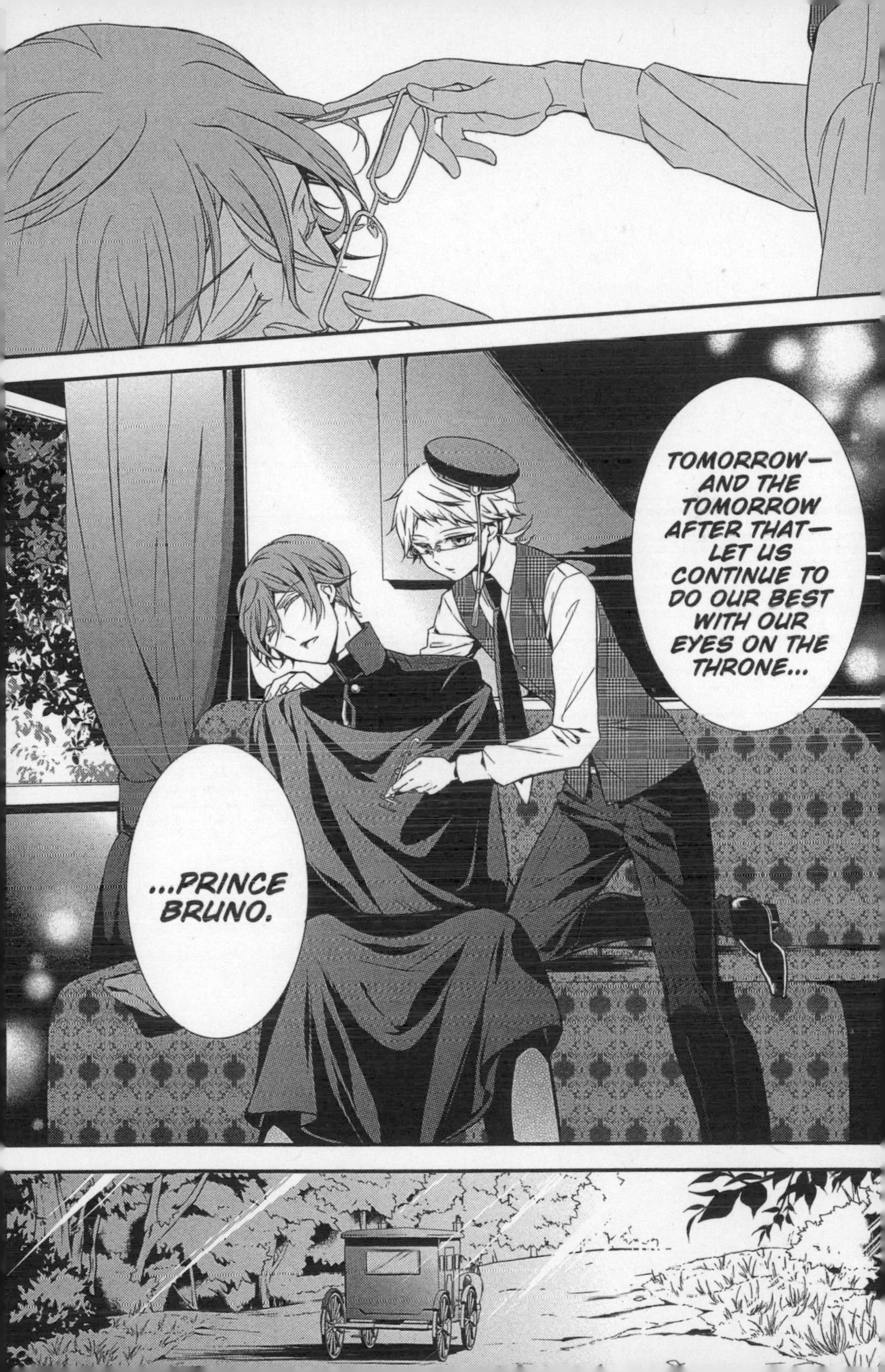
TOMORROW—AND THE TOMORROW AFTER THAT—LET US CONTINUE TO DO OUR BEST WITH OUR EYES ON THE THRONE...
...PRINCE BRUNO.

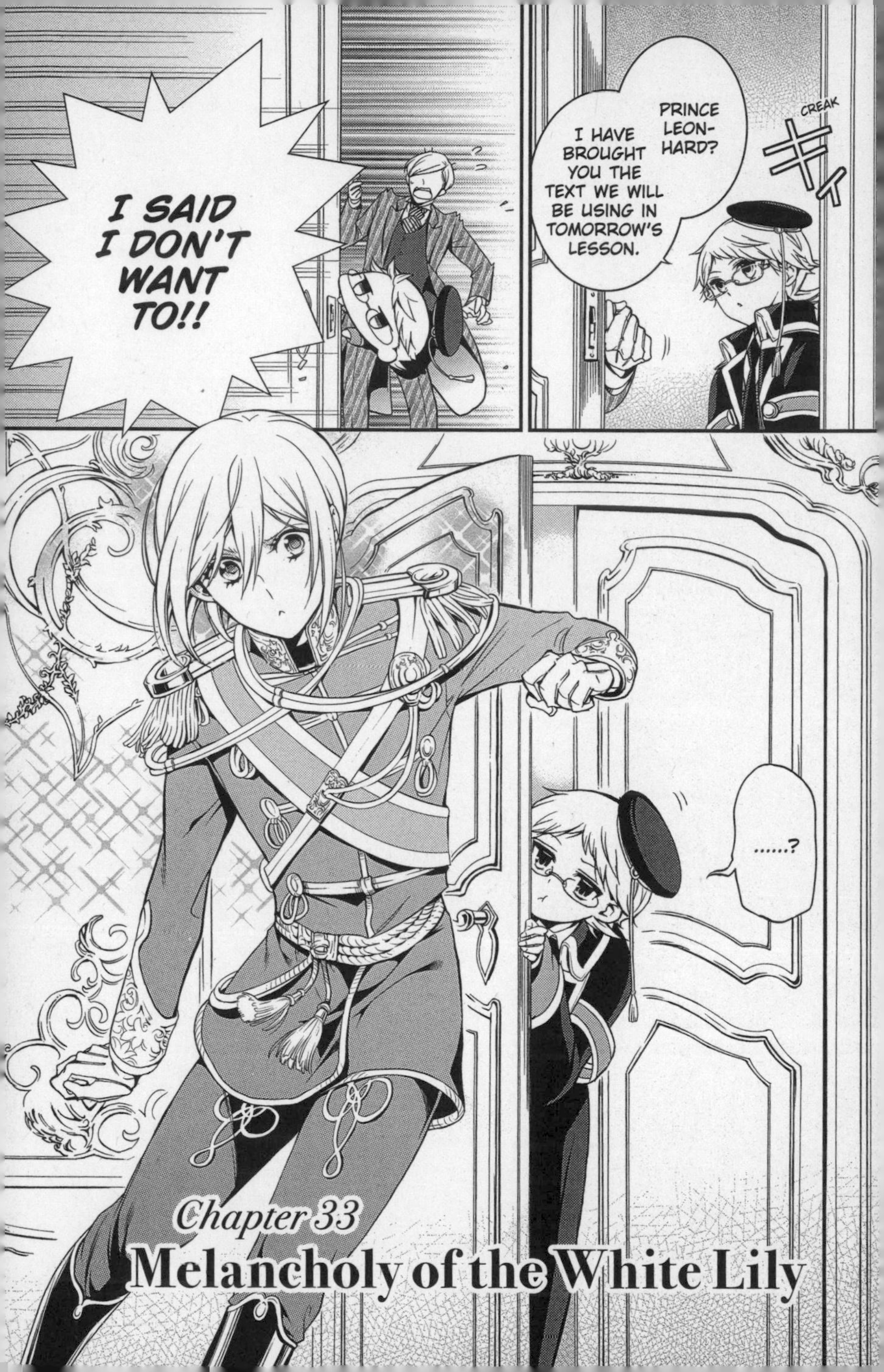
CREAK
PRINCE LEONHARD?
I HAVE BROUGHT YOU THE TEXT WE WILL BE USING IN TOMORROW'S LESSON.
I SAID I DON'T WANT TO!!
......?
Chapter 33
Melancholy of the White Lily

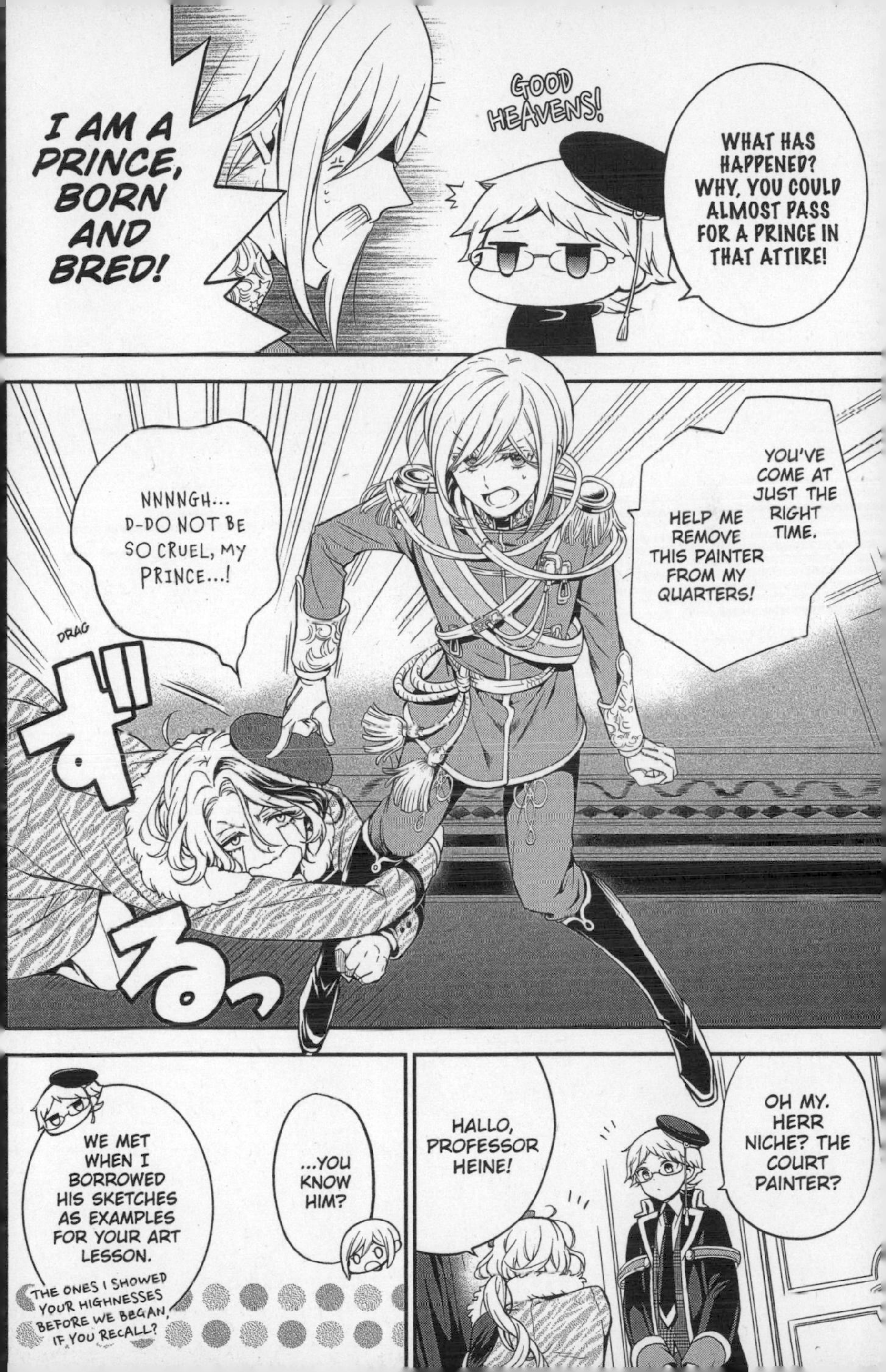
GOOD HEAVENS!
WHAT HAS HAPPENED? WHY, YOU COULD ALMOST PASS FOR A PRINCE IN THAT ATTIRE!
I AM A PRINCE, BORN AND BRED!
YOU'VE COME AT JUST THE RIGHT TIME.
HELP ME REMOVE THIS PAINTER FROM MY QUARTERS!
NNNNGH... D-DO NOT BE SO CRUEL, MY PRINCE...!
DRAG
OH MY. HERR NICHE? THE COURT PAINTER?
HALLO, PROFESSOR HEINE!
...YOU KNOW HIM?
WE MET WHEN I BORROWED HIS SKETCHES AS EXAMPLES FOR YOUR ART LESSON.
THE ONES I SHOWED YOUR HIGHNESSES BEFORE WE BEGAN, IF YOU RECALL?

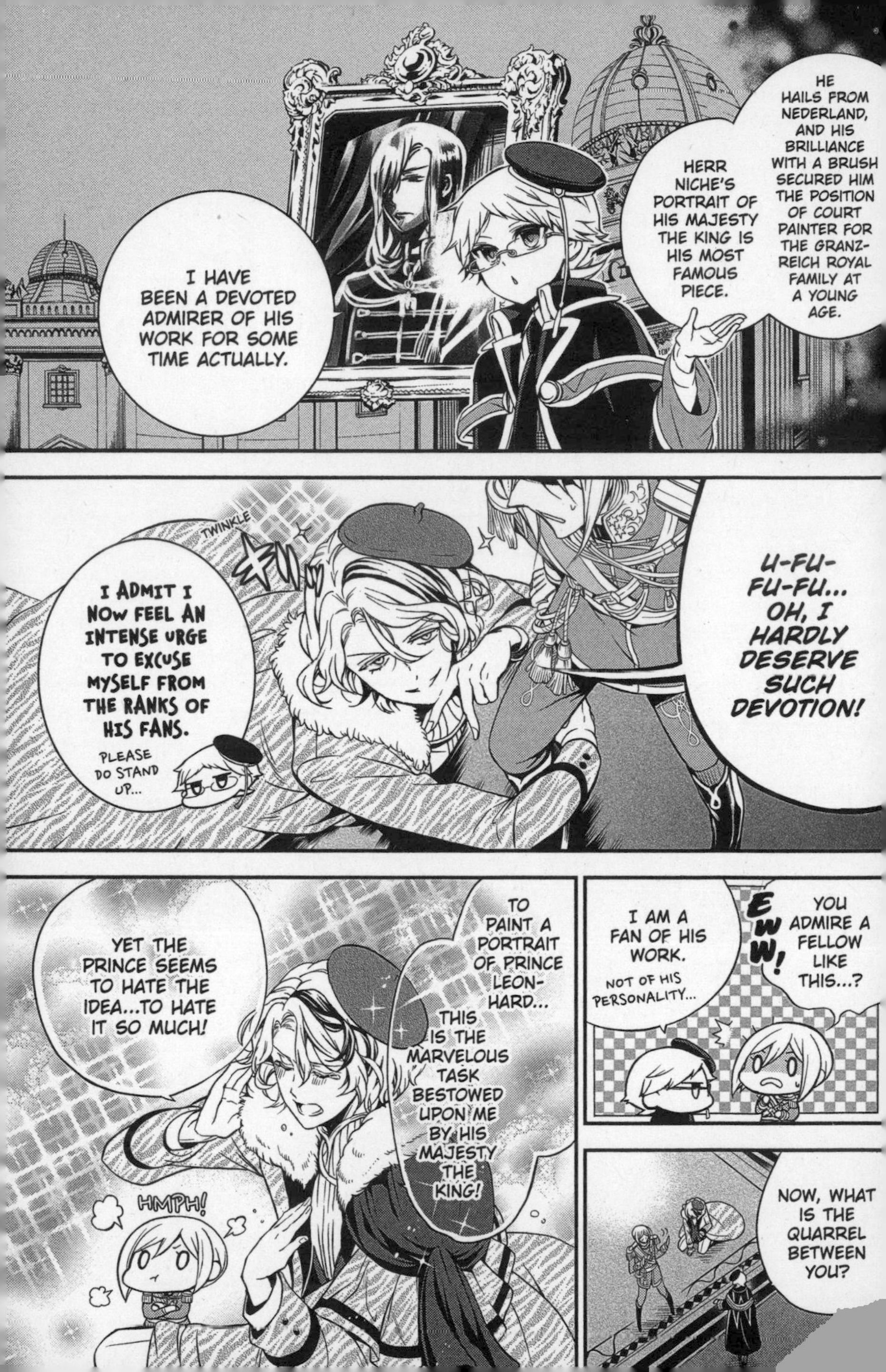
HE HAILS FROM NEDERLAND, AND HIS BRILLIANCE WITH A BRUSH SECURED HIM THE POSITION OF COURT PAINTER FOR THE GRANZREICH ROYAL FAMILY AT A YOUNG AGE.
HERR NICHE'S PORTRAIT OF HIS MAJESTY THE KING IS HIS MOST FAMOUS PIECE.
I HAVE BEEN A DEVOTED ADMIRER OF HIS WORK FOR SOME TIME ACTUALLY.
U-FU-FU-FU... OH, I HARDLY DESERVE SUCH DEVOTION!
TWINKLE
I ADMIT I NOW FEEL AN INTENSE URGE TO EXCUSE MYSELF FROM THE RANKS OF HIS FANS.
PLEASE DO STAND UP...
YOU ADMIRE A FELLOW LIKE THIS...?
EWW!
I AM A FAN OF HIS WORK.
NOT OF HIS PERSONALITY...
NOW, WHAT IS THE QUARREL BETWEEN YOU?
TO PAINT A PORTRAIT OF PRINCE LEONHARD...
THIS IS THE MARVELOUS TASK BESTOWED UPON ME BY HIS MAJESTY THE KING!
YET THE PRINCE SEEMS TO HATE THE IDEA...TO HATE IT SO MUCH!
HMPH!

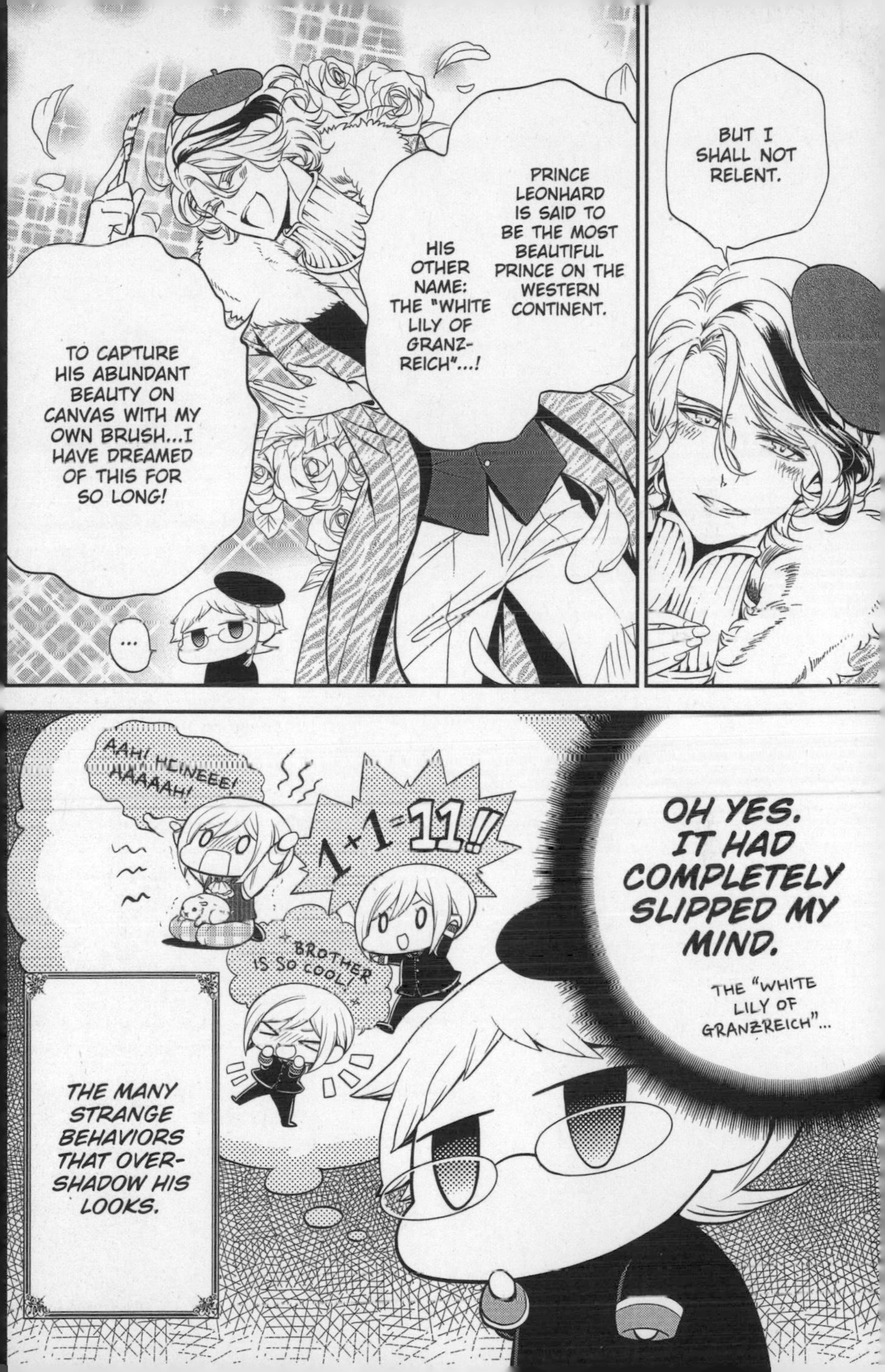
BUT I SHALL NOT RELENT.
PRINCE LEONHARD IS SAID TO BE THE MOST BEAUTIFUL PRINCE ON THE WESTERN CONTINENT.
HIS OTHER NAME: THE "WHITE LILY OF GRANZ-REICH"...!
TO CAPTURE HIS ABUNDANT BEAUTY ON CANVAS WITH MY OWN BRUSH...I HAVE DREAMED OF THIS FOR SO LONG!
...
OH YES. IT HAD COMPLETELY SLIPPED MY MIND.
THE "WHITE LILY OF GRANZREICH"...
AAH! HEINEEE! HAAAAAH!
1+1=11!!
BROTHER IS SO COOL!
THE MANY STRANGE BEHAVIORS THAT OVER-SHADOW HIS LOOKS.

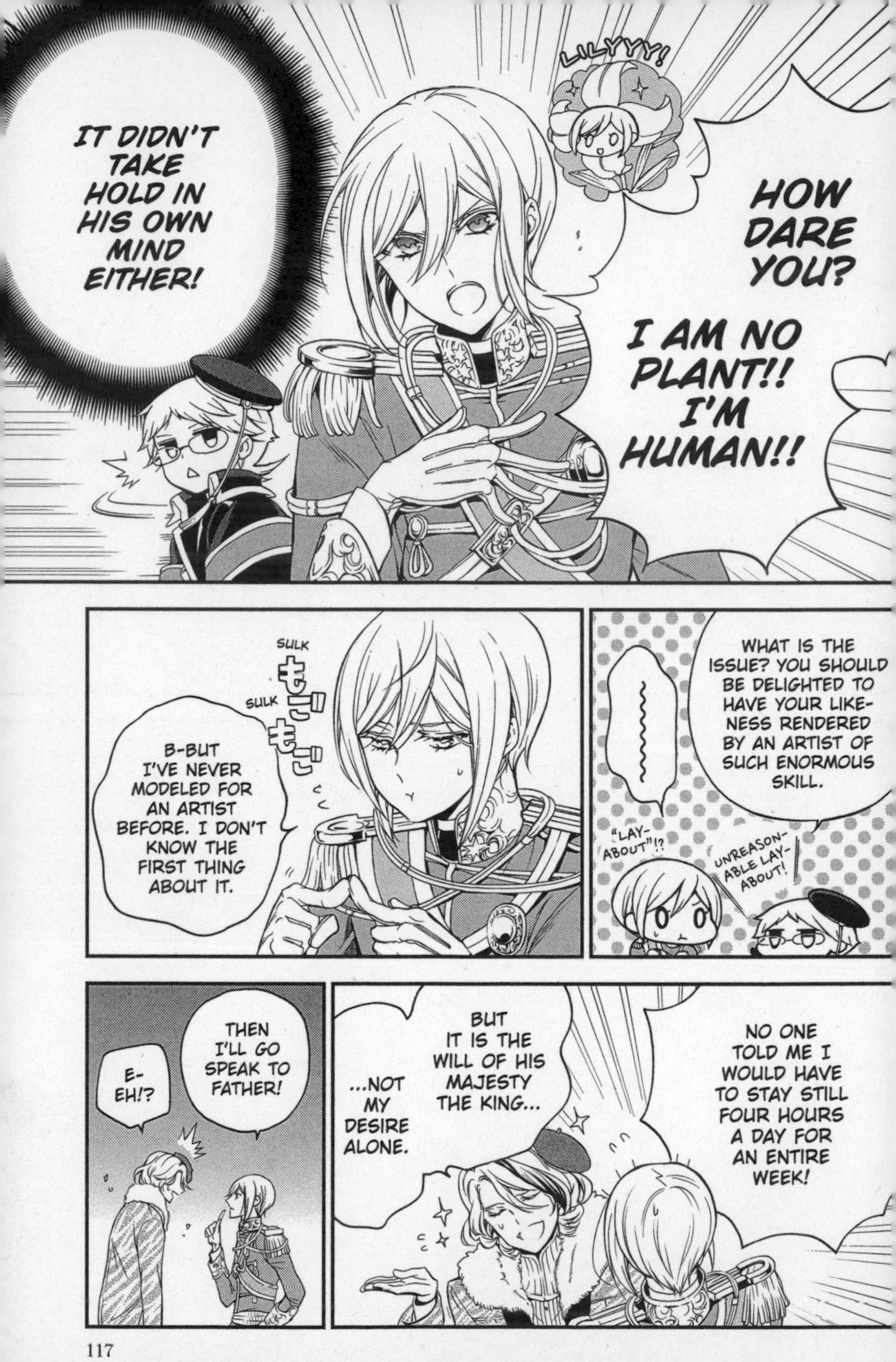
LILYYY!
HOW DARE YOU?
I AM NO PLANT!! I'M HUMAN!!
IT DIDN'T TAKE HOLD IN HIS OWN MIND EITHER!
WHAT IS THE ISSUE? YOU SHOULD BE DELIGHTED TO HAVE YOUR LIKENESS RENDERED BY AN ARTIST OF SUCH ENORMOUS SKILL.
UNREASONABLE LAYABOUT!
"LAY-ABOUT"!?
SULK
もご
SULK
もご
B-BUT I'VE NEVER MODELED FOR AN ARTIST BEFORE. I DON'T KNOW THE FIRST THING ABOUT IT.
NO ONE TOLD ME I WOULD HAVE TO STAY STILL FOUR HOURS A DAY FOR AN ENTIRE WEEK!
BUT IT IS THE WILL OF HIS MAJESTY THE KING...
...NOT MY DESIRE ALONE.
THEN I'LL GO SPEAK TO FATHER!
E-EH!?

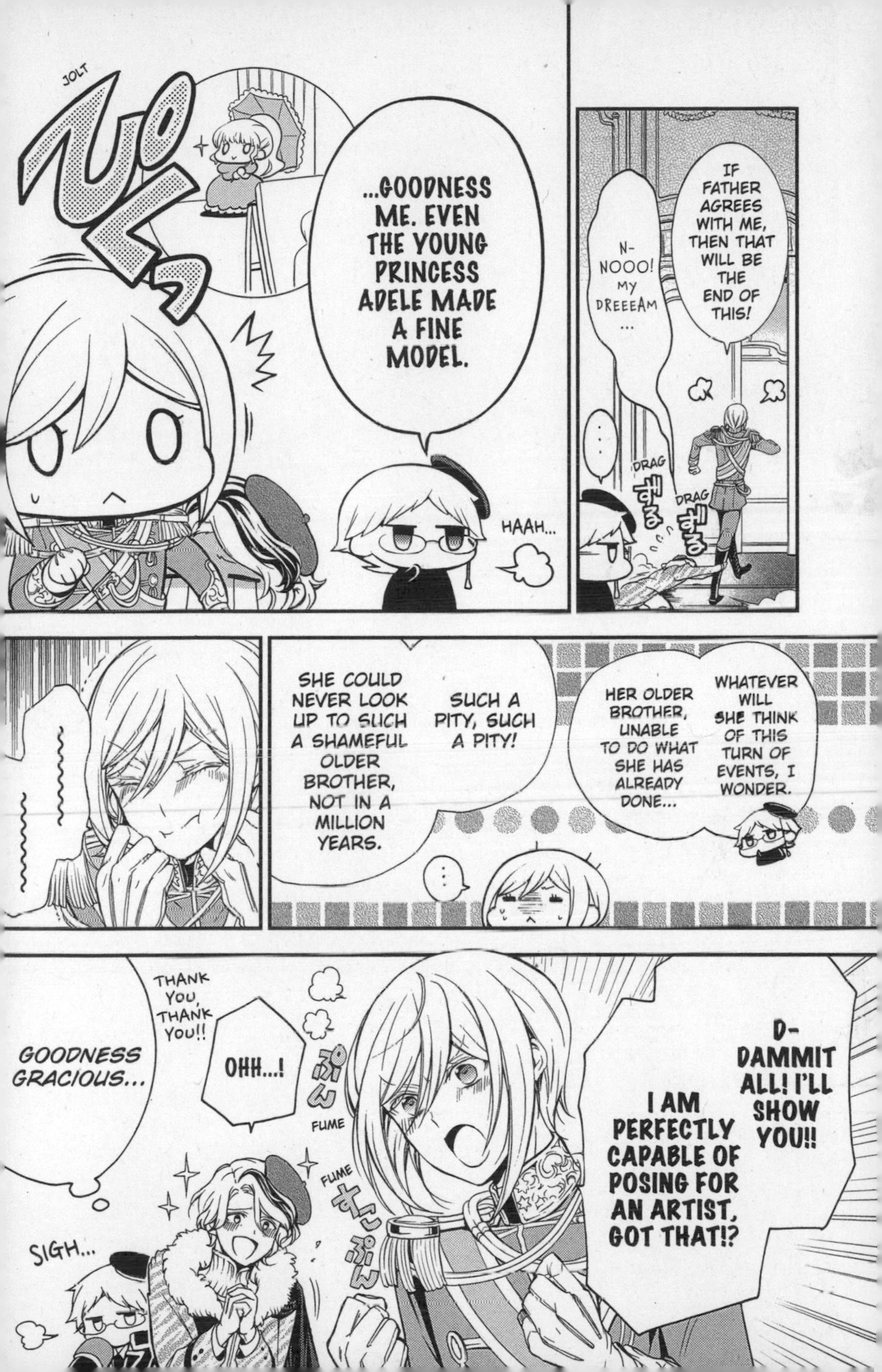
IF FATHER AGREES WITH ME, THEN THAT WILL BE THE END OF THIS!
N-NOOO! MY DREEEAM...
...
DRAG
DRAG
JOLT
...GOODNESS ME. EVEN THE YOUNG PRINCESS ADELE MADE A FINE MODEL.
HAAH...
WHATEVER WILL SHE THINK OF THIS TURN OF EVENTS, I WONDER.
HER OLDER BROTHER, UNABLE TO DO WHAT SHE HAS ALREADY DONE...
SUCH A PITY, SUCH A PITY!
SHE COULD NEVER LOOK UP TO SUCH A SHAMEFUL OLDER BROTHER, NOT IN A MILLION YEARS.
...
D-DAMMIT ALL! I'LL SHOW YOU!!
I AM PERFECTLY CAPABLE OF POSING FOR AN ARTIST, GOT THAT!?
FUME
FUME
OHH...!
THANK YOU, THANK YOU!!
GOODNESS GRACIOUS...
SIGH...

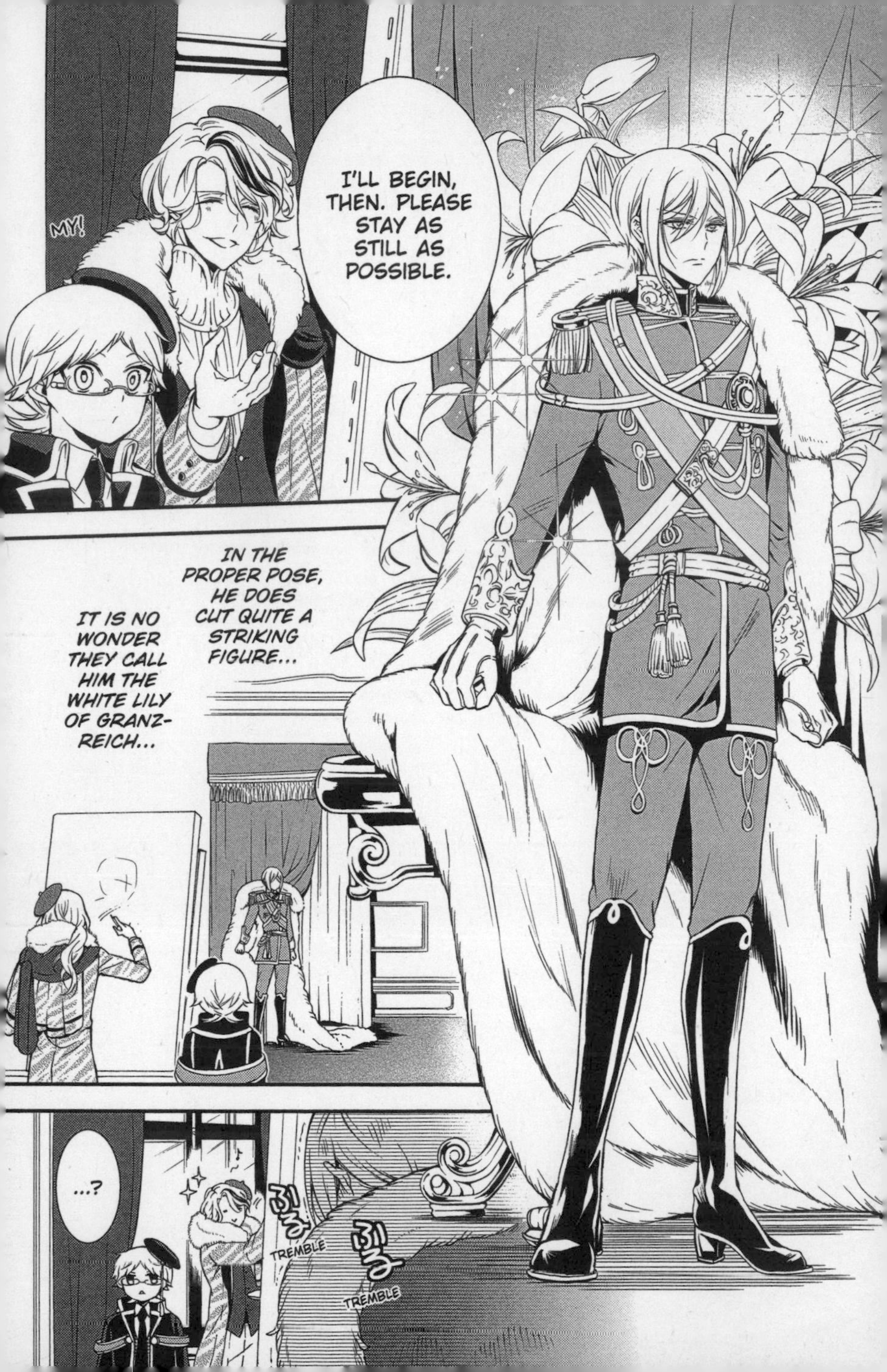
I'LL BEGIN, THEN. PLEASE STAY AS STILL AS POSSIBLE.
MY!
IN THE PROPER POSE, HE DOES CUT QUITE A STRIKING FIGURE...
IT IS NO WONDER THEY CALL HIM THE WHITE LILY OF GRANZ-REICH...
...?
ぷる
TREMBLE
ぷる
TREMBLE

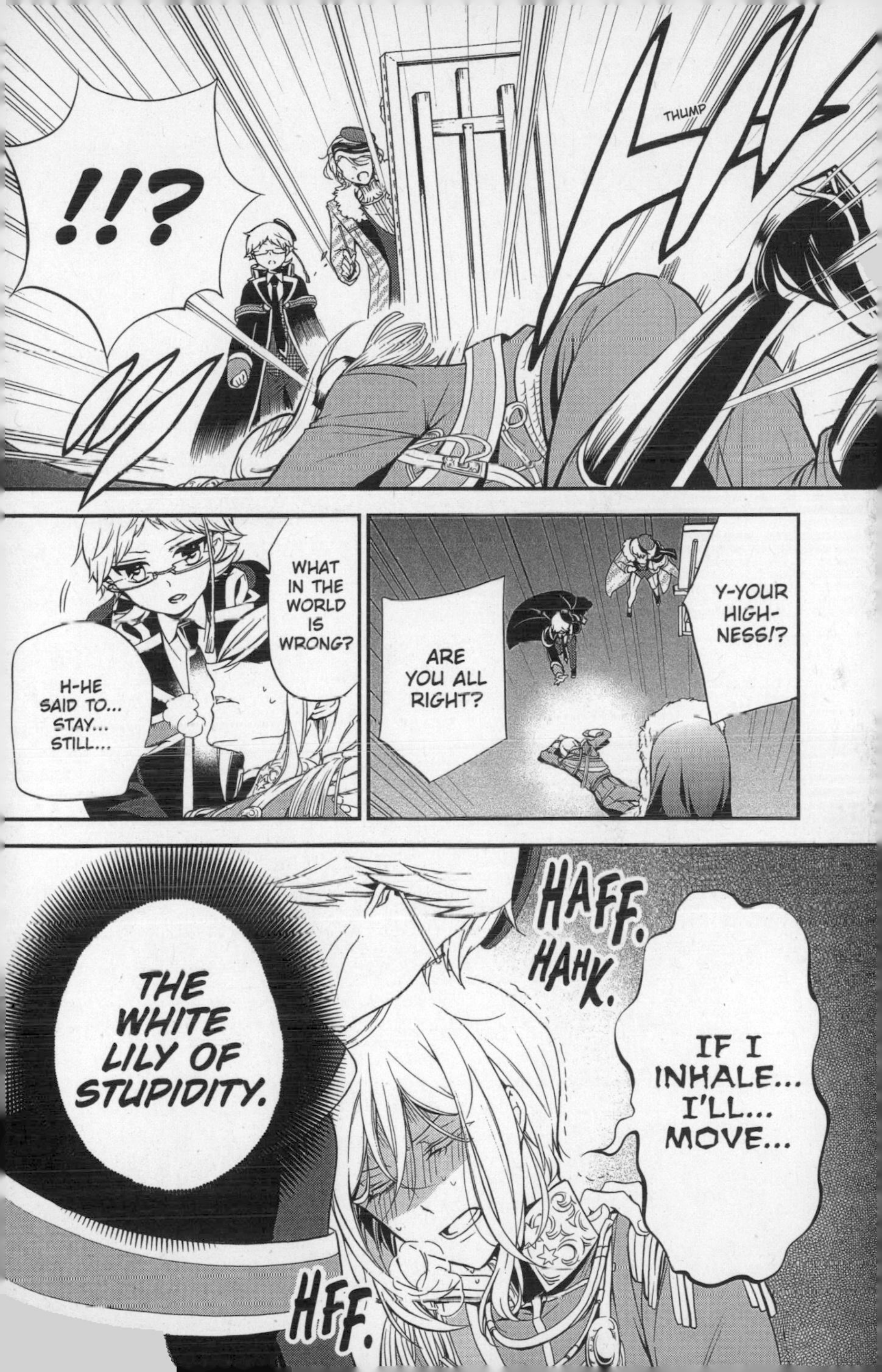
THUMP
!!?
Y-YOUR HIGH-NESS!?
ARE YOU ALL RIGHT?
WHAT IN THE WORLD IS WRONG?
H-HE SAID TO... STAY... STILL...
HAFF.
HAHK.
IF I INHALE... I'LL... MOVE...
THE WHITE LILY OF STUPIDITY.
HFF.

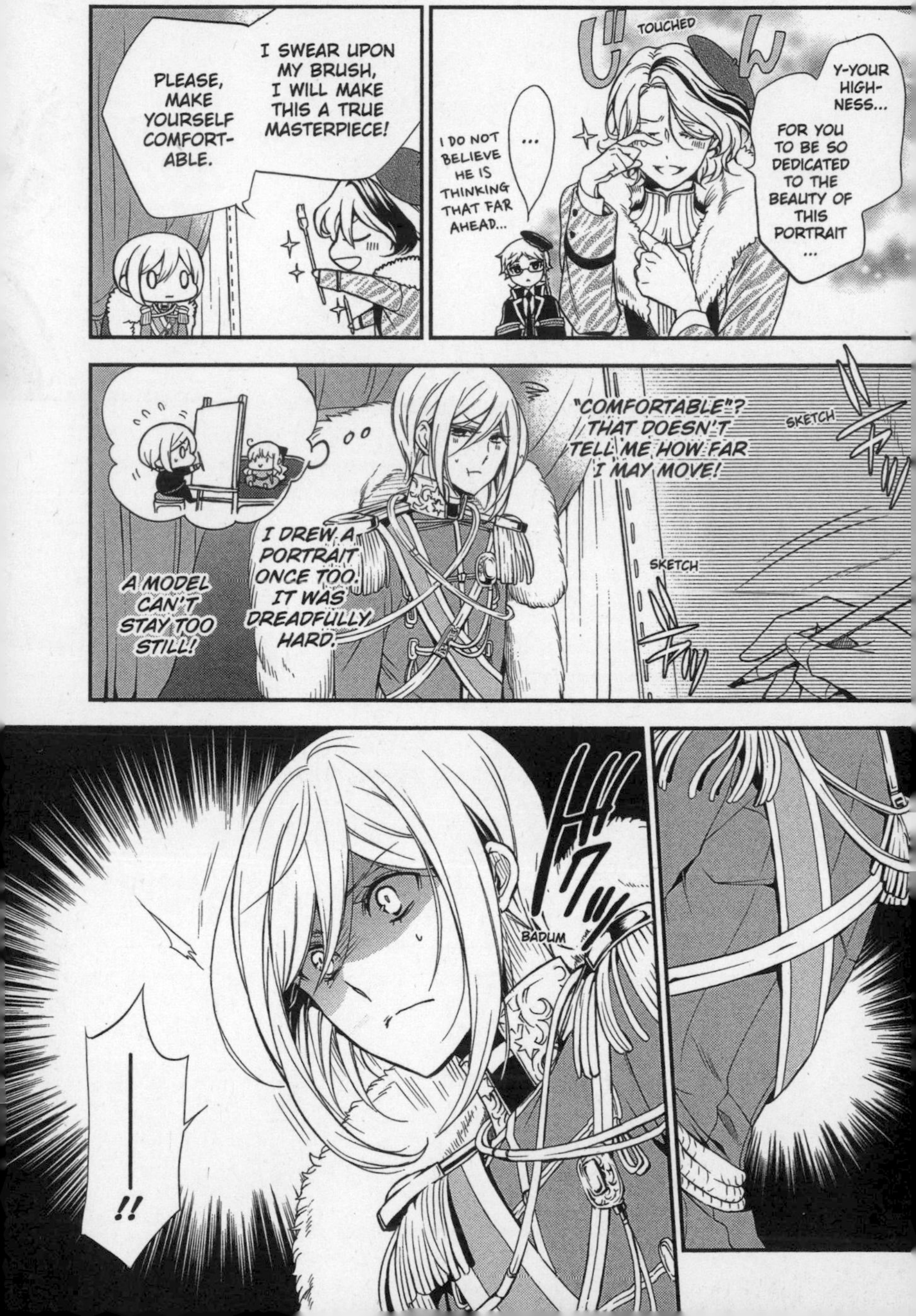
TOUCHED
Y-YOUR HIGHNESS...
FOR YOU TO BE SO DEDICATED TO THE BEAUTY OF THIS PORTRAIT...
...
I DO NOT BELIEVE HE IS THINKING THAT FAR AHEAD...
I SWEAR UPON MY BRUSH, I WILL MAKE THIS A TRUE MASTERPIECE!
PLEASE, MAKE YOURSELF COMFORTABLE.
SKETCH
"COMFORTABLE"? THAT DOESN'T TELL ME HOW FAR I MAY MOVE!
SKETCH
I DREW A PORTRAIT ONCE TOO. IT WAS DREADFULLY HARD.
A MODEL CAN'T STAY TOO STILL!
BADUM
!!

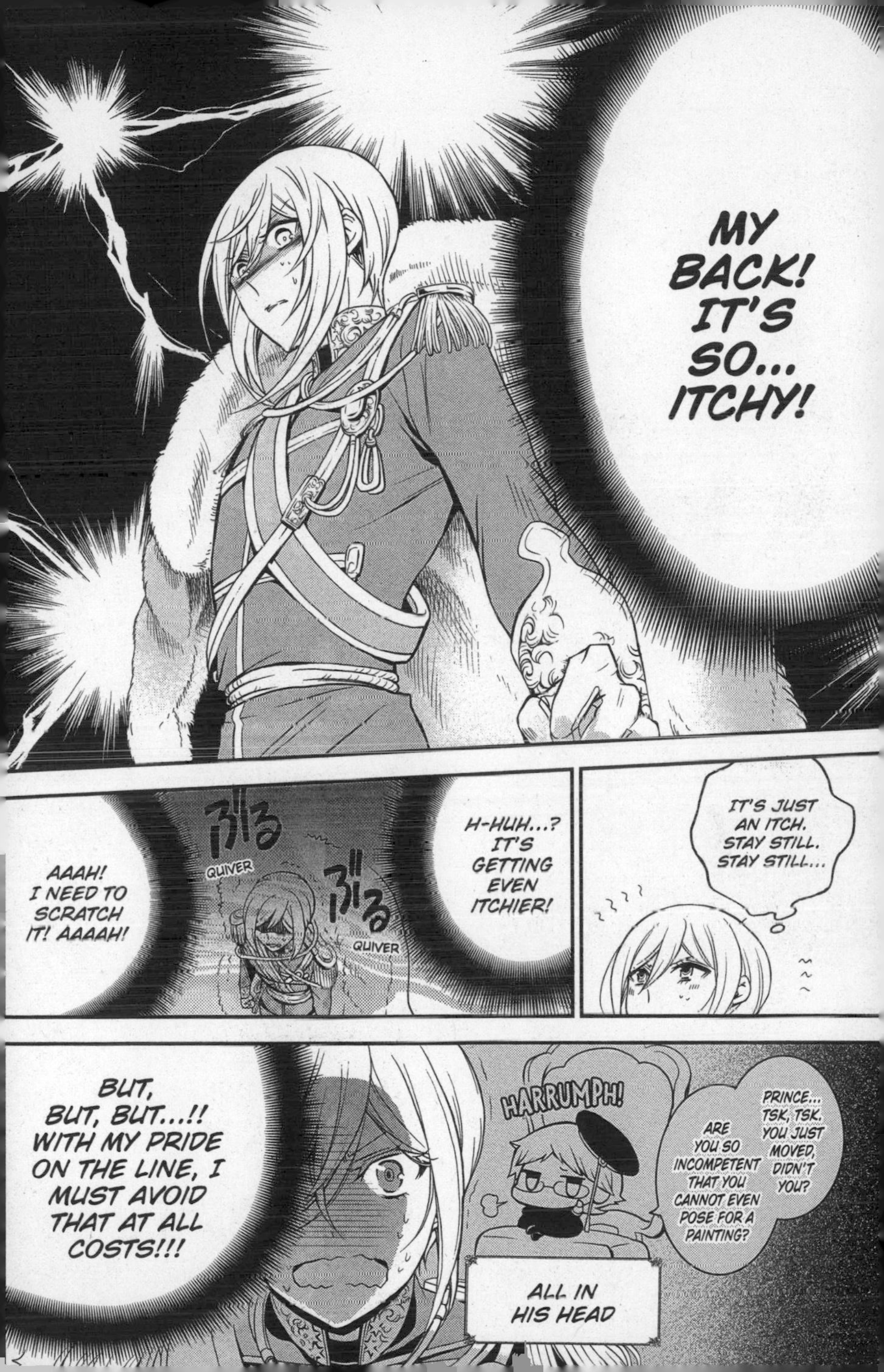
MY BACK! IT'S SO... ITCHY!
IT'S JUST AN ITCH. STAY STILL. STAY STILL...
H-HUH...? IT'S GETTING EVEN ITCHIER!
ぶる
QUIVER
ぶる
QUIVER
AAAH! I NEED TO SCRATCH IT! AAAAH!
PRINCE... TSK, TSK. YOU JUST MOVED, DIDN'T YOU?
ARE YOU SO INCOMPETENT THAT YOU CANNOT EVEN POSE FOR A PAINTING?
HARRUMPH!
ALL IN HIS HEAD
BUT, BUT, BUT...!! WITH MY PRIDE ON THE LINE, I MUST AVOID THAT AT ALL COSTS!!!

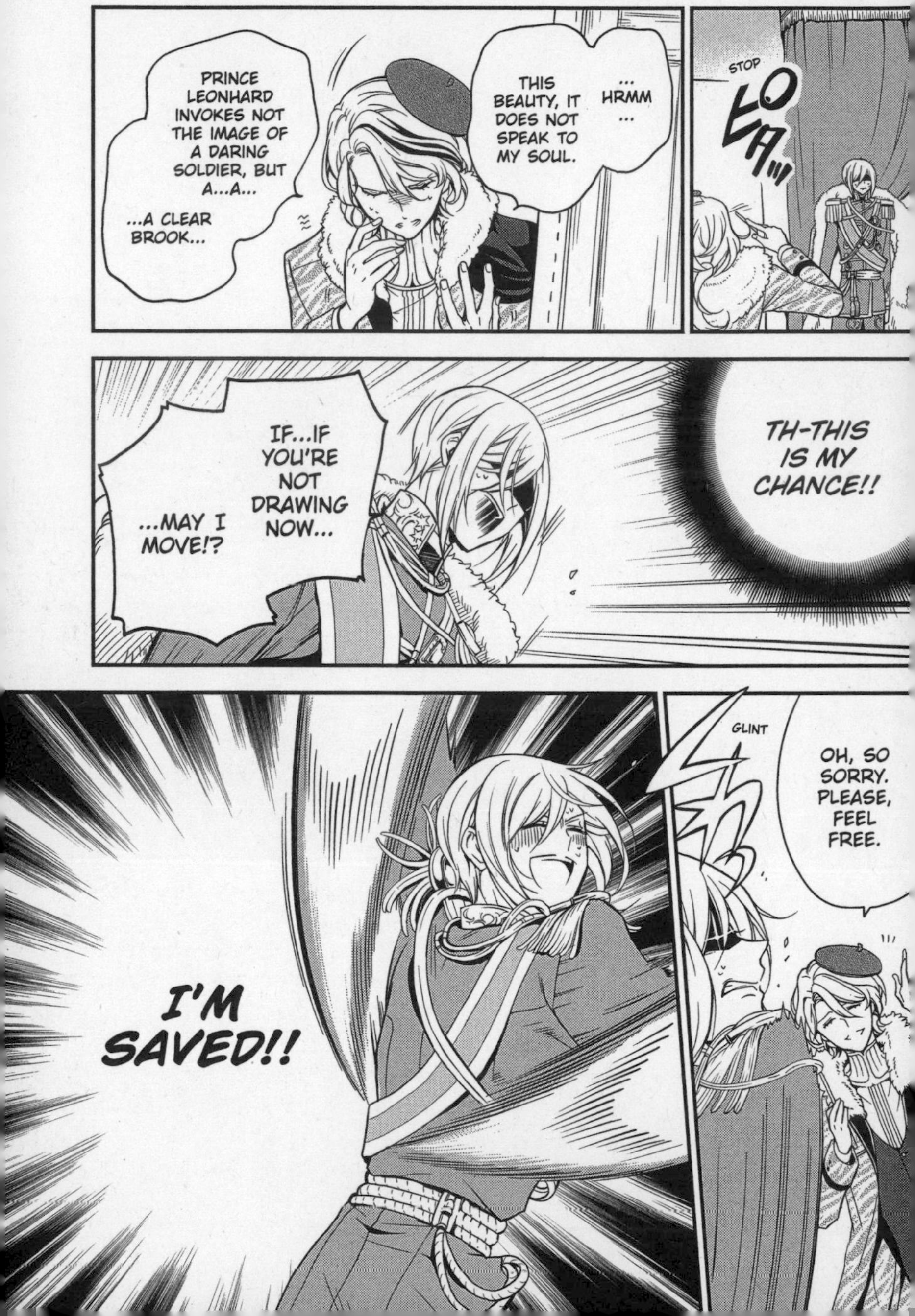
STOP
...HRMM...
THIS BEAUTY, IT DOES NOT SPEAK TO MY SOUL.
PRINCE LEONHARD INVOKES NOT THE IMAGE OF A DARING SOLDIER, BUT A...A...
...A CLEAR BROOK...
TH-THIS IS MY CHANCE!!
IF...IF YOU'RE NOT DRAWING NOW...
...MAY I MOVE!?
GLINT
OH, SO SORRY. PLEASE, FEEL FREE.
I'M SAVED!!

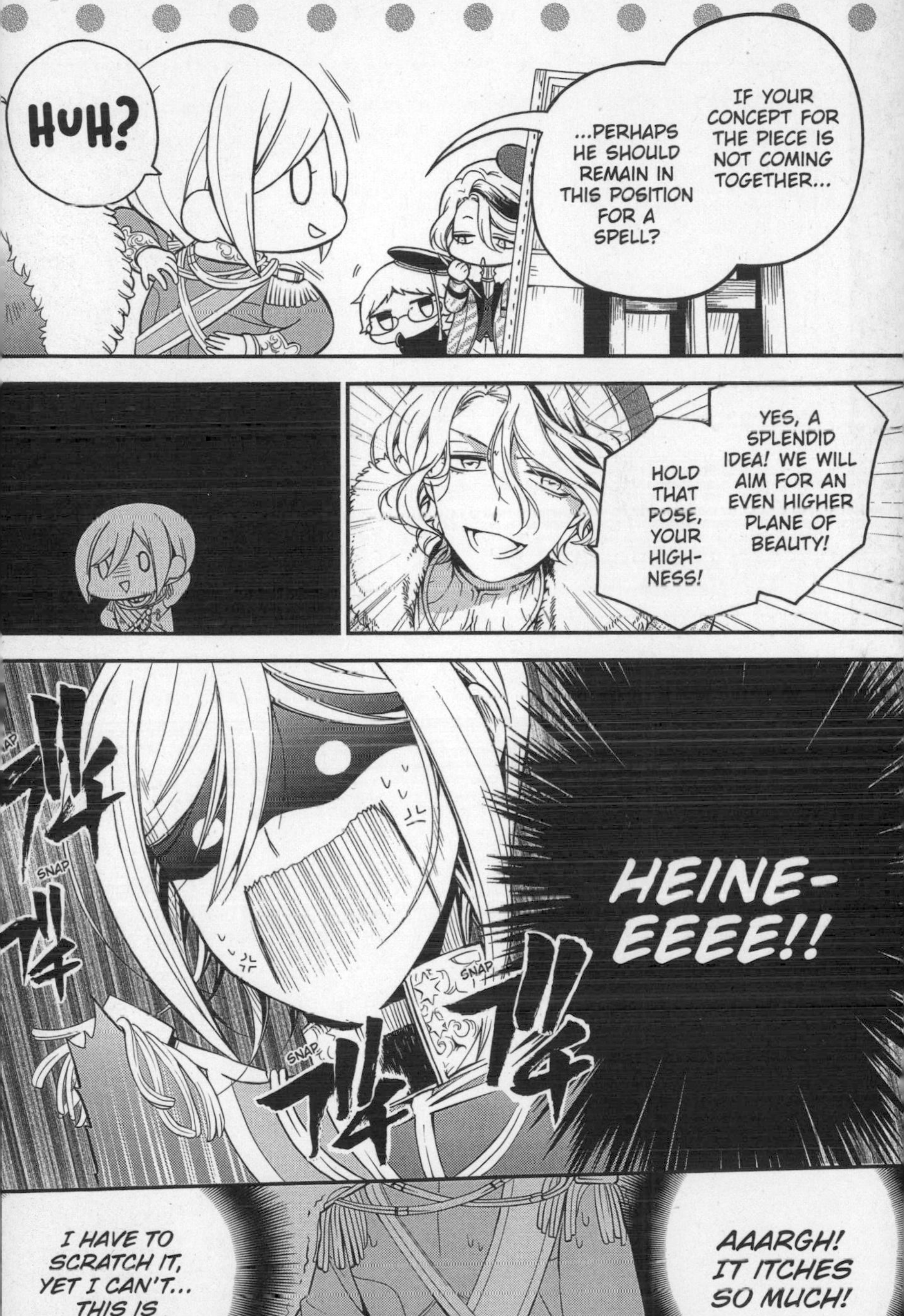
IF YOUR CONCEPT FOR THE PIECE IS NOT COMING TOGETHER...
...PERHAPS HE SHOULD REMAIN IN THIS POSITION FOR A SPELL?
HUH?
YES, A SPLENDID IDEA! WE WILL AIM FOR AN EVEN HIGHER PLANE OF BEAUTY!
HOLD THAT POSE, YOUR HIGHNESS!
HEINE-EEEE!!
SNAP
SNAP
SNAP
SNAP
AAARGH! IT ITCHES SO MUCH!
I HAVE TO SCRATCH IT, YET I CAN'T... THIS IS TORTURE!

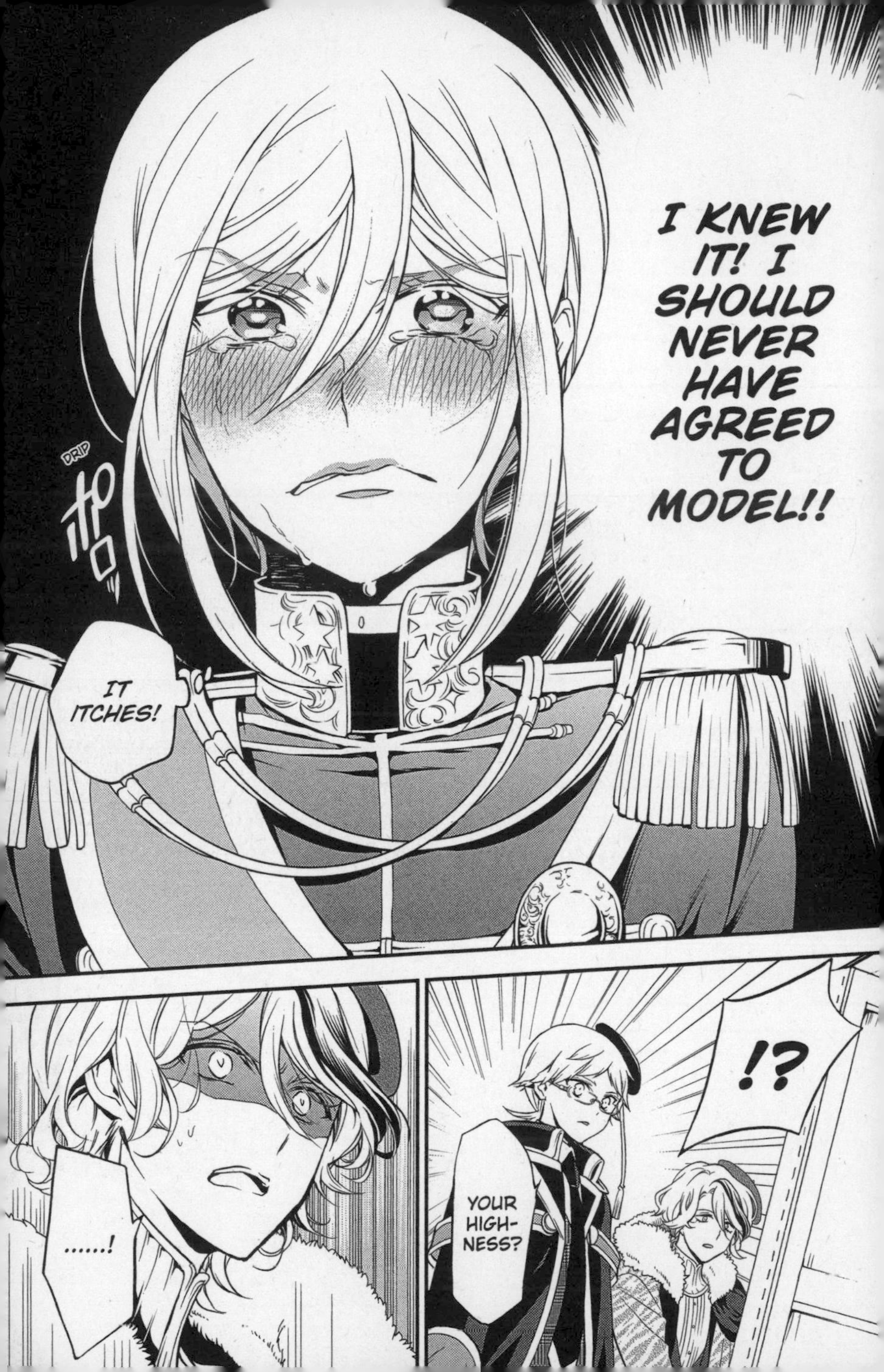
I KNEW IT! I SHOULD NEVER HAVE AGREED TO MODEL!!
DRIP
IT ITCHES!
!?
YOUR HIGH-NESS?
......!

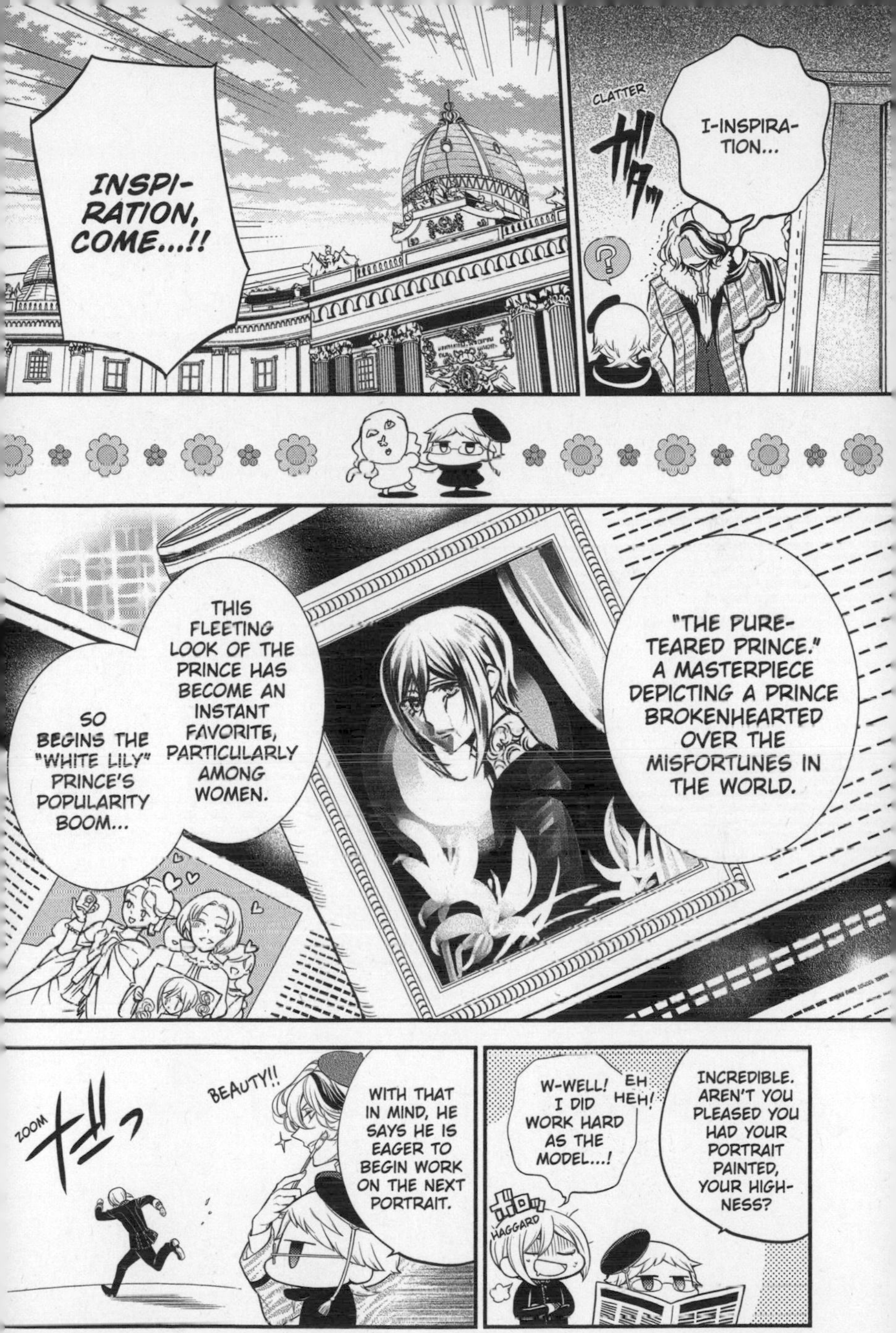
CLATTER
I-INSPIRA-TION...
INSPI-RATION, COME...!!
"THE PURE-TEARED PRINCE." A MASTERPIECE DEPICTING A PRINCE BROKENHEARTED OVER THE MISFORTUNES IN THE WORLD.
THIS FLEETING LOOK OF THE PRINCE HAS BECOME AN INSTANT FAVORITE, PARTICULARLY AMONG WOMEN.
SO BEGINS THE "WHITE LILY" PRINCE'S POPULARITY BOOM...
INCREDIBLE. AREN'T YOU PLEASED YOU HAD YOUR PORTRAIT PAINTED, YOUR HIGH-NESS?
W-WELL! I DID WORK HARD AS THE MODEL...!
EH HEH!
HAGGARD
WITH THAT IN MIND, HE SAYS HE IS EAGER TO BEGIN WORK ON THE NEXT PORTRAIT.
BEAUTY!!
ZOOM

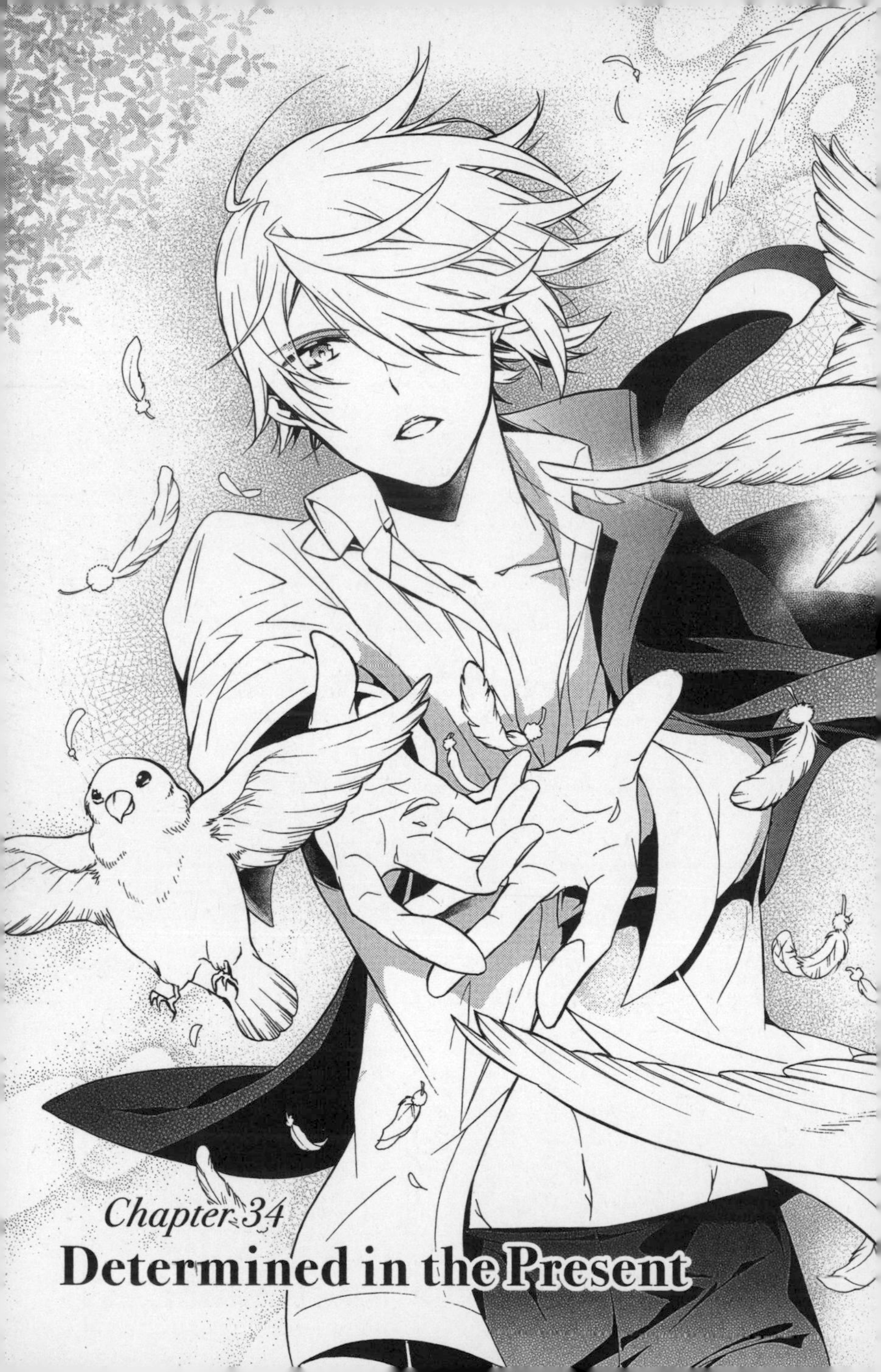

Chapter 34
Determined in the Present

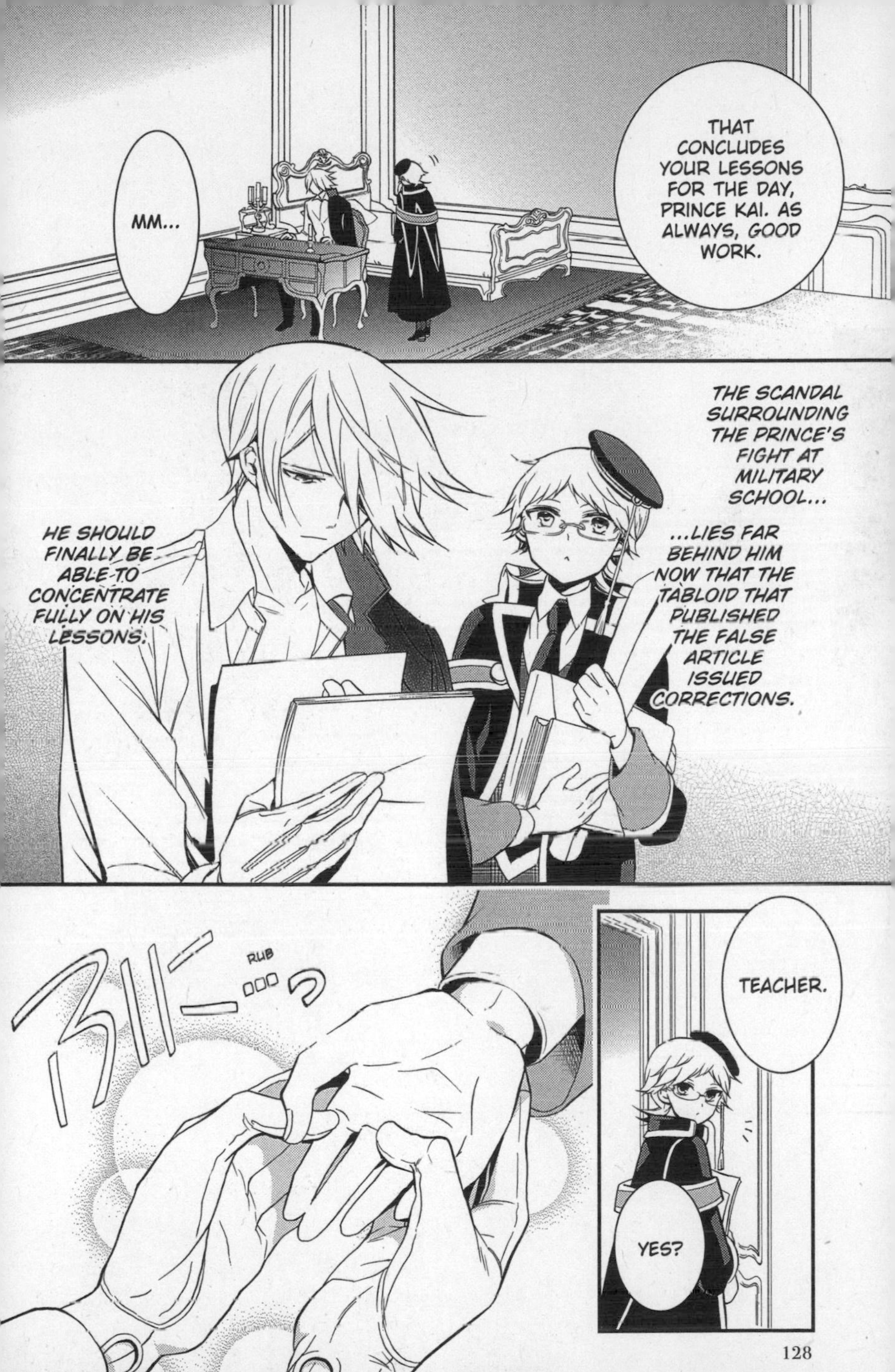
THAT CONCLUDES YOUR LESSONS FOR THE DAY, PRINCE KAI. AS ALWAYS, GOOD WORK.
MM...
THE SCANDAL SURROUNDING THE PRINCE'S FIGHT AT MILITARY SCHOOL...
...LIES FAR BEHIND HIM NOW THAT THE TABLOID THAT PUBLISHED THE FALSE ARTICLE ISSUED CORRECTIONS.
HE SHOULD FINALLY BE ABLE TO CONCENTRATE FULLY ON HIS LESSONS.
TEACHER.
YES?
RUB

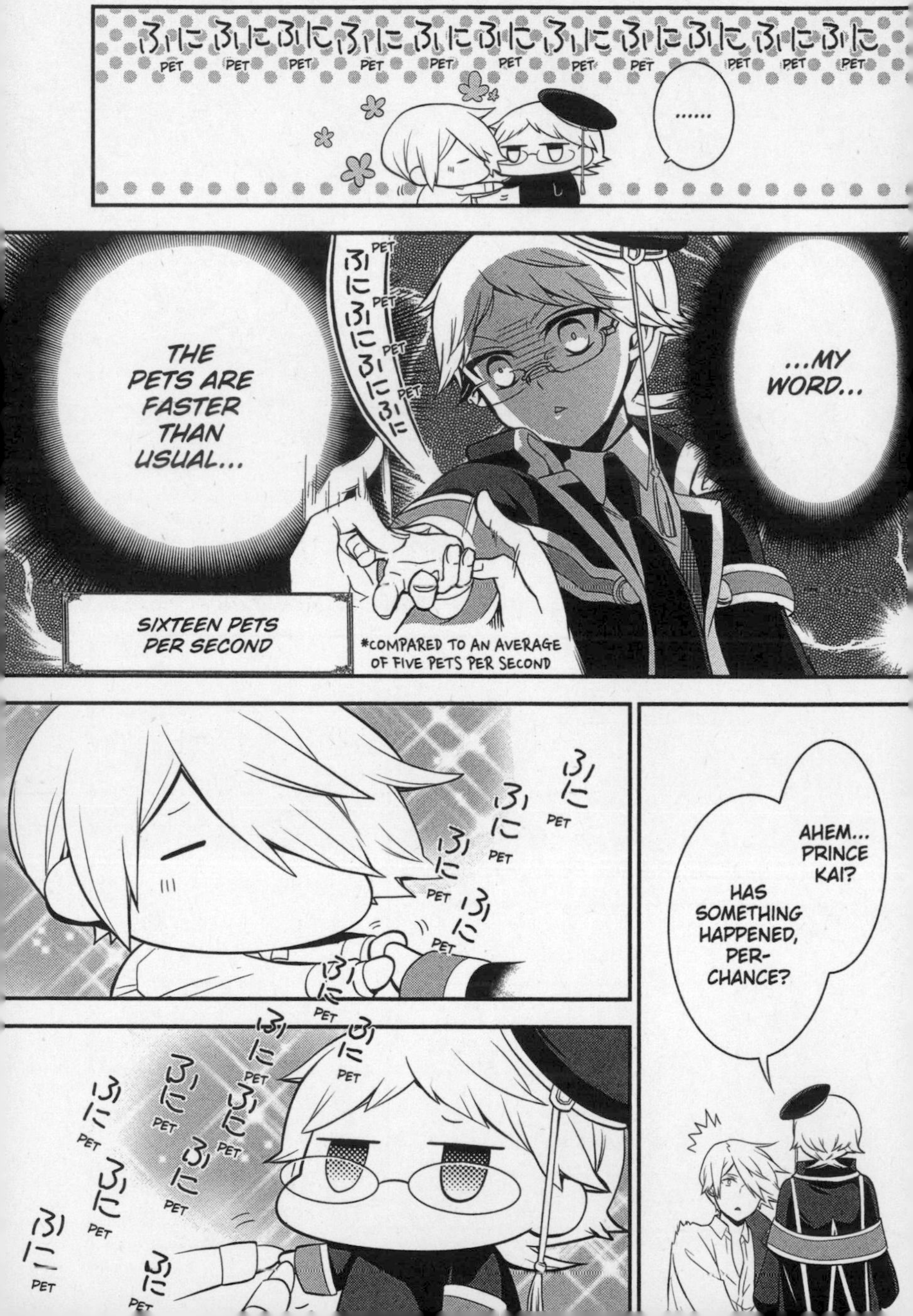
ふにふにふにふにふにふにふにふにふにふにふに
PET PET PET PET PET PET PET PET PET PET PET
......
...MY WORD...
THE PETS ARE FASTER THAN USUAL...
ふにふにふにふに
PET PET PET PET
SIXTEEN PETS PER SECOND
*COMPARED TO AN AVERAGE OF FIVE PETS PER SECOND
AHEM... PRINCE KAI?
HAS SOMETHING HAPPENED, PER-CHANCE?
ふに ふに ふに ふに ふに
PET PET PET PET PET
ふに ふに ふに ふに ふに ふに ふに ふに
PET PET PET PET PET PET PET PET

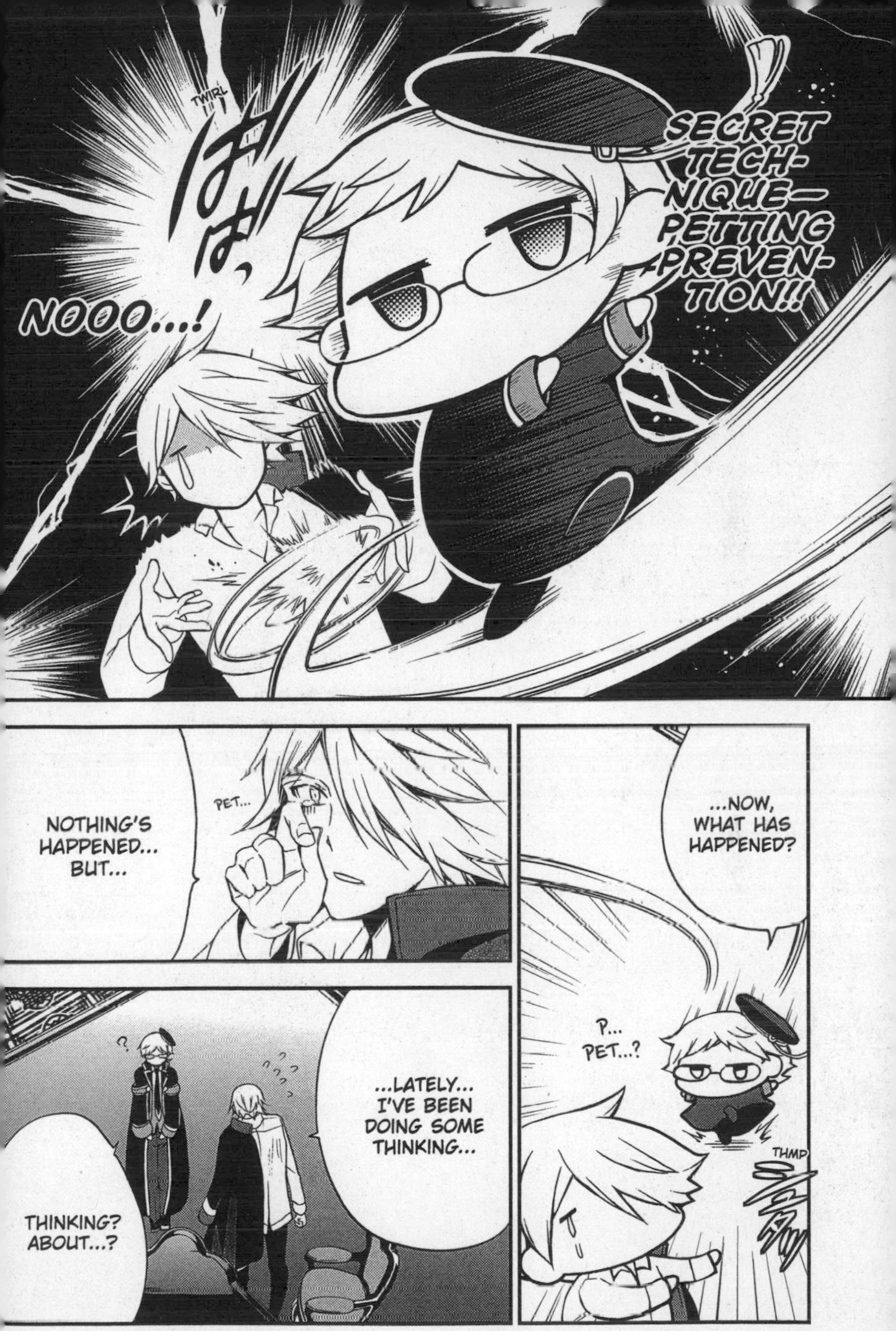

SECRET TECH-NIQUE—PETTING PREVEN-TION!!
TWIRL
ぱぱっ
NOOO...!
...NOW, WHAT HAS HAPPENED?
P... PET...?
THMP
PET...
NOTHING'S HAPPENED... BUT...
...LATELY... I'VE BEEN DOING SOME THINKING...
THINKING? ABOUT...?

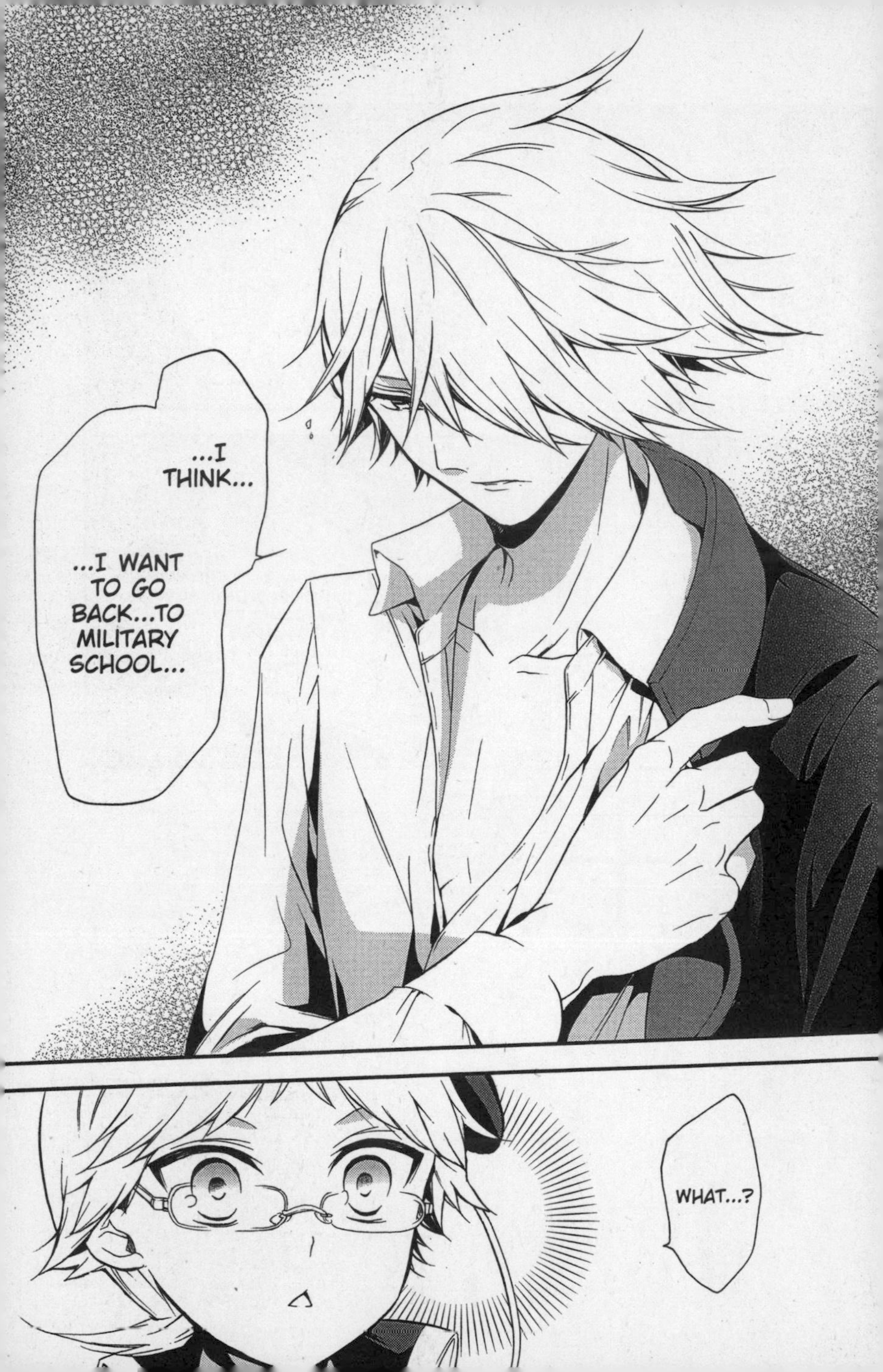
...I THINK...
...I WANT TO GO BACK...TO MILITARY SCHOOL...
WHAT...?

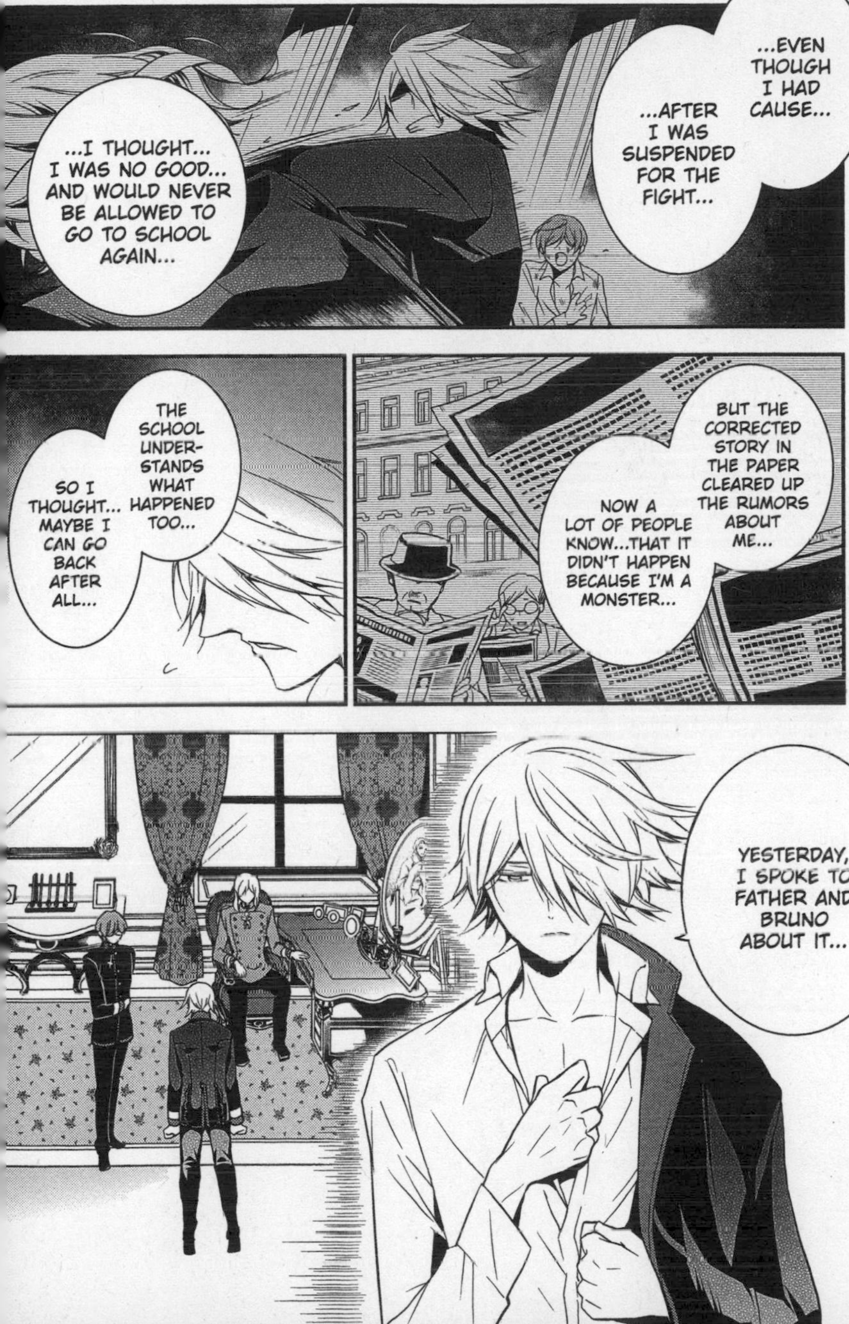
...EVEN THOUGH I HAD CAUSE...
...AFTER I WAS SUSPENDED FOR THE FIGHT...
...I THOUGHT... I WAS NO GOOD... AND WOULD NEVER BE ALLOWED TO GO TO SCHOOL AGAIN...
BUT THE CORRECTED STORY IN THE PAPER CLEARED UP THE RUMORS ABOUT ME...
NOW A LOT OF PEOPLE KNOW...THAT IT DIDN'T HAPPEN BECAUSE I'M A MONSTER...
THE SCHOOL UNDERSTANDS WHAT HAPPENED TOO...
SO I THOUGHT... MAYBE I CAN GO BACK AFTER ALL...
YESTERDAY, I SPOKE TO FATHER AND BRUNO ABOUT IT...

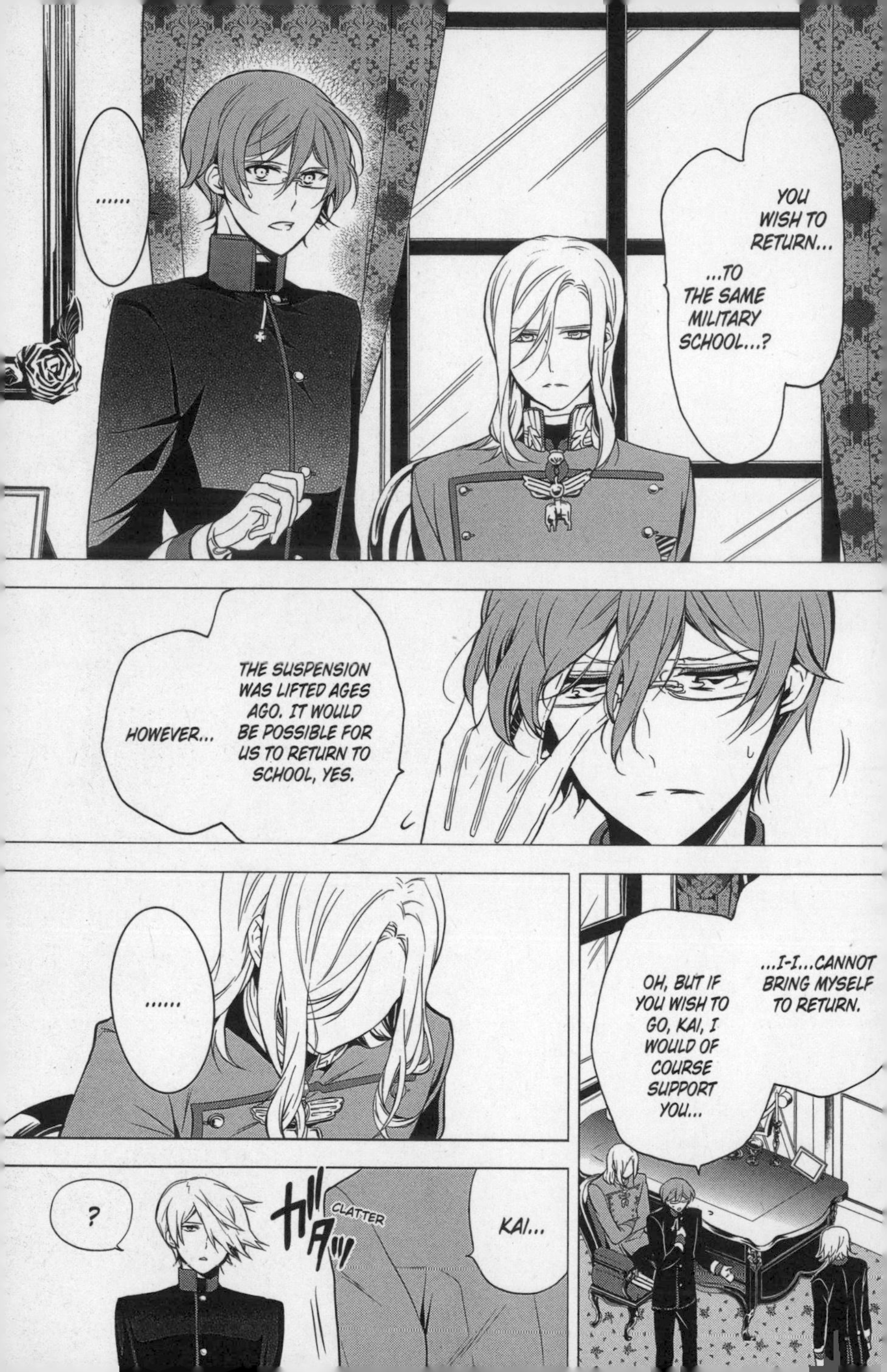
YOU WISH TO RETURN...
...TO THE SAME MILITARY SCHOOL...?
......
THE SUSPENSION WAS LIFTED AGES AGO. IT WOULD BE POSSIBLE FOR US TO RETURN TO SCHOOL, YES.
HOWEVER...
...I-I...CANNOT BRING MYSELF TO RETURN.
OH, BUT IF YOU WISH TO GO, KAI, I WOULD OF COURSE SUPPORT YOU...
......
KAI...
ガタッ
CLATTER
?

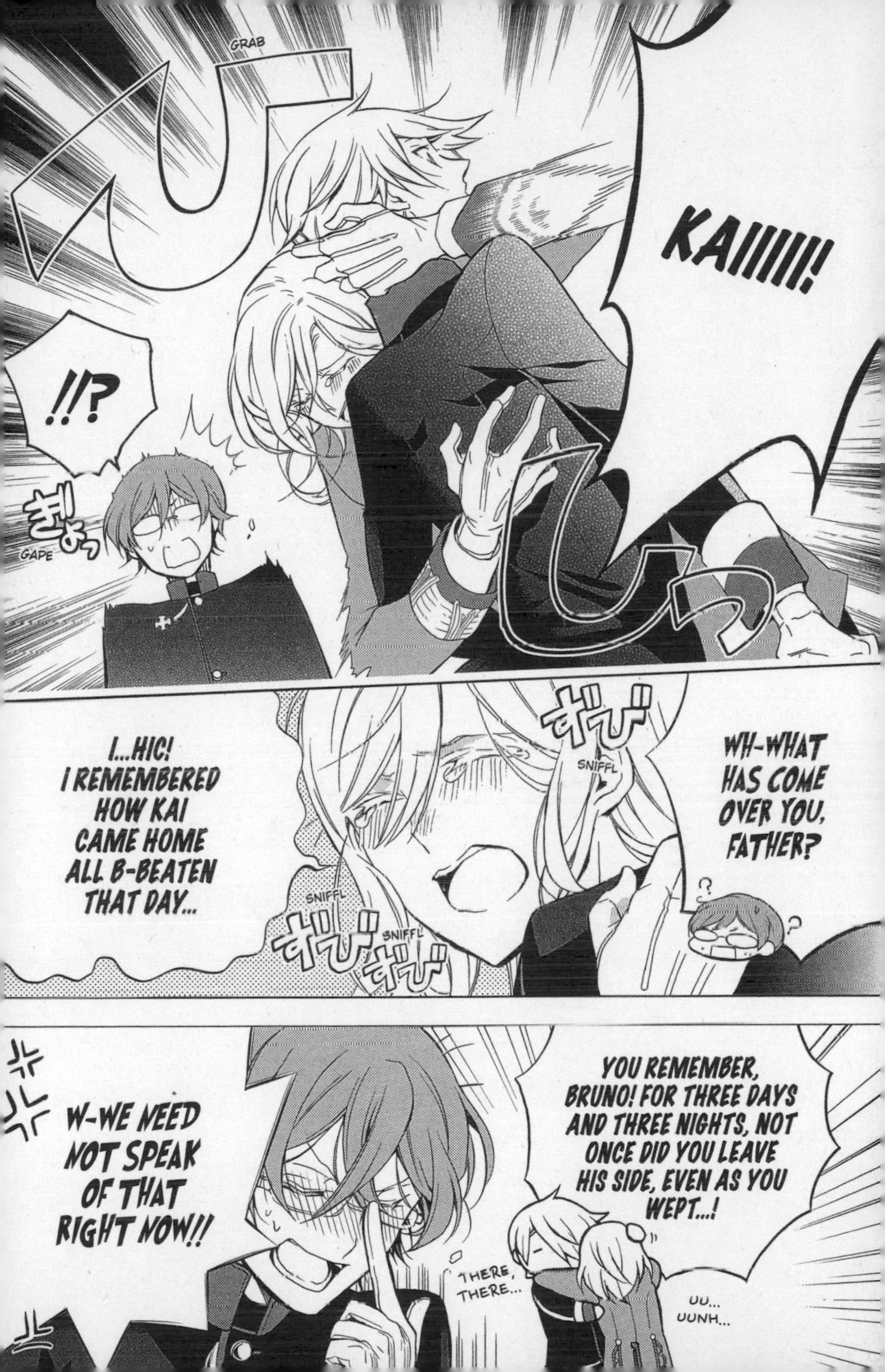
KAIIIIII!
GRAB
!!?
ぎょっ
GAPE
WH-WHAT HAS COME OVER YOU, FATHER?
ずび
SNIFFL
I...HIC! I REMEMBERED HOW KAI CAME HOME ALL B-BEATEN THAT DAY...
SNIFFL
ずびずび
SNIFFL
YOU REMEMBER, BRUNO! FOR THREE DAYS AND THREE NIGHTS, NOT ONCE DID YOU LEAVE HIS SIDE, EVEN AS YOU WEPT...!
UU... UUNH...
THERE, THERE...
W-WE NEED NOT SPEAK OF THAT RIGHT NOW!!

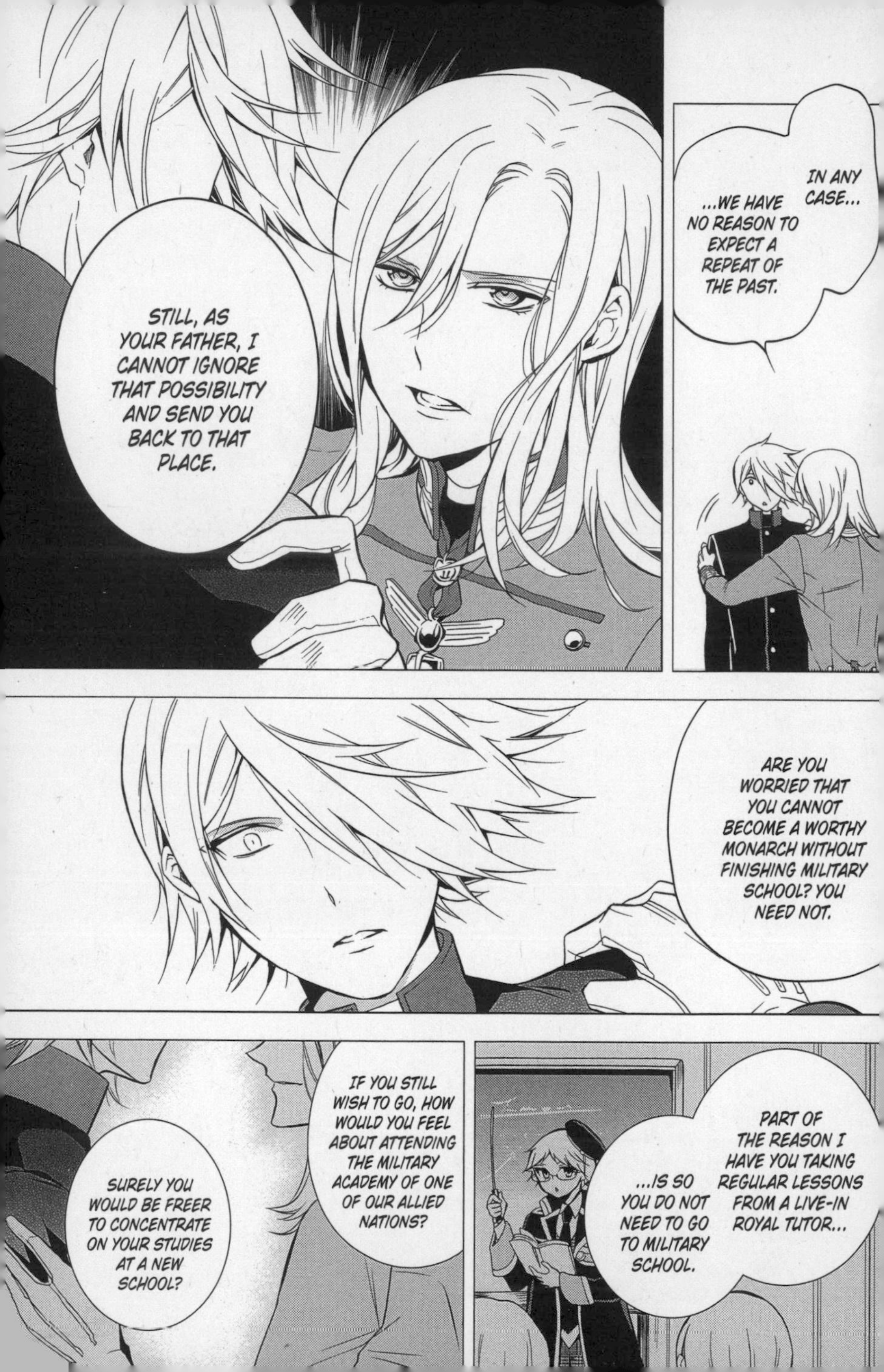
IN ANY CASE...
...WE HAVE NO REASON TO EXPECT A REPEAT OF THE PAST.
STILL, AS YOUR FATHER, I CANNOT IGNORE THAT POSSIBILITY AND SEND YOU BACK TO THAT PLACE.
ARE YOU WORRIED THAT YOU CANNOT BECOME A WORTHY MONARCH WITHOUT FINISHING MILITARY SCHOOL? YOU NEED NOT.
PART OF THE REASON I HAVE YOU TAKING REGULAR LESSONS FROM A LIVE-IN ROYAL TUTOR...
...IS SO YOU DO NOT NEED TO GO TO MILITARY SCHOOL.
IF YOU STILL WISH TO GO, HOW WOULD YOU FEEL ABOUT ATTENDING THE MILITARY ACADEMY OF ONE OF OUR ALLIED NATIONS?
SURELY YOU WOULD BE FREER TO CONCENTRATE ON YOUR STUDIES AT A NEW SCHOOL?

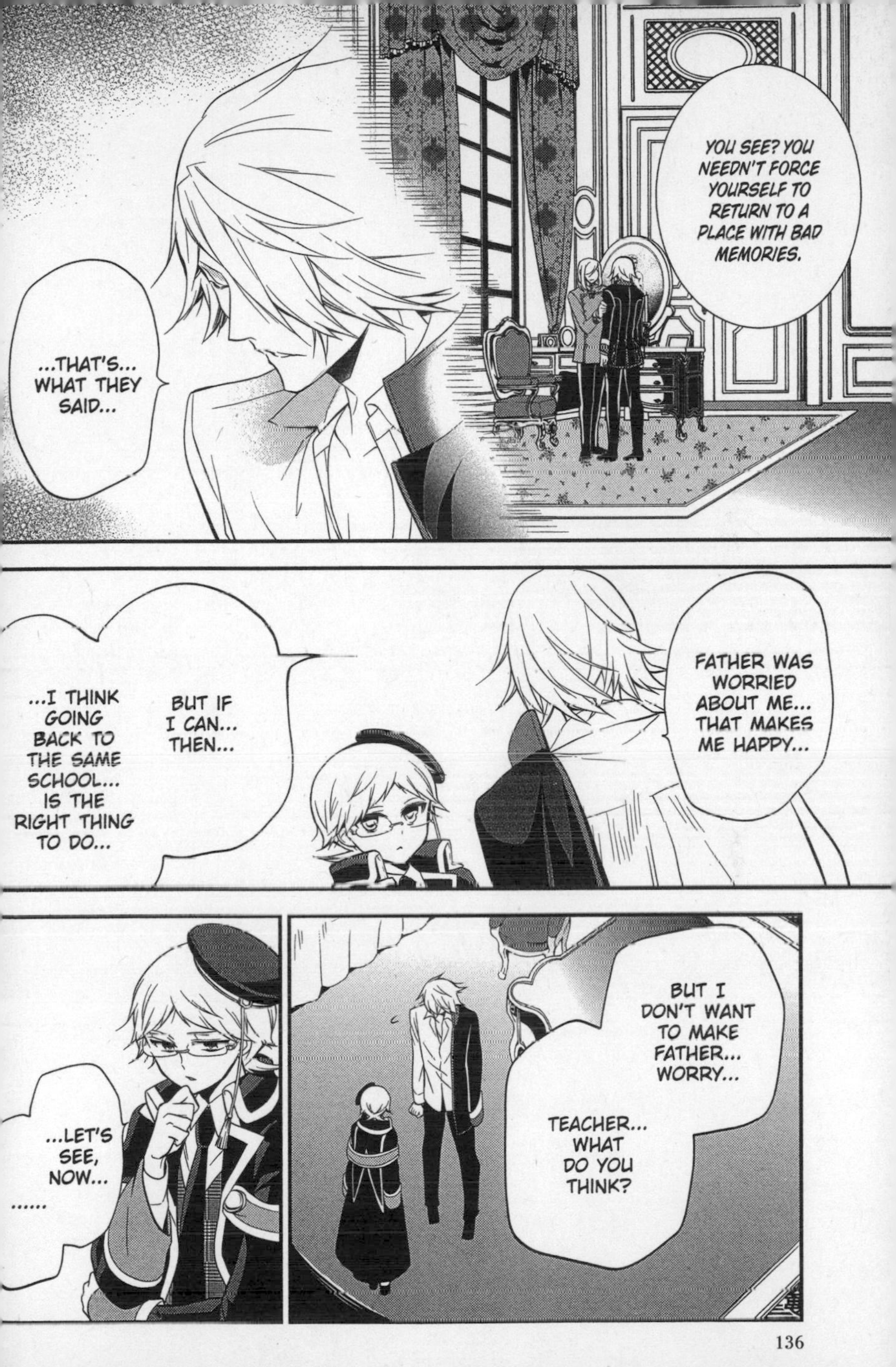
YOU SEE? YOU NEEDN'T FORCE YOURSELF TO RETURN TO A PLACE WITH BAD MEMORIES.
...THAT'S... WHAT THEY SAID...
FATHER WAS WORRIED ABOUT ME... THAT MAKES ME HAPPY...
BUT IF I CAN... THEN...
...I THINK GOING BACK TO THE SAME SCHOOL... IS THE RIGHT THING TO DO...
BUT I DON'T WANT TO MAKE FATHER... WORRY...
TEACHER... WHAT DO YOU THINK?
...LET'S SEE, NOW...
......

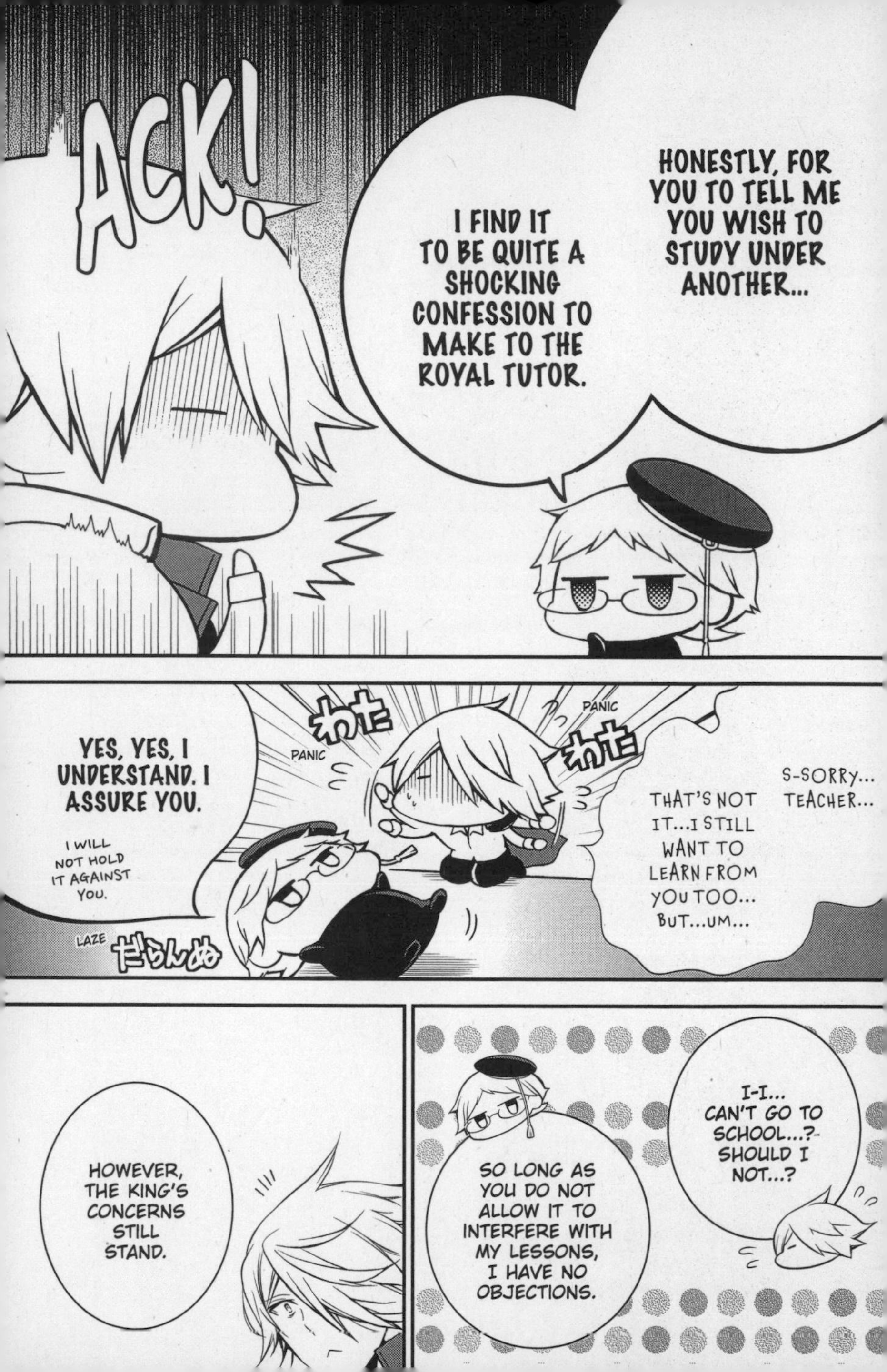
HONESTLY, FOR YOU TO TELL ME YOU WISH TO STUDY UNDER ANOTHER...
I FIND IT TO BE QUITE A SHOCKING CONFESSION TO MAKE TO THE ROYAL TUTOR.
ACK!
S-SORRY... TEACHER...
THAT'S NOT IT...I STILL WANT TO LEARN FROM YOU TOO... BUT...UM...
PANIC
わた
PANIC
わた
YES, YES, I UNDERSTAND. I ASSURE YOU.
I WILL NOT HOLD IT AGAINST YOU.
LAZE
だらんぬ
I-I... CAN'T GO TO SCHOOL...? SHOULD I NOT...?
SO LONG AS YOU DO NOT ALLOW IT TO INTERFERE WITH MY LESSONS, I HAVE NO OBJECTIONS.
HOWEVER, THE KING'S CONCERNS STILL STAND.

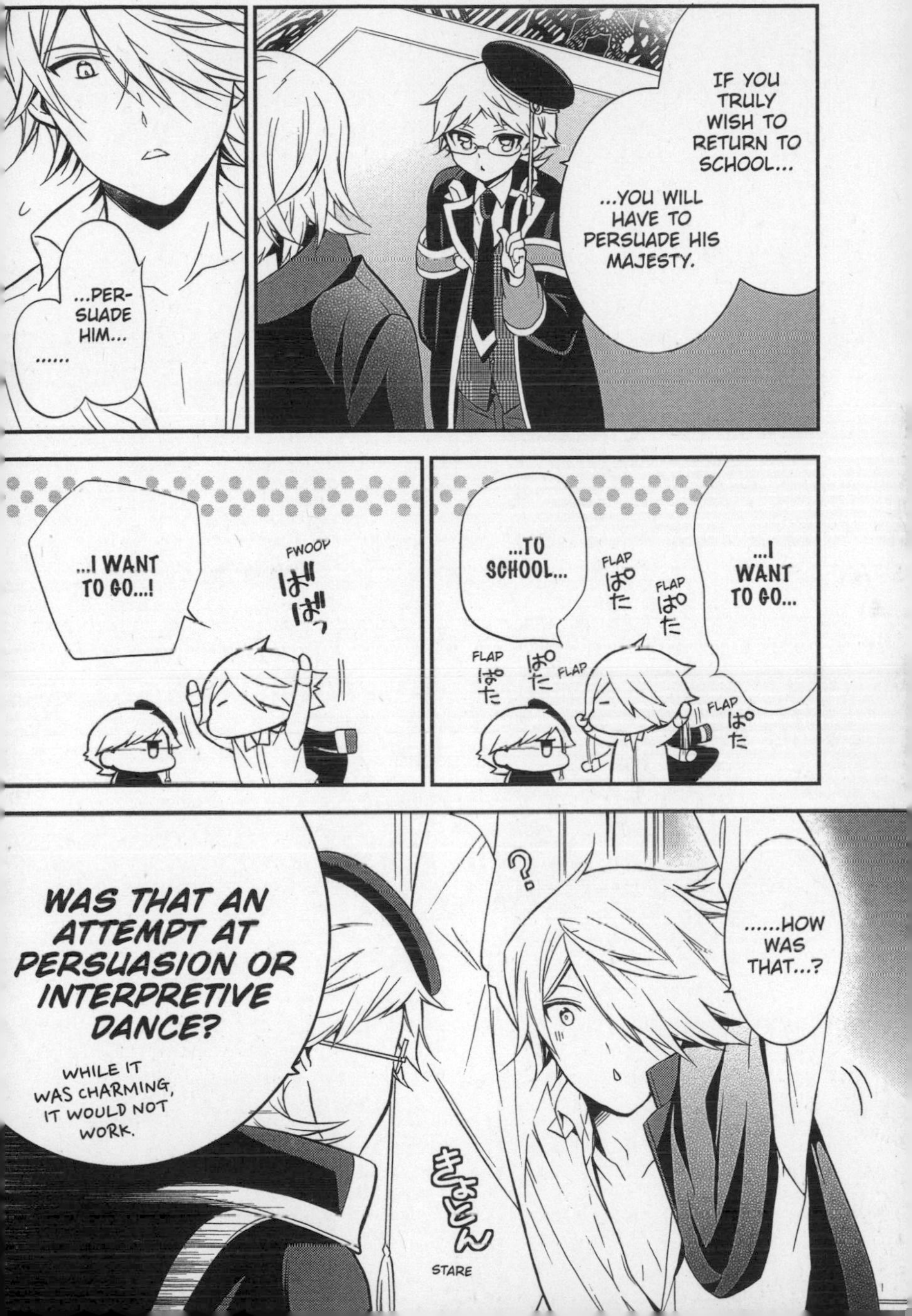
IF YOU TRULY WISH TO RETURN TO SCHOOL...
...YOU WILL HAVE TO PERSUADE HIS MAJESTY.
...PER-SUADE HIM...
......
...I WANT TO GO...
FLAP ぱた
FLAP ぱた
...TO SCHOOL...
FLAP ぱた
FLAP ぱた
FLAP ぱた
FWOOP ばばっ
...I WANT TO GO...!
......HOW WAS THAT...?
?
きょとん
STARE
WAS THAT AN ATTEMPT AT PERSUASION OR INTERPRETIVE DANCE?
WHILE IT WAS CHARMING, IT WOULD NOT WORK.

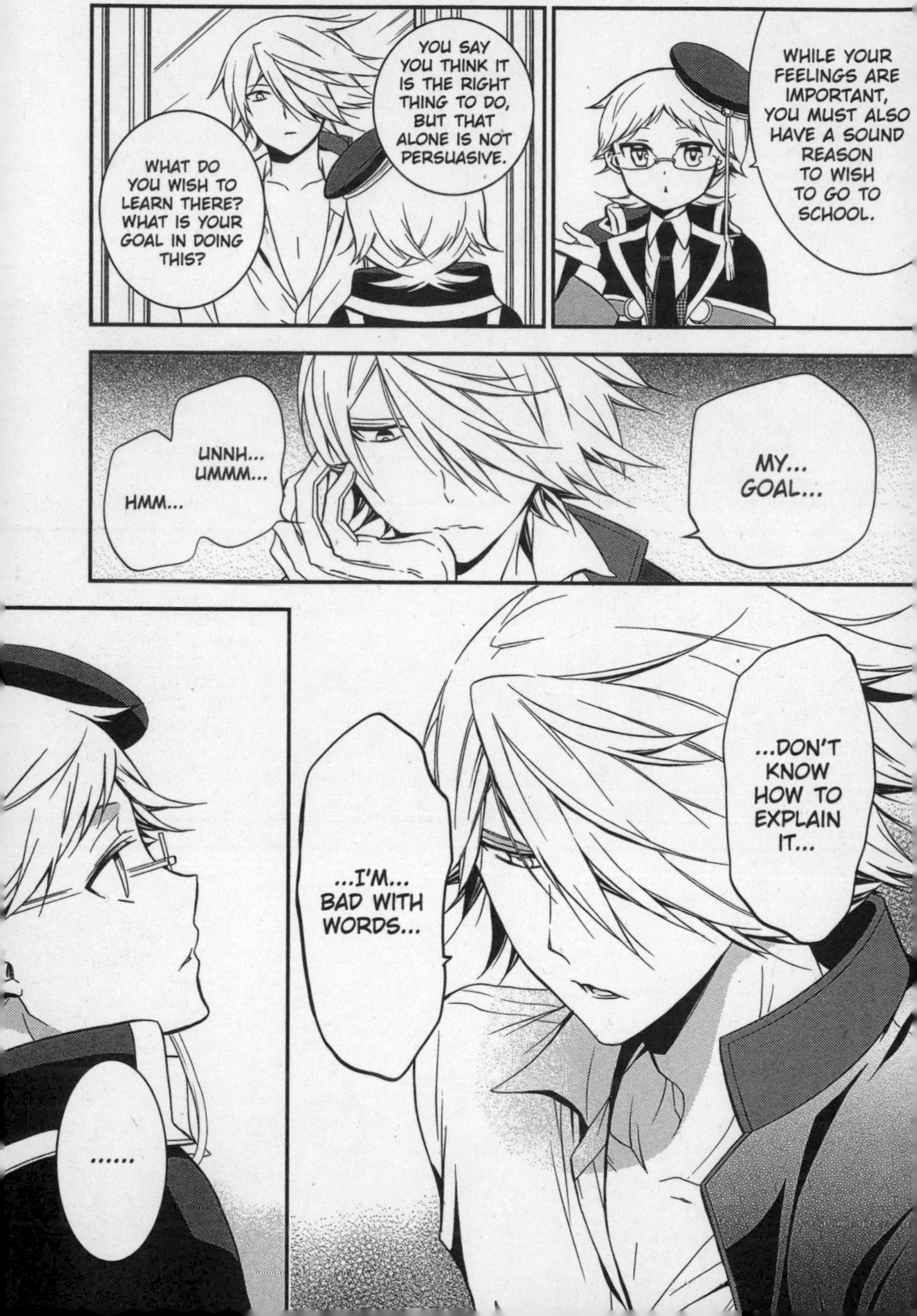
WHILE YOUR FEELINGS ARE IMPORTANT, YOU MUST ALSO HAVE A SOUND REASON TO WISH TO GO TO SCHOOL.
YOU SAY YOU THINK IT IS THE RIGHT THING TO DO, BUT THAT ALONE IS NOT PERSUASIVE.
WHAT DO YOU WISH TO LEARN THERE? WHAT IS YOUR GOAL IN DOING THIS?
MY... GOAL...
UNNH... UMMM... HMM...
...DON'T KNOW HOW TO EXPLAIN IT...
...I'M... BAD WITH WORDS...
......

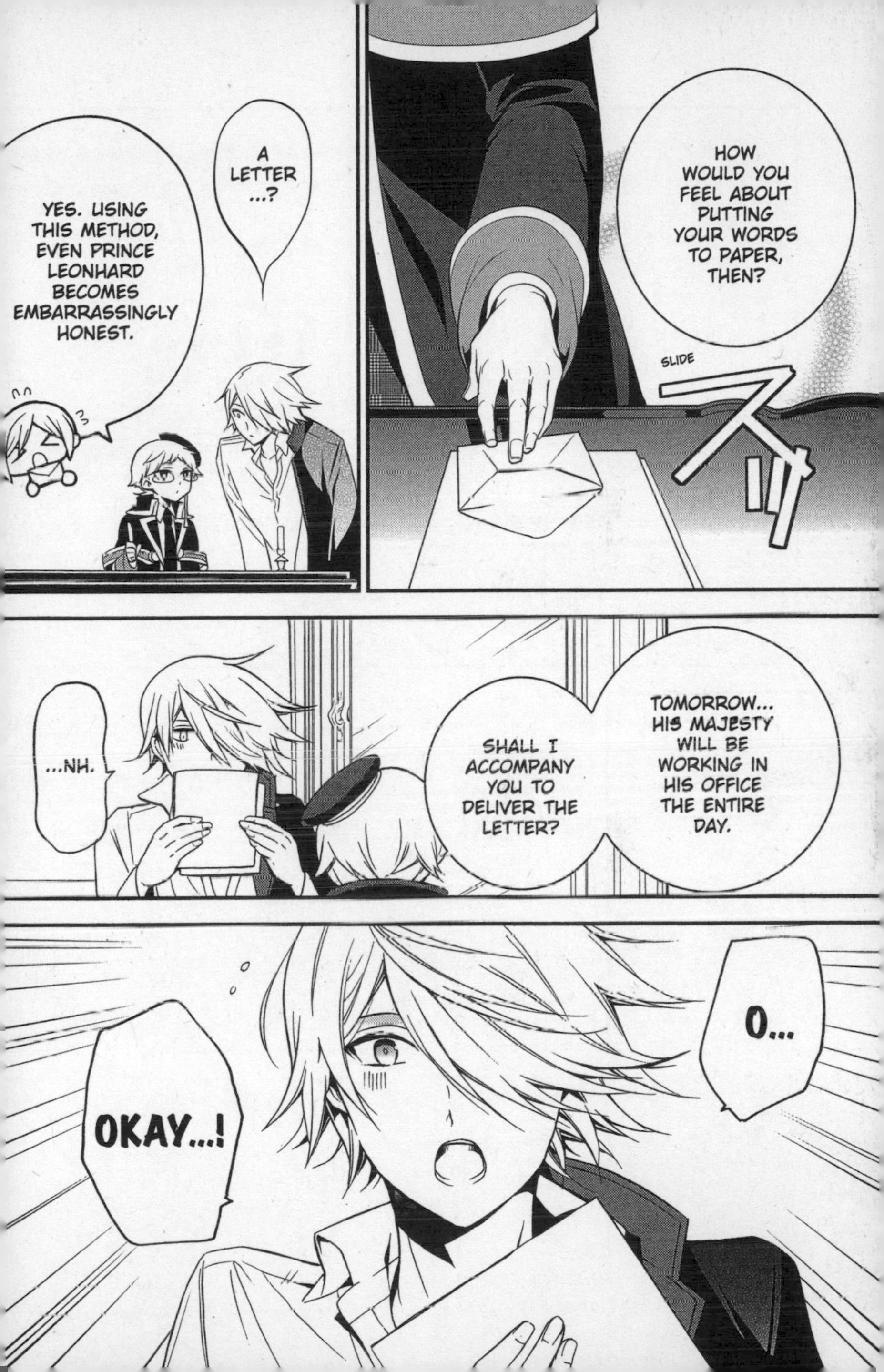
HOW WOULD YOU FEEL ABOUT PUTTING YOUR WORDS TO PAPER, THEN?
SLIDE
A LETTER ...?
YES. USING THIS METHOD, EVEN PRINCE LEONHARD BECOMES EMBARRASSINGLY HONEST.
TOMORROW... HIS MAJESTY WILL BE WORKING IN HIS OFFICE THE ENTIRE DAY.
SHALL I ACCOMPANY YOU TO DELIVER THE LETTER?
...NH.
O...
OKAY...!

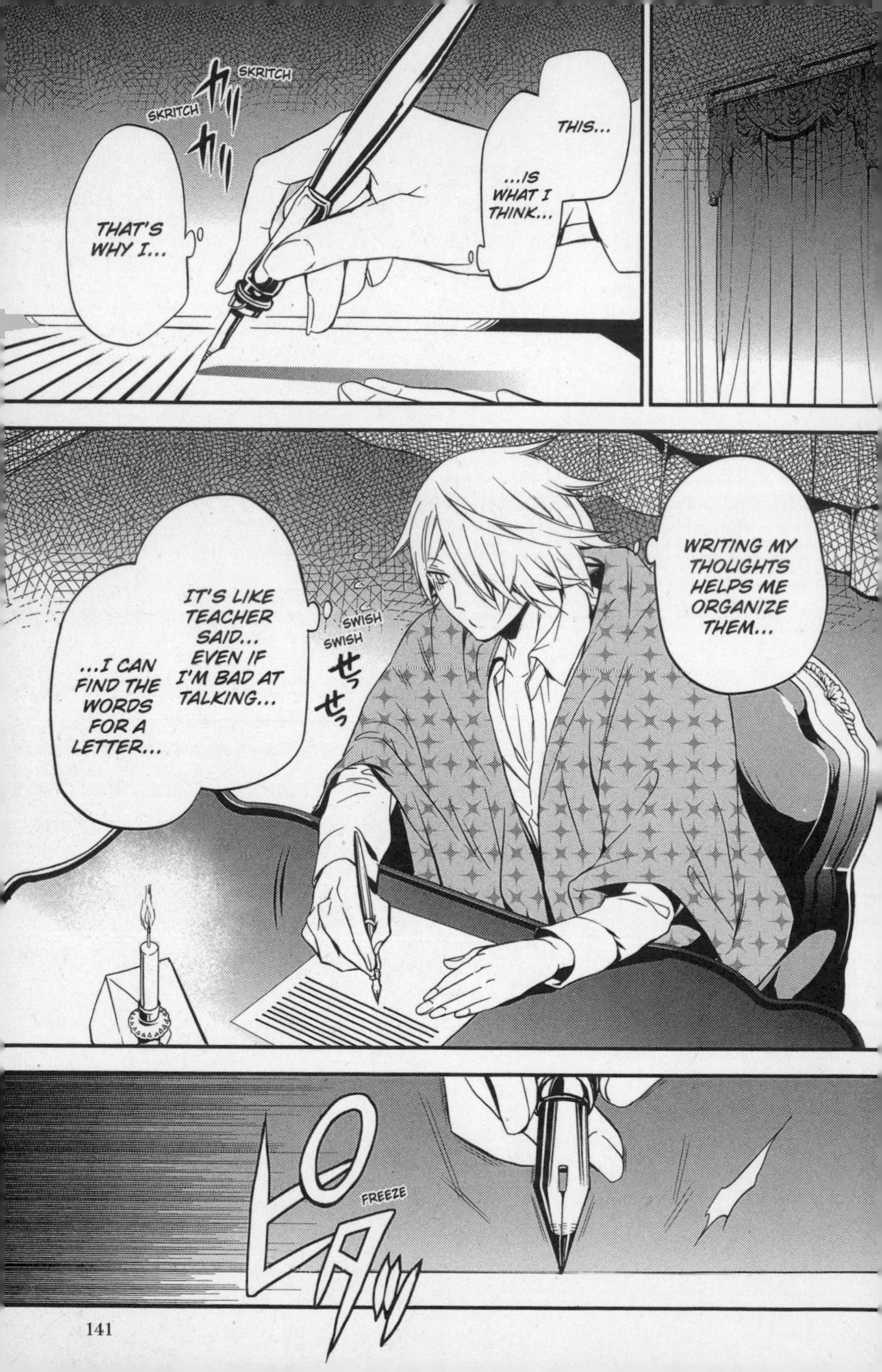
THIS...
...IS WHAT I THINK...
SKRITCH
SKRITCH
THAT'S WHY I...
WRITING MY THOUGHTS HELPS ME ORGANIZE THEM...
SWISH
SWISH
IT'S LIKE TEACHER SAID... EVEN IF I'M BAD AT TALKING...
...I CAN FIND THE WORDS FOR A LETTER...
FREEZE

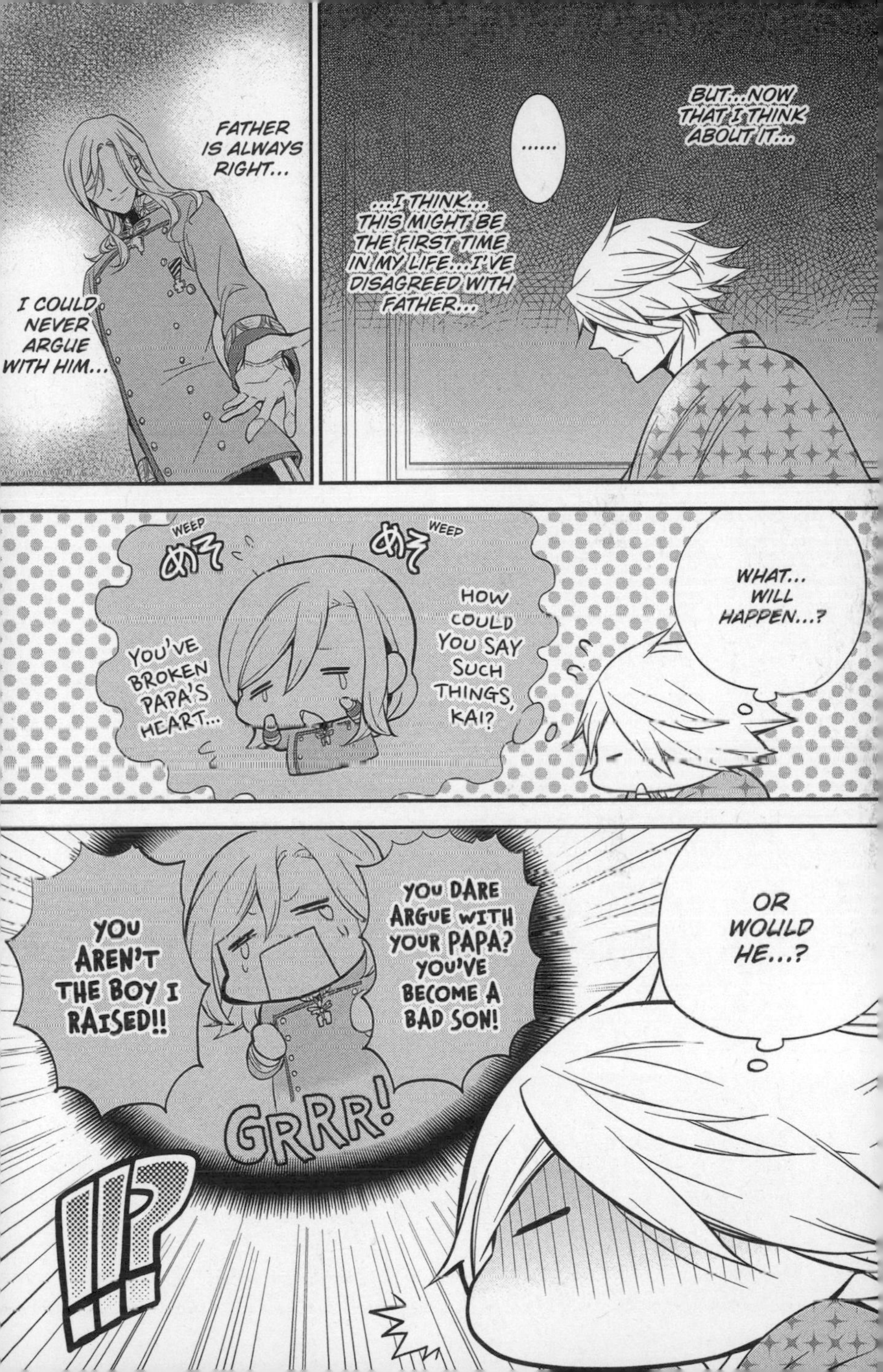
BUT...NOW THAT I THINK ABOUT IT...
......
...I THINK... THIS MIGHT BE THE FIRST TIME IN MY LIFE...I'VE DISAGREED WITH FATHER...
FATHER IS ALWAYS RIGHT...
I COULD NEVER ARGUE WITH HIM...
WHAT... WILL HAPPEN...?
WEEP めそ
WEEP めそ
HOW COULD YOU SAY SUCH THINGS, KAI?
YOU'VE BROKEN PAPA'S HEART...
OR WOULD HE...?
YOU DARE ARGUE WITH YOUR PAPA? YOU'VE BECOME A BAD SON!
YOU AREN'T THE BOY I RAISED!!
GRRR!
!!?

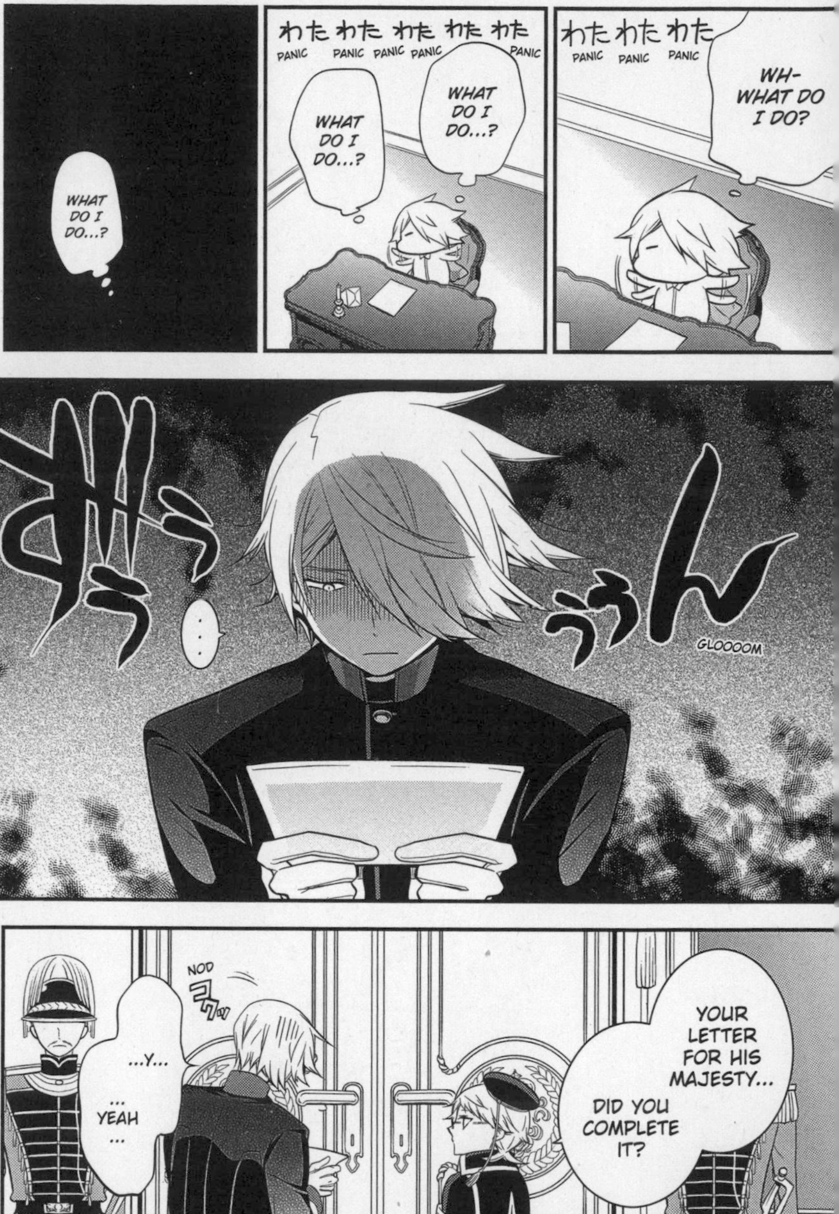
わた わた わた
PANIC PANIC PANIC
WH- WHAT DO I DO?
わた わた わた わた わた
PANIC PANIC PANIC PANIC PANIC
WHAT DO I DO...?
WHAT DO I DO...?
WHAT DO I DO...?
...
GLOOOOM
YOUR LETTER FOR HIS MAJESTY...
DID YOU COMPLETE IT?
NOD
...Y...
... YEAH ...

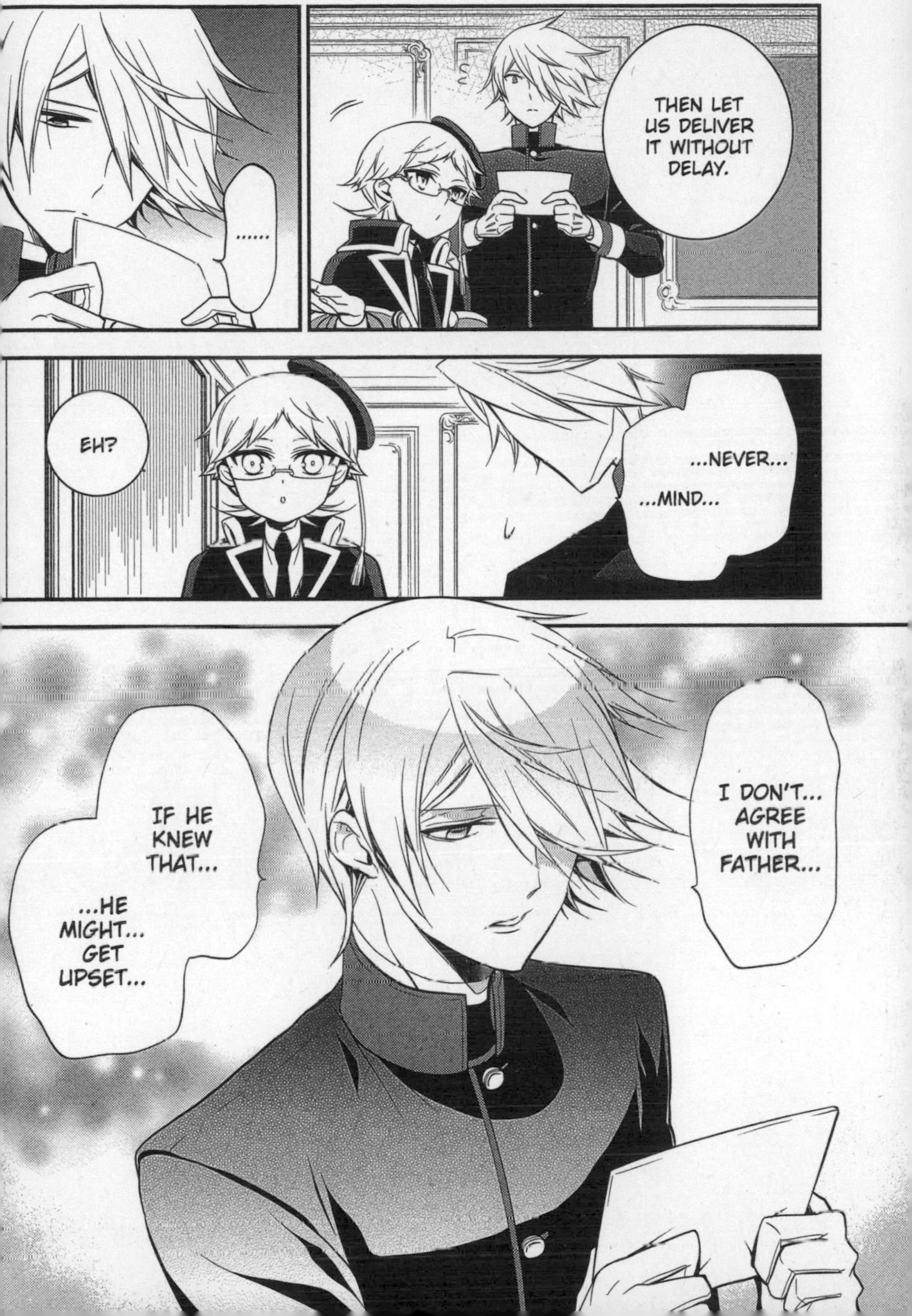
THEN LET US DELIVER IT WITHOUT DELAY.
......
...NEVER...
...MIND...
EH?
I DON'T... AGREE WITH FATHER...
IF HE KNEW THAT...
...HE MIGHT... GET UPSET...

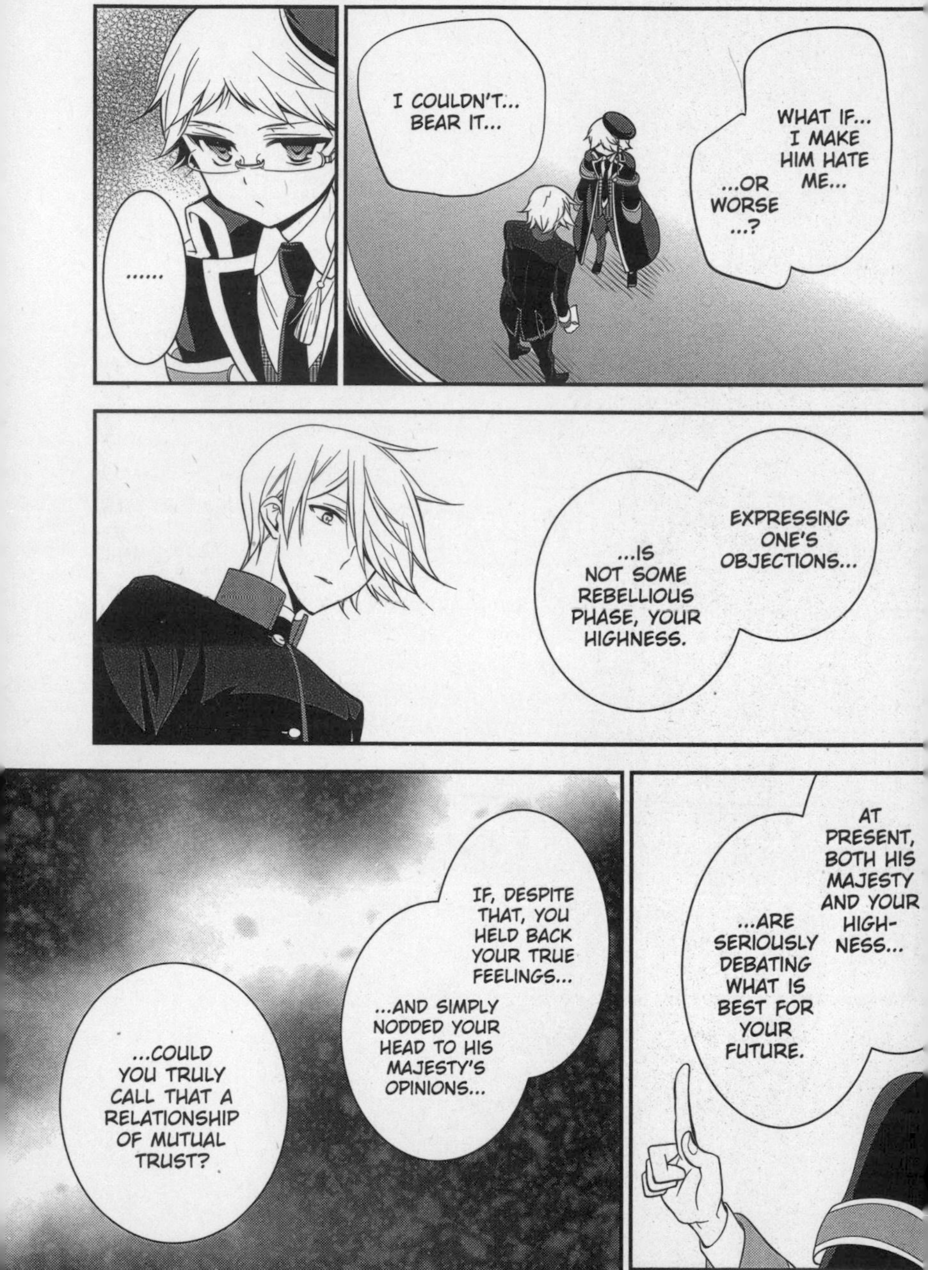
WHAT IF... I MAKE HIM HATE ME...
...OR WORSE ...?
I COULDN'T... BEAR IT...
......
EXPRESSING ONE'S OBJECTIONS...
...IS NOT SOME REBELLIOUS PHASE, YOUR HIGHNESS.
AT PRESENT, BOTH HIS MAJESTY AND YOUR HIGH-NESS...
...ARE SERIOUSLY DEBATING WHAT IS BEST FOR YOUR FUTURE.
IF, DESPITE THAT, YOU HELD BACK YOUR TRUE FEELINGS...
...AND SIMPLY NODDED YOUR HEAD TO HIS MAJESTY'S OPINIONS...
...COULD YOU TRULY CALL THAT A RELATIONSHIP OF MUTUAL TRUST?

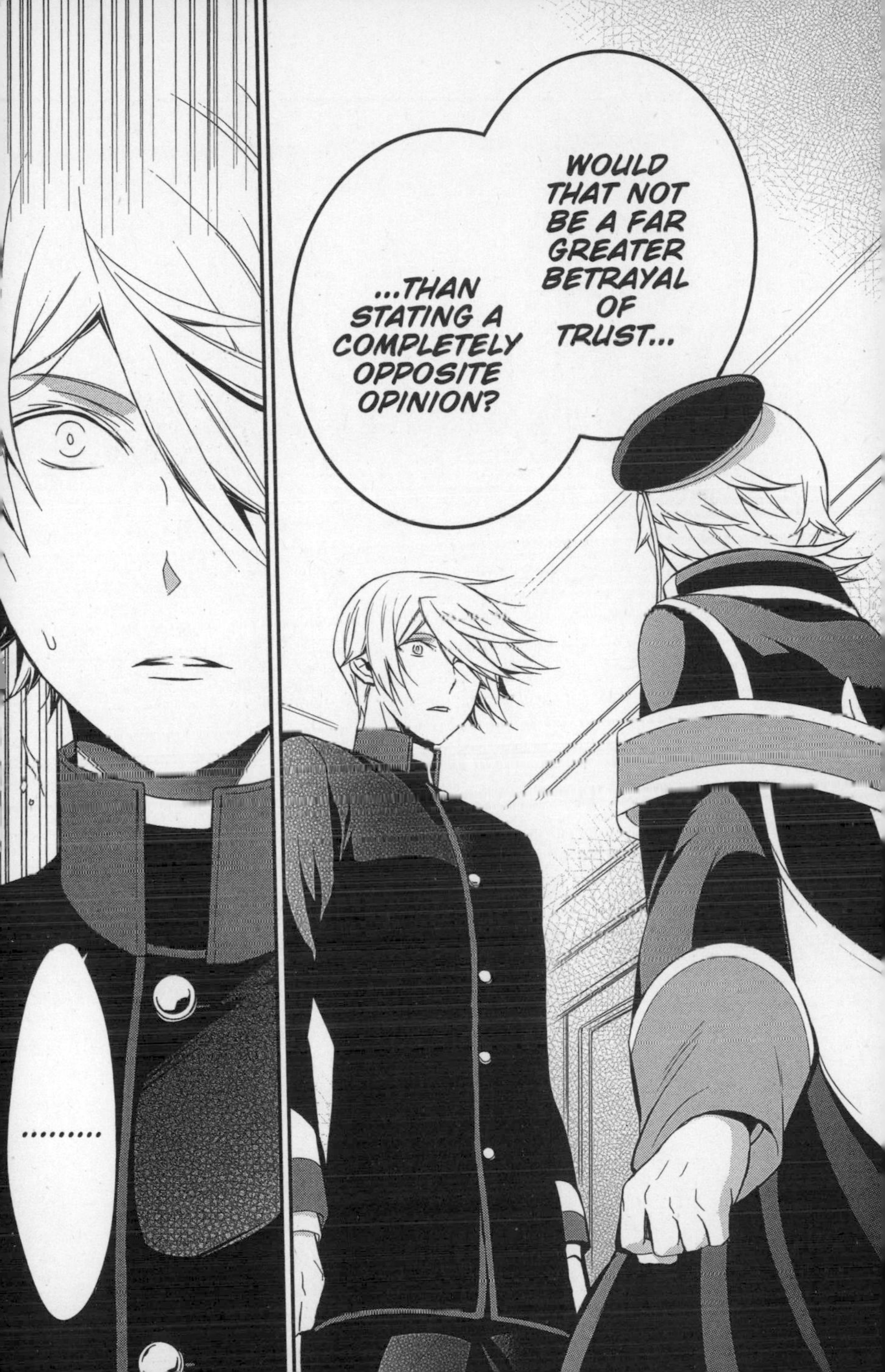
WOULD THAT NOT BE A FAR GREATER BETRAYAL OF TRUST...
...THAN STATING A COMPLETELY OPPOSITE OPINION?
....

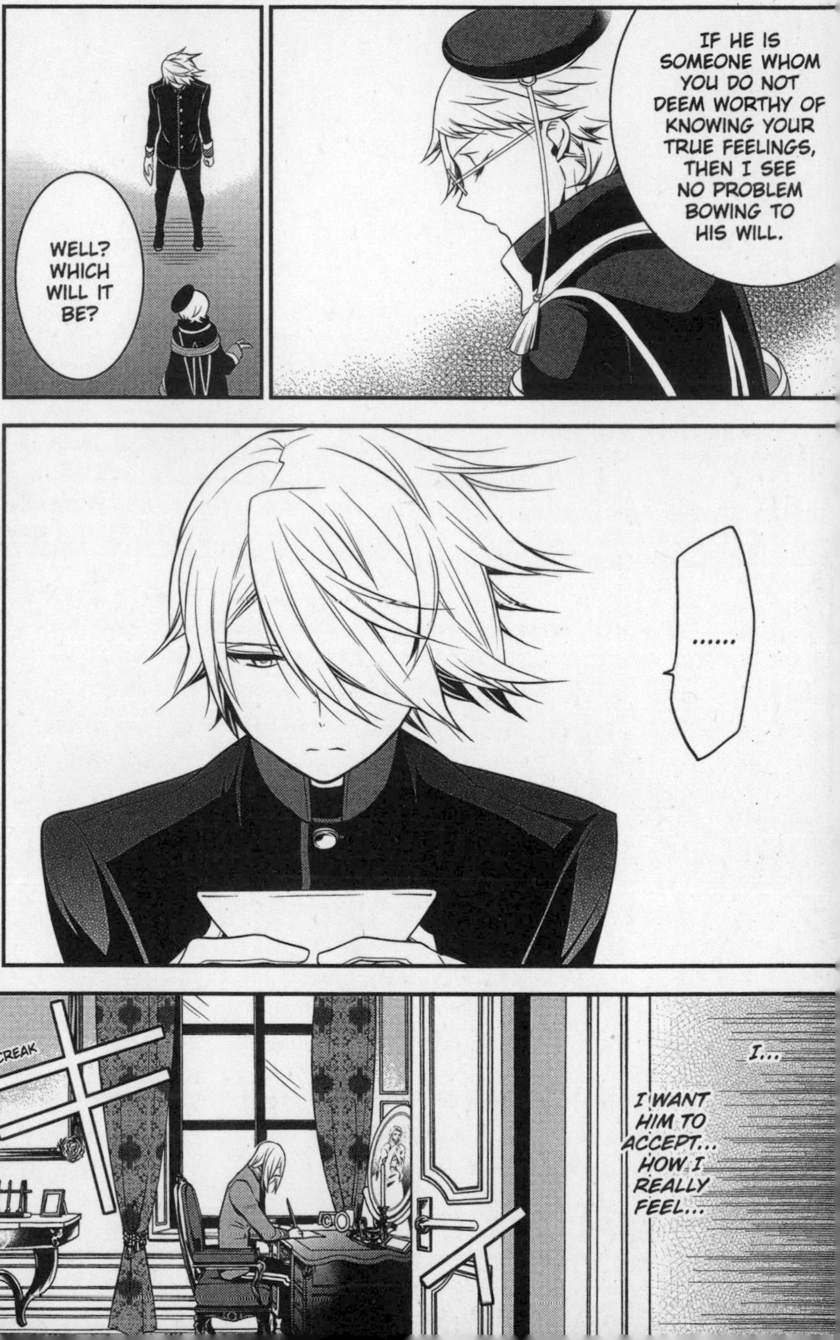
IF HE IS SOMEONE WHOM YOU DO NOT DEEM WORTHY OF KNOWING YOUR TRUE FEELINGS, THEN I SEE NO PROBLEM BOWING TO HIS WILL.
WELL? WHICH WILL IT BE?
......
I...
I WANT HIM TO ACCEPT... HOW I REALLY FEEL...
CREAK

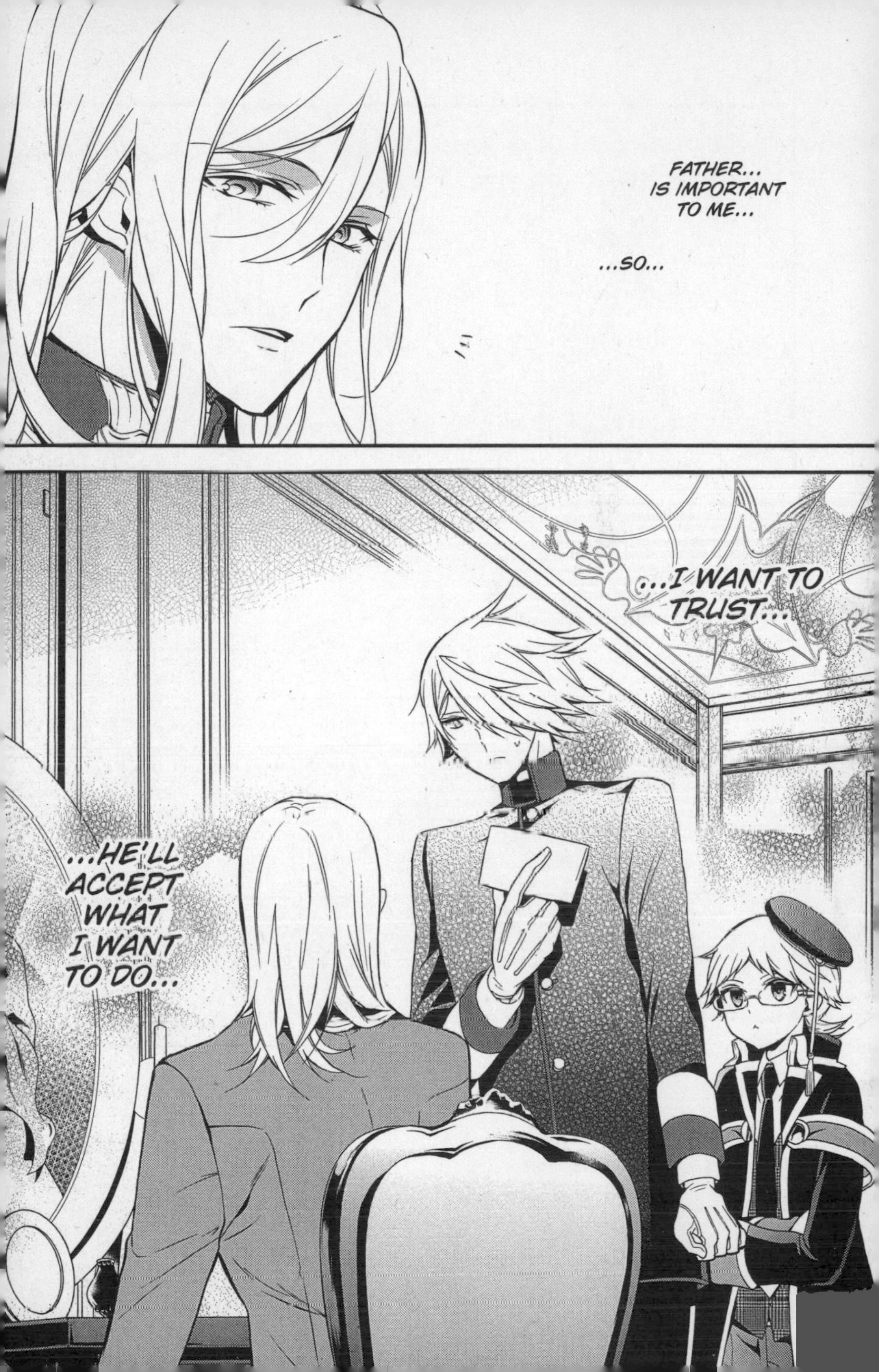
FATHER... IS IMPORTANT TO ME...
...SO...
...I WANT TO TRUST...
...HE'LL ACCEPT WHAT I WANT TO DO...

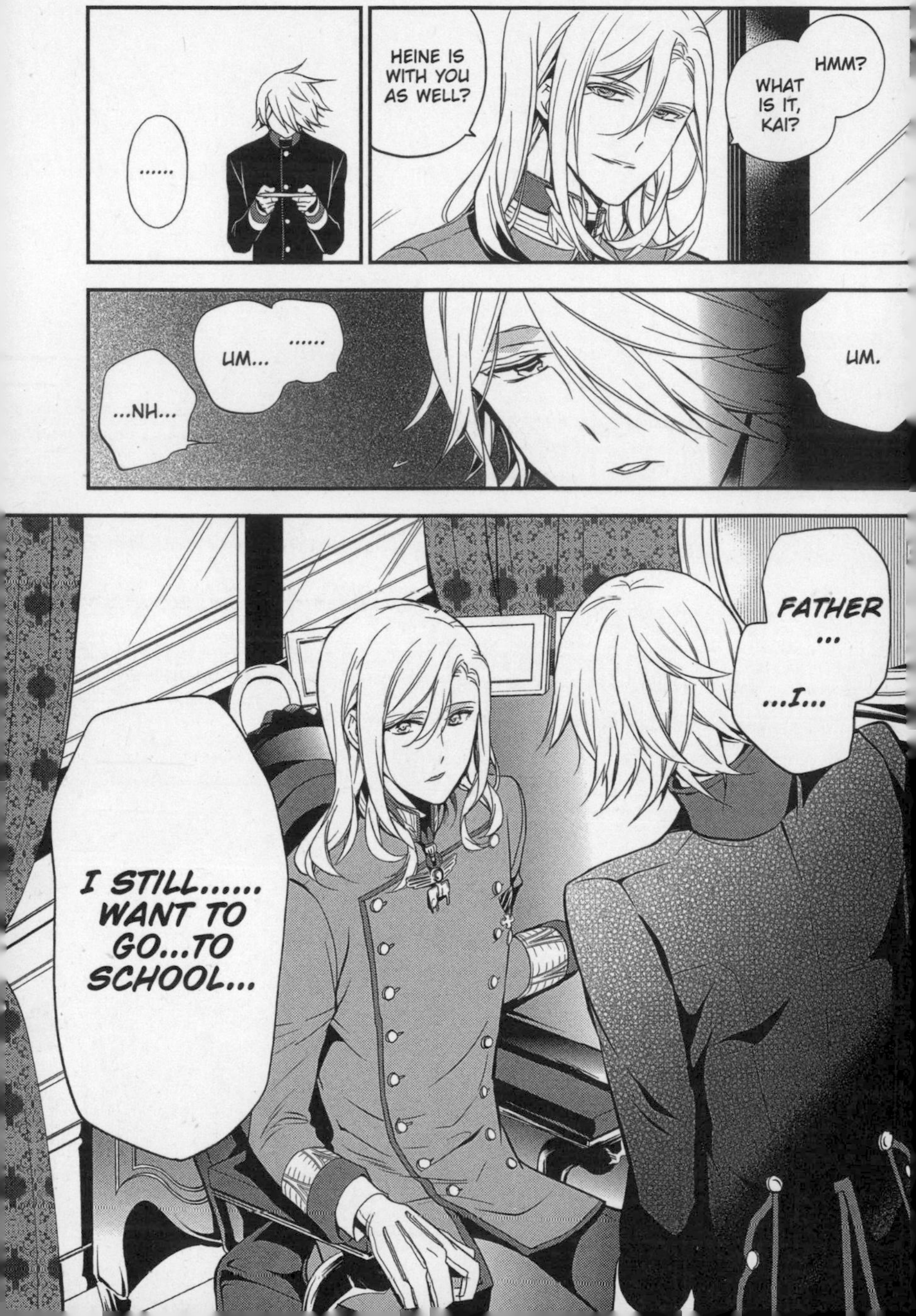
HMM? WHAT IS IT, KAI?
HEINE IS WITH YOU AS WELL?
......
UM.
......
UM...
...NH...
FATHER ...
...I...
I STILL...... WANT TO GO...TO SCHOOL...

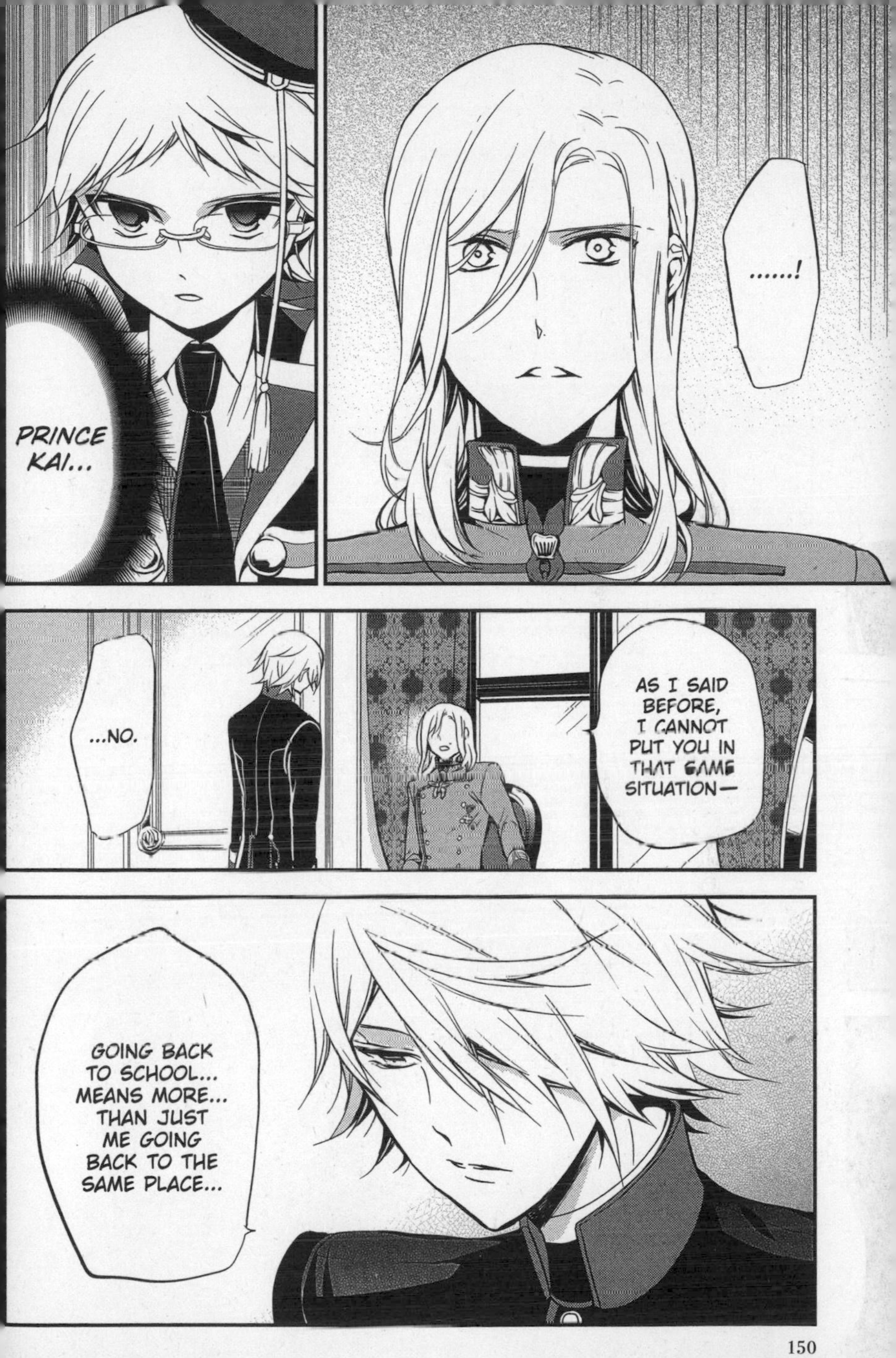
......!
PRINCE KAI...
AS I SAID BEFORE, I CANNOT PUT YOU IN THAT SAME SITUATION—
...NO.
GOING BACK TO SCHOOL... MEANS MORE... THAN JUST ME GOING BACK TO THE SAME PLACE...

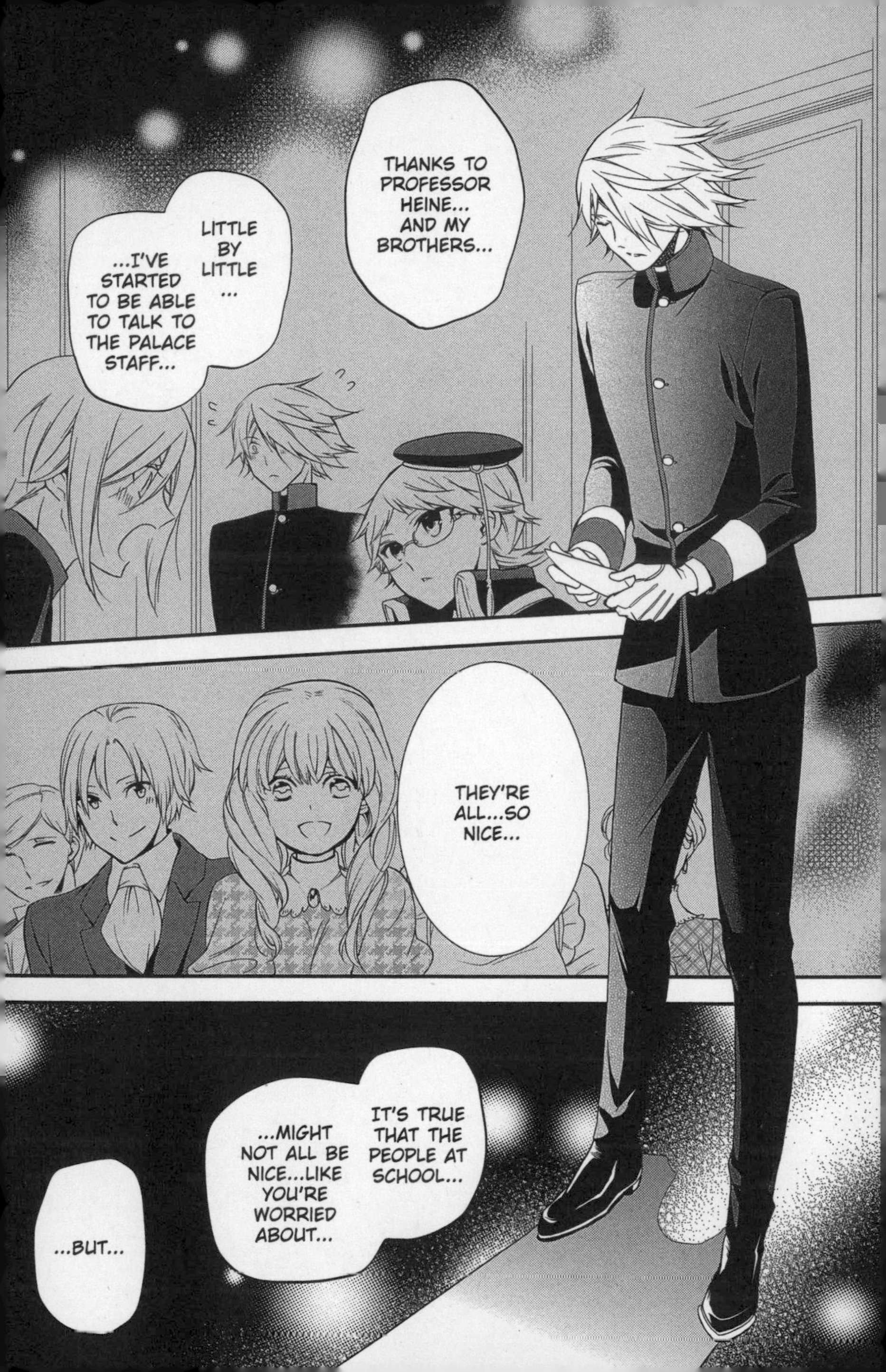
THANKS TO PROFESSOR HEINE... AND MY BROTHERS...
LITTLE BY LITTLE...
...I'VE STARTED TO BE ABLE TO TALK TO THE PALACE STAFF...
THEY'RE ALL...SO NICE...
IT'S TRUE THAT THE PEOPLE AT SCHOOL...
...MIGHT NOT ALL BE NICE...LIKE YOU'RE WORRIED ABOUT...
...BUT...

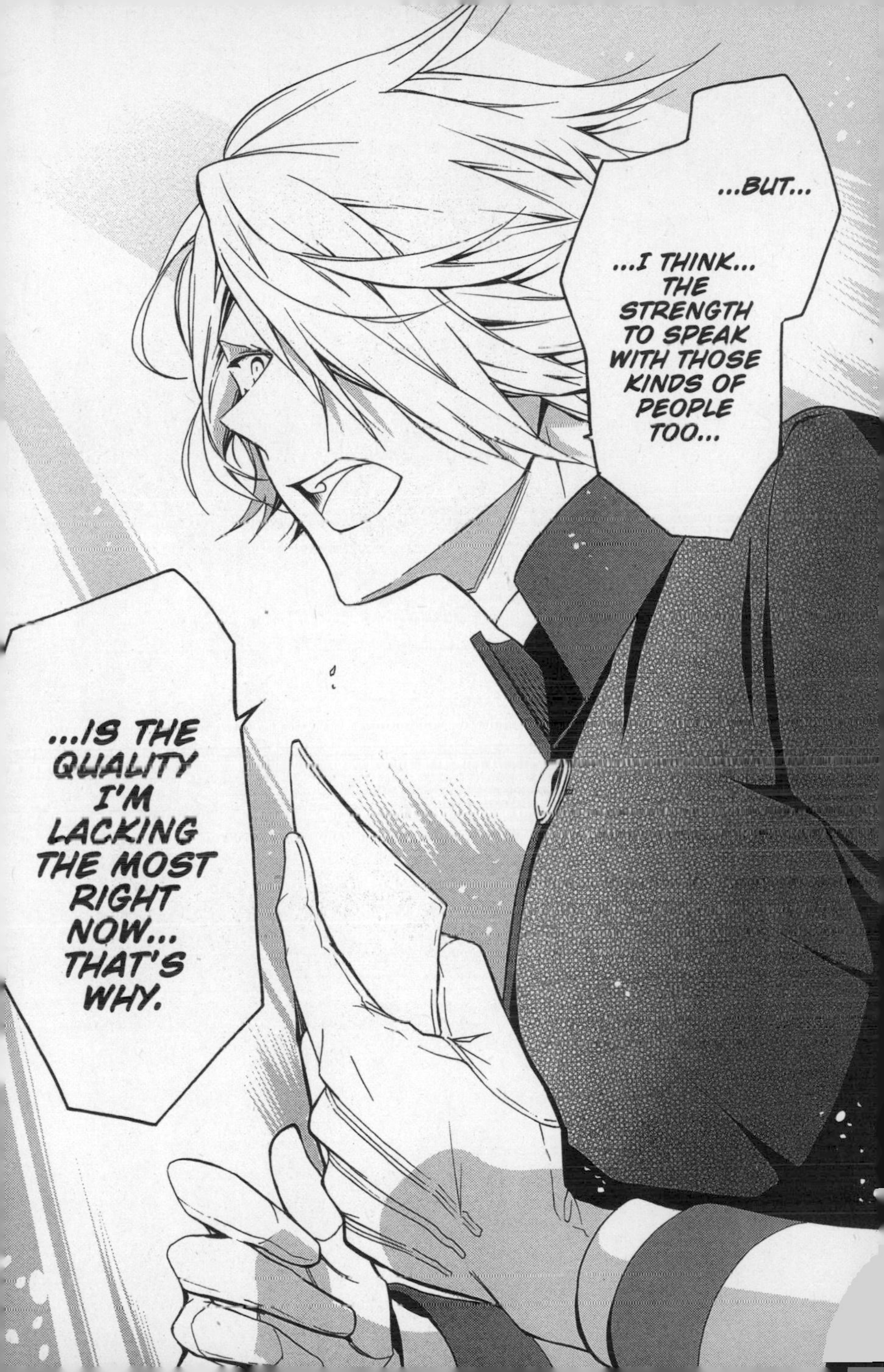
...BUT...
...I THINK... THE STRENGTH TO SPEAK WITH THOSE KINDS OF PEOPLE TOO...
...IS THE QUALITY I'M LACKING THE MOST RIGHT NOW... THAT'S WHY.

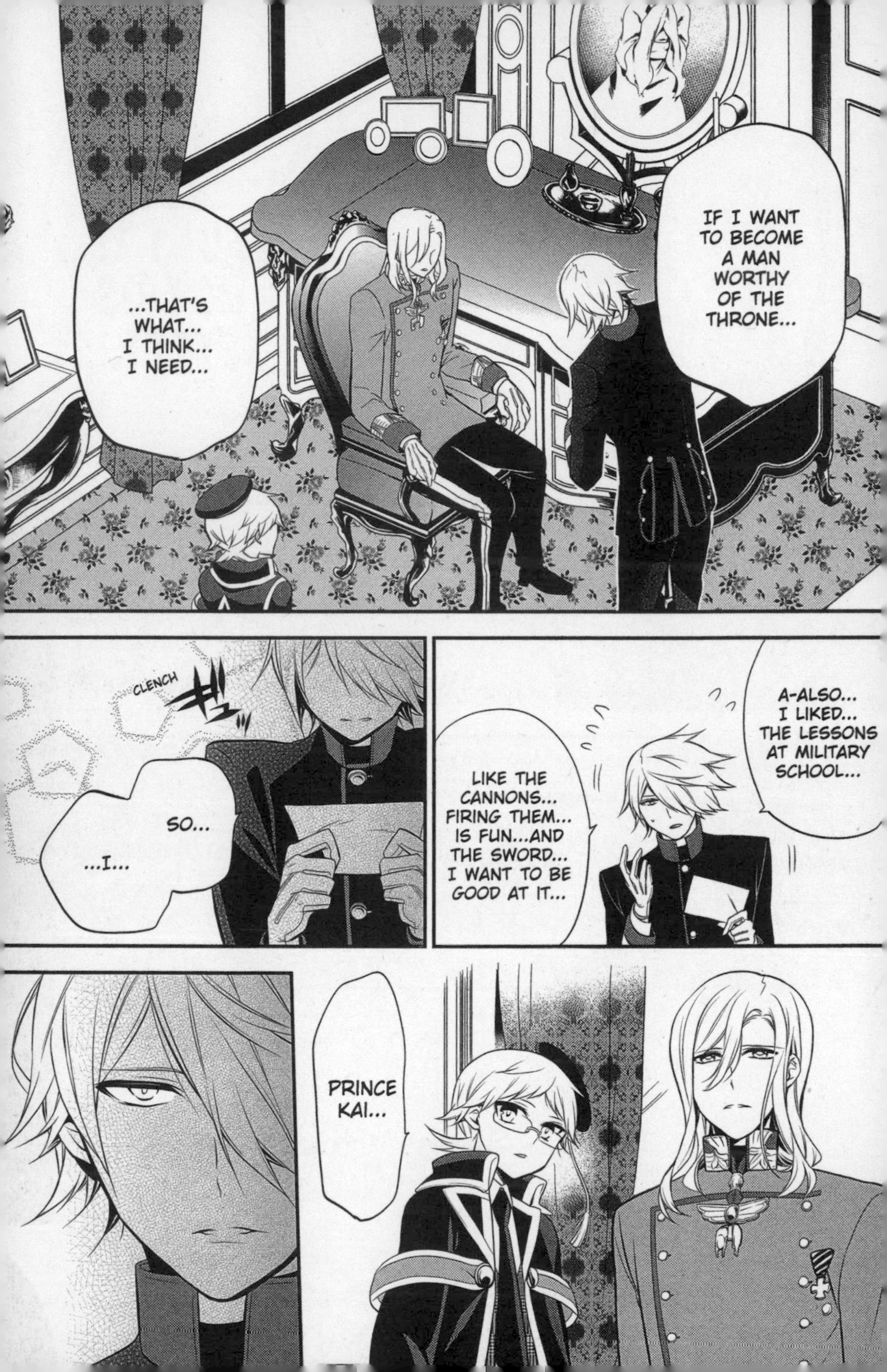
IF I WANT TO BECOME A MAN WORTHY OF THE THRONE...
...THAT'S WHAT... I THINK... I NEED...
A-ALSO... I LIKED... THE LESSONS AT MILITARY SCHOOL...
LIKE THE CANNONS... FIRING THEM... IS FUN...AND THE SWORD... I WANT TO BE GOOD AT IT...
CLENCH
SO...
...I...
PRINCE KAI...

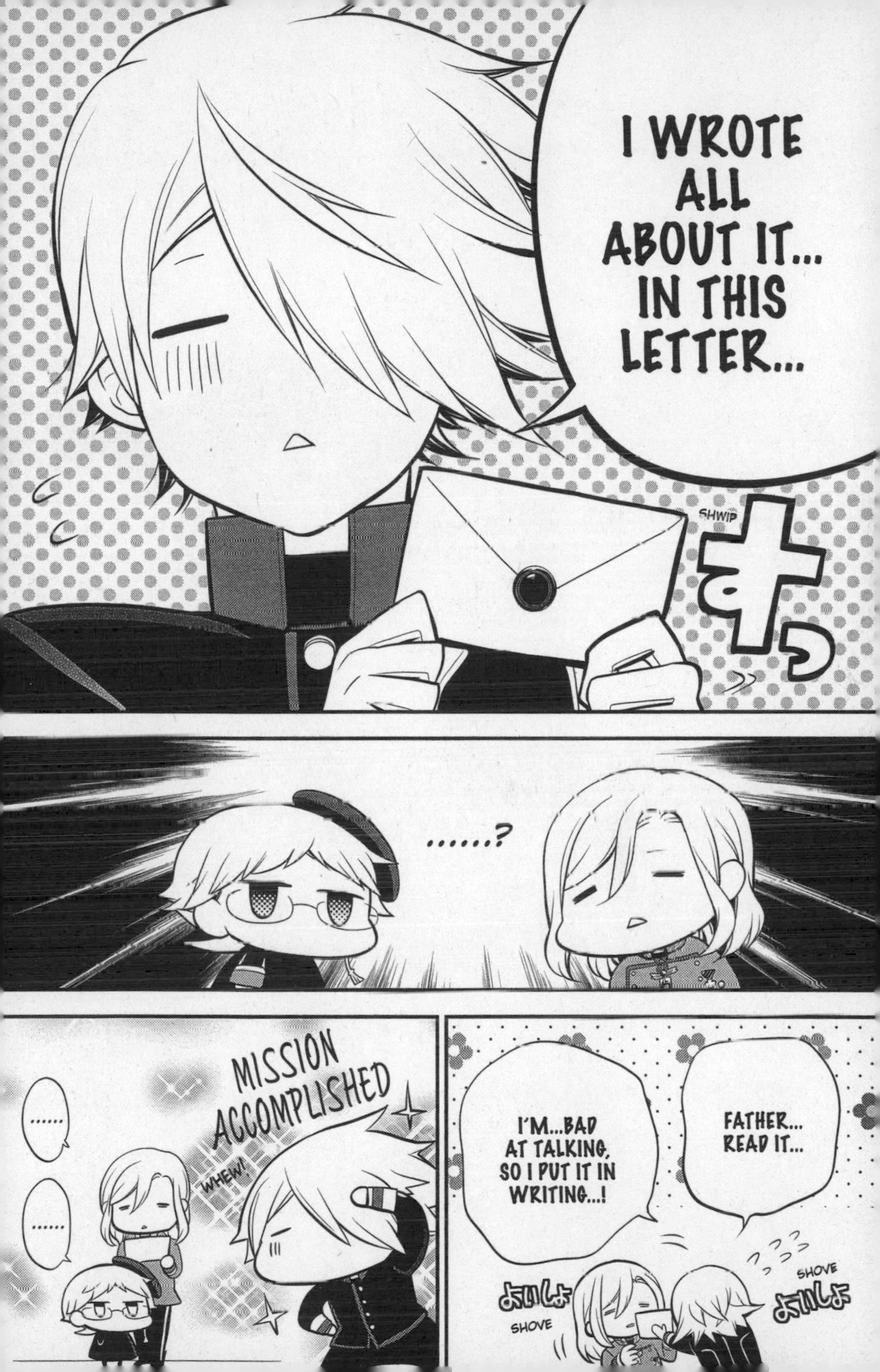
I WROTE ALL ABOUT IT... IN THIS LETTER...
SHWIP
すっ
......?
FATHER... READ IT...
I'M...BAD AT TALKING, SO I PUT IT IN WRITING...!
SHOVE
よいしょ
SHOVE
よいしょ
MISSION ACCOMPLISHED
WHEW!
......
......

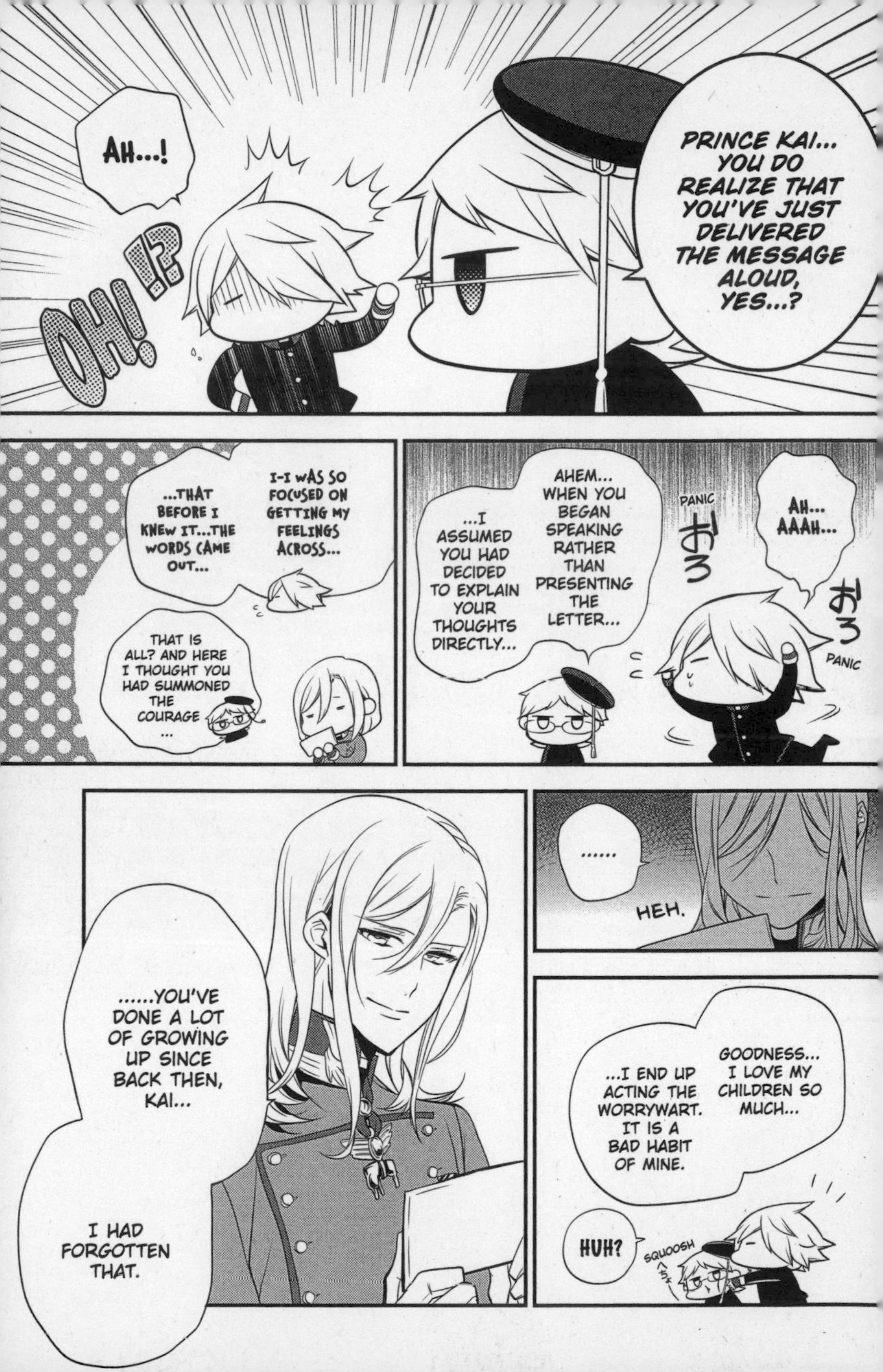
PRINCE KAI... YOU DO REALIZE THAT YOU'VE JUST DELIVERED THE MESSAGE ALOUD, YES...?
AH...!
OH!?
AH... AAAH...
PANIC
おろ
おろ
PANIC
AHEM... WHEN YOU BEGAN SPEAKING RATHER THAN PRESENTING THE LETTER...
...I ASSUMED YOU HAD DECIDED TO EXPLAIN YOUR THOUGHTS DIRECTLY...
I-I WAS SO FOCUSED ON GETTING MY FEELINGS ACROSS...
...THAT BEFORE I KNEW IT...THE WORDS CAME OUT...
THAT IS ALL? AND HERE I THOUGHT YOU HAD SUMMONED THE COURAGE ...
......
HEH.
GOODNESS... I LOVE MY CHILDREN SO MUCH...
...I END UP ACTING THE WORRYWART. IT IS A BAD HABIT OF MINE.
HUH?
SQUOOSH
......YOU'VE DONE A LOT OF GROWING UP SINCE BACK THEN, KAI...
I HAD FORGOTTEN THAT.

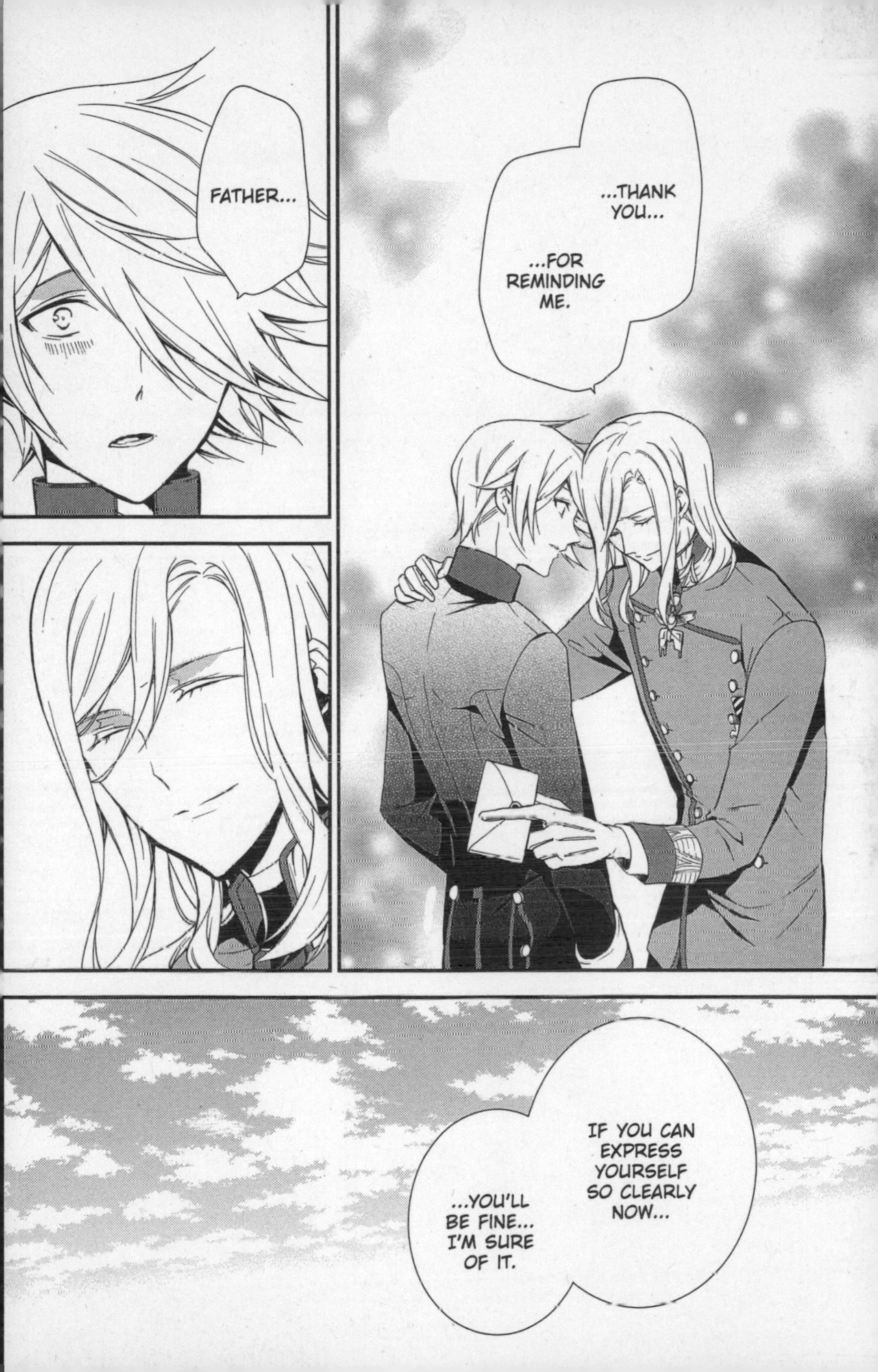
...THANK YOU...
...FOR REMINDING ME.
FATHER...
IF YOU CAN EXPRESS YOURSELF SO CLEARLY NOW...
...YOU'LL BE FINE... I'M SURE OF IT.

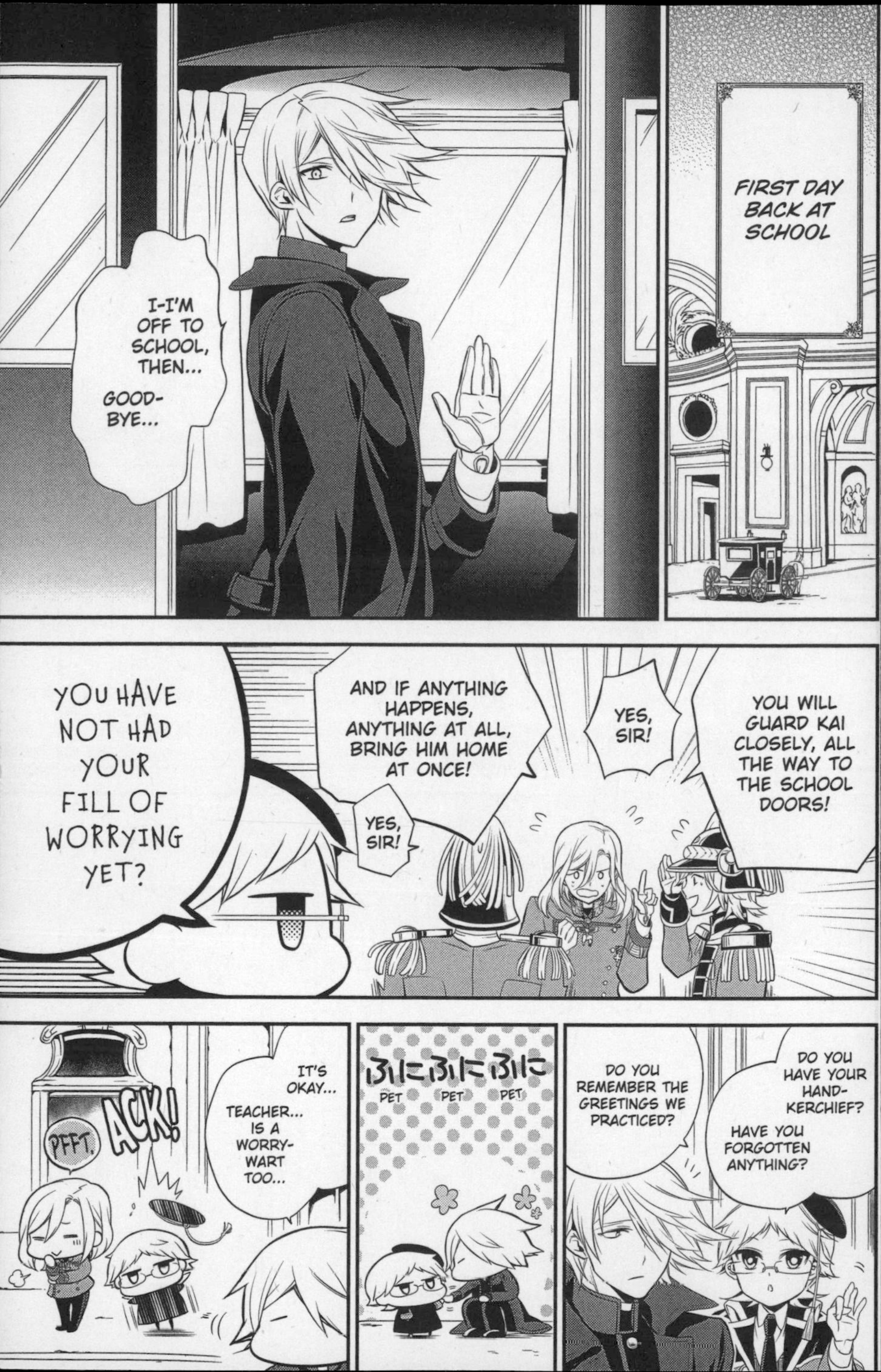
FIRST DAY BACK AT SCHOOL
I-I'M OFF TO SCHOOL, THEN...
GOOD-BYE...
YOU WILL GUARD KAI CLOSELY, ALL THE WAY TO THE SCHOOL DOORS!
YES, SIR!
AND IF ANYTHING HAPPENS, ANYTHING AT ALL, BRING HIM HOME AT ONCE!
YES, SIR!
YOU HAVE NOT HAD YOUR FILL OF WORRYING YET?
DO YOU HAVE YOUR HAND-KERCHIEF?
HAVE YOU FORGOTTEN ANYTHING?
DO YOU REMEMBER THE GREETINGS WE PRACTICED?
ふにふにふに
PET PET PET
IT'S OKAY...
TEACHER... IS A WORRY-WART TOO...
ACK!
PFFT.

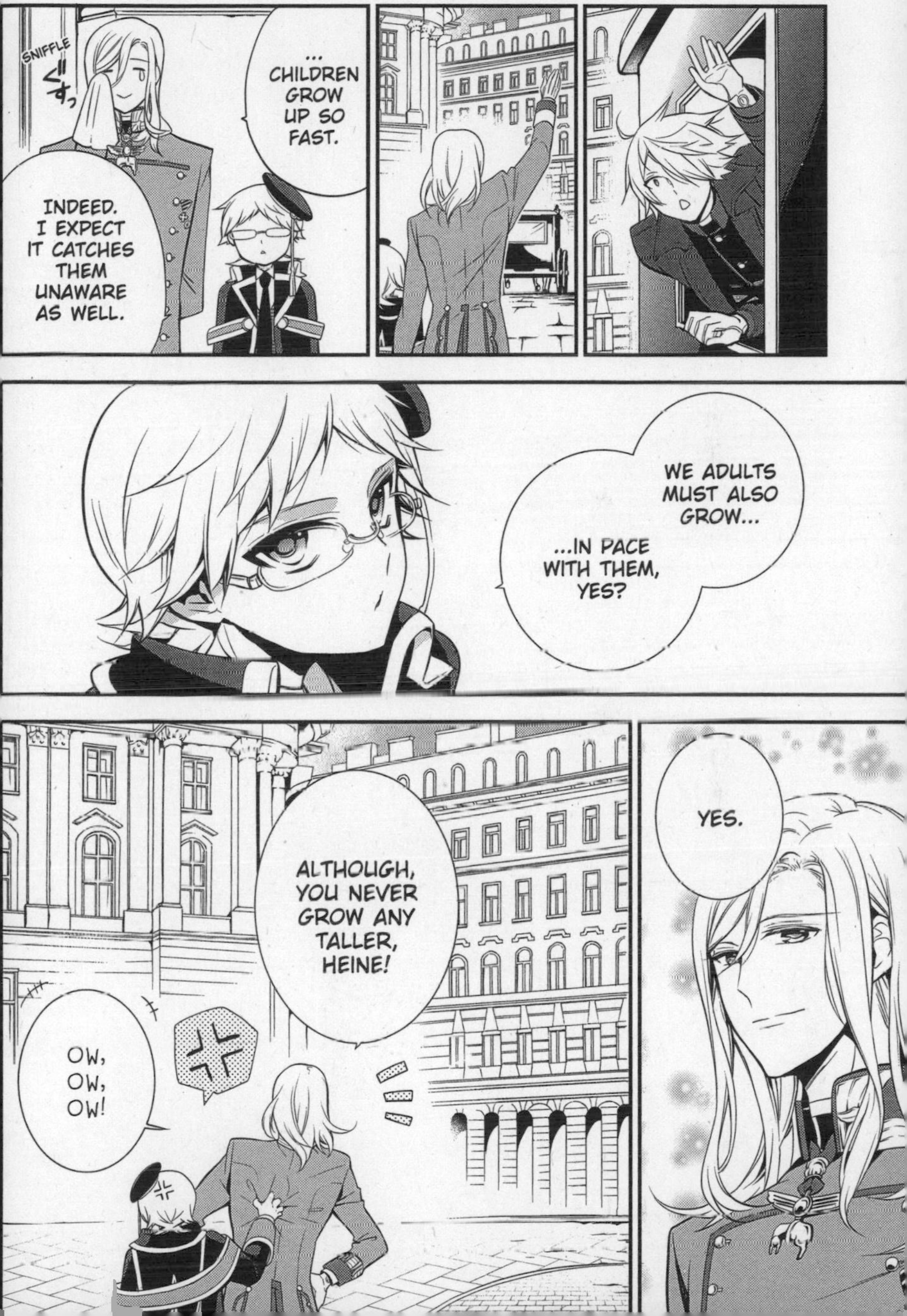
...CHILDREN GROW UP SO FAST.
SNIFFLE
ぐずっ
INDEED. I EXPECT IT CATCHES THEM UNAWARE AS WELL.
WE ADULTS MUST ALSO GROW...
...IN PACE WITH THEM, YES?
YES.
ALTHOUGH, YOU NEVER GROW ANY TALLER, HEINE!
OW, OW, OW!

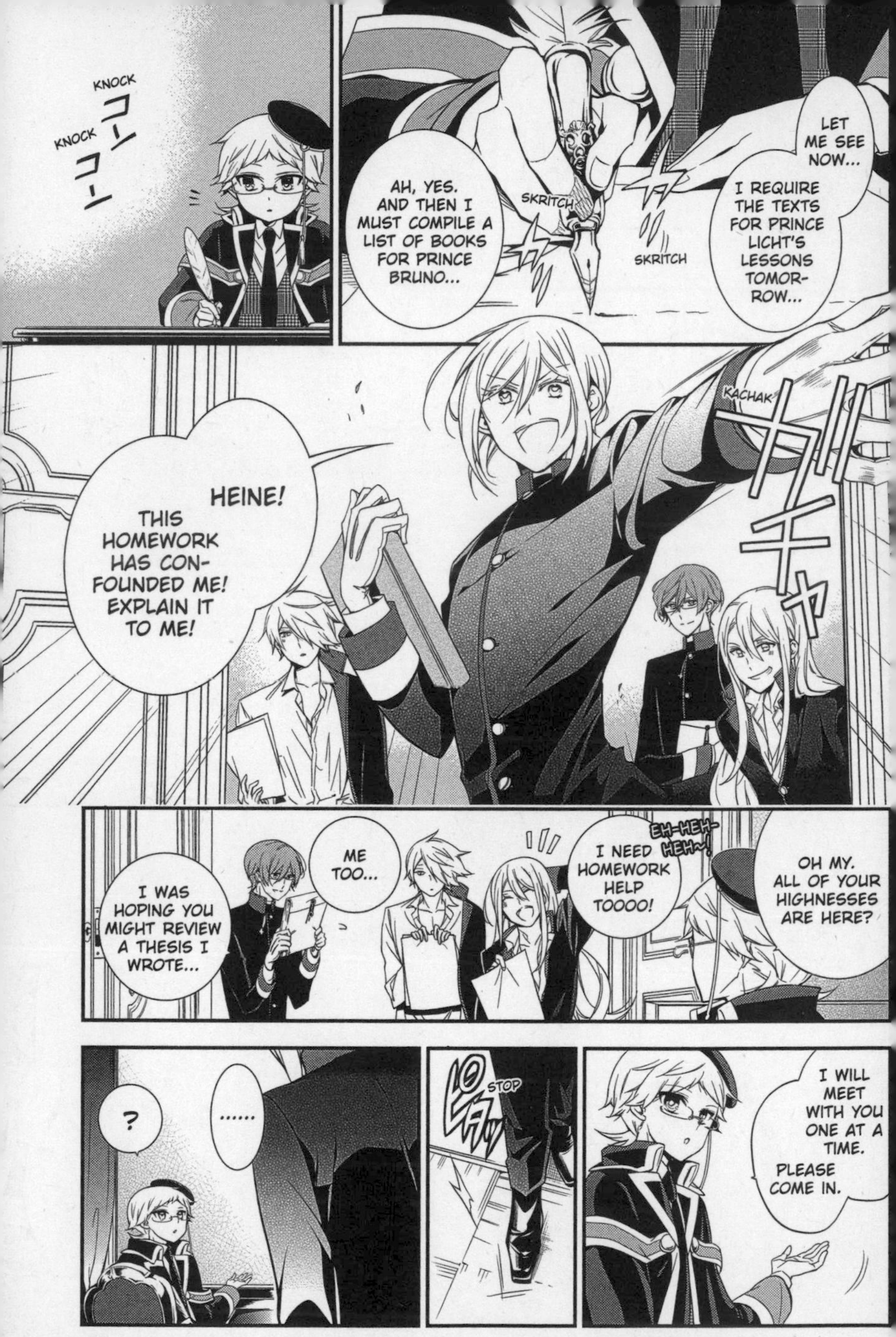

LET ME SEE NOW... I REQUIRE THE TEXTS FOR PRINCE LICHT'S LESSONS TOMORROW...
SKRITCH
SKRITCH
AH, YES. AND THEN I MUST COMPILE A LIST OF BOOKS FOR PRINCE BRUNO...
KNOCK
KNOCK
コンコン
KACHAK
HEINE! THIS HOMEWORK HAS CONFOUNDED ME! EXPLAIN IT TO ME!
OH MY. ALL OF YOUR HIGHNESSES ARE HERE?
EH-HEH-HEH~!
I NEED HOMEWORK HELP TOOOO!
ME TOO...
I WAS HOPING YOU MIGHT REVIEW A THESIS I WROTE...
I WILL MEET WITH YOU ONE AT A TIME. PLEASE COME IN.
STOP
......
?

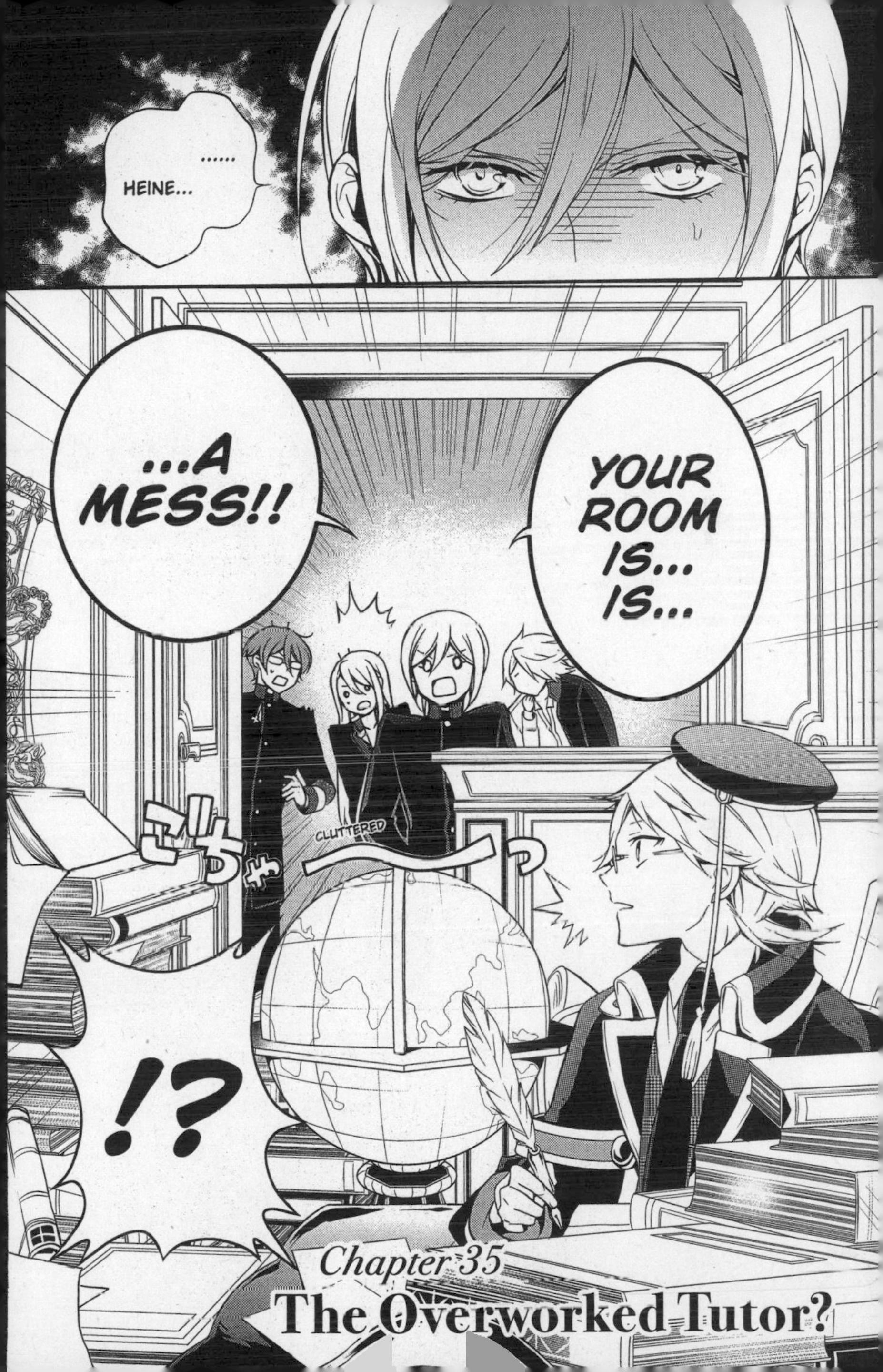
......
HEINE...
YOUR ROOM IS... IS...
...A MESS!!
CLUTTERED
!?

Chapter 35
The Overworked Tutor?

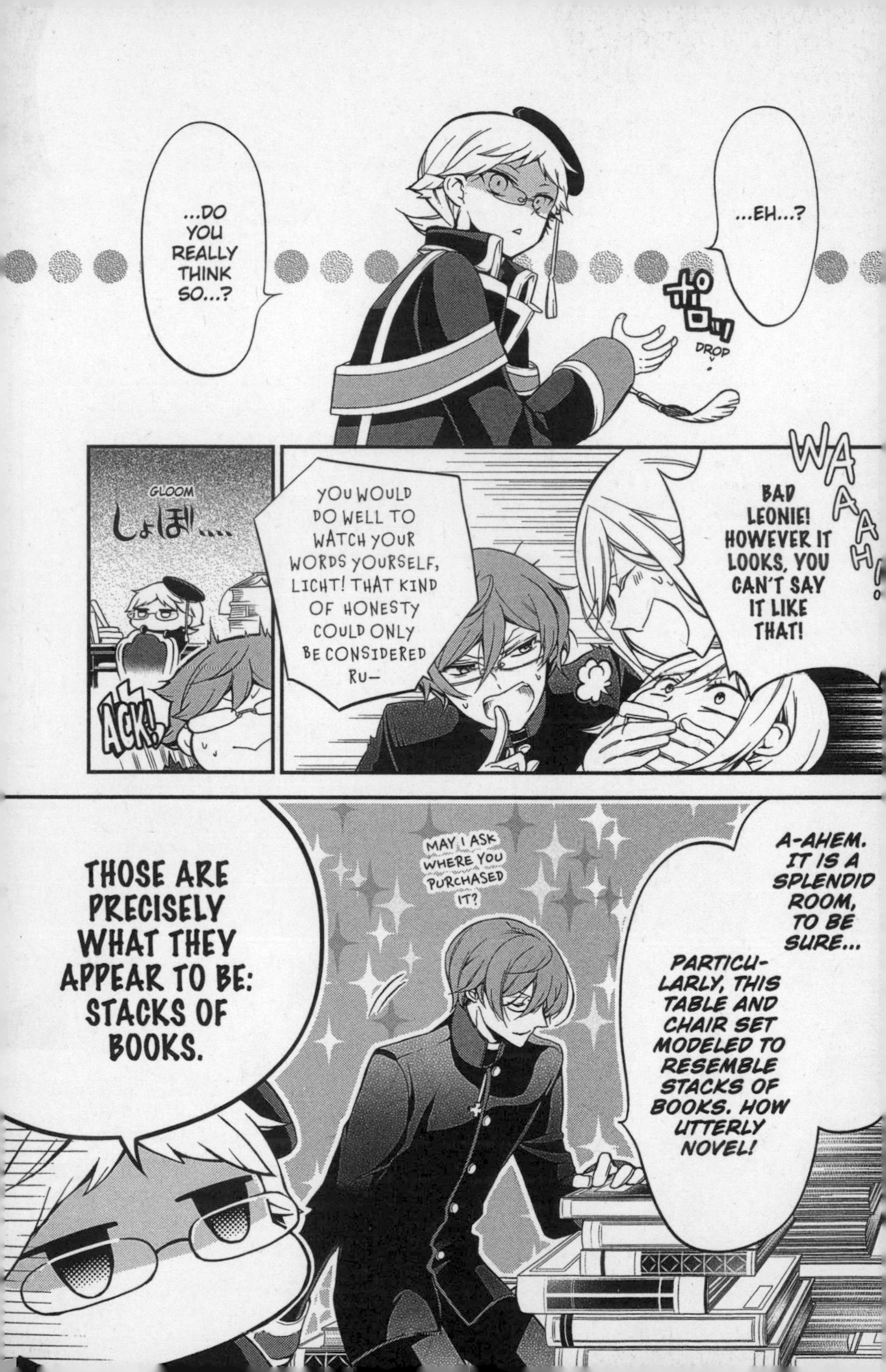
...EH...?
ポロッ
DROP
...DO YOU REALLY THINK SO...?
WAAAAH!
BAD LEONIE! HOWEVER IT LOOKS, YOU CAN'T SAY IT LIKE THAT!
YOU WOULD DO WELL TO WATCH YOUR WORDS YOURSELF, LICHT! THAT KIND OF HONESTY COULD ONLY BE CONSIDERED RU—
GLOOM
しょぼ.....
ACK!
A-AHEM. IT IS A SPLENDID ROOM, TO BE SURE...
PARTICU-LARLY, THIS TABLE AND CHAIR SET MODELED TO RESEMBLE STACKS OF BOOKS. HOW UTTERLY NOVEL!
MAY I ASK WHERE YOU PURCHASED IT?
THOSE ARE PRECISELY WHAT THEY APPEAR TO BE: STACKS OF BOOKS.

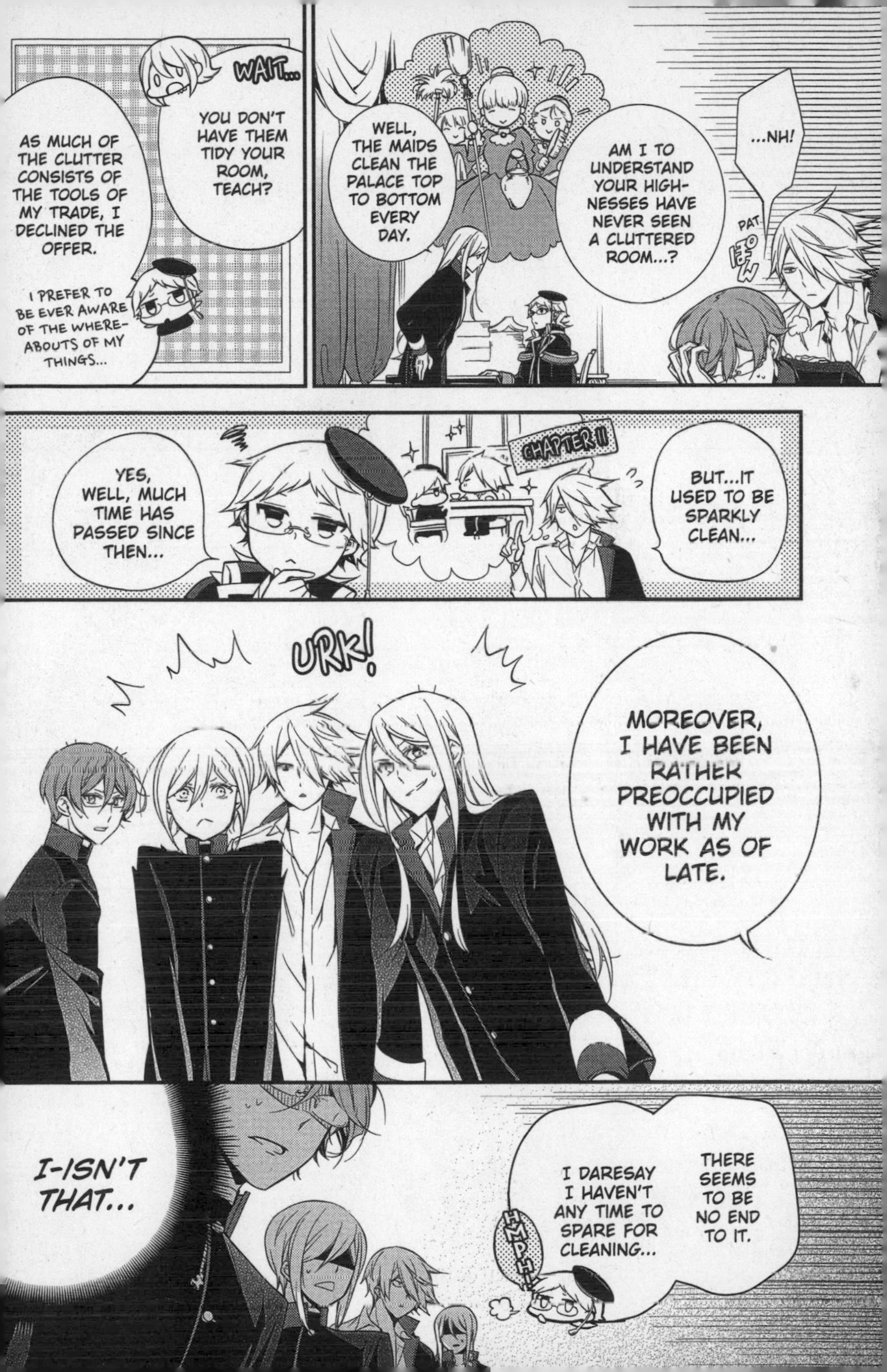
...NH!
PAT
AM I TO UNDERSTAND YOUR HIGHNESSES HAVE NEVER SEEN A CLUTTERED ROOM...?
WELL, THE MAIDS CLEAN THE PALACE TOP TO BOTTOM EVERY DAY.
WAIT...
YOU DON'T HAVE THEM TIDY YOUR ROOM, TEACH?
AS MUCH OF THE CLUTTER CONSISTS OF THE TOOLS OF MY TRADE, I DECLINED THE OFFER.
I PREFER TO BE EVER AWARE OF THE WHEREABOUTS OF MY THINGS...
BUT...IT USED TO BE SPARKLY CLEAN...
CHAPTER 11
YES, WELL, MUCH TIME HAS PASSED SINCE THEN...
MOREOVER, I HAVE BEEN RATHER PREOCCUPIED WITH MY WORK AS OF LATE.
URK!
THERE SEEMS TO BE NO END TO IT.
I DARESAY I HAVEN'T ANY TIME TO SPARE FOR CLEANING...
HMPH!
I-ISN'T THAT...

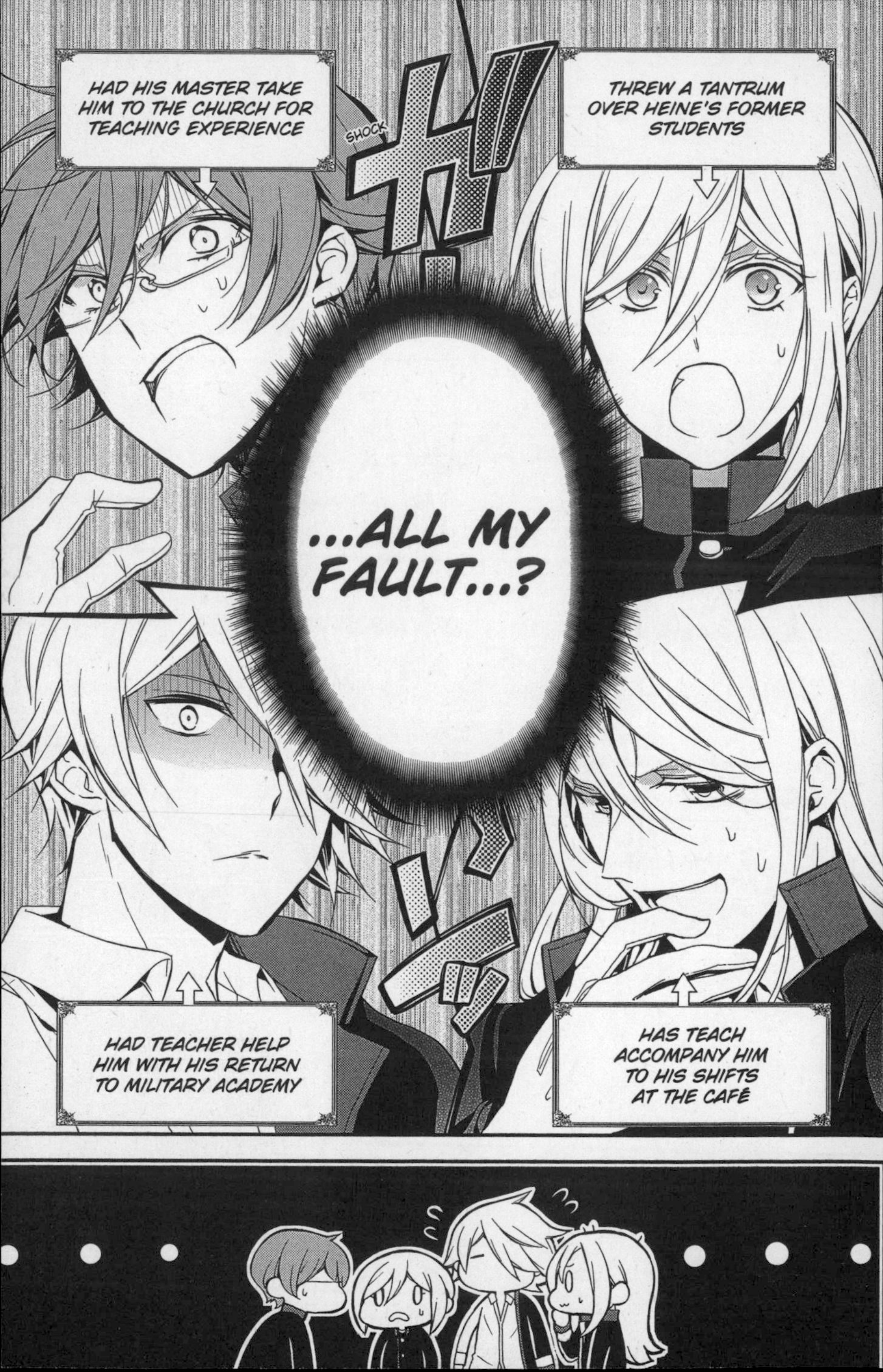
THREW A TANTRUM OVER HEINE'S FORMER STUDENTS
SHOCK
HAD HIS MASTER TAKE HIM TO THE CHURCH FOR TEACHING EXPERIENCE
...ALL MY FAULT...?
HAS TEACH ACCOMPANY HIM TO HIS SHIFTS AT THE CAFÉ
HAD TEACHER HELP HIM WITH HIS RETURN TO MILITARY ACADEMY

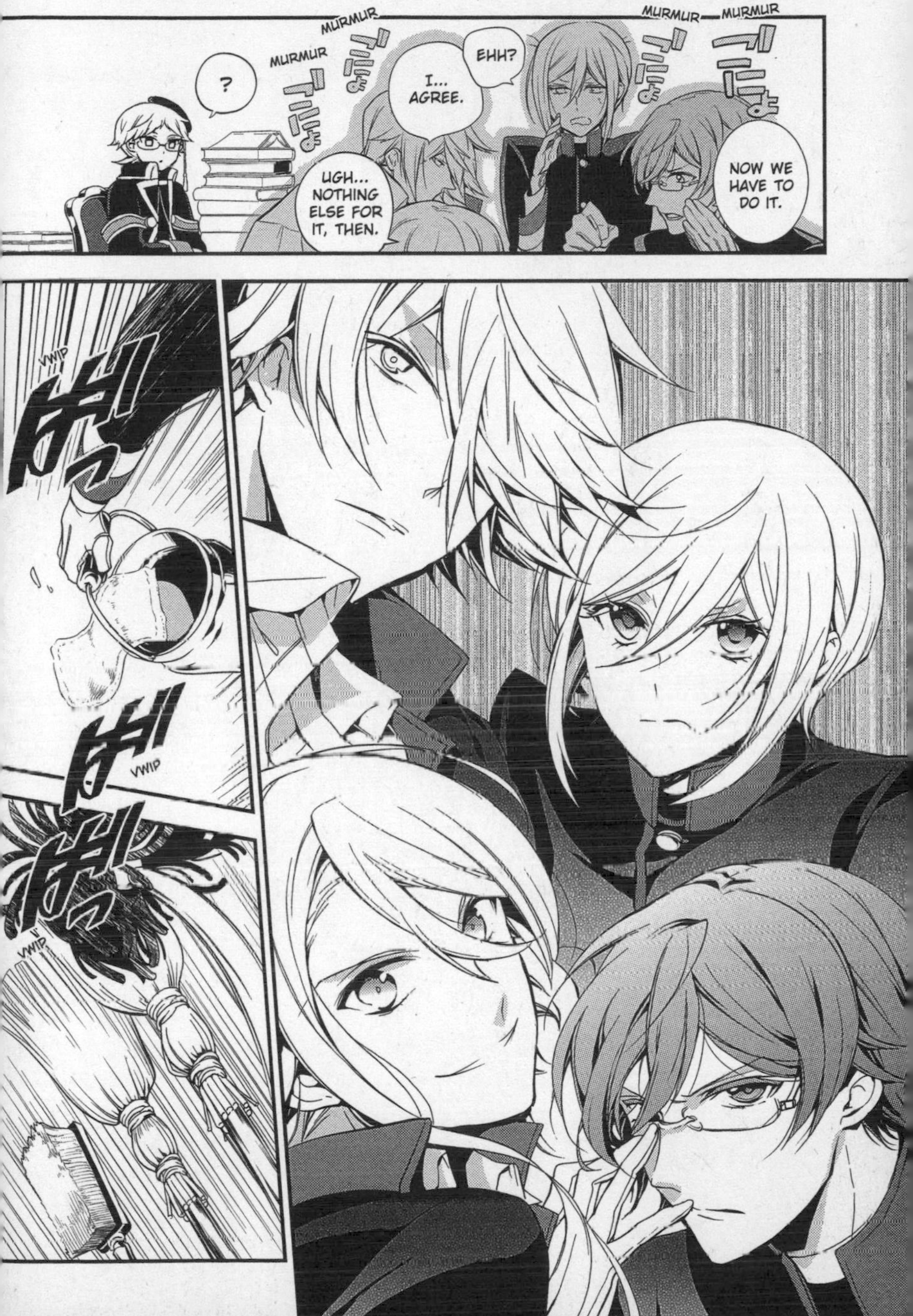
MURMUR
MURMUR
NOW WE HAVE TO DO IT.
EHH?
I... AGREE.
MURMUR
MURMUR
UGH... NOTHING ELSE FOR IT, THEN.
?
VWIP
VWIP
VWIP

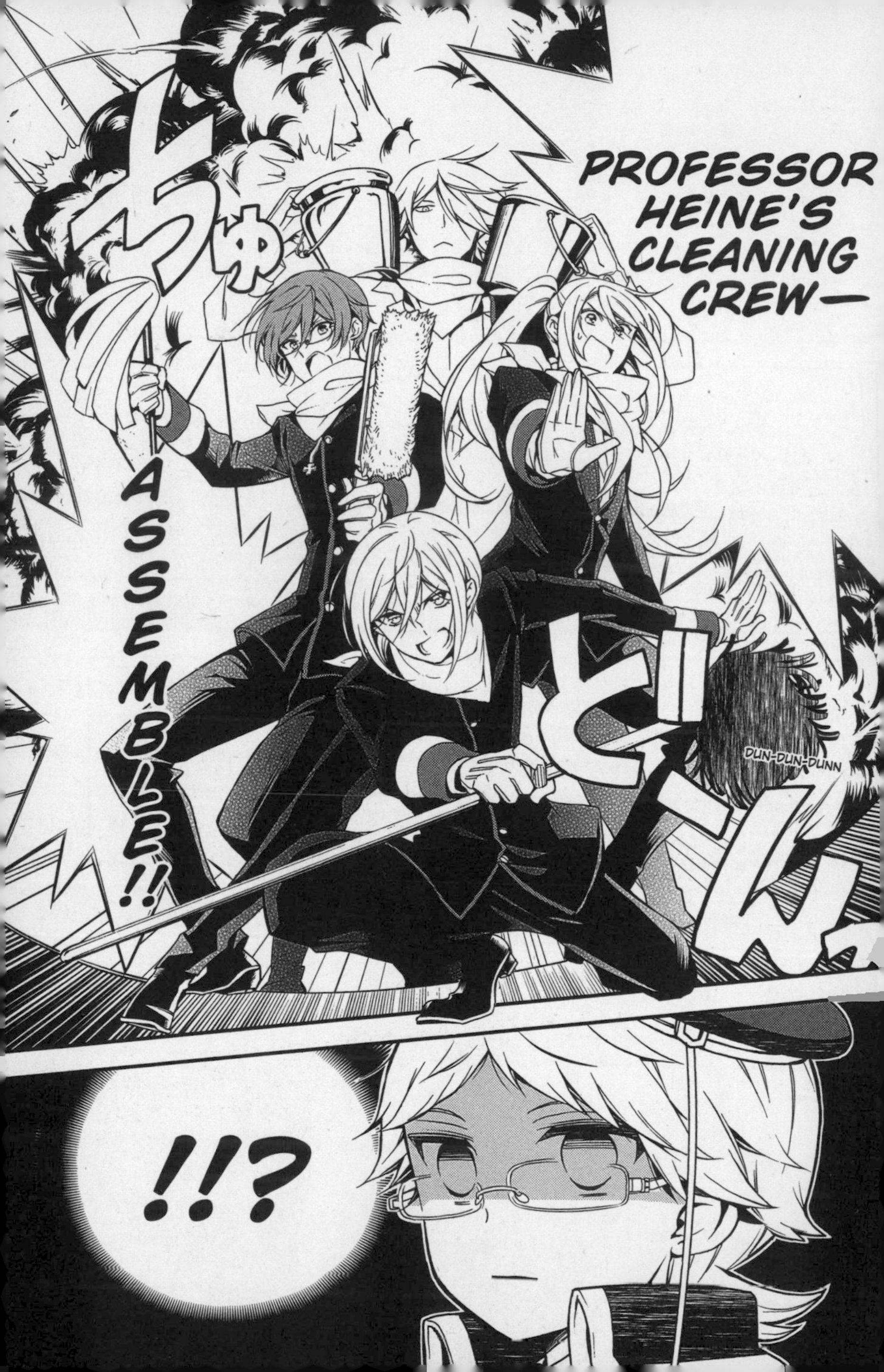
PROFESSOR HEINE'S CLEANING CREW—
ASSEMBLE!!
DUN-DUN-DUNN
!!?

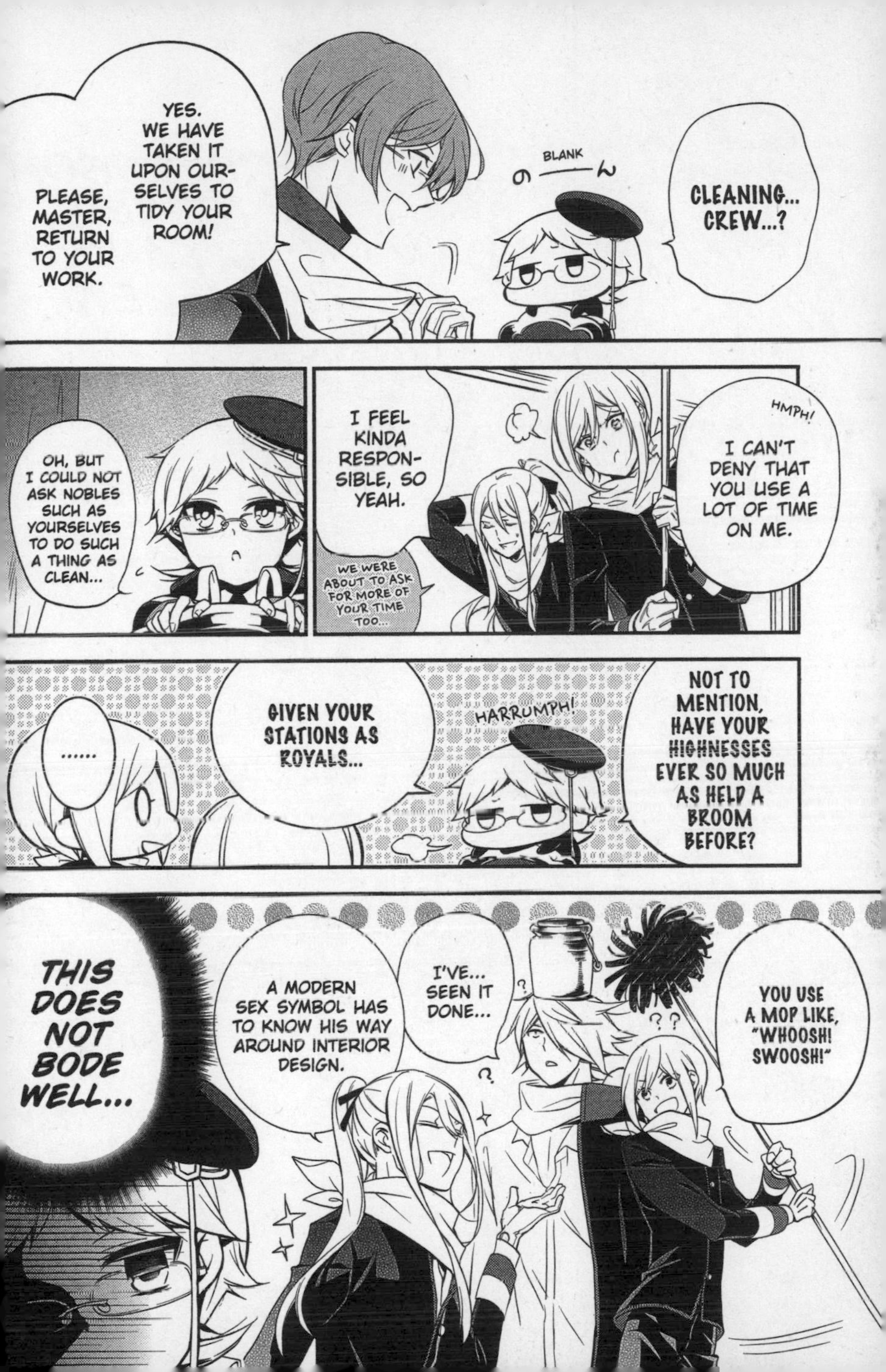
CLEANING... CREW...?
BLANK
の―ん
YES. WE HAVE TAKEN IT UPON OURSELVES TO TIDY YOUR ROOM!
PLEASE, MASTER, RETURN TO YOUR WORK.
HMPH!
I CAN'T DENY THAT YOU USE A LOT OF TIME ON ME.
I FEEL KINDA RESPONSIBLE, SO YEAH.
WE WERE ABOUT TO ASK FOR MORE OF YOUR TIME TOO...
OH, BUT I COULD NOT ASK NOBLES SUCH AS YOURSELVES TO DO SUCH A THING AS CLEAN...
NOT TO MENTION, HAVE YOUR HIGHNESSES EVER SO MUCH AS HELD A BROOM BEFORE?
HARRUMPH!
GIVEN YOUR STATIONS AS ROYALS...
......
YOU USE A MOP LIKE, "WHOOSH! SWOOSH!"
I'VE... SEEN IT DONE...
A MODERN SEX SYMBOL HAS TO KNOW HIS WAY AROUND INTERIOR DESIGN.
THIS DOES NOT BODE WELL...

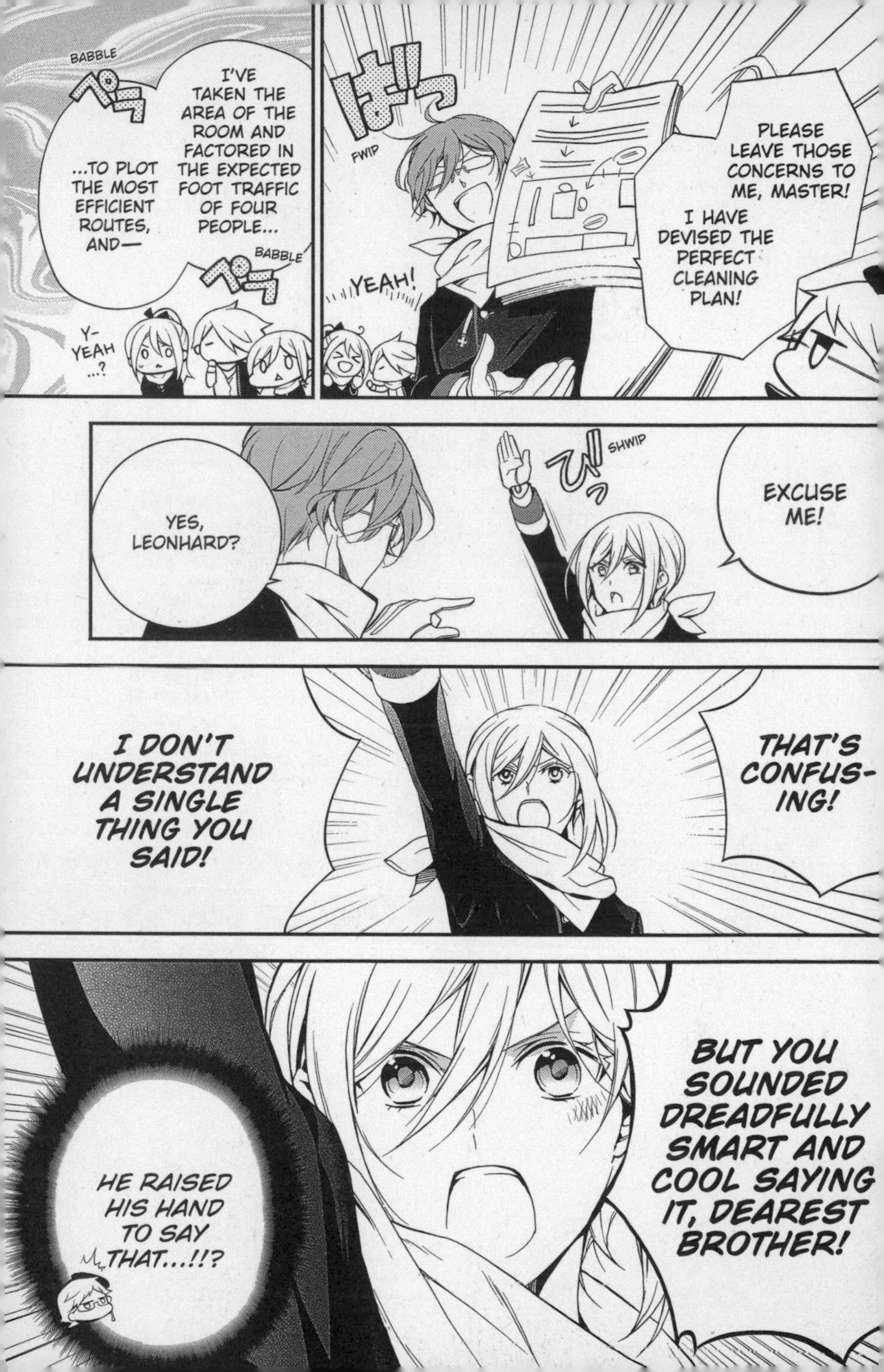
PLEASE LEAVE THOSE CONCERNS TO ME, MASTER!
I HAVE DEVISED THE PERFECT CLEANING PLAN!
FWIP
YEAH!
BABBLE
I'VE TAKEN THE AREA OF THE ROOM AND FACTORED IN THE EXPECTED FOOT TRAFFIC OF FOUR PEOPLE...
...TO PLOT THE MOST EFFICIENT ROUTES, AND—
BABBLE
Y-YEAH ...?
EXCUSE ME!
SHWIP
YES, LEONHARD?
THAT'S CONFUS-ING!
I DON'T UNDERSTAND A SINGLE THING YOU SAID!
BUT YOU SOUNDED DREADFULLY SMART AND COOL SAYING IT, DEAREST BROTHER!
HE RAISED HIS HAND TO SAY THAT...!!?

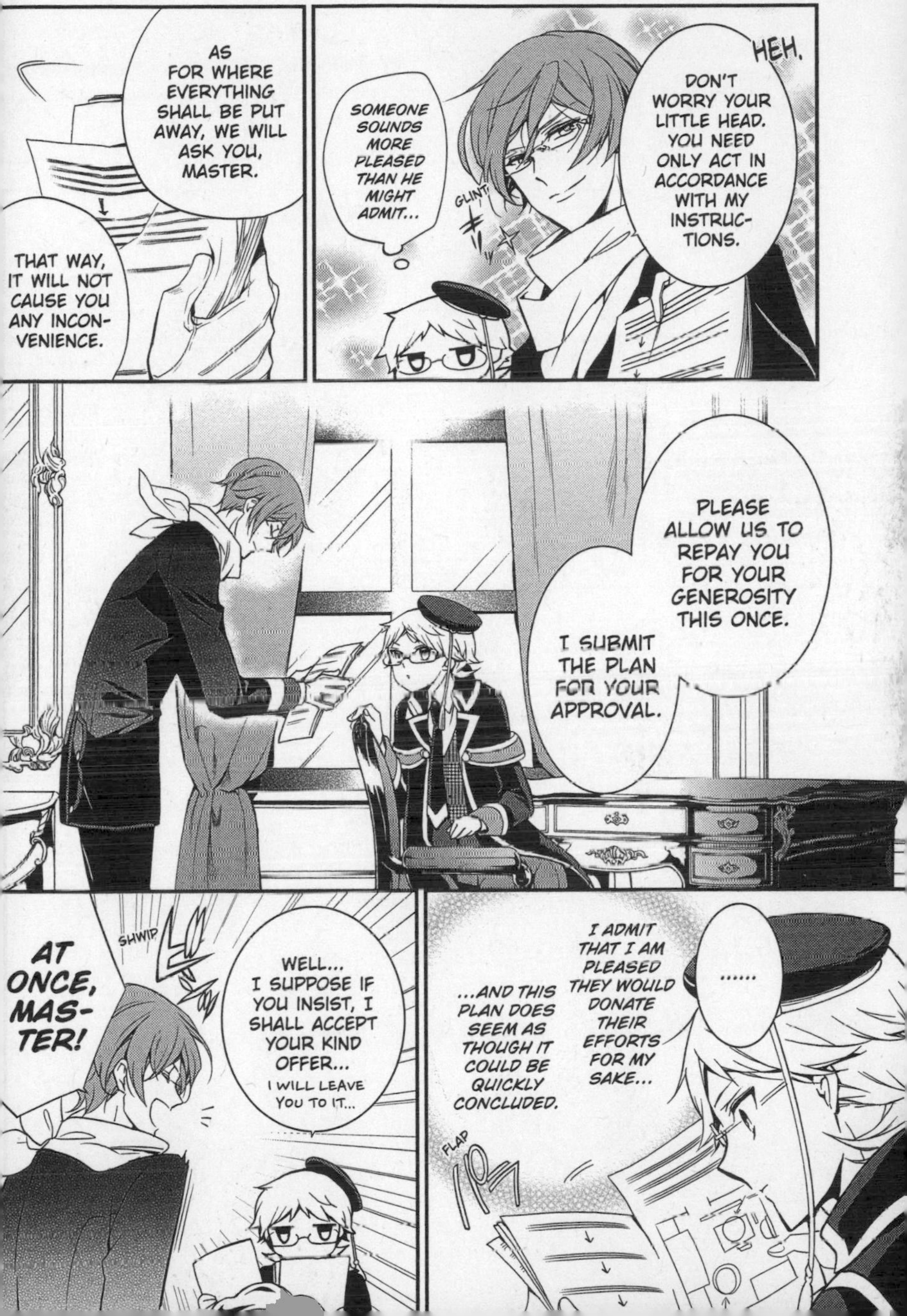
HEH.
DON'T WORRY YOUR LITTLE HEAD. YOU NEED ONLY ACT IN ACCORDANCE WITH MY INSTRUCTIONS.
GLINT
SOMEONE SOUNDS MORE PLEASED THAN HE MIGHT ADMIT...
AS FOR WHERE EVERYTHING SHALL BE PUT AWAY, WE WILL ASK YOU, MASTER.
THAT WAY, IT WILL NOT CAUSE YOU ANY INCONVENIENCE.
PLEASE ALLOW US TO REPAY YOU FOR YOUR GENEROSITY THIS ONCE.
I SUBMIT THE PLAN FOR YOUR APPROVAL.
......
I ADMIT THAT I AM PLEASED THEY WOULD DONATE THEIR EFFORTS FOR MY SAKE...
...AND THIS PLAN DOES SEEM AS THOUGH IT COULD BE QUICKLY CONCLUDED.
FLAP
WELL... I SUPPOSE IF YOU INSIST, I SHALL ACCEPT YOUR KIND OFFER...
I WILL LEAVE YOU TO IT...
SHWIP
AT ONCE, MASTER!

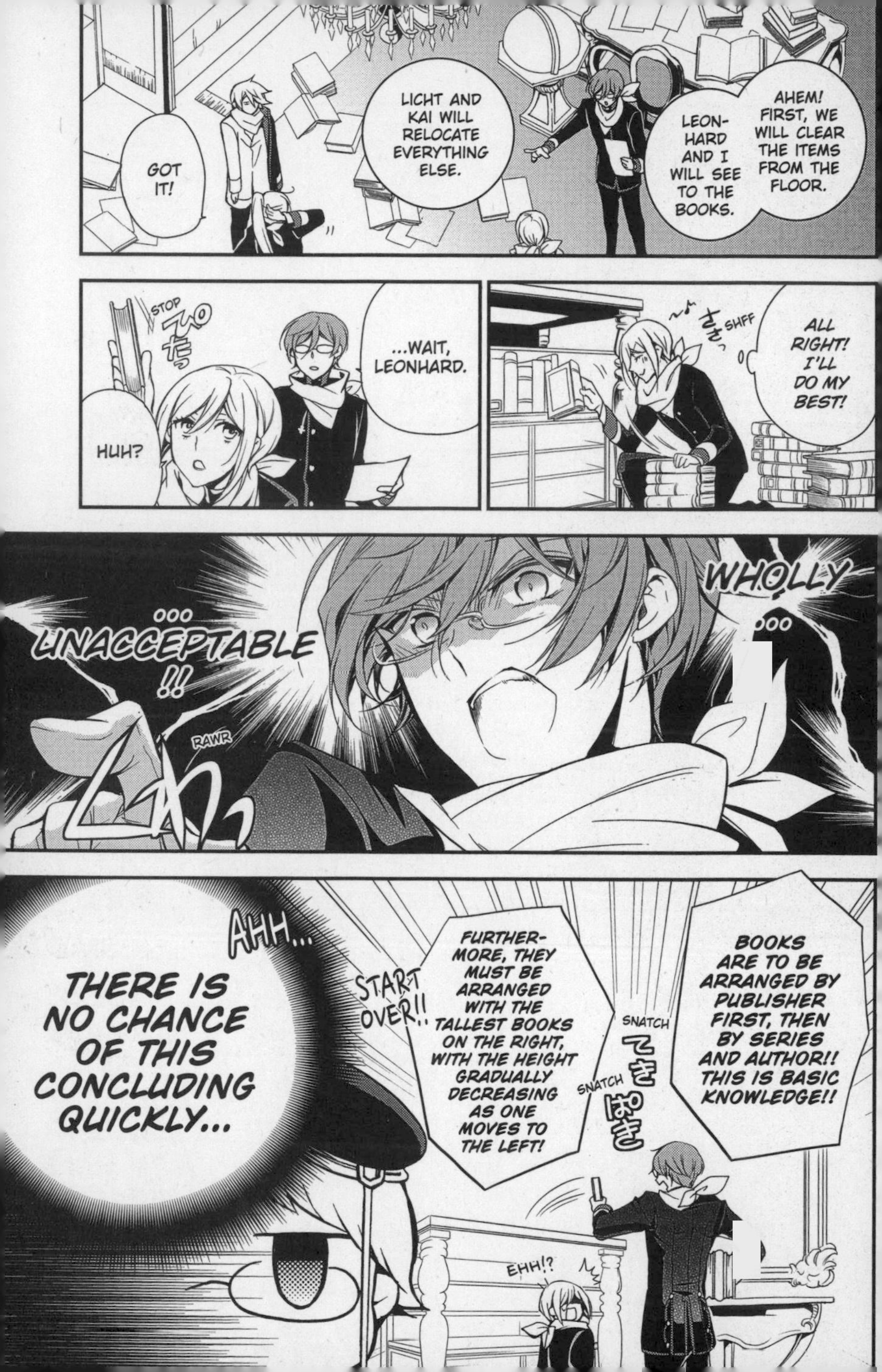
AHEM! FIRST, WE WILL CLEAR THE ITEMS FROM THE FLOOR.
LEON-HARD AND I WILL SEE TO THE BOOKS.
LICHT AND KAI WILL RELOCATE EVERYTHING ELSE.
GOT IT!
ALL RIGHT! I'LL DO MY BEST!
さっ
SHFF
...WAIT, LEONHARD.
ぴたっ
STOP
HUH?
WHOLLY
UNACCEPTABLE!!
RAWR
BOOKS ARE TO BE ARRANGED BY PUBLISHER FIRST, THEN BY SERIES AND AUTHOR!! THIS IS BASIC KNOWLEDGE!!
てき
SNATCH
ぱき
SNATCH
FURTHER-MORE, THEY MUST BE ARRANGED WITH THE TALLEST BOOKS ON THE RIGHT, WITH THE HEIGHT GRADUALLY DECREASING AS ONE MOVES TO THE LEFT!
START OVER!!
EHH!?
AHH...
THERE IS NO CHANCE OF THIS CONCLUDING QUICKLY...

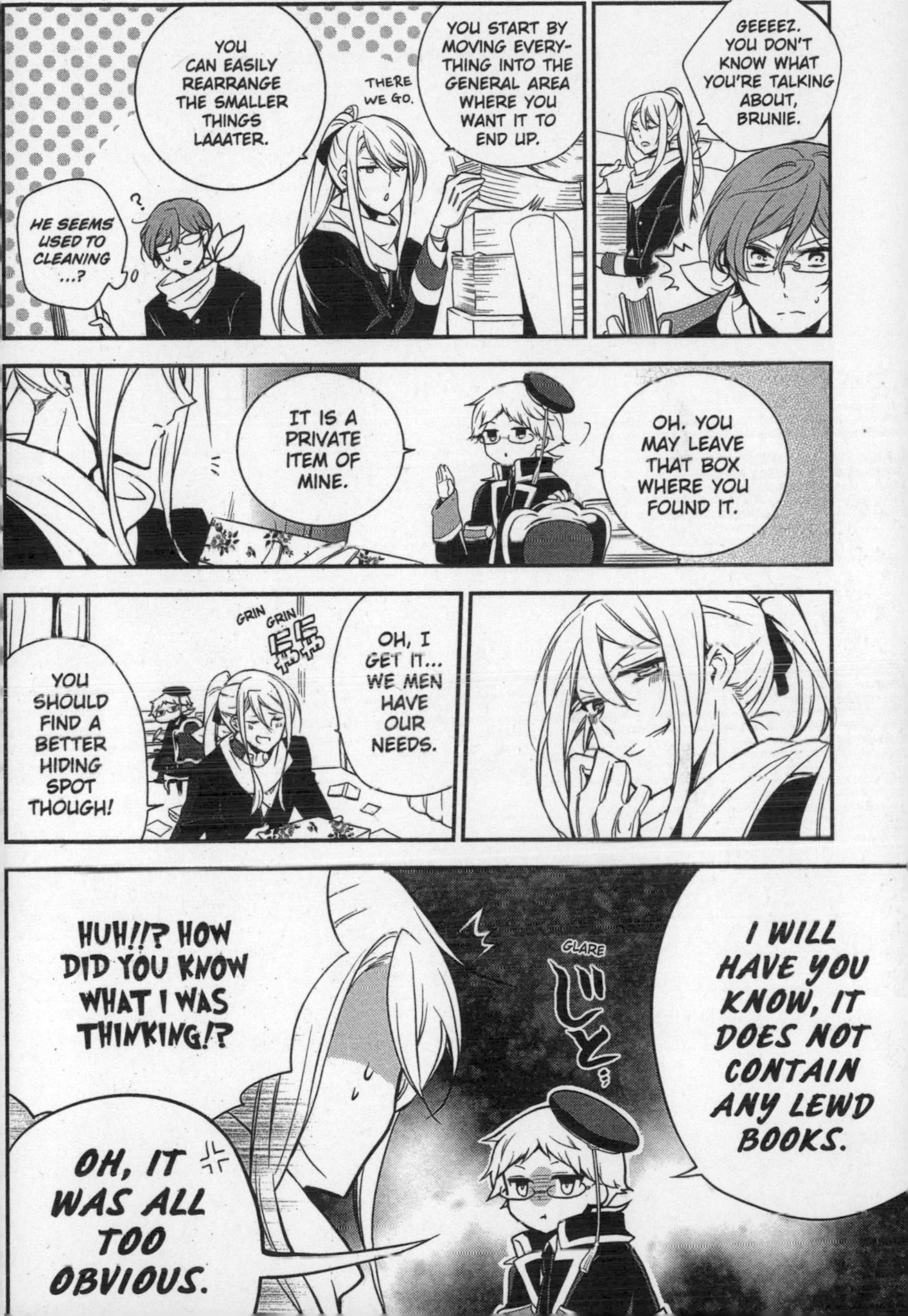
GEEEEZ. YOU DON'T KNOW WHAT YOU'RE TALKING ABOUT, BRUNIE.
YOU START BY MOVING EVERYTHING INTO THE GENERAL AREA WHERE YOU WANT IT TO END UP.
THERE WE GO.
YOU CAN EASILY REARRANGE THE SMALLER THINGS LAAATER.
?
HE SEEMS USED TO CLEANING ...?
OH. YOU MAY LEAVE THAT BOX WHERE YOU FOUND IT.
IT IS A PRIVATE ITEM OF MINE.
OH, I GET IT... WE MEN HAVE OUR NEEDS.
GRIN GRIN
YOU SHOULD FIND A BETTER HIDING SPOT THOUGH!
I WILL HAVE YOU KNOW, IT DOES NOT CONTAIN ANY LEWD BOOKS.
GLARE
HUH!!? HOW DID YOU KNOW WHAT I WAS THINKING!?
OH, IT WAS ALL TOO OBVIOUS.

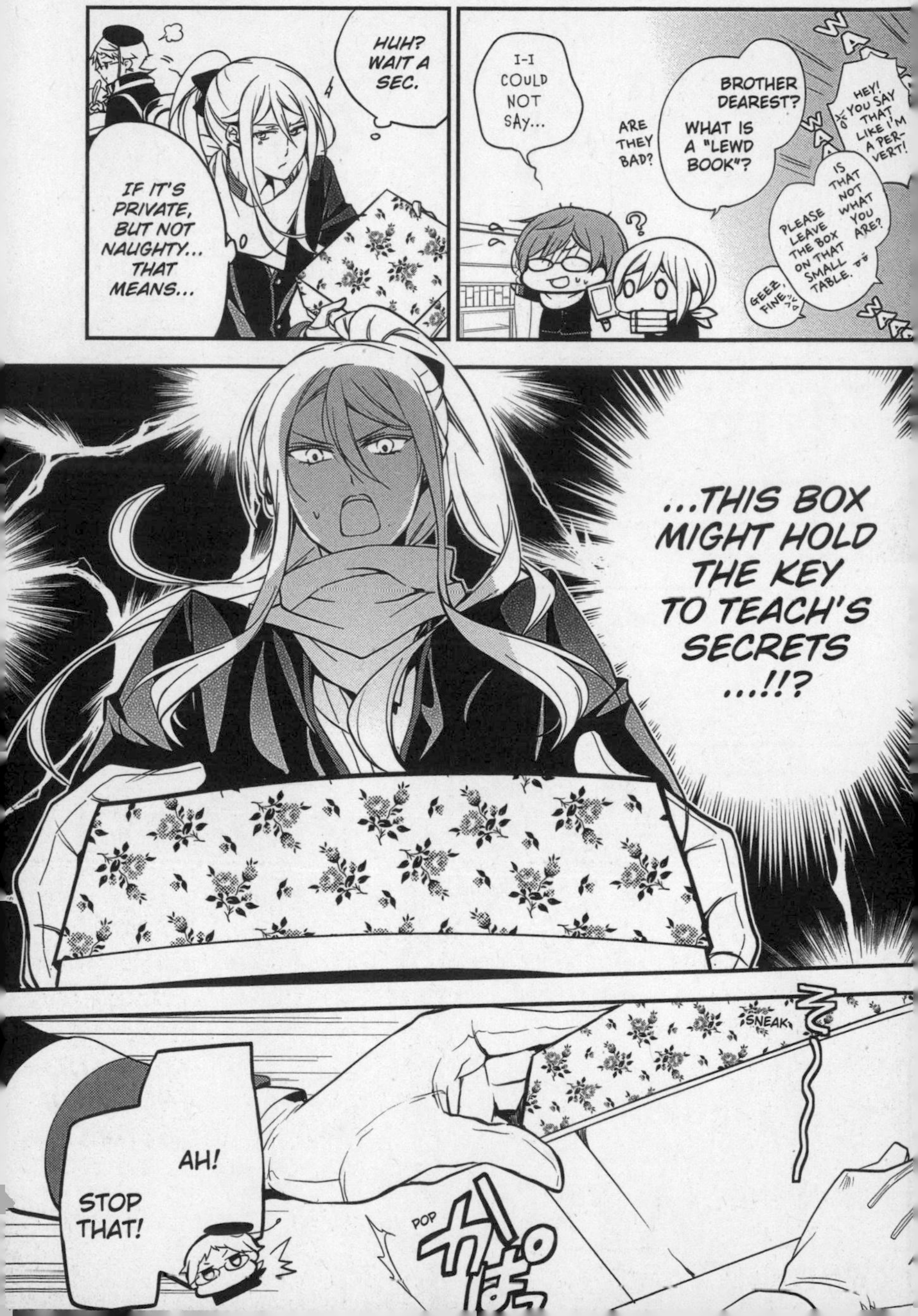
HEY! YOU SAY THAT LIKE I'M A PER-VERT!
BROTHER DEAREST? WHAT IS A "LEWD BOOK"?
IS THAT NOT WHAT YOU ARE?
PLEASE LEAVE THE BOX ON THAT SMALL TABLE.
ARE THEY BAD?
I-I COULD NOT SAY...
GEEZ, FINE.
HUH? WAIT A SEC.
IF IT'S PRIVATE, BUT NOT NAUGHTY... THAT MEANS...
...THIS BOX MIGHT HOLD THE KEY TO TEACH'S SECRETS ...!!?
SNEAK
POP
AH!
STOP THAT!

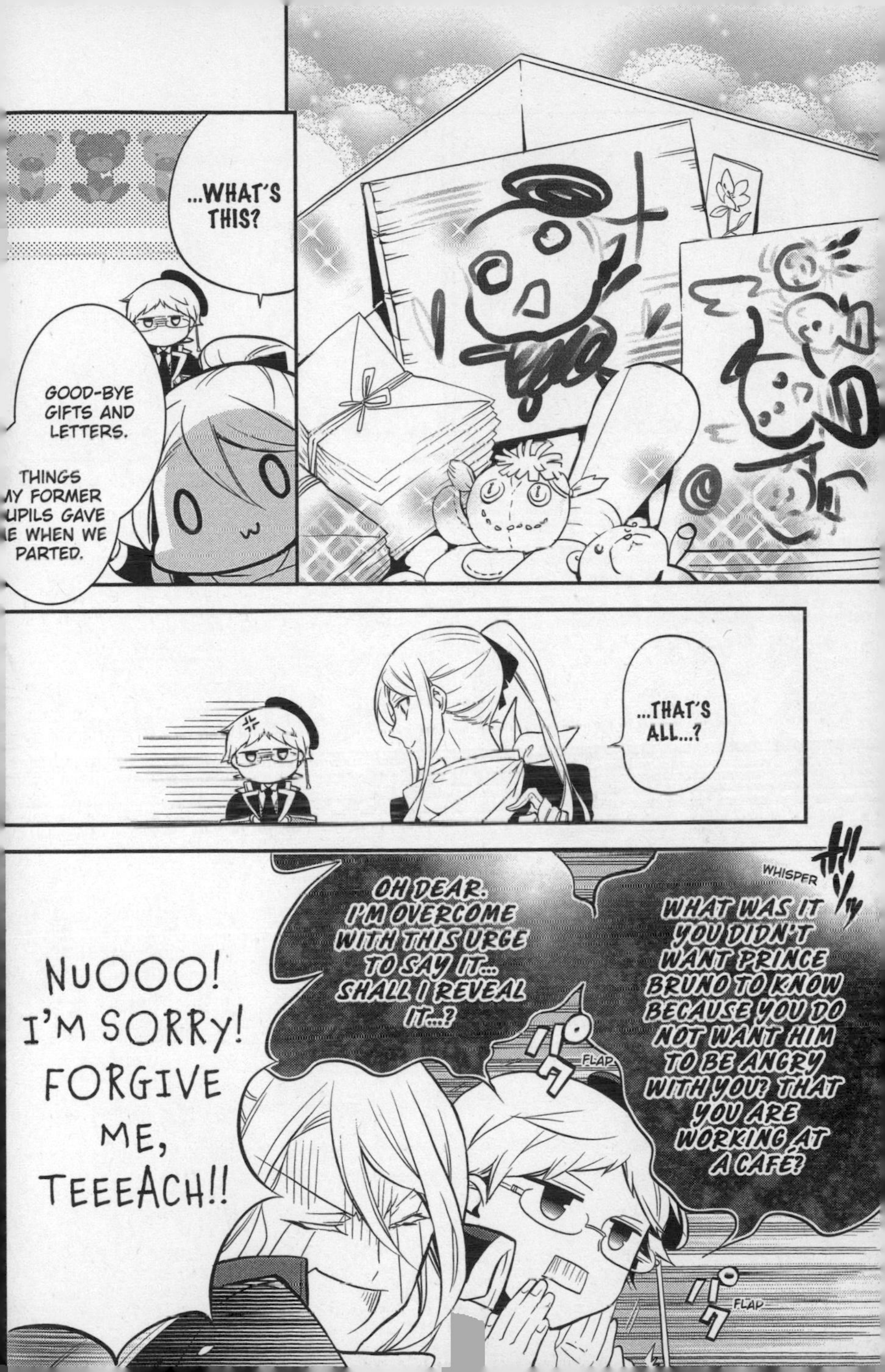
...WHAT'S THIS?
GOOD-BYE GIFTS AND LETTERS.
THINGS MY FORMER UPILS GAVE E WHEN WE PARTED.
...THAT'S ALL...?
WHISPER
WHAT WAS IT YOU DIDN'T WANT PRINCE BRUNO TO KNOW BECAUSE YOU DO NOT WANT HIM TO BE ANGRY WITH YOU? THAT YOU ARE WORKING AT A CAFÉ?
OH DEAR. I'M OVERCOME WITH THIS URGE TO SAY IT... SHALL I REVEAL IT...?
FLAP
FLAP
NUOOO! I'M SORRY! FORGIVE ME, TEEEACH!!

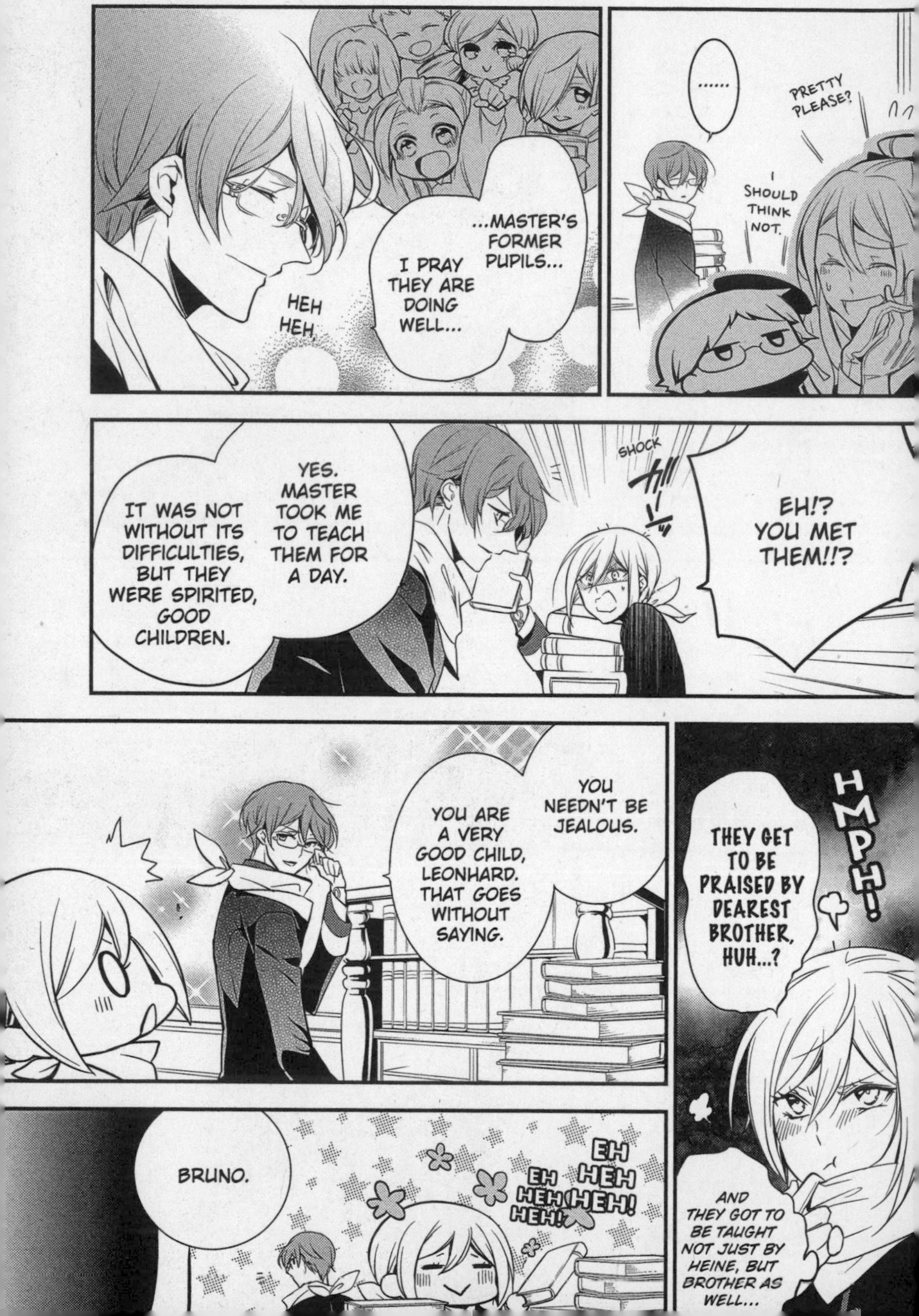
……
PRETTY PLEASE?
I SHOULD THINK NOT.
...MASTER'S FORMER PUPILS...
I PRAY THEY ARE DOING WELL...
HEH HEH
EH!? YOU MET THEM!!?
SHOCK
YES. MASTER TOOK ME TO TEACH THEM FOR A DAY.
IT WAS NOT WITHOUT ITS DIFFICULTIES, BUT THEY WERE SPIRITED, GOOD CHILDREN.
HMPH!
THEY GET TO BE PRAISED BY DEAREST BROTHER, HUH...?
AND THEY GOT TO BE TAUGHT NOT JUST BY HEINE, BUT BROTHER AS WELL...
YOU NEEDN'T BE JEALOUS.
YOU ARE A VERY GOOD CHILD, LEONHARD. THAT GOES WITHOUT SAYING.
EH HEH HEH!
EH HEH HEH!
BRUNO.

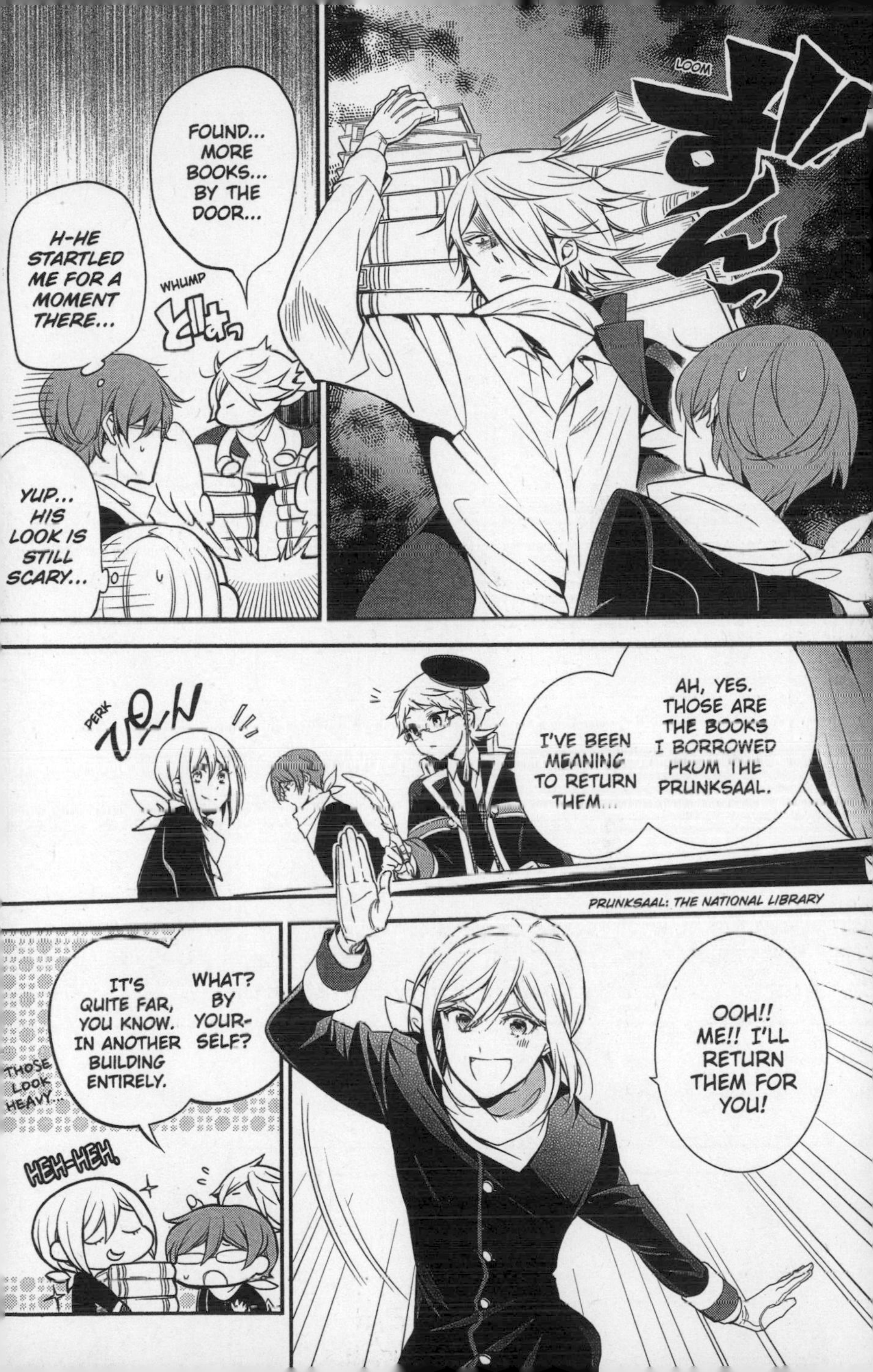
LOOM
FOUND... MORE BOOKS... BY THE DOOR...
WHUMP
H-HE STARTLED ME FOR A MOMENT THERE...
YUP... HIS LOOK IS STILL SCARY...
AH, YES. THOSE ARE THE BOOKS I BORROWED FROM THE PRUNKSAAL.
I'VE BEEN MEANING TO RETURN THEM...
PERK
PRUNKSAAL: THE NATIONAL LIBRARY
OOH!! ME!! I'LL RETURN THEM FOR YOU!
WHAT? BY YOURSELF?
IT'S QUITE FAR, YOU KNOW. IN ANOTHER BUILDING ENTIRELY.
THOSE LOOK HEAVY...
HEH-HEH.

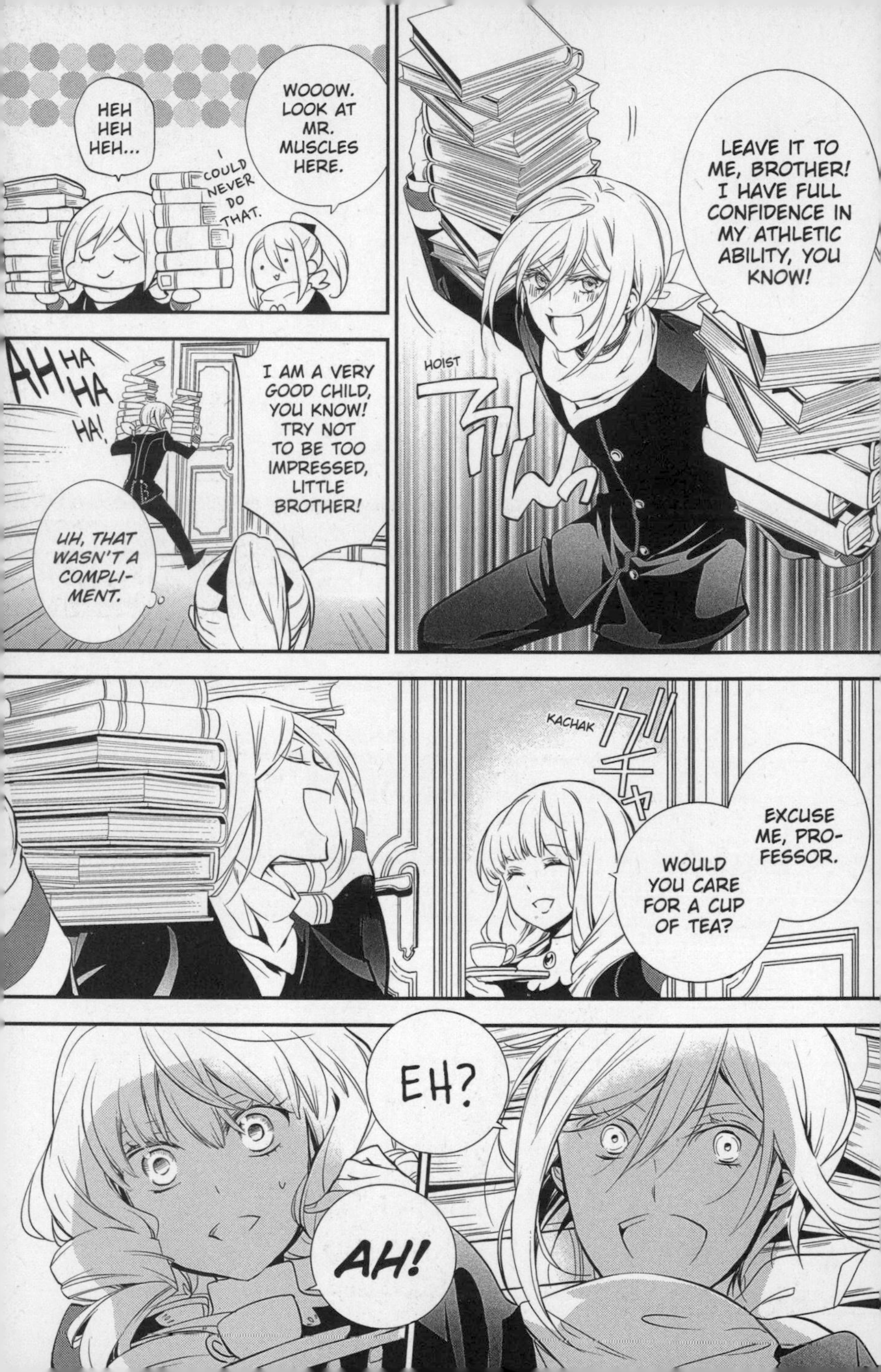
LEAVE IT TO ME, BROTHER! I HAVE FULL CONFIDENCE IN MY ATHLETIC ABILITY, YOU KNOW!
HOIST
WOOOW. LOOK AT MR. MUSCLES HERE.
I COULD NEVER DO THAT.
HEH HEH HEH...
I AM A VERY GOOD CHILD, YOU KNOW! TRY NOT TO BE TOO IMPRESSED, LITTLE BROTHER!
AH HA HA HA!
UH, THAT WASN'T A COMPLIMENT.
KACHAK
EXCUSE ME, PRO-FESSOR.
WOULD YOU CARE FOR A CUP OF TEA?
EH?
AH!

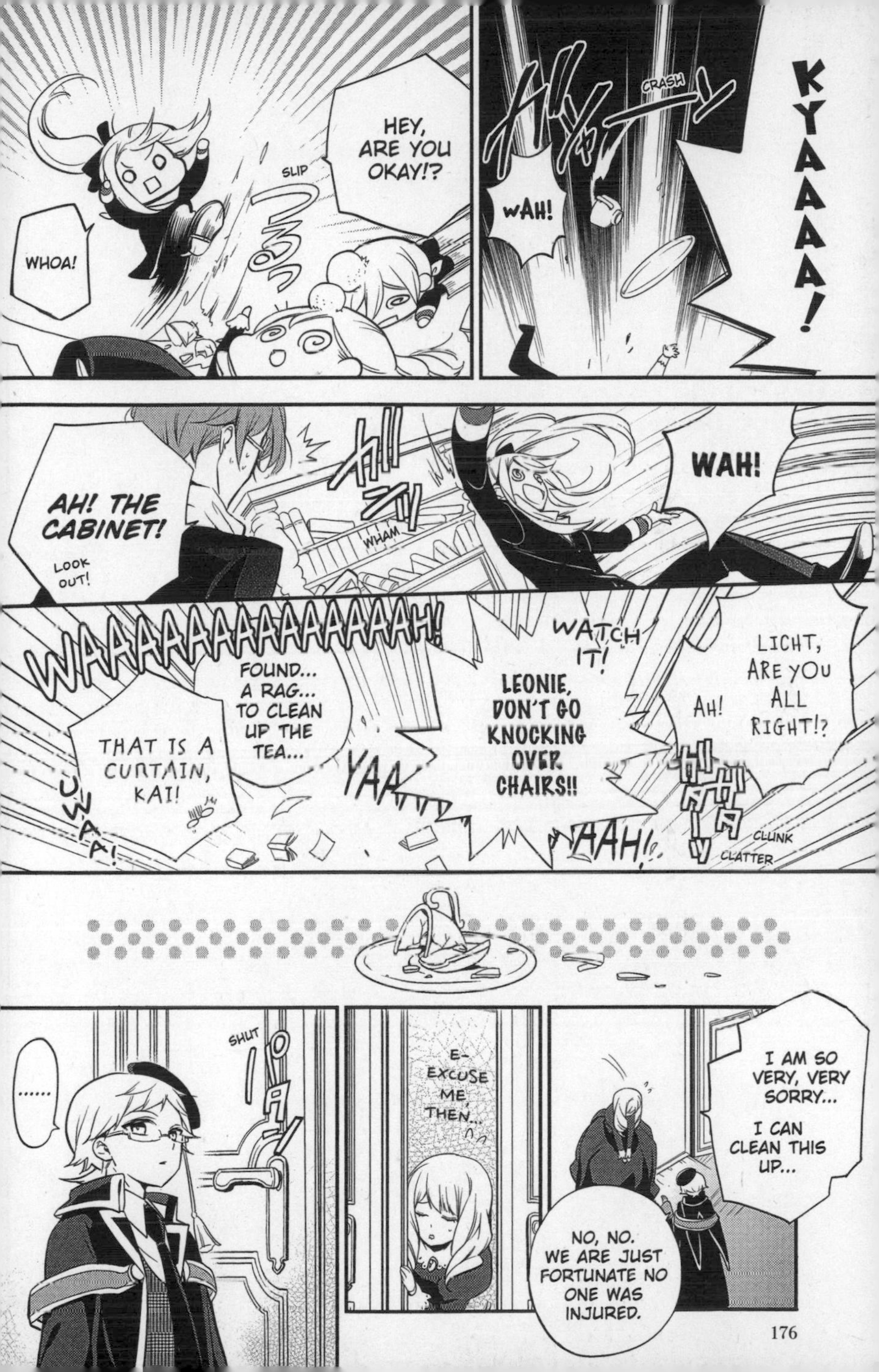
CRASH
KYAAAA!
WAH!
HEY, ARE YOU OKAY!?
SLIP
WHOA!
WAH!
WHAM
AH! THE CABINET!
LOOK OUT!
LICHT, ARE YOU ALL RIGHT!?
AH!
CLUNK
CLATTER
WATCH IT!
LEONIE, DON'T GO KNOCKING OVER CHAIRS!!
WAAAAAAAAAAAAAAH!
FOUND... A RAG... TO CLEAN UP THE TEA...
THAT IS A CURTAIN, KAI!
UWAA!
YAAAAH!
I AM SO VERY, VERY SORRY...
I CAN CLEAN THIS UP...
NO, NO. WE ARE JUST FORTUNATE NO ONE WAS INJURED.
E-EXCUSE ME, THEN...
SHUT
......

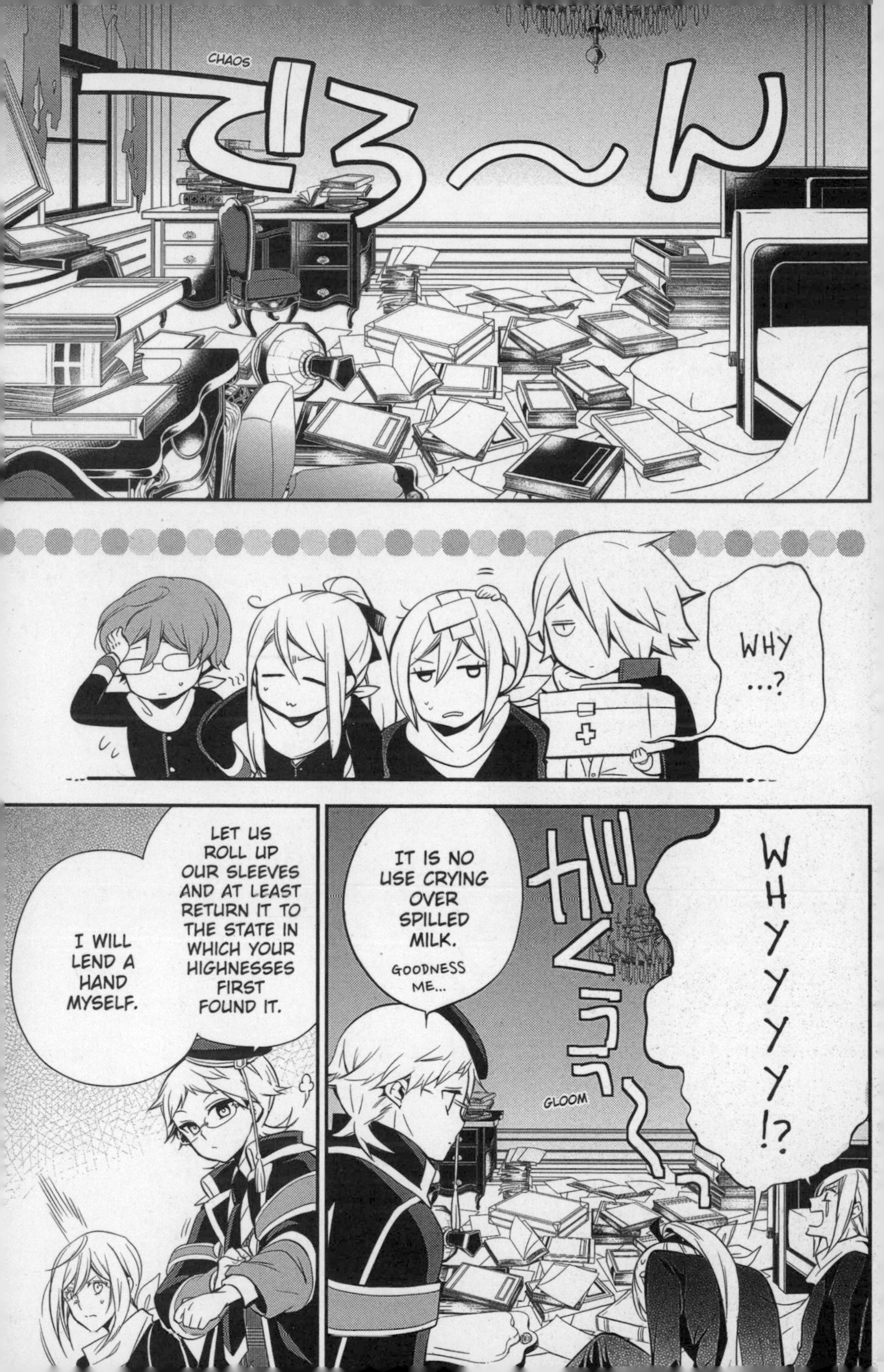
CHAOS
でろ～ん
WHY ...?
WHYYYYY!?
GLOOM
IT IS NO USE CRYING OVER SPILLED MILK.
GOODNESS ME...
LET US ROLL UP OUR SLEEVES AND AT LEAST RETURN IT TO THE STATE IN WHICH YOUR HIGHNESSES FIRST FOUND IT.
I WILL LEND A HAND MYSELF.

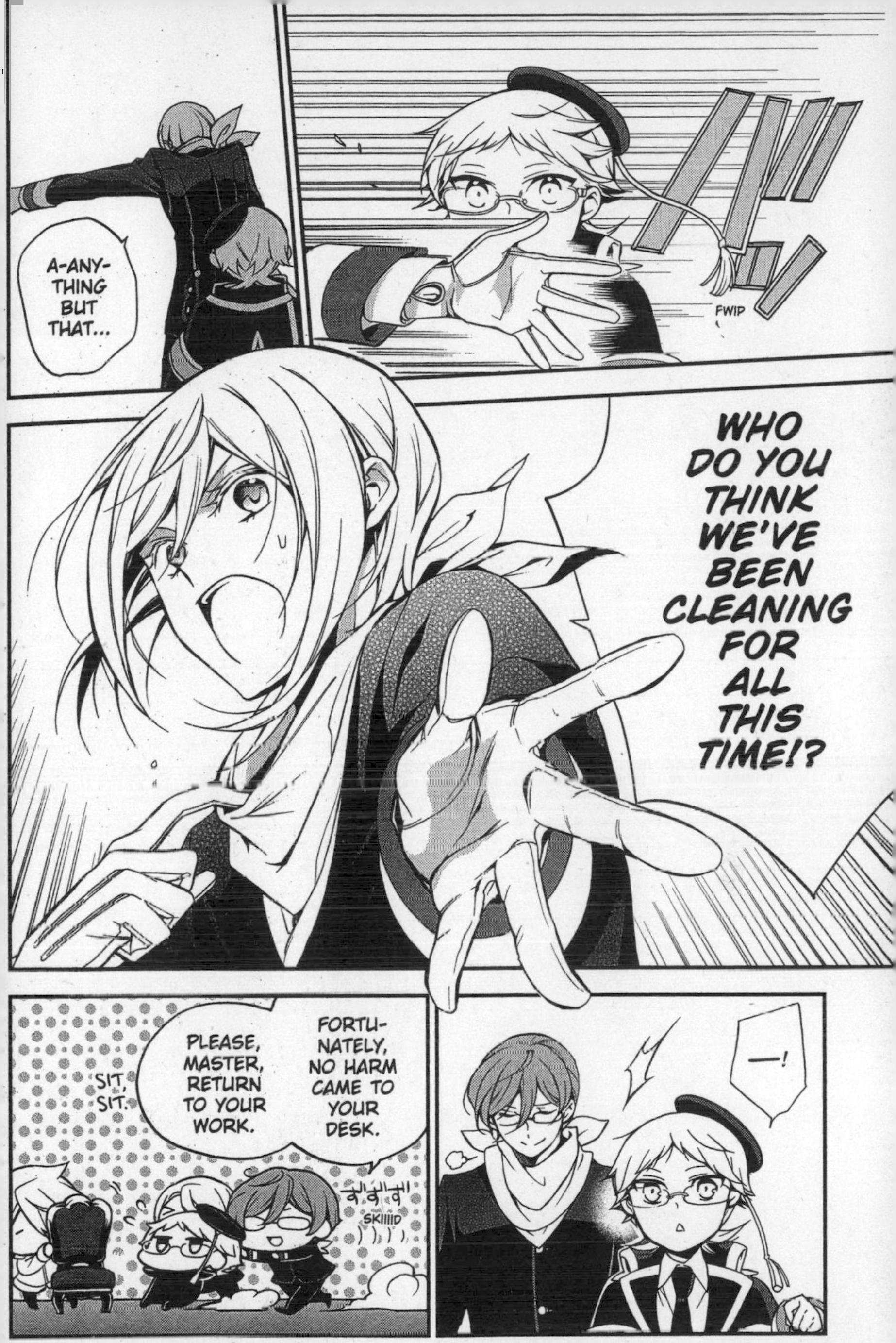
FWIP
A-ANY-THING BUT THAT...
WHO DO YOU THINK WE'VE BEEN CLEANING FOR ALL THIS TIME!?
—!
FORTU-NATELY, NO HARM CAME TO YOUR DESK.
PLEASE, MASTER, RETURN TO YOUR WORK.
SIT, SIT.
すすす
SKIIIID

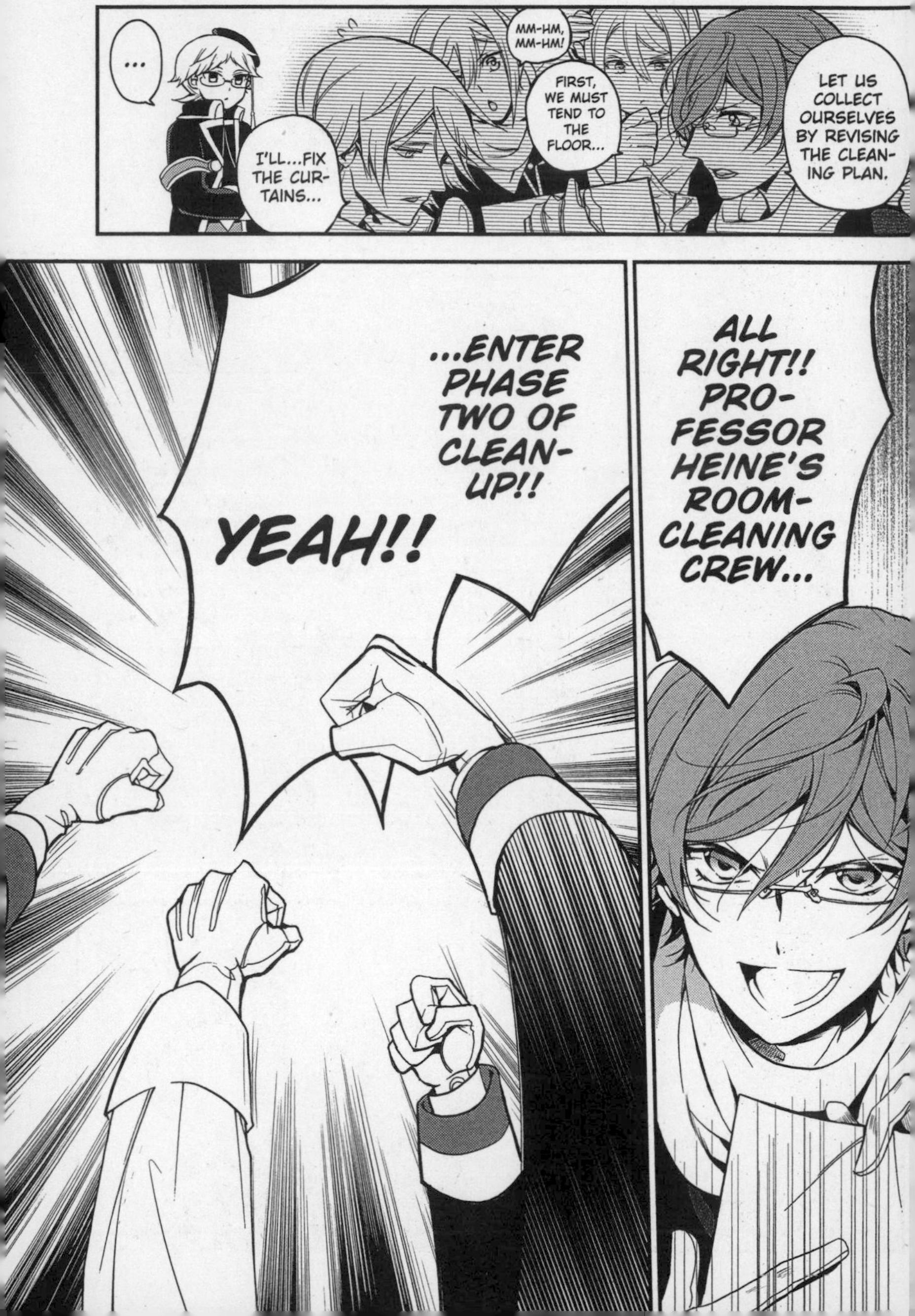
LET US COLLECT OURSELVES BY REVISING THE CLEAN-ING PLAN.
FIRST, WE MUST TEND TO THE FLOOR...
MM-HM, MM-HM!
I'LL...FIX THE CUR-TAINS...
...
ALL RIGHT!! PRO-FESSOR HEINE'S ROOM-CLEANING CREW...
...ENTER PHASE TWO OF CLEAN-UP!!
YEAH!!

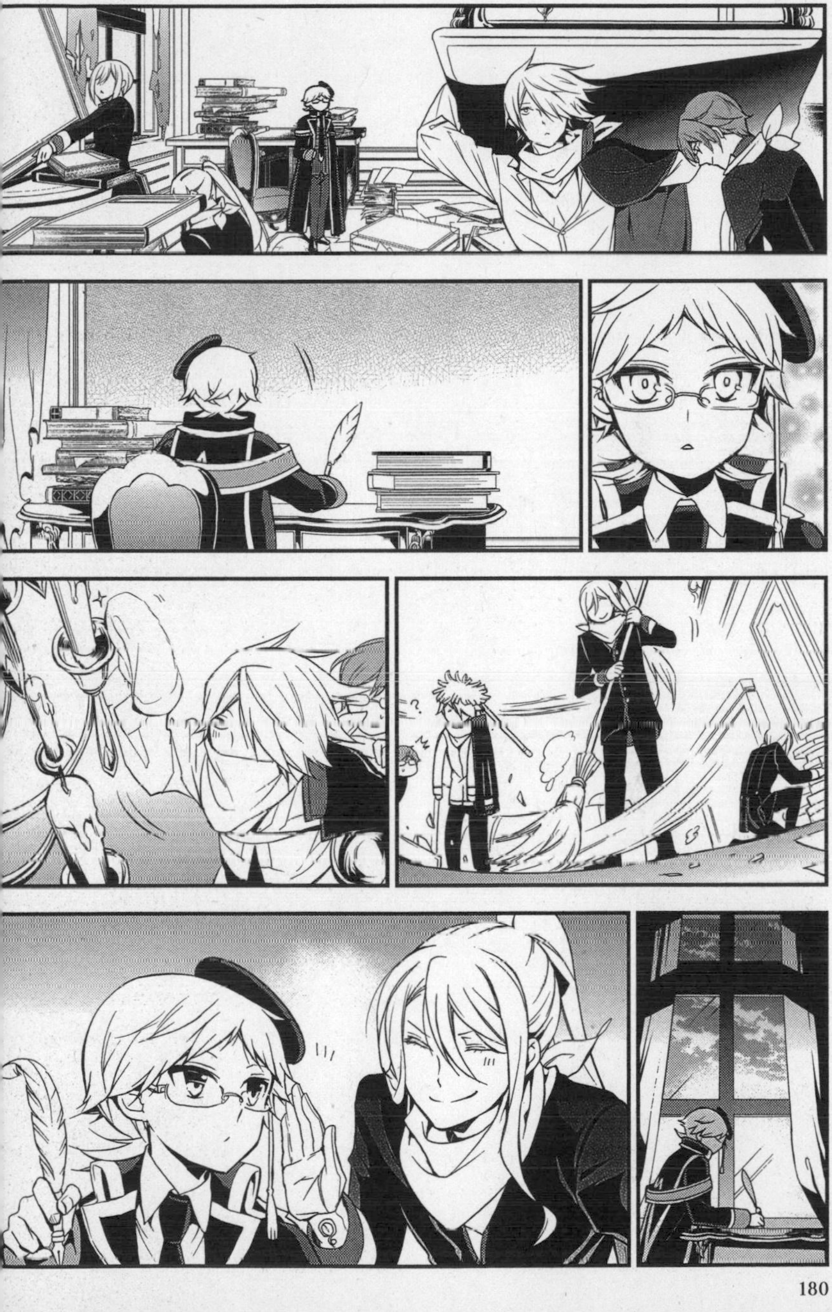

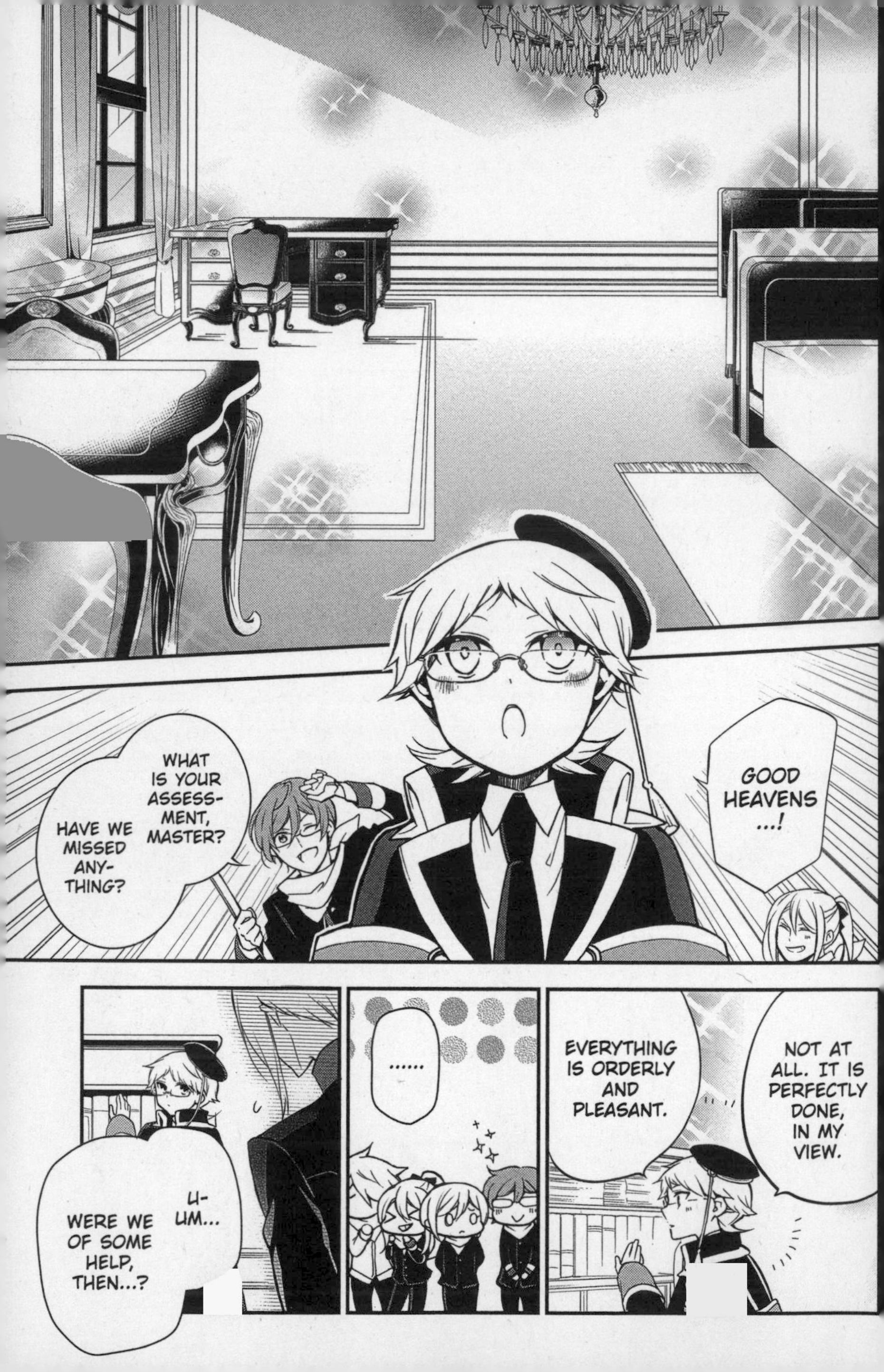
GOOD HEAVENS ...!
WHAT IS YOUR ASSESSMENT, MASTER?
HAVE WE MISSED ANYTHING?
NOT AT ALL. IT IS PERFECTLY DONE, IN MY VIEW.
EVERYTHING IS ORDERLY AND PLEASANT.
......
U-UM...
WERE WE OF SOME HELP, THEN...?

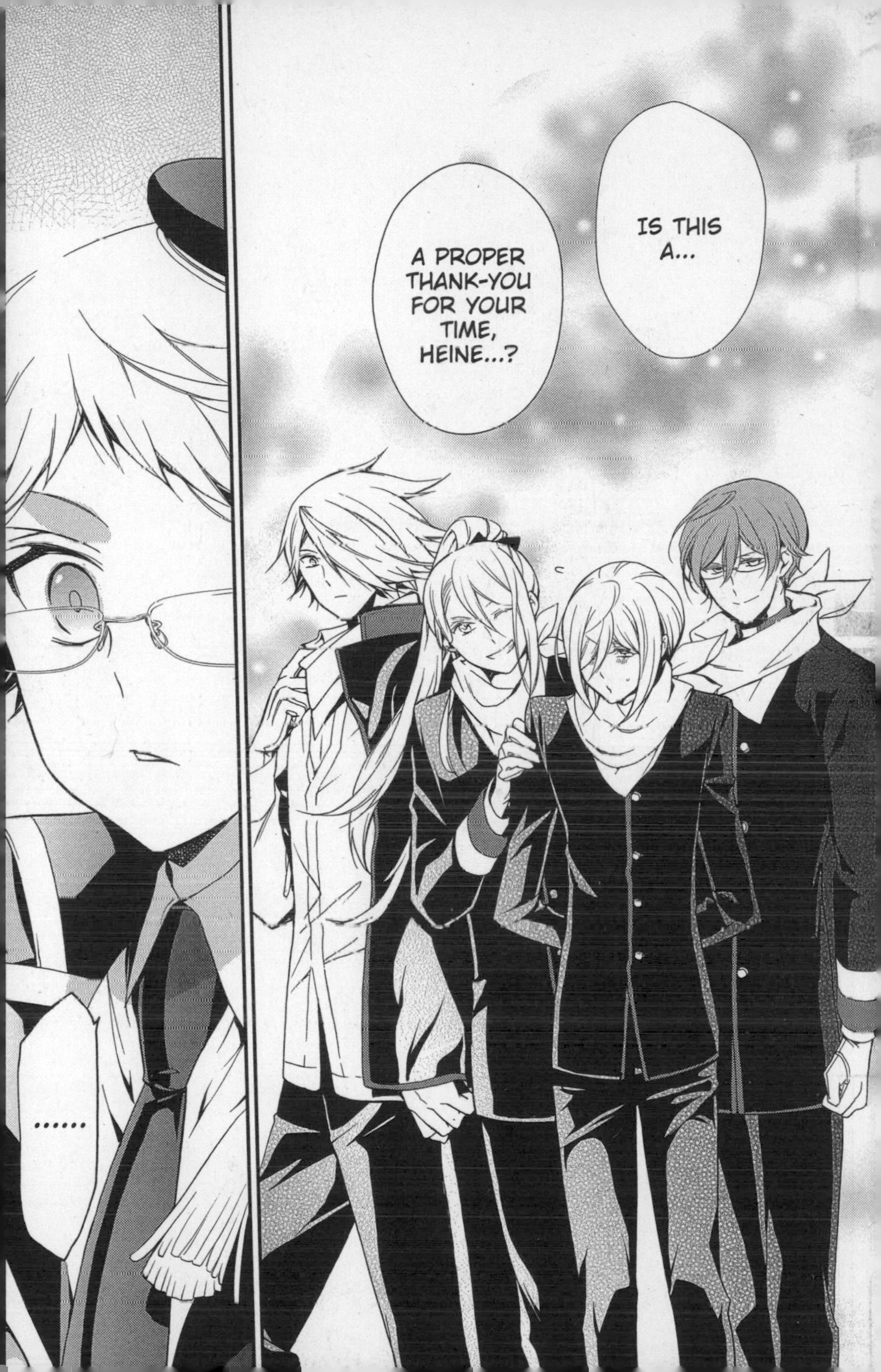
IS THIS A...
A PROPER THANK-YOU FOR YOUR TIME, HEINE...?
......

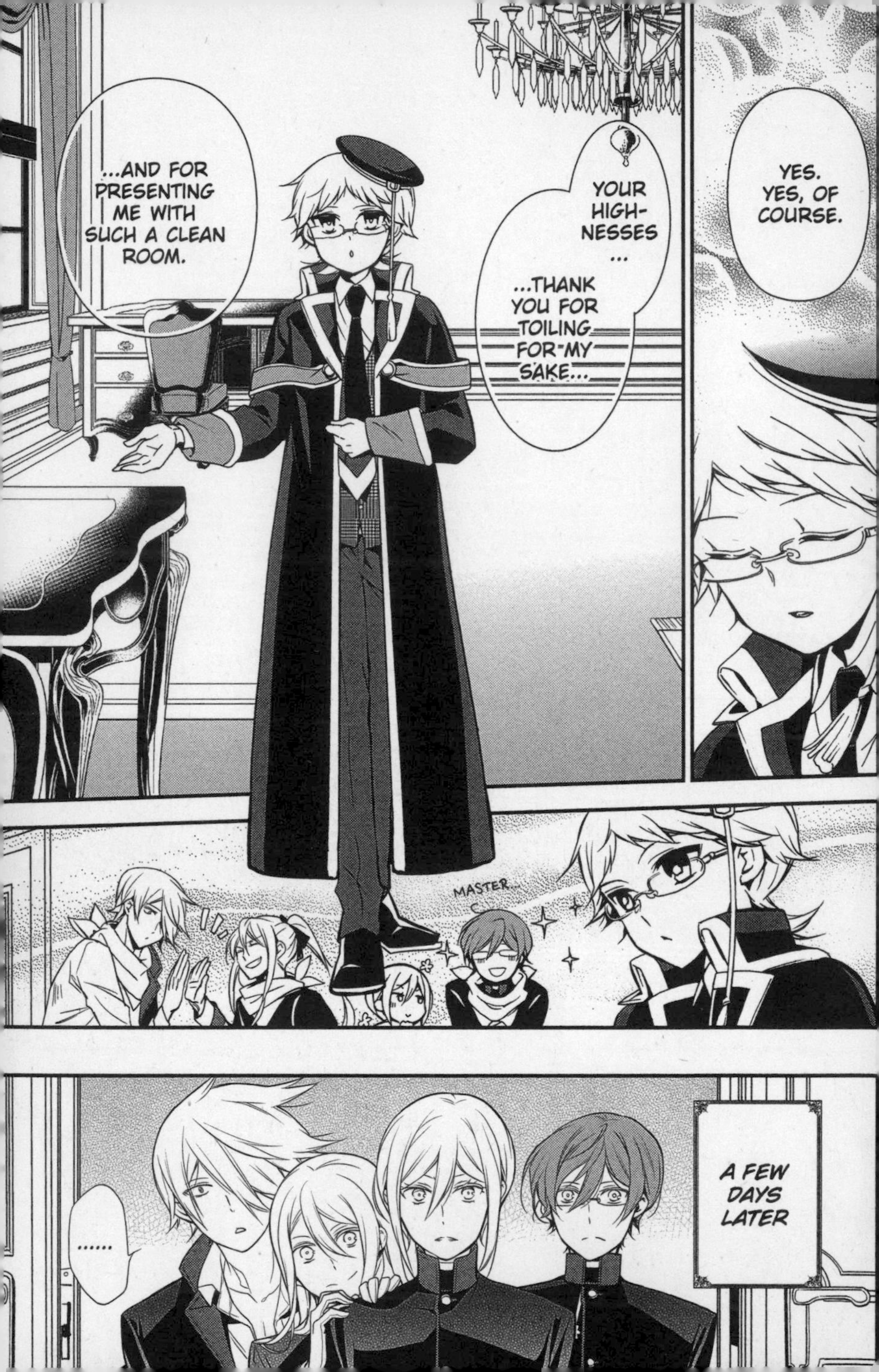
YES. YES, OF COURSE.
YOUR HIGH-NESSES...
...THANK YOU FOR TOILING FOR MY SAKE...
...AND FOR PRESENTING ME WITH SUCH A CLEAN ROOM.
MASTER...
A FEW DAYS LATER
......

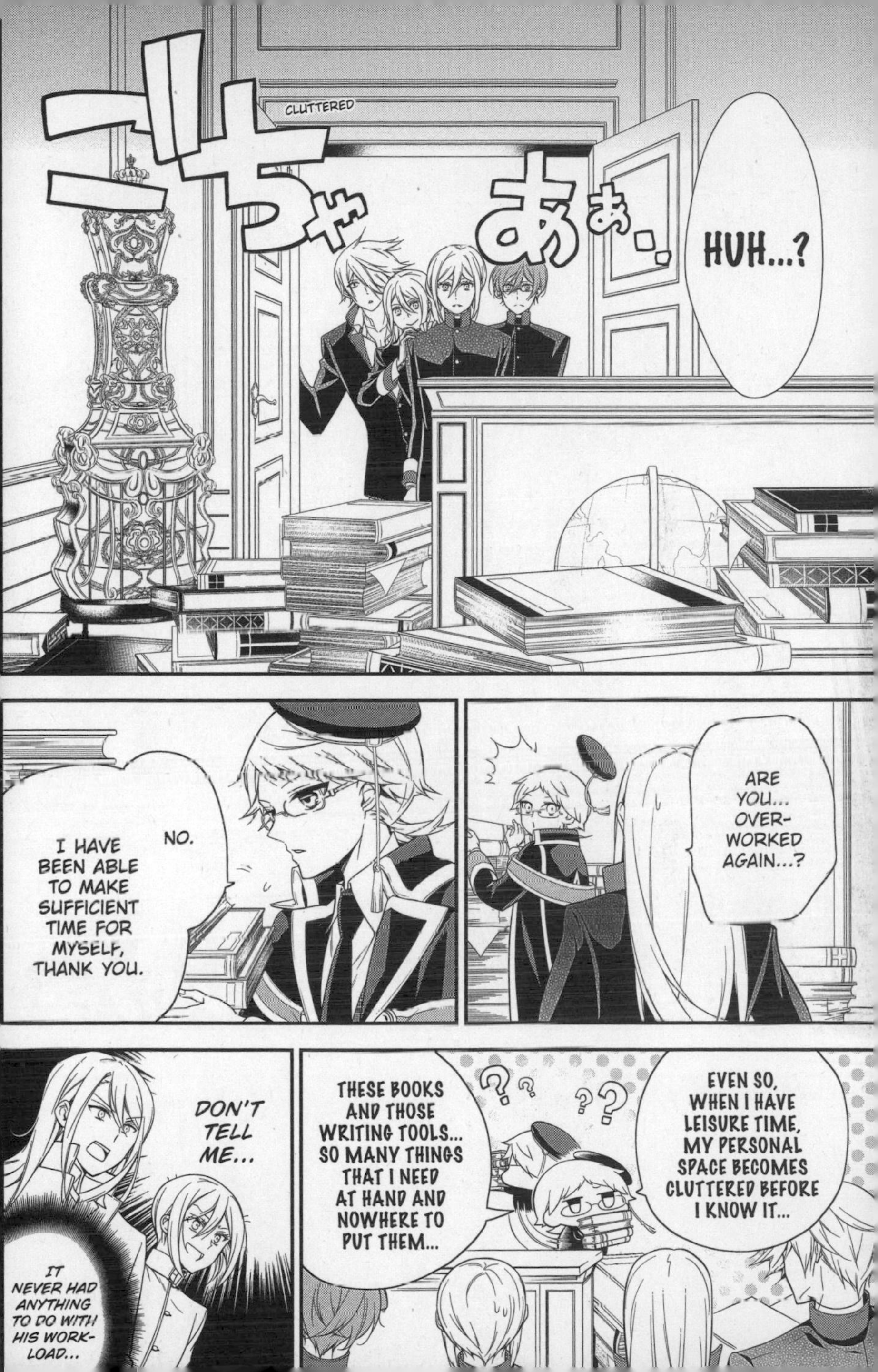
ごちゃあぁ。。
CLUTTERED
HUH...?
ARE YOU... OVER-WORKED AGAIN...?
NO.
I HAVE BEEN ABLE TO MAKE SUFFICIENT TIME FOR MYSELF, THANK YOU.
EVEN SO, WHEN I HAVE LEISURE TIME, MY PERSONAL SPACE BECOMES CLUTTERED BEFORE I KNOW IT...
THESE BOOKS AND THOSE WRITING TOOLS... SO MANY THINGS THAT I NEED AT HAND AND NOWHERE TO PUT THEM...
DON'T TELL ME...
IT NEVER HAD ANYTHING TO DO WITH HIS WORK-LOAD...

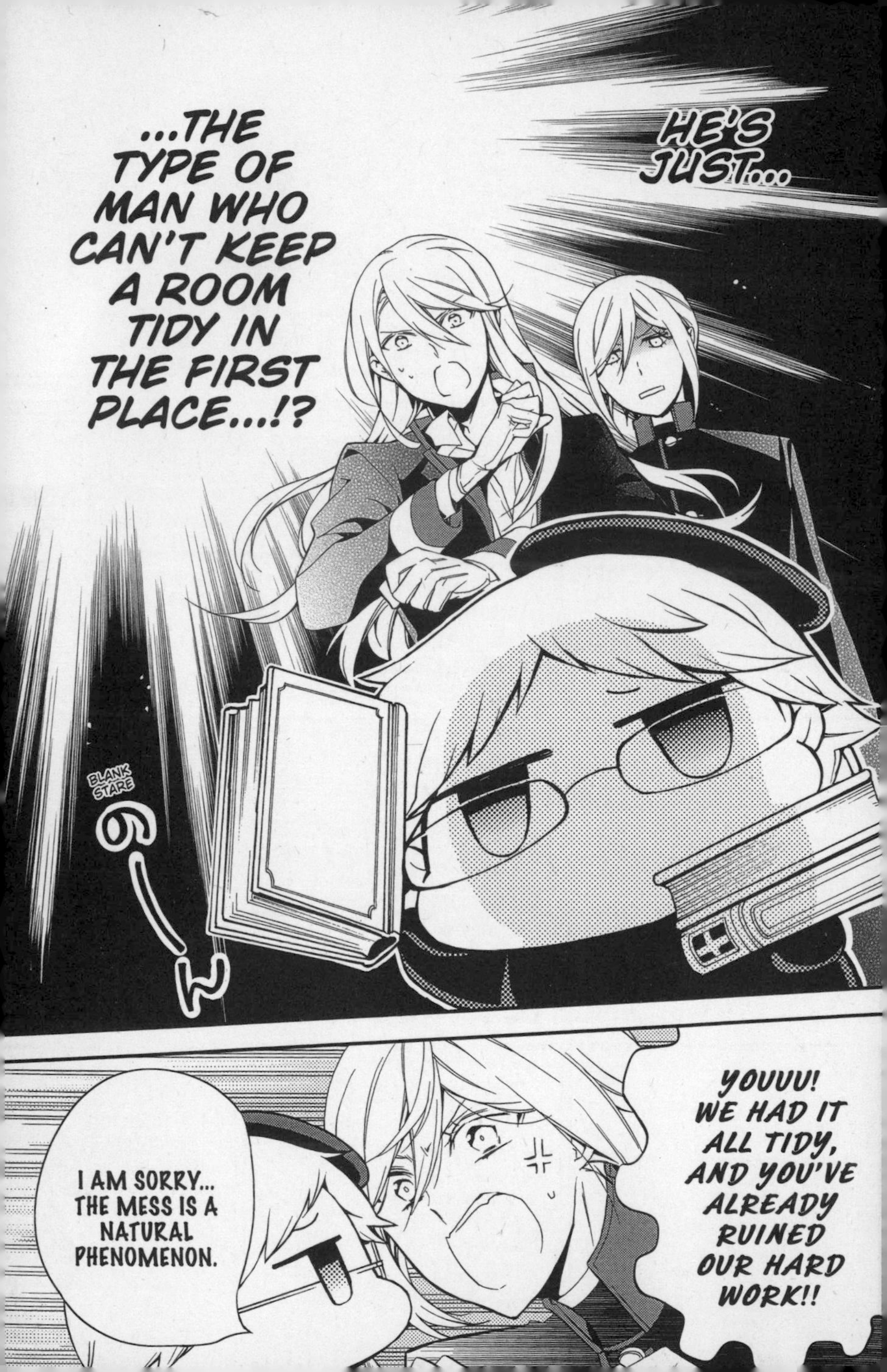
HE'S JUST...
...THE TYPE OF MAN WHO CAN'T KEEP A ROOM TIDY IN THE FIRST PLACE...!?
BLANK STARE
YOUUU! WE HAD IT ALL TIDY, AND YOU'VE ALREADY RUINED OUR HARD WORK!!
I AM SORRY... THE MESS IS A NATURAL PHENOMENON.

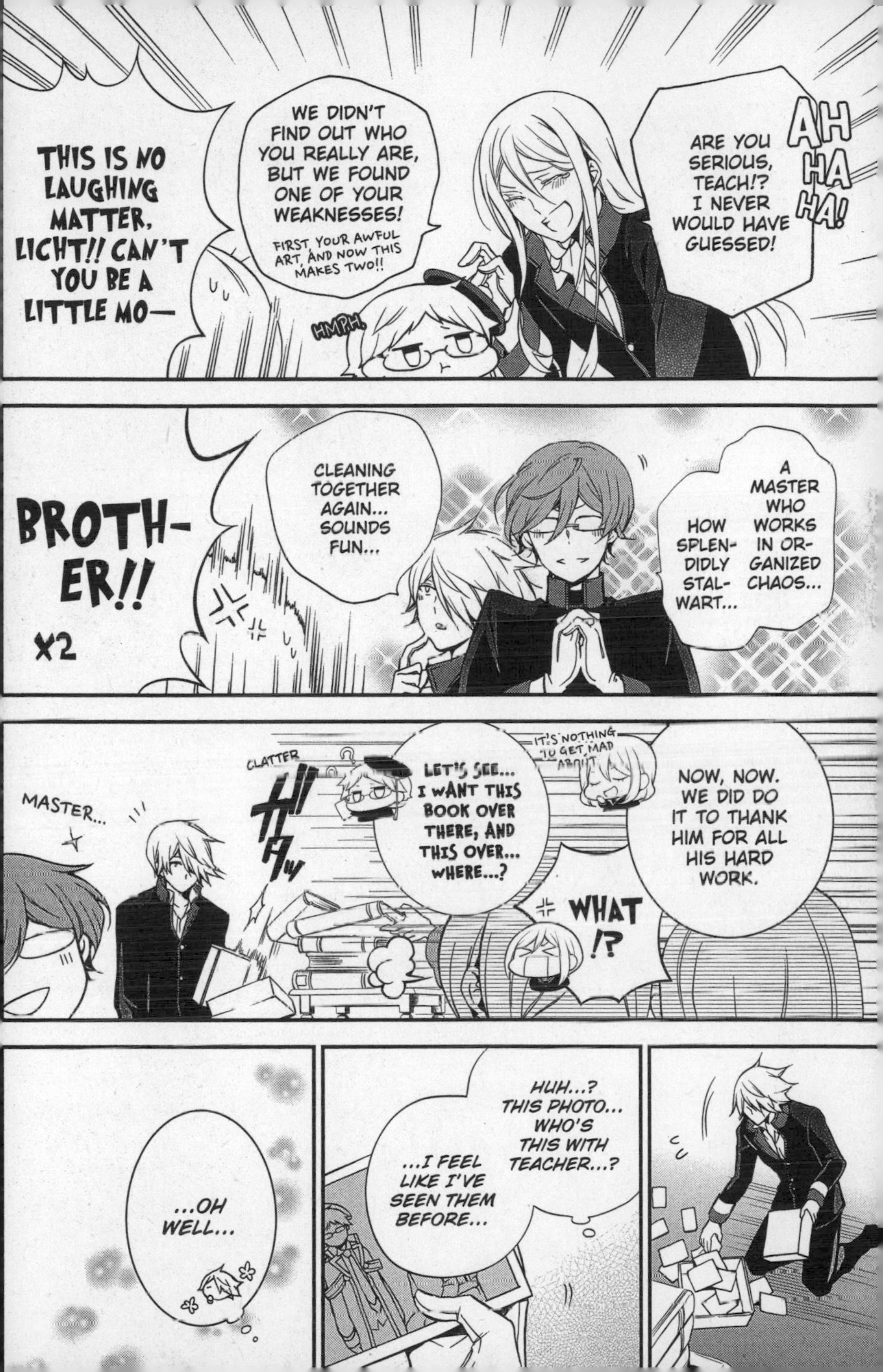
AH HA HA!
ARE YOU SERIOUS, TEACH!? I NEVER WOULD HAVE GUESSED!
WE DIDN'T FIND OUT WHO YOU REALLY ARE, BUT WE FOUND ONE OF YOUR WEAKNESSES!
FIRST YOUR AWFUL ART, AND NOW THIS MAKES TWO!!
HMPH.
THIS IS NO LAUGHING MATTER, LICHT!! CAN'T YOU BE A LITTLE MO—
A MASTER WHO WORKS IN ORGANIZED CHAOS...
HOW SPLENDIDLY STALWART...
CLEANING TOGETHER AGAIN... SOUNDS FUN...
BROTHER!!
x2
NOW, NOW. WE DID DO IT TO THANK HIM FOR ALL HIS HARD WORK.
IT'S NOTHING TO GET MAD ABOUT
WHAT!?
LET'S SEE... I WANT THIS BOOK OVER THERE, AND THIS OVER... WHERE...?
CLATTER
MASTER...
HUH...? THIS PHOTO... WHO'S THIS WITH TEACHER...?
...I FEEL LIKE I'VE SEEN THEM BEFORE...
...OH WELL...

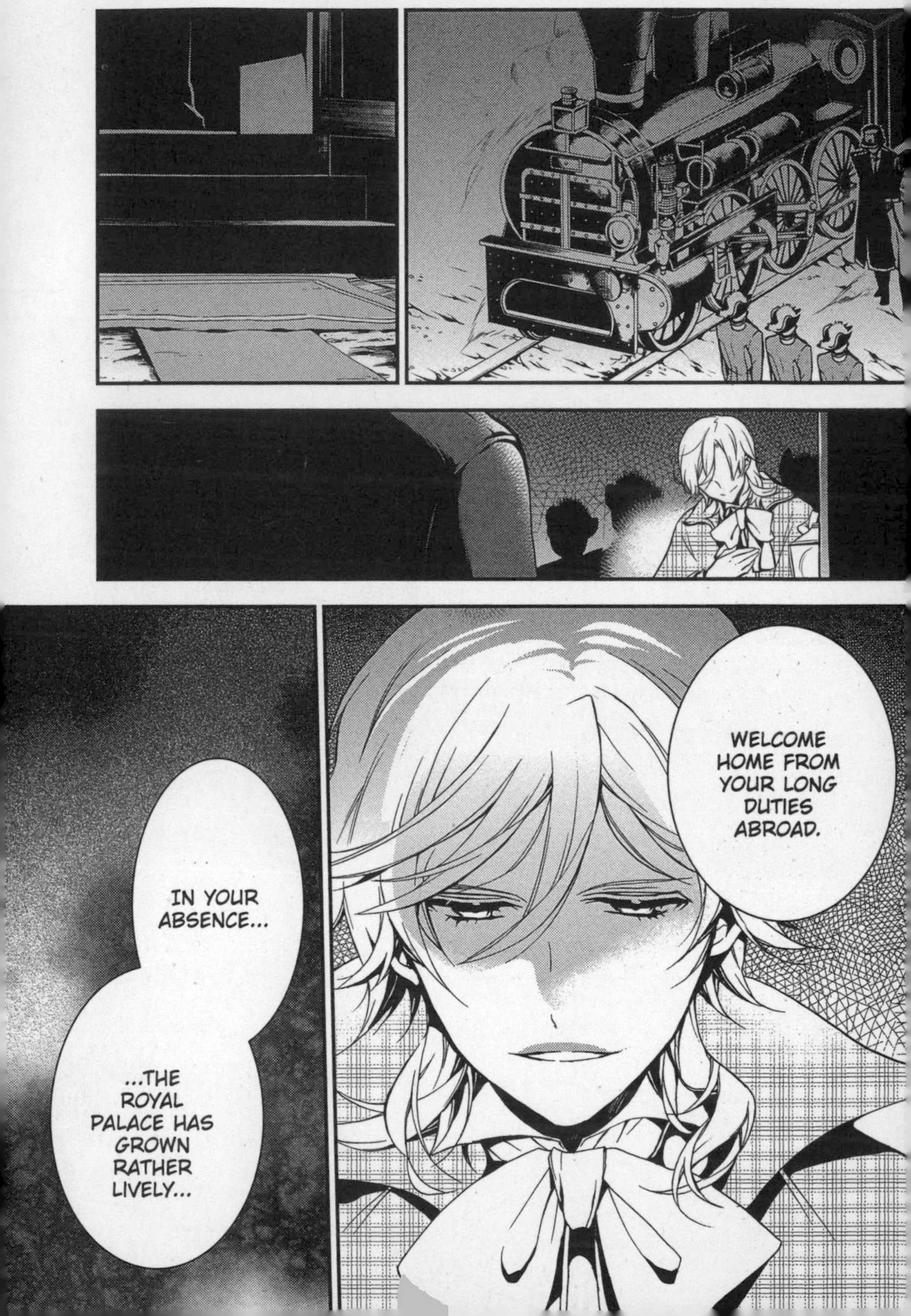
WELCOME HOME FROM YOUR LONG DUTIES ABROAD.
IN YOUR ABSENCE...
...THE ROYAL PALACE HAS GROWN RATHER LIVELY...

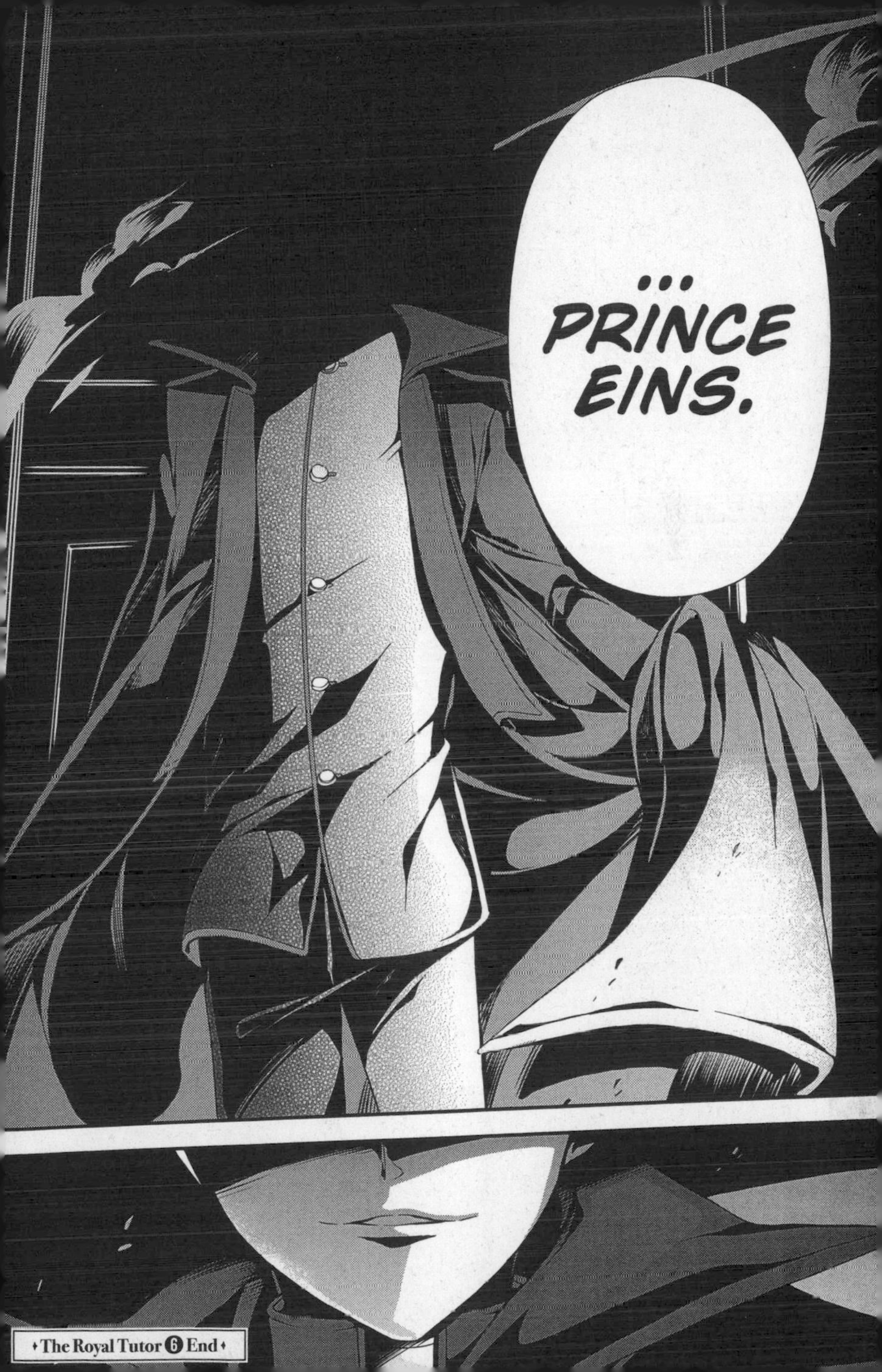
...PRINCE EINS.

•The Royal Tutor ⑥ End•

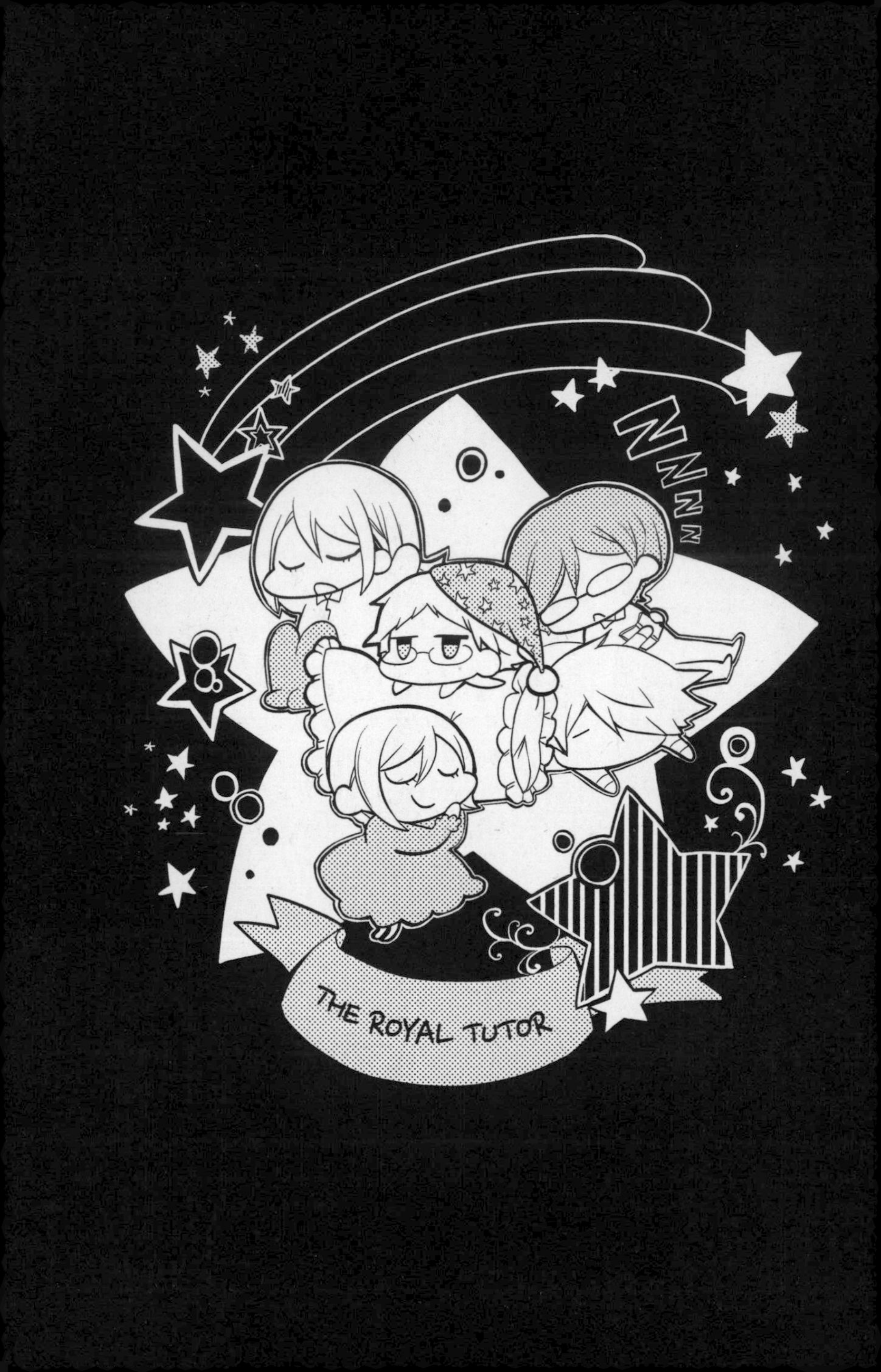

ZZZZZ
THE ROYAL TUTOR

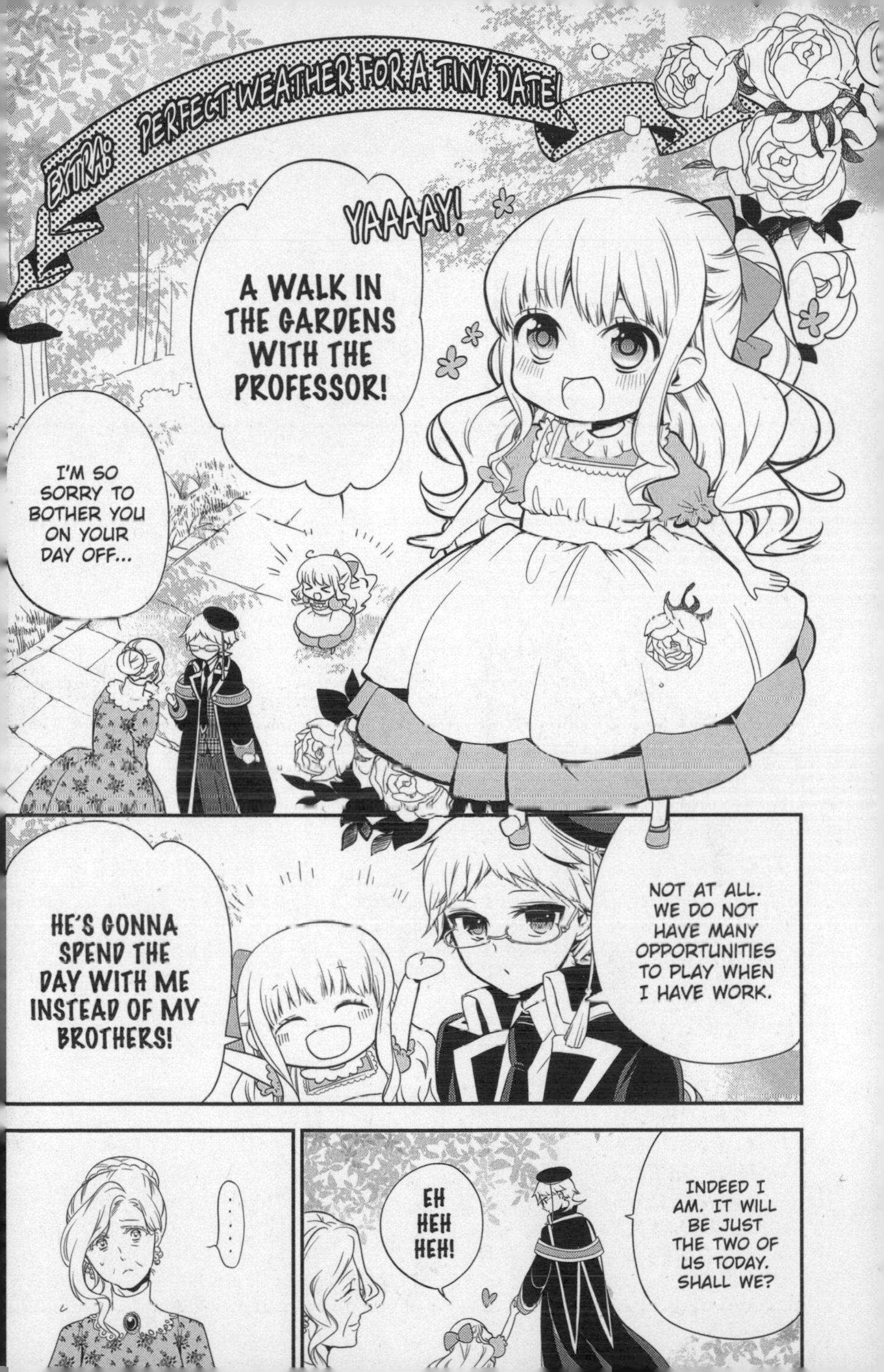
EXTRA: PERFECT WEATHER FOR A TINY DATE!
YAAAAY!
A WALK IN THE GARDENS WITH THE PROFESSOR!
I'M SO SORRY TO BOTHER YOU ON YOUR DAY OFF...
NOT AT ALL. WE DO NOT HAVE MANY OPPORTUNITIES TO PLAY WHEN I HAVE WORK.
HE'S GONNA SPEND THE DAY WITH ME INSTEAD OF MY BROTHERS!
INDEED I AM. IT WILL BE JUST THE TWO OF US TODAY. SHALL WE?
EH HEH HEH!
.....

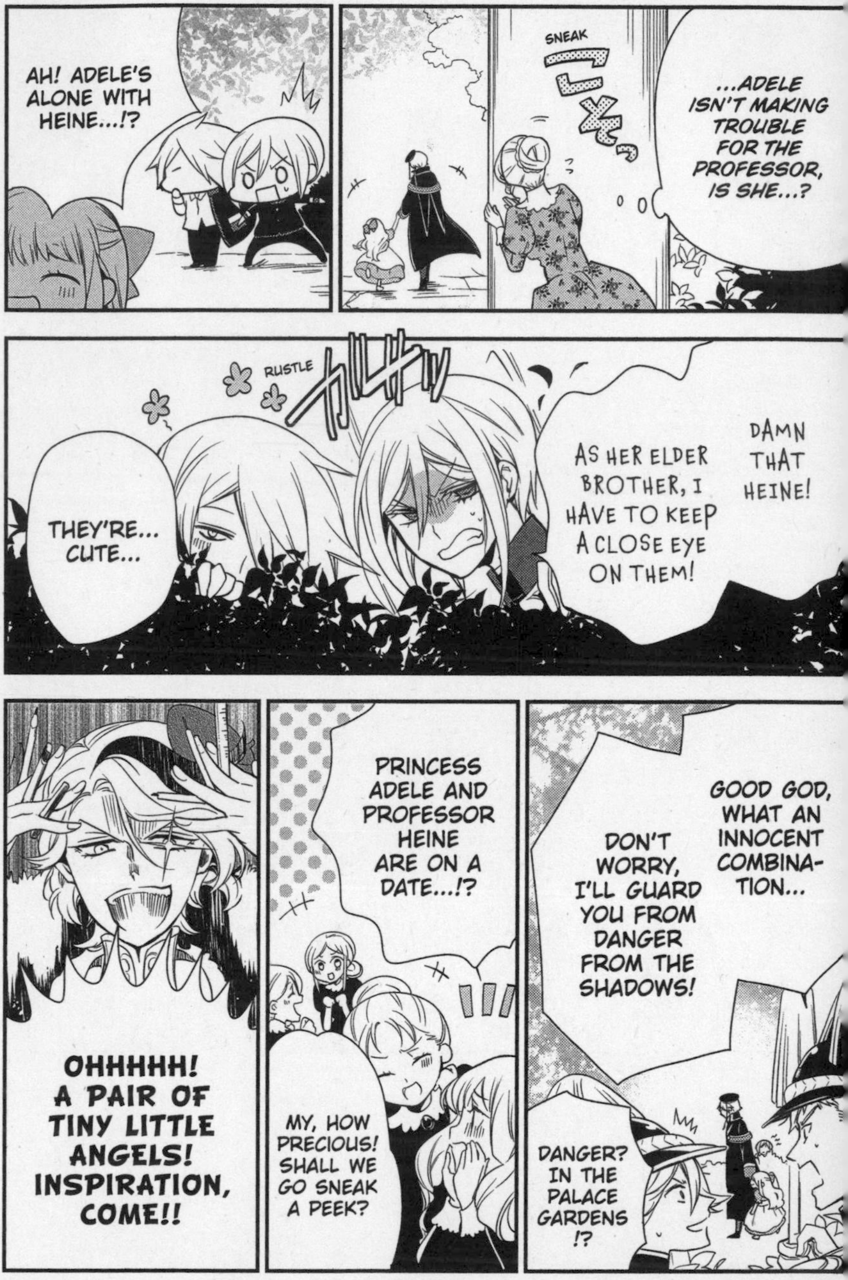
SNEAK
...ADELE ISN'T MAKING TROUBLE FOR THE PROFESSOR, IS SHE...?
AH! ADELE'S ALONE WITH HEINE...!?
DAMN THAT HEINE!
AS HER ELDER BROTHER, I HAVE TO KEEP A CLOSE EYE ON THEM!
RUSTLE
THEY'RE... CUTE...
GOOD GOD, WHAT AN INNOCENT COMBINA-TION...
DON'T WORRY, I'LL GUARD YOU FROM DANGER FROM THE SHADOWS!
DANGER? IN THE PALACE GARDENS !?
PRINCESS ADELE AND PROFESSOR HEINE ARE ON A DATE...!?
MY, HOW PRECIOUS! SHALL WE GO SNEAK A PEEK?
OHHHHH! A PAIR OF TINY LITTLE ANGELS! INSPIRATION, COME!!

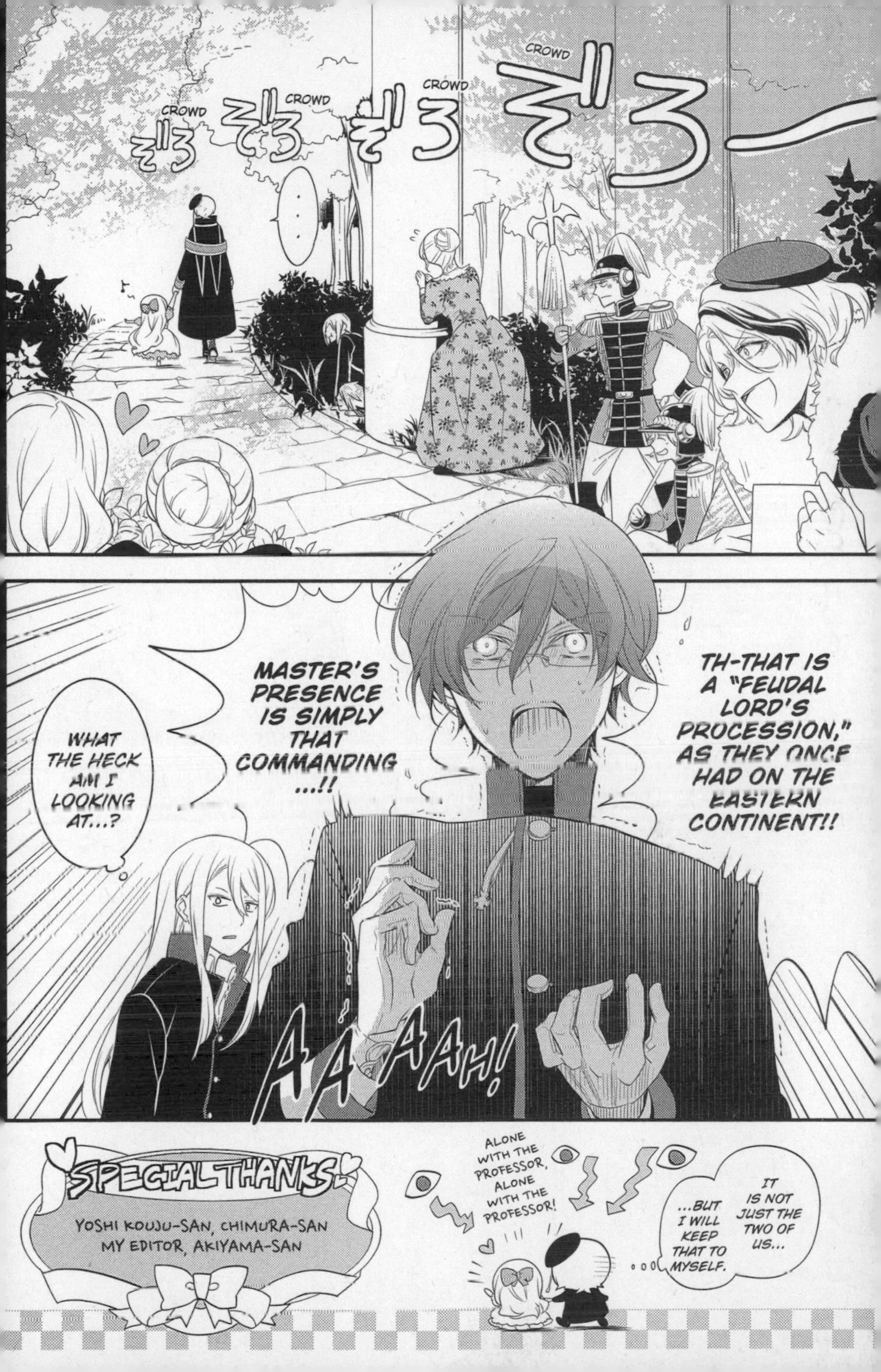
CROWD
CROWD
CROWD
CROWD
...
TH-THAT IS A "FEUDAL LORD'S PROCESSION," AS THEY ONCE HAD ON THE EASTERN CONTINENT!!
MASTER'S PRESENCE IS SIMPLY THAT COMMANDING ...!!
WHAT THE HECK AM I LOOKING AT...?
AAAAH!
IT IS NOT JUST THE TWO OF US...
...BUT I WILL KEEP THAT TO MYSELF.
ALONE WITH THE PROFESSOR, ALONE WITH THE PROFESSOR!
SPECIAL THANKS
YOSHI KOUJU-SAN, CHIMURA-SAN
MY EDITOR, AKIYAMA-SAN

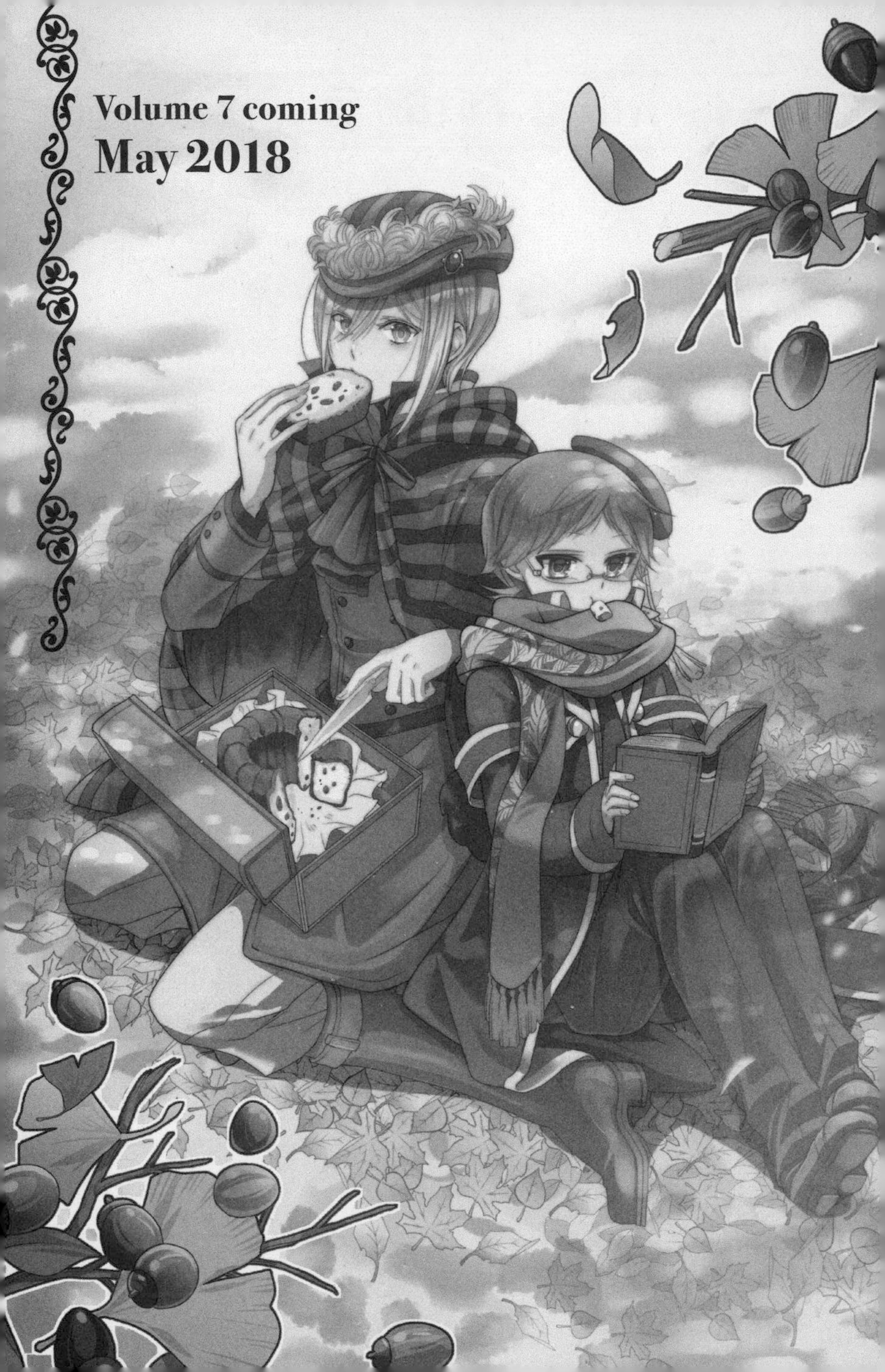
Volume 7 coming
May 2018

The Royal Tutor ❻

Higasa Akai

Translation: Amanda Haley • Lettering: Abigail Blackman

THE ROYAL TUTOR Vol. 6 © 2016 Higasa Akai / SQUARE ENIX CO., LTD. First published in Japan in 2016 by SQUARE ENIX CO., LTD. English translation rights arranged with SQUARE ENIX CO., LTD. and Yen Press, LLC through Tuttle-Mori Agency, Inc., Tokyo.

English translation © 2018 by SQUARE ENIX CO., LTD.

Yen Press
1290 Avenue of the Americas
New York, NY 10104

Visit us at yenpress.com
facebook.com/yenpress
twitter.com/yenpress
yenpress.tumblr.com
instagram.com/yenpress

First Yen Press Edition: March 2018
The chapters in this volume were originally published as eBooks by Yen Press.

Yen Press is an imprint of Yen Press, LLC.
The Yen Press name and logo are trademarks of Yen Press, LLC.

Library of Congress Control Number: 2017938422

ISBNs: 978-0-316-44663-1 (paperback)
       978-0-316-44668-6 (ebook)

10 9 8 7 6 5 4 3 2 1

BVC

Printed in the United States of America